ACTING ONE/ ACTING TWO

FIFTH EDITION

Robert Cohen

UNIVERSITY OF CALIFORNIA, IRVINE

Boston   Burr Ridge, IL   Dubuque, IA   New York
San Francisco   St. Louis   Bangkok   Bogotá   Caracas   Kuala Lumpur
Lisbon   London   Madrid   Mexico City   Milan   Montreal   New Delhi
Santiago   Seoul   Singapore   Sydney   Taipei   Toronto

The McGraw·Hill Companies

ACTING ONE / ACTING TWO, FIFTH EDITION
Published by McGraw-Hill, an imprint of The McGraw-Hill Companies, Inc., 1221
Avenue of the Americas, New York, NY 10020. Copyright © 2008 by Robert Cohen.
All rights reserved. No part of this publication may be reproduced or distributed in
any form or by any means, or stored in a database or retrieval system, without the
prior written consent of The McGraw-Hill Companies, Inc., including, but not limited
to, in any network or other electronic storage or transmission, or broadcast for
distance learning.

This book is printed on acid-free paper.

10 11 12 LKV 24 23 22

ISBN: 978-0-07-328854-3
MHID: 0-07-328854-3

Editor in Chief: Emily Barrosse
Publisher: Chris Freitag
Development Editor: Beth Ebenstein
Production Editor: Aaron Downey, Matrix Productions Inc.
Manuscript Editor: Patricia Herbst
Senior Designer: Preston Thomas
Senior Production Supervisor: Richard DeVitto

This book was set in 10/12 Sabon by Laserwords, and printed on 45# New Era Matte
Plus by Lakeside Book Company.

Library of Congress Cataloging-in-Publication Data

Cohen, Robert
    Acting One / Acting Two. Robert Cohen—5th ed.
        p. cm.
    Includes index.
        ISBN-13: 978-0-07-328854-3; ISBN-10: 0-07-328854-3
    1. Acting. 2. Advanced Acting. I. Title: Acting 1 /Acting 2. II. Title.

PN2061.C582   2008
792'.028—dc21
                                        2006054235

www.mhhe.com

To my past, present, and future colleagues
at UC Irvine

CONTENTS

P R E F A C E

Acting One/Acting Two is a comprehensive study of acting, from the most basic interactions between human characters like ourselves, covered in *Acting One,* to extending ourselves into other styles and characterizations, which is the subject of *Acting Two.* Although these topics are treated here in two separate "books," the fundamental principles unifying these texts are the core subject of *Acting One/Acting Two*—as well as of my entire teaching and directing career.

Playing "ourselves" and playing "others" are intimately bound. Every role, no matter how realistic or ordinary, scripted or improvised, is a performance of style and character—if only because it must sustain the attention of people gathered to see it. And every "stylized" role, even in Greek tragedy or Japanese *kabuki,* is ultimately based on human interaction, even if only between actor and audience. So while these texts are separated for pedagogical reasons (and *Acting One* is separately available in a paperback edition), it is their living symbiosis that becomes the fuel of great acting—in every variety of play existing or imaginable.

Acting One, of which this is the fifth edition, is a beginning acting text. It is devoted to the basics of acting as taught in the United States and most other countries, and it includes lessons and exercises that will teach you how to act and interact in realistic modern plays—plays set within your own area of life experience and using speech patterns much like your own or well known to you from daily speech. After an introduction on the actor's preparation, and a basic exercise, *Acting One* introduces the four core principles of acting: how to play a character's Goal, Tactics, and Expectations in association with Other characters. These words are capitalized here because in Lesson 8 they are introduced as an acronym—GOTE—for easy recollection. "Getting your GOTE" becomes, then, a foundation for all the remaining lessons in *Acting One*—on rehearsing, performing, making choices, integrating voice and body, analyzing scenes, and so forth—and the starting point, which you need never abandon, for *Acting Two.*

Acting Two takes you beyond modern and realistic dramas. It provides an approach to acting in *any* play—including works set in radically different cultures (some ancient, some futuristic, some imaginary) and written in radically different theatrical and linguistic styles. It teaches an approach to playing any sort of character in such dramas—kings and queens, fairies and gods, killers and malcontents, the aged and illiterate. Whereas *Acting One* asks you to act honestly and convincingly in your own world, *Acting Two* asks you to act, no less honestly and convincingly, in a world you have never yet experienced. *Acting Two* thus invites you to enter, in Shakespeare's words, a "brave new world that has *such people* in it!"

Accompanying the text of *Acting One* are many quotations from well-regarded professional actors on their approach to basic acting principles. *Acting Two*, in contrast, is accompanied by visual illustrations of the world you will enter when performing in, say, the plays of Sophocles, Shakespeare, Shaw, Brecht, or Ionesco (to take five of the dozen-plus playwrights from all eras specifically detailed in that book). *Acting Two* (which is the second edition—substantially revised—of the book first published as *Advanced Acting*) is about extending yourself into new worlds while still employing all the basic components of GOTE from your own heart's core.

ACKNOWLEDGMENTS

In the preparation of this edition, I am very pleased to acknowledge the assistance of the outstanding theatre photographers whose work now appears in these pages: Laurencine Lot in Paris, Geraint Lewis in London, Joan Marcus in New York, Michal Daniel in Minneapolis, Phil Channing in Santa Barbara, Nina Krieger in Williamstown, Massachusetts, and Henry DiRocco and Ken Werther in Los Angeles.

I am in debt to the theatre press offices at Williamstown Theatre Festival (Juliet Flynt) and South Coast Repertory (Vanessa Nelson), as well as to the marvelous scholar / mask-maker Chris Vervain in the U.K.

I also deeply appreciate the guidance of my editors at McGraw-Hill; namely Chris Freitag, Caroline Ryan, Jon-David Hague, Gina Boedecker, and Beth Ebenstein, along with the keen-eyed work of Melissa Williams as the book's publication manager, Aaron Downey at Matrix Productions as the production editor, and the wonderful copyeditor, Patricia Herbst, who carefully massaged the text with an assured, yet always graceful, hand.

And, when this book actually appears in print, I will at last know the names (below) of the reviewers of the previous editions, whose thoughtful suggestions are reflected in the following pages; I therefore give my deepest and warmest gratitude to the heretofore anonymous Patrick J. Fennell, Saddleback College; Nina LeNoir, Minnesota State University, Mankato; David Mann, University of South Florida; and Murray McGibbon, Indiana University.

ACTING ONE

I

Preparation for Acting

CAN ACTING BE TAUGHT?

Of course acting can be taught. In the United States, acting is taught regularly in literally thousands of colleges, conservatories, workshops, and professional studios. Nearly all young actors coming into the profession have studied acting in some formal manner, and many professional actors continue their training for years beyond their successful entry into the profession. Thus, acting is not only taught but also learned.

Of course, reading any certain list of books, or studying with any particular teacher or teachers, or enrolling in any particular training program will not guarantee that you will become a great actor or even a fair one. Fine acting demands a rare combination of talents: intelligence, imagination, psychological freedom, physical dexterity, vocal strength and flexibility, emotional depth, and an ability to learn from mistakes, criticism, and observation. It also requires certain personal prowess, which might appear from time to time as wit, charm, self-confidence, assuredness, honesty, audacity, charisma,

3

passionate intensity, and compelling candor. These characteristics cannot be taught, directly, in anything resembling their entirety: They are acquired, if at all, as much through life experience as by training for the stage.

What can be taught is a beginning to the art of acting. This is something more than merely pointing you at the stage and something less than giving you a fully codified set of rules and regulations. It is a method of helping you to get the most out of yourself and to train your acting instrument—primarily your voice and body—into a more workable, more exciting, apparatus. And it is a method that will help you learn from life and apply what you learn to the art of translating life into art: the art of the theatre. Providing this beginning is the goal of *Acting One*.

1

Preparing to Act

Relaxation

Every actor knows the importance of relaxation, for it is the necessary starting place for acting. Relaxation is both physical and mental; it allows the
body to respond freshly and the mind to create spontaneously. A relaxed
actor can do anything; a tense actor is always constrained.

Relaxation cannot be forced, but it can be induced or self-induced.
Simple stretching exercises—rolling the head in large circles, bending the
body forward and back, and moving the fingers, hands, arms, and legs in
figure-eight patterns—are excellent warm-up techniques that both tone
body muscles and release physical tensions. Bouncing lightly on the balls of
the feet; vigorously shaking the arms, hands, face, and torso; and rapidly
shadowboxing or rope-jumping also limber and relax the body. Almost all
actors develop physical regimens of exercises like these to use before rehearsals and performances, and you should too. Many acting classes begin
with such warm-ups. If yours doesn't, you can do your own warm-up
beforehand.

Mental relaxation is a matter of putting out of mind the day-to-day affairs
of life so that you can concentrate more directly and fully on the problems of
acting and on the situation of the characters you will play. Inasmuch as acting
is, among other things, a complex mental activity, the more freedom you have

from your own daily preoccupations, the more deeply you will be able to involve yourself with your acting situation, even during periods of extreme stress in your personal life. Physical exercise is often a help to achieving this mental relaxation; so are meditation, yoga, thinking about pleasant images, or "playing" soothing music in your head. One of the best ways of achieving mental relaxation in an acting class is simply to look around you and study what you see. What color are the walls? How many people are in the class? Does your teacher wear contact lenses? Are the other students as nervous as you? Who brought their books to class today? Since most mental tension comes from thinking about ourselves (and how we might be failing to measure up), thinking about other people helps us to relax and put the world in a better perspective.

LET YOUR BODY GO

Young actors first work through tension because it's the only thing they know. But it's most inefficient. Do exercises where you let every muscle in your body go, one at a time. Then your body is ready to react to whatever command you give it; your thoughts and emotions will resonate with truth.

LAURENCE OLIVIER, ADVISING THE YOUNG ANTHONY HOPKINS

Relaxation is the starting point for acting, not the ending point. Don't ever confuse relaxation with "not thinking." Relaxation is not stupor; it is a state of openness and receptivity to your surroundings—a state unmarked by extreme preoccupation or worry. Go ahead and think all you want, but don't burrow into your thoughts and dwell on yourself. Relax with your eyes wide open, with your senses fully awake, and with the idea of taking in all you can.

◆ E X E R C I S E   1–1

Relaxation

Stand easily, legs slightly apart, with enough room around you to stretch your arms in all directions.

While inhaling, extend your arms fully upward and outward. On your exhale, release your arms totally and let them drop to your sides. Release all the tension in your fingers, then your wrists, then your elbows, then your shoulders.

Repeat the preceding exercise four times. Starting with the third repetition go up on your toes as you inhale, and let your heels drop as you exhale. Try to extend your arms and to rise farther each time, and release your fingers, wrists, elbows, and shoulders farther as well.

Shake out your left leg for three full breaths, then your right leg; then repeat. Roll your neck around from left to right on the repeat.

Hands on hips, shudder your body and release all tension while taking five deep breaths. Avoid hyperventilating.

From the same position, rotate your body all the way to the left and then to the right three times. Then, hands still on hips, bow forward as far as you can, vertebra by vertebra, with your arms hanging to the floor, releasing all tension in your back, shoulders, arms, and fingers as you do so. Hang there for a long moment, taking a deep breath and enjoying the release. Slowly come back up, one vertebra at a time, until you are standing tall and freely erect. Do not compete with the persons next to you! This is a relaxation exercise, not a test of strength, speed, or agility.

Swing twice more to the left and the right, and bow a final time, shuddering your body as you come up.

On a full breath, exhale while saying "HUH, bubba buh, bubba buh, bubba buh!" Do it four more times, a bit louder each time.

On a full breath, exhale while saying "Brekka korex, korex, korex, korex." Repeat three more times, a bit louder each time. (This line, by the way, is an approximation of the "croaking chorus" of *The Frogs* by Aristophanes—a play twenty-five hundred years old!)

Do this line three *more* times, this time croaking each "korex" a tiny bit louder than the one immediately before it, as "Brekka korex. Korex! Korex!! KOREX!!!"

Exhale on "HUH, bubba buh, bubba buh, bubba buh!" while twisting your body left and right. Continue twisting with "Brekka korex, korex, korex, korex!" Alternate the speeches while twisting and bowing three more times.

Run in place—or jump an imaginary rope—for fifteen breaths.

Go up on your toes and extend your arms fully one last time; then release and collapse gently into a relaxed standing position. You're done.

Trust

Trust is also a precondition for acting. Because acting is something you do with, and in front of, other people, anxiety about those people can eat into your ability to act. Trust, like relaxation, cannot be forced, but you can't sit around waiting for it to arrive, either. Trust is a mutual relationship between you and your fellow actor–students—a relationship marked by giving, sharing, and common concern.

You must take the initiative here, because isolation and apathy invest the first classroom meeting with deadly inertia, and only the determined efforts of you and your fellows will break down the walls of carefully nurtured egotism and suspicion that characterize most groups of arbitrarily gathered strangers. If you can find your acting partner interesting, it will make you interested and interesting; if you find your partner fascinating, it will make you fascinated and fascinating. It is to your advantage to seek out what is admirable and wonderful in your fellow actors, the qualities that will make them prized companions and colleagues and will make you a lively partner dramatically engaged with them.

A word about competition: The theatre is a highly competitive business at the upper levels, which means that you will need companions and colleagues all the more. The intensely personal moments that characterize the greatest performances rarely come forth in a climate of contention or antagonism or through the isolation of seemingly self-sufficient individual actors. Rapport among actors, developed through trusting ensemble work, is the context of fine performance.

Actor trust means, at bottom, that you are comfortable with your fellows and they with you. It is the feeling that you can make a fool of yourself without embarrassment and can be emotionally open without getting stepped on. Acting exposes personal vulnerabilities (good acting does, anyway). An atmosphere of trust ensures that those exposures are not callously rubbed raw—that indeed they will become, if anything, therapeutic rather than humiliating and enjoyable rather than discouraging.

Trust develops first out of self-confidence and out of shared activities among the acting group. Trust exercises and games are often used; even children's games are frequently brought into classes or rehearsals by teachers and directors sensitive to the need for mutual trust. Pure socializing has its important place in the work of actors, both in class and in the professional world. Mutual massage or mutual back rubs are also beneficial, both for trust and for relaxation. An excellent basic warm-up involving both is the following "spine lengthening" exercise adapted from the Alexander technique (see Lesson 18).

◆ E x e r c i s e   1–2

Spine Lengthening

Pair with a partner. One person lies down on a mat, face up, knees raised. The other gently pulls the supine actor's head away from the torso, tilting the chin down slightly at the same time. Going around the supine body, the massaging actor gently pulls one limb at a time away from the torso center, pulling along the limb, and then at the extremities, returning to the head after each limb.

At the end of the massage, the actor is rolled to one side and invited to curl into a fetal position. The actor can then be gently raised to an erect position, his or her head is lifted up and away one last time, and the actors reverse positions. This exercise induces a sense of well-being in addition to relaxation and trust; each actor will feel about two inches taller at the end of it.

Neither trust nor relaxation comes about automatically, and for some people neither will come easily at all. Each of us brings different fears and tensions into our work. In general, the more you can focus away from yourself, and can recognize the uniqueness and beauty of the persons around you, and can respond to the world with wonder rather than with irritation and envy, the more you will be in the creative state that will permit you to act deeply, fully, and with spirit.

Exuberance

Acting—in nearly all of its forms—requires a level of performance energy that more sedentary activities, like writing or studying, ordinarily do not. It also requires, during actual moments of performance, a positive and uncritical attitude so that you can carry through your performance tasks with confidence rather than self-doubt. Putting these two together—energy and positive attitude—we may say that acting requires a level of spirited exuberance and a willingness to make a fool of yourself in public if need be, neither of which is often seen elsewhere in daily academic life.

Such exhibitionism (as it is sometimes called) does not come easily, and we all come to acting with social conditioning that inhibits public displays of exuberance. No one need immediately start shouting, grimacing, acting-up, and acting-out in public to prove that he or she is an actor, but regular public performance activities, such as singing in a choir or musical, reading aloud in class or in staged play-readings, giving political speeches for class elections, teaching classes, or even speaking in classroom discussions are all useful in developing performance energy and exuberant expression. Here's a simple exercise that helps break barriers as well.

◆ E X E R C I S E   1–3

BAM-POW, Dance, Sing

1. Shadowbox

Make two fists, and bouncing from foot to foot, with one fist (normally the right) held up to protect your chin, jab at an imaginary opponent with the other, extending your arm fully each time. As you do this, shout "BAM!" with every blow.

Continue to bounce from foot to foot, dodging your imaginary opponent's imaginary blows ("Rope-a-dope," Muhammad Ali called this). When you see an (imaginary) opening, hit your opponent with your other fist—a potentially knockout punch known as a cross (a "right cross" if done with your right fist). With every cross, shout "POW!"

Use your "Bams" and "Pows" to cheer yourself on, to frighten your opponent into submission, and to encourage others to cheer for you (which will frighten your opponent even more). Exult in your (imaginary) victory. Attract a crowd.

2. Dance

Balancing on the balls of your feet, step forward on one foot while extending the same arm, wrist forward, in the same direction, letting your fingers follow after the wrist has reached its maximum extension. The movement is identical to throwing a Frisbee. At the moment when the fingers follow (or the imaginary Frisbee is released), cry "Dance!" Repeat with the other leg and arm, and keep repeating, in alternation, crying "Dance!" with each move.

Continue, switching to the word "Ballet!" As you step on your right foot, go up on your toes on your left foot, and vice versa. Say the word "ballet" in a way that encourages others to appreciate the beauty of ballet (whether or not you find it beautiful).

Continue, switching to the word "L'amour!" (the French word for "love," pronounced "la-MOOR!") and imagining that you are casting beautiful flower petals—as love tokens—at the feet of beautiful persons. Say the word "L'amour" in a way that encourages others to think you a wonderful and imaginative lover (whether or not you think you are).

Exult in your magnificent ballet moves and your beautiful tossing of flower petals.

(Feel like a fool yet? Good; you're doing fine. But in acting, you'll have to do equally ridiculous things—and believe in them! This is just to get you started.)

3. Sing

With your feet planted firmly on the ground, and with one hand on your belly and the other extended before you, sing an aria whose notes you invent and whose sole lyric consists of several repetitions of the word "Aria!"

Exult in your operatic splendor. Hear cries of "Bravo!" in your head.

Continue, switching to "HUH, bubba buh, bubba buh, bubba buh!" Don't just do these exercises; do them *exuberantly!*

Discipline

DISCIPLINE

To be an actor in the theatre is to teach yourself and keep yourself disciplined and honorable. And if you do that, you get a chance to fly in this kind of emotional paradise that acting can be. Acting is just as hard as ditch digging. And if you do all the yeoman work, inspiration will come.

FRANK LANGELLA

It goes without saying that an actor must be a disciplined artist. Inasmuch as the theatre is a collaborative art, discipline is essential to the effectiveness of the collaboration. Without discipline, trust disappears. If you can't trust your fellow actor to show up for rehearsal, you can't trust her or him to be sensitive to your feelings.

As a result, theatre artists must be particularly punctual and responsible, must meet all of their obligations on time (and *precisely* on time), and must be fully prepared to expend their energies in the pursuit of high standards of artistic effort. That "the show must go on" is a well-known cliché does not detract from its serious importance in the theatre world. Theatre is not a casual activity, and the intensity of the theatrical experience is made possible only by the dedication and commitment of theatre artists to collaborate fully and responsibly with each other on a continuing basis. Discipline makes you someone who can be counted upon, and it makes you able to count upon the commitment of others. There is no better place to start learning artistic discipline than in an acting class.

Criticism

Every actor, from the beginner to the veteran professional, must learn to come to grips with criticism. There is no way around it. Criticism comes from instructors, fellow students, audiences, directors, the press, neighbors, parents, friends, competitors, and avowed enemies. Some is constructive, some instructive, some destructive, and some entirely beside the point. Some you will find useful; some you will find inane; some you will inevitably find unfair. And let's make no mistake about it: Criticism hurts. Anybody who says it doesn't is either a fool or a liar.

The reason criticism hurts the actor more than it hurts other artists is that the art of the actor comes directly out of the actor himself or herself;

therefore, criticism of the actor usually takes the form of criticism of the actor's voice, movement, feelings (or seeming lack of feelings), expression, or personality. Some so-called criticisms of acting published in widely read magazines take the form of vitriolic attacks on the personal appearance or mannerisms of an actor. It is understandable, therefore, that actors in general tend to take criticism personally—and that's why it hurts.

The best way to relate to criticism of your work is to profit from it. As a beginner, you must realize that you have much to learn and that persons with some experience in the theatre can be of great help to you. While well-intended and constructive criticism is obviously going to be the most helpful to you, you can learn from callous criticism as well—as long as you filter it properly. The important things are not to take criticism too personally and not to waste a lot of time defending yourself. In the long run, it means little if the criticism is fair or unfair. If you can learn from it, use it. If you can't learn from it, forget it. All criticism is subjective in the final analysis, and you're not going to please everybody. You should be aiming at steady growth, greater comfort onstage, and greater freedom to go out on one emotional limb after another. Any suggestions or critiques that you can turn to your advantage are not only to be dealt with, they should be sought after with persistence. The finest actors do not try to avoid criticism; they solicit it.

A Playful Attitude

> ⚑ OPEN AND PLAYFUL
>
> *I was fairly playful, and I think that, really, the space to be in as an actor is open and playful and listening and exploring.*
>
> SUSAN SARANDON, ON WHAT LED HER INTO ACTING

Acting is a serious, but never a solemn, art. While its historic roots may lie partly in religious worship, they lie equally in "play," which includes child's play and acting-out (if not acting-up). In acting, you must develop a healthy balance between disciplined commitment and creative playing, and between studying the reality around you and investigating the imagination within you. Like play, theatre is entertaining—not only for the audience but for you the actors (players) as well. Theatre provides you a very special entertainment, one rooted in deep involvement, energetic effort, and creative improvisation, all within a focused framework. Theatre is mind filling, just like volleyball, chess, and Ping-Pong. Indeed, acting alternates with sports as the chief object of our leisure-time attention; and acting and sports—plays and play—are surprisingly similar activities. For this reason, beginning acting classes—as well as some professional acting ensembles—often begin their work with a few games.

Acting is work, but it is also play. If you forget that, you lose a crucial aspect of this very subtle art.

Freedom

Finally, the actor must learn to be free—free from physical and psychological inhibition—and must learn to enjoy that freedom. The actor must be free to think, feel, touch, and be touched. Above all, the actor's imagination must be unhindered. Relaxation, trust, discipline, and an effective response to criticism all play a part in this—relaxation and trust because they promote uninhibited interaction, discipline because it establishes a limit to gratuitous encroachment of the actor's physical privacy (preventing, for example, unwarranted sexual groping), and a response to criticism that allows the actor to grow, not shrivel, from his or her experience.

The free actor can imagine anything. Fantasy is the actor's playground; unbridled fantasy is the prerequisite to playing Romeo or Juliet, George or Martha. An actor afraid to fantasize, afraid to imagine the unimaginable, is an actor unacceptably bound to a narrow spectrum of emotional life. Plays and scenes may be outwardly mild; inwardly they are usually stormy and violent. The actor's mind must be able to play freely with the inner turmoil of the character: The actor's mind must be open to lust, terror, joy, and exaltation by turns—and must be open to playing the actions that emanate from those mental states.

Acting is emotionally risky. Indeed, one of the joys of acting is in taking those risks. The exercises and suggestions that follow in this book, and experience that will ensue in any acting class, will lead into these emotionally risky areas. An actor obdurately refusing to follow that lead—an actor who, instead, retreats behind a fixed image of herself or himself—is not free to act.

Preparation

You may begin to study acting at any age. Indeed, the study of acting is invariably a prerequisite to the study of other theatre arts, such as directing; it is also a useful preparation for public speaking, politics, law, business, and any profession where self-expression and communication are important.

But there are some useful things that you can do or study before beginning to act. Dance, in any fashion, is most helpful to the beginning actor because it teaches a physical mode of performance. Athletics also provides a good background for acting because of the energy it demands and because of the public nature of its exhibition. Singing, poetry reading (and writing), and storytelling are exceptionally helpful because they involve language and performance and getting at the heart of feelings in a constructive way. Reading (novels, plays, and biographies) helps the young actor to understand the complexities of human life, including varieties of human experience not immediately observable in the actor's environment. And of course, theatregoing is a prime preparation for acting: seeing the potentials of performance, and seeing the work of accomplished actors firsthand.

Summary

The precursors to acting—relaxation, trust, exuberance, discipline, the response to criticism, a playful attitude, freedom to act, and prior preparation—do not simply appear on command; nor need you have them in your hip pocket before your first class in acting. They are developed continually in a beginning actor's work, and they need refreshing throughout an actor's career. They will stand you in good stead whether you become an actor or not, for they are also useful preparations for the interactions of daily life, for relationships of every order, whether personal or professional. And they are the sort of basic goals you should check yourself out on regularly as you pursue your studies toward artistic advancement in the theatre or elsewhere.

L E S S O N

2

What Is Acting?

◆ E X E R C I S E   2–1

Pledge Your Allegiance to a Flag*

Imagine there is an American flag on the front wall of your classroom. Pledge allegiance to it. Here are the words:

I pledge allegiance to the flag of the United States of America, and to the republic for which it stands: one nation, under God, indivisible, with liberty and justice for all.

Go ahead.

* * *

Good. Now repeat the exercise, *very sincerely.* When you finish, as before, don't move or talk; just keep looking at the imaginary flag. Go ahead.

* * *

Keep looking at the flag.

_____

* This exercise might best be led by an instructor prior to the first assignment out of this book. A video of the author conducting this exercise may be purchased on VHS cassette from Insight Media (www.insight-media.com) or on DVD from First Light Video (www.firstlightvideo.com).

Now imagine the following situation: You are not and have never been an American citizen, nor have visited America, nor indeed have ever been outside your own country, which is across an ocean from America. The country where you have lived your entire life has, in the past years, come under the rule of a tyrannical regime that regularly persecutes—for no reason—people of your race or ethnic origin. This persecution has gotten much worse in recent months. Goon squads are driving through your village arresting people at will. You hear cries of torture from a military post right outside of town. There is no mail, television, radio, telephone, or communications from the outside world, and you are not allowed to criticize the regime to your friends or even your family. And yesterday your little sister was picked up by the goon squad and driven away, screaming for help.

You have decided you must leave your country by any means. You sneak out of your town in the dead of night, with nothing but the clothes you are wearing, and walk toward the distant ocean. Eventually you manage to get on a boat headed to the United States. After a long, miserable crossing, you now, miraculously, find yourself standing on the sand of a beach, facing inland. In front of you is a hill, covered in green grass; on the top of the hill flies an American flag.

You have never seen a real American flag, but you have seen pictures of it. You believe America to be a land of freedom, justice, and democracy, and you decide you will, before proceeding farther, *write your own prose-poem offering to become an ally of all Americans.* Your prose-poem will declare not only your allegiance to this cloth symbol of the United States, but also your bond with its democratic government and free citizens.

Still facing this (imaginary) flag, make your pledge to it: However, *the words of your prose-poem just happen to be the identical words of the Pledge of Allegiance cited above.* But these are your own words now, and you are making them up as you say them.

On your own time, and without making any effort to say this prose-poem in unison with anyone else, go ahead.

* * *

Keep looking at the flag.

Now give the pledge one more time: This time, when you come across the four words or phrases described below, think of the possible alternatives—the sort of words you might previously have said under these circumstances, or could otherwise say—before you *choose* the one precise word that is in the pledge as you have twice now given it. These words or phrases are:

"**allegiance**" In your former country, you had to pledge your "obedience." But that wouldn't be right here: You're going to be an "ally" of the flag, not a slave to it. On the other hand, what's the single word that means "an ally of"? You don't remember saying this word ever in your life, but you know it: It's "allegiance." So your thinking (in parentheses) that accompanies these first words is something like: "I pledge . . . (not obedience but, ummm . . .) allegiance . . ."

"United States of America" When you and your friends talked about this country in earlier times, you always said "America" or "USA" or "the US." But that seems a little too informal at this moment, doesn't it, when you are pledging to be an ally of it?

"republic" What were those definitions of governmental forms we heard about in school? Dictatorship, monarchy, empire . . . no, America is probably a . . . "republic."

"under God" In your old country, your nation was ruled by the tyrant, and the army, and the rich, and the upper class, or the favored ethnic group. Your new nation, to which you would pledge allegiance, would recognize only one higher power—*if any*—and thus would only find itself "under God."

Pledge your allegiance this time as before, but *choosing*—immediately before you speak them—these four words or phrases from your list of possible alternatives.

On your own time, as before, go ahead.

* * *

Keep looking at the flag.

Now you are going to give the pledge one more time, exactly as before, except that this time when you come to the word **"United"** in the country's name you are going to reflect on the fact that what became the United States was originally a group of independent states—and the people in them—that *chose* to unite and that now *you* have chosen to unite with them. As you say the word "United," then, let the people *behind* the flag, who have already united with each other, know that you are coming to unite with them.

And how about the people standing next to you? For the first time, *listen* to them and discover that they, too, seem to be pledging their allegiance—in words that sound amazingly like yours.

You must now realize you are not an isolated escapee from another land but, rather, part of a *group* of emigrants, all fleeing to a country that promises liberty and justice—not just to you, but to *all*.

So—without looking at these other people—start *blending* your voice with the voices around you. *Unite* with them. Make clear to your fellow emigrants—purely by the sound of your voice—that you hear them and that you are willing to help them and gain their help as well, in a united cause.

And when you come to the words **"one nation,"** say this phrase in unison with those around you, making this a united pledge rather than your own solo effort.

And when you come to the word **"indivisible,"** let everybody on the beach know that you will *not let this group be divided again.* The dictator in your home country, by not permitting the freedom of assembly or letting people communicate with each other, kept the citizens isolated: Persuade your fellow emigrants that you will never let this happen again.

And when you come to the words **"for all,"** insist to everyone—both beside you on the beach and three thousand miles behind the flag—that you will work to provide universal freedom and justice for all Americans, including the American you plan to become.

So, starting on your own time, and beginning to listen and blend with the others on "United," go ahead.

* * *

Now one more time.

Bend down and, with the hand you ordinarily throw with, pick up some imaginary sand pebbles from the beach. Stand back up.

This time you are going to make your pledge exactly as before, except that at the words **"with liberty"** you are going to turn around and face the ocean you have just crossed and, beyond that, the country from which you have fled. Thousands of miles from you are the goons that picked up your little sister. As well as the dictator who ordered them to perform those horrific deeds. As well as those friends and family members you left behind.

Send your word **"liberty"** *all the way across the ocean* so that your friends and family can hear it—and can hear that you have made it across the ocean to a land that gives you the liberty to make a pledge such as this one.

Send your words **"and justice"** to them as well—and also to the goons and the dictator and indeed the entire population of your country, so that they will know that justice does still exist in the world, which means that the days of the goons and dictators are numbered.

And with the words **"for all,"** *throw* your sand pebbles all the way across the ocean, so as to blind the goons, and at the same time to float as a signal of hope—angel dust if you will—upon your sister and your captive friends.

Go ahead.

* * *

That's all. The exercise is over.

What was the difference between the first pledging of allegiance and the last?

If you are like the thousands of persons who have participated in this exercise, you will have noticed many if not all of the following changes that occurred:

◆ The speech was more *emotional*. From a mere rote recitation, it moved to an expression of real feeling.

◆ The words were invested with *meaning*. What were at first vaguely understood concepts became specific political or personal principles.

◆ You felt a sense of *connection* with other people, both the real ones next to you and the unseen, imaginary ones planted in the improvisation.

◆ You felt connected *personally* to the words you were saying, which seemed to come not just out of your mouth, but out of your active mind as well.

◆ You felt more *creative*, the creator and not merely the reciter of the text.

◆ You felt *active*, not passive.

◆ You felt your emotions *grow* during the speech, rather than being static.

◆ You experienced *exhilaration* by the end, whereas the first time you only felt dutiful or even (when asked to pledge "sincerely") a sense of failure.

◆ Technically, your pledge was, in general, *louder,* and by the end it had built to an accelerating crescendo. The same was true for the pledges you heard others saying.

◆ Also technically, the *inflections* (pitch changes), which had always gone downward between phrases (after "allegiance" and "flag," for example) now often went upward, both for you and your fellow students.

This exercise shows exactly *what acting is.*

Acting is taking a memorized text, almost always written by someone else, and investing it with your own personal feelings, intelligence, communicative skills, interest in other people, and personality. All of these are brought out by *living the situation* that the dramatic character—in this case, an immigrant to the United States—experiences.

And, as it happens, the above-bulleted "changes" in your reading from the first to the last pledge all represent what most people call "good theatre" and "good acting": namely, acting that is emotionally vivid, intellectually precise, interpersonally communicative, personally authentic, creative, active, growing, and with variation, momentum, and uplift.

Notice that none of these changes happened when you were simply asked, on the second time through, to "be sincere." Indeed, you probably felt a sense of failure at that request ("Wasn't I sincere the first time?") and again in the pledge that followed, since you were made self-conscious about your level of sincerity (and being sincere basically means not "trying to put on an act," which the "be sincere" command makes you do).

Sincerity, and good acting (and of course *great* acting), comes from fully throwing yourself into a situation, not "putting on an act."

Please note: This exercise is not about your or your author's politics! It is not about America or your belief (or disbelief) in God! It is only about *acting*. The improvisation is sheer fiction. If your ancestors came to the United States on slave ships, they moved from relative freedom to unspeakable oppression. Other immigrants came for business or family reasons; still others emigrated thousands of years ago, across the Bering Sea, long before anyone had conceived of "America." And no one can seriously believe that America has provided liberty or justice for *everyone—all the time*. All you are asked to do, in this exercise, is *act the role* of a person who has had, and is having, the described experience. And you are asked to *imagine* that you could throw sand pebbles across an ocean, which of course can happen only in fantasy. Acting, and the imagination that powers it, create all the bulleted points listed above.

Summary

So, by *experiencing* this improvisation, you have learned—by doing it—the most basic nature of acting. You have taken a memorized text, written by someone else,* and, by accepting, elaborating on, and playing a situation, invested it with your own person. Almost everything in the rest of the book will build upon what you have experienced in this fundamental exercise.

---

* The Pledge of Allegiance was written by Francis Bellamy, a staff writer for *Youth's Companion;* it was first published in the magazine's September 8, 1892, issue. The phrase "under God" was added by Congress in 1954.

II

The Actor's Approach

ACTING IS A PROCESS INVOLVING CERTAIN TRANSFORMATIONS: A PERSON is transformed into an actor; an actor is transformed into a character. This process is not sudden or magical (although it may at times appear to be both); rather, it is gradual and deliberate.

The actor's approach is the series of steps the actor takes in that process. They are steps of exploring, feeling, trying, and doing; together they form a set of experiences. Every actor, from the beginner to the veteran professional, goes through these experiences. Every actor re-creates the process of acting with every performance.

The actor's approach, therefore, is a process of self-transformation—of moving out of oneself and getting into a role or into a work of art. It is a series of first steps that, like all first steps, are very challenging.

Goal and Obstacle

Fundamental Principle

There is one fundamental principle in acting. It's that the actor must always play toward a goal. This is because characters, who resemble persons in life, are pursuing goals. *The actor acts by pursuing—often vigorously—the presumed goal of the character.*

Sometimes this goal is called the *objective*. Often, in the pages that follow, it is also called the *victory*. Some other teachers use the word *intention*, or *purpose*, or *want*. It doesn't really matter what it is called, as long as you pursue it. This is what makes acting represent life; it's what makes acting lifelike.

There is a corollary to this principle. It's that in a play the goal should be fairly difficult to achieve. This is what makes acting dramatic. "To take a breath" may be a real-life goal, but in everyday situations it is not difficult enough to engage our energies or to be interesting to an audience. If you were under water, however, "to take a breath" would be a goal sufficiently difficult to be dramatic.

Therefore, the actor must pursue a *goal* (e.g., "to take a breath") in the context of an *obstacle* (e.g., "you are under water"). You want to marry—a person who is reluctant. You want to overthrow—an adversary who is powerful. You want to win the race—despite your sprained ankle.

The goal is what you—your character—wants.

The obstacle is what stands in your way.

> ⚑ GOAL
> _____
>
> *The actor's intention is the only thing that counts. Everything else is just talk.*
>
> WILLIAM H. MACY

You have to try hard to achieve your goal, despite your obstacle.

This ties you to your character and makes your acting both lifelike and dramatic.

◆ E X E R C I S E   **3–1**

Reaching

Stand on your right foot; reach as high as you can with your left hand. Reverse: Stand on your left foot and reach with your right hand.

By itself, reaching is not an acting exercise. It is merely a physical exercise, or a calisthenic.

◆ E X E R C I S E   **3–2**

Reaching for Goals

Imagine that there is something you greatly desire above your head: a beautiful jewel, or a bowl of strawberries, or "the key to your true love's heart." Now, reach again!

When you are reaching for a goal, your action is purposeful and you are emotionally, physiologically committed. You reach farther, more intently, more energetically. You reach so hard that you pull yourself off balance. You bounce on the balls of your feet. You are not merely following an instruction, you are trying to *do* something. You are intent upon achieving your goal: You want something and you want it badly. All these words—*purposeful, doing, trying, intent, winning, want*—are useful in describing the playing for goals. The actor's energetic pursuit of the character's goal is what makes the action of a play acting, not demonstrating; dynamic, not static.

In reaching, you are working against an obstacle: your own physical limitations. You can stretch only so far against the pull of gravity. Now, intensify that obstacle:

◆ E X E R C I S E   3–3

Overcoming an Obstacle

Imagine that you are sick to your stomach and fearful of losing control of your bowels. Reach up as in Exercise 3–2—only the more you reach, the sicker you feel. The more excited you get at reaching for your bowl of strawberries, the more fearful you become that you will publicly embarrass yourself.

In Exercise 3–3, your simple act of reaching has become an emotionally complex experience, even profound. You are acting.

There is no exercise, no acting challenge, that cannot be seen as a confrontation between an obstacle and an actor's pursuit of a goal. The job of the actor is to find and pursue goals in every role, even in every training exercise or calisthenic, and also to find and challenge the obstacles that stand in the way. Finding goals and obstacles sometimes involves research, but it always involves imagination. Frequently, imagination, properly focused, is all that is needed to transform simple, everyday acts into acting.

Imagination is the breeding ground for fantasy, and an actor's fantasy is often the source of his or her most compelling goals and obstacles. What did you think when you read "the key to your true love's heart"? Did you take that literally or figuratively? Would the image of Rapunzel in her tower prison or Leonardo DiCaprio in chains have made you reach higher and harder? The actor's job is not just to find goals and obstacles but to create them—and to create them with such vividness and enthusiasm that they can lead to an exciting and clearly defined performance, even in a simple exercise.

📓 OBSTACLE

For an action to be dramatic, it needs a counter-balancing obstacle; so make sure you know what it is.

JON JORY

Self-Consciousness

If playing toward goals and playing against obstacles are the fundamental principles of acting, self-consciousness is the actor's greatest enemy. Standing up and being observed, being "on display" for the presumably critical eyes of others, is a terrifying prospect to most of us.

◆ E X E R C I S E   3–4

Doing vs. Being

Do the following actions in order. Allow thirty seconds for each numbered command.

1. Stand up in front of the group.

2. Be dignified.

3. Look sexy.

4. Relax.

5. Count the number of men you see.

6. Count the number of women faster than you counted the men. If you succeed, you'll win a prize!

Chances are that the first two minutes of that exercise were agonizing. Being publicly commanded to "be dignified" or "look sexy" fills us with terror; how certainly we will fail! And how can we relax with all those people looking at us? How can we *really* relax—on cue? But counting the men—that's *doing* something; the focus moves away from us and onto the watchers. And counting the women—fast, so as to win a prize (even an imaginary prize)—that's *energetic* doing; that's even almost fun!

The actor cannot simply "be" something or somebody onstage, or simply "look" a certain way, without being acutely self-conscious, unbearably self-aware of being or looking. Nor can the actor be ordered to relax, because relaxing—real relaxing—means not worrying about obeying anybody's orders. The only way for an actor to avoid self-consciousness—and to truly relax—is to do something. And the more actors feel they are doing something important (as, for example, trying to win a prize), the more they relax into the task and think about things other than themselves.

Projection

Self-consciousness is your focus on yourself; projection is your focus on others, on the outside world, and your efforts to project your concerns outside yourself. Projection is also your ability to project your voice, to be heard by others, to *make yourself heard* by others. Projection, therefore, is basically the opposite of self-consciousness; it is the ability to escape the prison of yourself (self-doubt, self-indulgence, selfishness) and to enter into active, productive social intercourse. Every actor must learn this skill quite thoroughly.

◆ E X E R C I S E   3–5

Resonating

Do the following actions in order.

1. Face the wall and say "ahhhhhh."

2. Recognize that sound is simply the vibration of molecules. Face the wall, say "ahhhhhh," and feel the vibration in your throat.

3. Recognize that sound resonates and that sound may set up sympathetic vibrations in other objects. Face the wall, say "ahhhhhhh," and try to make the molecules in the wall vibrate in harmony with your voice.

The three steps in Exercise 3–5 lead you from self-consciousness to projection. In the first, you are simply making sound. In the second, you are making sound with a purpose: to feel your own vibration. In the third, you are making sound with a purpose that *extends beyond yourself:* In other words, you are projecting your sound purposefully; you are pursuing a goal (trying to make the wall vibrate) and struggling against an obstacle (the firmness of the wall). It does not matter if the wall vibrates or not. (Actually, the wall does vibrate, but there's no way you can measure this.) The point is that you have created and acted upon a goal, using a real object (the wall), your voice, and your imagination.

Did your voice change on the third step? Of course it did. It became louder, more resonant, and more forceful. Chances are that you opened your jaw wider, dropped your Adam's apple lower in your throat, and straightened your posture. You may not know it, but these are exactly what a voice teacher would instruct you to do, and you have done it without thinking about anything except vibrating a wall!

◆ E X E R C I S E   3–6

Resonating (A Continuation)

Pair with a partner and space yourself away from others as much as possible. By turns, say "ahhhhhh" to the partner, with the goal of vibrating your partner's spine with the sound of your voice. With your fingers, feel your partner's spine to see if you can feel the actual vibrations. Try different ranges of your vocal pitch, different kinds of vocal sounds, and different positions of your body. Try to feel the vibrations as much as you can.

In Exercise 3–6, you are projecting sound not to a wall but to another person. Moreover, you are trying to sense the physical effects of that projection. Your concentration has gone entirely from the sound of your voice to the physical effect your voice has on your partner, and now your consciousness is not self-directed but other-directed. This exercise has led you to a moment—however simple—of "pure" acting: person-to-person communication at the most fundamental level.

Some acting moments in plays are precisely this: one character holding, cuddling, or embracing another, saying "ahhhhhh" as a way to lull the other character into relaxing, or into a romantic mood, or to settle the other character's nerves. Or the "ahhhhhh" could be an exclamation, accompanied by a raised sword, as Macbeth draws on Macduff, attempting (as his goal) to frighten him into submission. Not all acting involves lines, but all acting does involve person-to-person communication, at either the verbal or the nonverbal level.

In playing a role, of course, the actor must project more than just sound. Words, gestures, ideas, feelings, commands, personality—these are among the intangibles that the actor must convey to other actors and to the back of the house, that is, the audience. These projections all enter into the stream of communication that every actor both generates and receives. Projections are the means by which actors involve themselves with the activity around them—and turn their focus outward, away from self-conscious self-absorption.

◆ E X E R C I S E   3–7

Goals

Do the following tasks. Afterward, define the goal, define the obstacle, and discuss the degree to which your involvement in each task projected yourself into the world outside yourself and dispelled your self-consciousness.

1. Untie and remove your partner's shoes.

2. Find the 126th word on page 56 of this book.

3. Balance this book on your partner's head.

4. Find the wall or piece of furniture or other object that best resonates with the sound of your voice.

5. Find the best pitch of your voice to resonate that which you found in item 4.

6. Neaten your corner of the classroom.

7. Move people from one corner of the classroom to another.

Summary

The actor always plays toward a goal and against an obstacle. Concentration on achieving the goal reduces the actor's self-consciousness; moreover, it demands that the actor *project* by focusing on something or someone. The mutual projection between actors—a person-to-person communication—is the foundation of all acting, even the most complex or most highly stylized.

4

Acting with the "Other"

The Other

In most plays, the actors do not try to resonate walls; they try to have an impact on other people. Usually those other people are the other characters in the play. For the purposes of acting class, the "other" is your acting partner.

Probing deeply into other people is one of the essential tasks of the actor. This does not necessarily mean long talks into the night, social involvements, mutual therapy sessions, or the baring of personal secrets. It certainly does not mean forcing confessions or outside relationships on other actors. It does mean a willingness to look clearly and directly at your acting partner and to take in *the whole person* with whom you are acting.

◆ E X E R C I S E   4–1

Making Your Partner Smile

Pair with a partner. Stand opposite your partner and devote about twenty seconds to each of the tasks that follow. At the end of the list, change roles and repeat the exercise.

THE OTHER

I work very much with other people; I don't do a performance alone, and I want the other person to react with me and be honest with me. I need that desperately.

ESTELLE PARSONS

---

1. Study your partner's eyebrows.

2. Make your partner smile.

3. Study your partner's mouth.

4. Make your partner laugh.

5. Ask yourself: What makes my partner laugh?

6. Make your partner laugh *loudly*.

7. Study your partner's eyes.

8. Ask yourself: What does my partner see, looking at me?

9. Make your partner take you seriously.

10. Smile.

11. Take your partner's two hands.

12. See the four-year-old child your partner once was.

13. See the corpse your partner eventually will be.

14. Make your partner smile.

(While you're trying to make your partner smile, your partner should simply be studying your face, with the goal of trying to figure out how your mind works.)

When you try to make your partner smile, or laugh, or take you seriously, you are not merely "doing something." You are doing something to (or with) someone else—that is, you are participating in an interaction. All acting is interacting with other persons (even monologues, which are discussed at the end of this lesson).

Your acting partner is a person. He or she was an infant once and is as mortal as you are. Your acting partner (like you) is a sexual person, a fearful person, a caring person, and a person who has profound desires. In other words, your acting partner is not just "your acting partner." He or she is an individual and, potentially, a source of great inspiration for you.

The more fully you contact your acting partner, the more fully you will be acting. Acting is something you can never do entirely in isolation or entirely by yourself. In order to "live" onstage, you must first make the other characters, your acting partners, "live" in your mind. Your communication—your acting—will ultimately depend as much on them as on you and on the intensity with which you make yourself believe in them and care about them.

Interactive Dynamics

The actor's awareness of others is not merely a matter of dispassionate observation. Stage relationships that are properly dramatic must suggest a potential for dramatic change: usually the potential for love, on the one hand, or the potential for physical or psychological violence, on the other. These potentials are the dynamics of relationships. Because this potential for love or violence is always present, we say that the actors are vulnerable. Exercise 4–2 is a simple way of approaching actor-to-actor vulnerability.

◆ E X E R C I S E   4–2

Vulnerability

Pair with a partner and designate one of you to be A and the other B. Memorize and quickly "rehearse" this contentless scene. (A contentless scene is one in which the words, by themselves, do not clearly reveal any specific characters or plot; it is a scene that has no specified dramatic content.)

A: One.

B: Two.

A: Three.

B: Four.

A: Five.

B: Six.

A: Seven.

B: Eight.

A: Nine!

B: Ten!

"Perform" the scene while imagining each of these situations:

1. You have reason to believe that your acting partner may be planning to murder you and that he or she may have a concealed weapon.

2. You were separated from a beloved sibling when you were three years old, and you have reason to believe that your acting partner is that sibling.

3. Person A has reason to believe (1) above, and Person B has reason to believe (2).

4. Person B has reason to believe (1) above, and Person A has reason to believe (2).

Vulnerability, a crucial component of all acting, means that you are aware of the other actor as a complete person, and that you are also aware of *the potential good or harm that can come from the relationship* between you.

Interactive dynamics suggest that relationships are not merely static arrangements between agreeable people but are evolving interplays of mutuality and independence, attraction and separation, desire and fear. The person you meet in the cafeteria today *could* be your life companion twenty years from now; the person you are rehearsing a scene with *could* pull out a revolver and shoot you. The normal human impulse is to ignore such remote potentials. The actor's impulse, in an acting situation, should be to make them vivid, to create the dynamics of the relationship wherever possible and appropriate. Even a scene as content-free as "one, two, three . . . ten" can become a vivid and exciting drama if you explore the potential for both love and violence that might be imagined as existing between characters A and B and the vulnerability of the actors to those potentials.

◆ E X E R C I S E   4–3

Discovery

Pair with a partner and designate an A and a B. "Play" the following interchange. Try to discover as much as possible about your partner by studying his or her tone of voice, expression, and changes in breathing pattern, and by speculating on his or her possible thoughts or fantasies.

A: Can I see you on Monday?

B: How about Tuesday?

A: How about Wednesday?

▣ OUTWARD-DIRECTEDNESS

In "real life" the mother begging for her child's life, the criminal begging for a pardon, the atoning lover pleading for one last chance—these people give no attention whatever to their own state, and all attention to the state of that person from whom they require their object. This outward-directedness brings the actor in "real life" to a state of magnificent responsiveness and makes his progress thrilling to watch. On the stage, similarly, it is the progress of the outward-directed actor, who behaves with no regard to his personal state, but with all regard for the responses of his antagonists, which thrills the viewers.

DAVID MAMET

B: How about Thursday?

A: How about Friday?

B: How about Saturday?

A: How about Sunday?

B: OK, then, Sunday.

Don't make any effort to give clever readings, and don't worry about your own delivery of the lines. In fact, don't think about yourself at all. *Concentrate entirely on your partner* and on finding out what you can about him or her. Direct your focus sharply outward, not inward, and you will both lose your self-consciousness as an acting student performing for a grade and intensify your full engagement in winning an interpersonal goal.

Try this alternate scene, too, with the same instructions:

A: I know you will.

B: I know I won't.

A: I know you will.

B: I know I won't.

A: I know you will.

B: I know I won't.

A: I know you will.

B: I know I won't.

The dialogues in this exercise were chosen because they can be memorized instantly. Memorized dialogue from scenes that you work on later also can be used in this exercise, if you wish to return to it.

The Character

Here's an important question that may have occurred to you already: When you make your partner smile, or when you imagine your partner as a long-lost sibling, or when you ask your partner if he or she can see you on Sunday, is your partner a classmate, or an actor, or a character? Philosophers may answer that question in a variety of ways, but for you there is only one answer: *Your partner is always a character.* The moment an acting exercise begins, it exists within a theatrical context. At that point, all participants are characters, and all behavior is acting, or "playing."

This is a liberating answer. It means that the interactions between your partner and yourself take place within an overall context in which you have already agreed to "play," or to interact as characters. Therefore, you can experience your feelings fully; you can experience the depth of love, lust, violence, and ambition within a dramatic context (even in an exercise or improvisation) without committing yourself in any personal (outside-of-class) way. Indeed, you can explore the extremities—and profundities—of feelings within the "playing" arena and return to your more private personality when the exercise (or play or improvisation) is over. The ability to see your classmates as characters—which extends to seeing your best friend as Iago and your worst enemy as Romeo—is the ability to free your feelings so as to act vividly and intensely with other people.

Tactics

Tactics are the strategies of human communication; they are the active ingredients of dynamic interactions. Most of the tactics of everyday life are simple and benign, generated more by spontaneous impulse than by conscious plan. Smiling, for example, encourages agreement and tolerance; raising the level of the voice encourages compliance. Some tactics are used to seek the support of other characters; some to silence their opposition.

In the effort to achieve goals and overcome obstacles, the actor continually tries to put *pressure* on the other actors—who are, of course, characters in the play or scene. This pressure is real; it may be the seductiveness of a raised eyebrow, the menace of a clenched fist, or the bedazzlement of a brilliantly articulated argument, but it is a pressure felt by the other actors and by the audience alike. Your power in playing tactics will determine your authority and magnetism on stage.

◆ E X E R C I S E   4–4

Using Tactics

Pair with a partner. Imagine that the nonsense word *beetaratagang* means "Get out of here!" in some foreign language. Imagine that the nonsense word *cleridipity* means "Come over here" in the same language. Take turns playing the following situations.

1. Order your acting partner away by saying "beetaratagang!" to him or her.

2. Urge your acting partner to come toward you by saying "cleridipity" to him or her.

3. Send your partner away with "beetaratagang" and then draw him or her back with "cleridipity." Reverse.

To communicate with your partner, use body language, tone of voice, inflection, gesture, facial expression, threats of physical force, seductive postures—everything you can think of *except* physical contact.

Full contact with an acting partner depends on your willingness to engage in genuine emotional interaction with another person: to frighten, to encourage, to alarm, and to entertain your acting partner. The desire to achieve your goal, coupled with a willingness and ability to translate that desire into effective person-to-person behavior, creates the baseline of your acting performance. Your ability to make "beetaratagang" so unsettling as to force someone to go away, or to make "cleridipity" so evocative as to induce someone to approach you, is a primal acting ability, coming wholly from you and not from a text or a dramatic staging or interpretation.

◆ E X E R C I S E   4–5

One Two Three Four Five Six Seven

This exercise is intended to deepen your concentration and extend your repertoire of communication tactics. Trying is more important than succeeding in these tasks.

Without touching your partner, and using only the words "one two three four five six seven" on each task, try to elicit the following actions or feelings from your partner.

1. Make your partner sit down next to you.

2. Make your partner kneel before you.

3. Make your partner feel sorry for you.

4. Make your partner happy.

5. Make your partner nervous.

6. Make your partner aroused.

7. Make your partner feel chilled.

Monologues

How do you act with the "other" when there seems to be no other: in, for example, a monologue, soliloquy, or one-person show, where you are alone onstage with no one else—physically at least—listening to you? You might say you are talking "to yourself" or "thinking aloud" in these cases, but that's not a very dramatic solution, nor is it particularly true to life.

Before mulling this over further, try the following exercise, in which you invent an imaginary other to act with.

◆ E X E R C I S E   4–6

Inventing the Other

Do Exercises 4–4 and 4–5 without a partner but with the following "others" that you create in your imagination:

1. As a "rehearsal" where you practice how you would frighten a bully away by saying "beetaratagang!" to him or her. Practice it out loud and to a variety of imagined bullies, big and small.

2. Speak to an imagined god-figure (Zeus, let's say, or Buddha, or the Judeo-Christian-Islamic "God") in whom you believe or can imagine you believe. Try to bring this deity into your physical presence by saying "cleridipity" or "one two three four five six seven." Vary the deity: Replace Zeus with Venus, then Satan, then a revered ancestor or role

model of your own. Such an exercise is, in fact, essential for playing characters (Oedipus or Dr. Faustus, for example) who worship or fear higher powers.

3. Imagine you learn that your hated uncle has murdered your beloved father. You know you will have a chance to confront him in court. Rehearse pointing your finger at him and crying these words of public accusation: "Bloody, bawdy villain!" Rehearse the line several times, trying to find the most persuasive tone.

4. Imagine a god-figure hovering above or around you as you contemplate a life-threatening adventure. Pose this dilemma to the god: "To be or not to be, that is the question." See if the god—by word or silence or gust of wind—answers you in any way or gives you any hint as to your best course to follow. Repeat several times, imagining the god-figure in different forms.

5. Speak to an imaginary audience that you cannot see (as would be the case onstage, with stage lights in your eyes). Try to get listeners to answer this question:

> "What is a man,
> If his chief good and market of his time
> Be but to sleep and feed?"

See if—and how—they answer you. They won't answer, but keep trying to get them to do so, repeating your question three or four times.

The speeches in items 3, 4, and 5, as you probably know, are from soliloquies spoken by Shakespeare's Hamlet. All dramatic speeches, even monologues and soliloquies, are spoken to "someone" else, even though that someone may be nonpresent at the time, dead, otherworldly, or imagined. This subject is taken up more fully in Lesson 28. If you're interested in tackling such a speech now—for an upcoming audition, for example—you might skip ahead to that lesson.

Summary

Acting is not something you do by yourself; invariably it is something you do to, with, or for at least one other person. Most of what the audience eventually sees in an acting performance is a *relationship* between characters—a relationship created by you and your acting partner. In order for that relationship to be a dramatic one, it must be dynamic. The actors must be vulnerable to one another. A potential for good or harm—preferably for both—must be clearly implied by the relationship, and the actors, through the use of interpersonal tactics, must put pressure on each other to change or improve their relationship.

5

Beginning to Act

Contentless Scene

In the preceding pages we have introduced several foundations of acting: goals, obstacles, vulnerability, projection, and the person-to-person contact and tactical interplay that characterize dynamic relationships. These fundamentals can all be explored in a series of contentless scenes—so called because they are devoid of fixed plot or characterizations.

A contentless scene can be memorized quite rapidly—usually in about ten minutes. In a group situation, actors should pair up and memorize their parts aloud, one person of each pair memorizing part A, the other person memorizing part B. During memorization, no attempt should be made to create an interpretation with the lines or to "fix" readings or inflections of individual lines; the lines are to be learned simply by rote.

When the scene has been memorized, the actors should then switch partners so that each A is paired with a B with whom they have not rehearsed or spoken this dialogue. The contentless scenes may be performed many times. Switch partners each time, so that each time the scene is produced, it is produced without prior rehearsal between the paired actors.

◆ E X E R C I S E   5–1

Contentless Scene I

Perform this scene without rehearsal or planning of any kind. For each performance, however, use one of the seven situations on the following list.

Scene: "What did you do last night?"

A: Hi!

B: Hello.

A: How's everything?

B: Fine. I guess.

A: Do you know what time it is?

B: No. Not exactly.

A: Don't you have a watch?

B: Not on me.

A: Well?

B: Well what?

A: What did you do last night?

B: What do you mean?

A: What did you do last night?

B: Nothing.

A: Nothing?

B: I said, nothing!

A: I'm sorry I asked.

B: That's all right.

The Seven Situations

1. A is a parent; B is a teenager. The scene takes place at the breakfast table; B eating a bowl of cereal, A entering.

2. A and B (different sexes) are a young married couple. Last night, after an argument, B left the apartment. It is now the following morning. A is washing dishes. B returns.

3. A and B (same sex) are roommates. Both have been involved with the same boy (or girl) during the past few weeks, both are still interested in pursuing the relationship, and both are somewhat suspicious of the other's secrecy. They meet while returning to their room after a night's absence.

4. A and B are classmates who have been romantically interested in each other for some time. They meet in a cafeteria by accident, and A sits down next to B.

5. A and B (same sex) are auditioning for an important role. It is rumored that the director plays sexual favorites in casting. A and B meet at the bulletin board to await the announcement of callbacks.

6. A and B are siblings. B has recently been released from a psychiatric unit after a suicide attempt. After B has stayed out all night, A finds B in the waiting room of a bus depot.

7. A and B are friends. B has recently been released from a psychiatric unit after maniacally attacking a friend with a butcher knife. A, aware of this, comes upon B in an isolated spot.

When many variations on contentless scenes are performed, with the actors switching partners each time, several things become evident.

The content of the scene is created entirely by the given situation and the actors: The words become instruments of the action, not the dictator of plot, character, or behavior. Thus the acting becomes a way of creating a spontaneously changing relationship—and the plot develops entirely out of what happens between you and your acting partner.

The scene is happening in real time—that is, it is being *experienced* while it is being performed. One often talks, in acting, about "creating the illusion of the first time."* In Exercise 5–1, "the first time" is no illusion; you are indeed experiencing the interchange for the first time, live and unrehearsed.

You will find that there is nothing you can do in Exercise 5–1 to succeed "on your own." Whatever happens in the contentless scene depends not on you or on your acting partner, but on what happens between the two of you. Person-to-person contact, tactical interplay, projection, and vulnerability are demanded by the exercise itself. In these situations, feelings come to you naturally.

---

* The notion, first expressed by nineteenth-century American actor–playwright William Gillette, that acting should appear unrehearsed, that each speech should be delivered as though the character was uttering the words "for the first time."

The scene is unpredictable. One of the problems in the theatre is that scripts, by nature, are predictable: The last act has already been written and rehearsed when the curtain rises on Act 1. Exercise 5–1 helps you avoid—for a time at least—the problem of making a predictable scene look unpredictable: The scene *is* unpredictable, and neither you nor your acting partner knows, at the outset, how it is going to end. Such a condition keeps you alert, involved, and mentally active throughout the scene, often to an extraordinary degree.

Intensifiers

Exercise 5–1 can be repeated almost indefinitely, inasmuch as there are hundreds of possible situations and thousands of implications that will make every rendition fresh and different. The exercise can also be intensified by adding obstacles to the situations.

◆ E X E R C I S E   5–2

Intensifying

Replay the dialogue in Exercise 5–1 using one of the seven situations, plus one of the obstacles on the following list. Repeat the exercise by varying both situations and obstacles.

1. Your acting partner has been known to carry a revolver.

2. You feel sick to your stomach.

3. The odor in the room is noxious.

4. You suspect your acting partner is dying.

5. Your acting partner is partly deaf.

6. It is very cold.

7. Your acting partner seems sexually frustrated.

8. Your acting partner seems especially flushed.

9. You do not feel that you can stand up without losing control of your bowels.

10. You feel that if you speak loudly, you will start crying.

The intensifiers are not things that you play or that you have to show in any way. Indeed, they are actually obstacles that you will have to struggle *against:* against showing them and against their standing in your way. The struggle against obstacles makes you perform more intensely. When speaking to a partly deaf person, for example, you must speak louder and with clearer articulation. Obstacles cannot be so great that they inhibit action altogether (that is why we specify a *partly* deaf person), or so insignificant that you can forget about them entirely. They must be bold enough to make you work harder, and difficult enough to make your quest dramatically interesting.

Physicalizers

Sometimes extraordinary changes occur in scenes simply when the locale is changed or when the actors are asked to carry on some sort of underlying action, such as jogging. Physicalizing a scene frequently brings out subtler undertones and more poignant transitions; it also gets the acting "into the body" more than simply sitting and talking.

◆ E X E R C I S E   5–3

Varying Locale or Action

Replay the contentless scene in any of these physicalized variations:

1. While jogging

2. While setting the table together

3. While lying down at the beach

4. B lying in bed, A seated at foot of bed

5. While playing basketball

6. While arm wrestling

7. While dancing to music

8. While doing push-ups

9. While eating a real banana

10. While giving a back rub, one to the other

Invent your own variations!

◆ E X E R C I S E   5–4

Contentless Scene II

Memorize the following dialogue. Then, using the new dialogue, repeat Exercises 5–1, 5–2, and 5–3.

Scene: *"I'm going away."*

A: Hi!

B: Hello.

A: You all right?

B: Yes.

A: Are you sure?

B: Yes, I'm sure. A little headache, that's all.

A: Oh, good. You want some aspirin?

B: No. Don't be so helpful, OK?

A: You are upset.

B: Good Lord!

A: OK, OK. I thought you might want to talk.

B: About what?

A: About anything.

B: I'm going away.

A: What do you mean?

B: I'm going away, that's all.

A: Where?

B: Not far. Don't get excited.

A: When?

B: Now. *[Starts to leave]*

The situations in the previous scene will work here, but you can invent dozens of other situations as well.

Summary

The contentless scene—in which the dialogue is essentially ambiguous, trivial, or both—provides an opportunity to explore the playing of goals, tactics, and relationships in a fresh, improvisatory manner, without planning or rehearsing. The personal interaction can be intensified by establishing obstacles to the basic goals. Physicalizing the scenes may bring out subtle meanings and pointed moments that are valuable in an acting performance.

6

Tactics

Punishment and Reward

To the actor, goals are more than just wishes or daydreams. They are what the dramatic character actively wants to win, gain, acquire, or achieve. Acting, by definition, is *action,* and it is *active.* We in the audience do not want to see you simply thinking about your goals; we want to see you working hard to achieve them.

Characters pursue their goals just as real people do, by employing *tactics.* They argue, they persuade, they threaten, they seduce, and they inspire. They try to influence other characters in the play to support them and to discourage other characters from opposing them. Indeed, this is why drama is *dramatic.* Tactics are the moment-to-moment work of truly dramatic acting. Tactics drive and define the basic interactions of the play.

Do we use tactics in our own lives? Most of us would like to believe that we don't, that we simply live and let live without trying to manipulate our friends and acquaintances. But as we saw in Lesson 4, this is not the case. When someone is talking to us, we smile to invite more talking or look skeptical to shut the fellow up. We frown at a disobedient child and raise our voices to make sure our instructions are followed. Or we squat humbly at the feet of a celebrated guru and beam upward to indicate the respect that may draw forth a word of wisdom. These are interpersonal tactics, and we use them whenever we are in the presence of others.

Dogs, cats, and two-month-old babies use tactics too; any thinking species with needs and wants uses tactics to seek and achieve its moment-to-moment goals and victories. Acting requires that the actor learn how to play tactics forcefully, winsomely, and engagingly.

There are basically two kinds of tactics: those that threaten and those that induce—punishment and reward, in other words. Tactics that threaten say, "Do what I want or I'll make your life miserable." Tactics that induce say, "Do what I want and you'll be happier for it." Raising your voice is a threatening tactic, smiling an inductive tactic; both are common in everyday life and on the stage that mirrors life.

Playing Tactics

When you play tactics onstage, you *really* play them. When your character is trying to threaten another character, you try to threaten your acting partner. But if your character is trying to encourage warmth from another character, you make every effort to induce that warmth from the actor who is your partner.

But remember this ground rule: The actor must never physically or sexually abuse another actor during an exercise, a scene, or an improvisation. Any acting involving physical force, combat, or overt sexual behavior must be rehearsed and talked through until both actors are fully comfortable with it. It is often useful to have a general understanding of what constitutes sexual abuse in an exercise situation, as this definition may vary depending on the age, experience, and cultural milieu of the actors involved.

◆ E X E R C I S E   6–1

Frighten Your Partner

Pair with a partner. Using one of the phrases below, try to *actually frighten* your partner.

1. Shut up!

2. Get out of here!

3. Leave me alone!

4. Go to hell!

5. Go on, kill me!

Study your partner's expression. Has color or animation drained from his face? Does she seem to be trembling or fidgety? Are his eyes widening? Remember, it's not essential that you *succeed* in achieving these results, only that you *try* to achieve them—and that you *really* study your partner to find out whether you have in fact succeeded or failed (in which case, try harder!).

◆ E X E R C I S E   6–2

Building Intensity

Using the phrases in Exercise 6–1, again trying to frighten your partner, repeat each phrase three times, building your intensity each time, as in "Shut up! Shut up!!! SHUT UP!!!!!" You might even add a mild oath to the last invective, as "Shut up! Shut up!!! SHUT UP, DAMMIT!!!!" Try to increase your intensity in several ways—not   just by increasing your volume (although that will be part of it) but by a more vigorous pronunciation, an increasingly commanding (and threatening) physical presence, and a deepening emotional commitment to your goal.

◆ E X E R C I S E   6–3

Try to Make Your Partner Cry

Repeat Exercise 6–2 with a different partner, and try to make a tear well up in your partner's eye. Again, don't worry if this doesn't happen; the point is not to succeed but to try. Plays are filled with characters who don't succeed at their goals; actors need only to make the effort of the character—the genuine effort. Trying to make your partner cry gives your tactic a physiological reality. It gives you a specific and human psychophysical goal to pursue, and you will succeed—as an actor—merely by pursuing that goal convincingly. But really try. And try hard.

Trying to make the other actor cry is one of the strongest goals an actor can pursue, inasmuch as it brings to the surface thoughts and emotions, often repressed from childhood, that unlock a great deal of subconscious behavior. Our earliest tears stem from pain, rage, and fright—often the fright induced by a seemingly omnipotent parent—and any improvisation or dialogue that brings back those primal situations can be an immensely stimulating acting discovery. Trying to make somebody cry brings out qualities of behavior that are rarely seen in the classroom, and it liberates much of the inherent power of the performer. So don't be afraid of *really* trying to make your partner cry. It will make you a better actor—and your partner a better actor as well! (Professional actors never complain that their partners give them "too much," only that they don't give them "enough.") So come on to your partner with power and intensity. He or she will be the better for it, as will you.

FRIGHTEN HIM

The other actor is the most important thing in a scene. I'll try to frighten him or to make him laugh, because the better he is, the better I am and the better the scene is. If the scene stinks, everybody in it stinks. If I can make him have a couple of great moments, the scene is good and therefore I'm good.

JAMES CAAN

◆ E X E R C I S E   6-4

Movement and Contact

Repeat Exercise 6–3 several times, adding physical gestures and movements that intensify the pursuit of your victory. Use *agreed-upon* physical contact: a soft shove on your partner's shoulder or shoulders, seizing your partner's wrist, or slapping your partner's arms and torso. Be sure to use the physical business simply as a means of adding force and emphasis to your lines—not as a way of making your partner cry by inflicting real pain. The threatening tactics of an actor are psychological only; physical violence, onstage, is *always* simulated.

You will quickly tire of threatening or frightening exercises, which can be sustained only for a very short time in any event. Ordinarily they should be alternated with inductive exercises, such as this one.

◆ E X E R C I S E   6-5

Encourage Your Partner

Pair with a partner. Using one of the phrases below, try to encourage your partner to come closer to you, to sit down, or to engage in behavior that you suggest would be enjoyable.

1. Come on over here.

2. Sit down next to me.

3. I want to talk with you.

4. I have something I think you'd like.

5. Please . . .

6. [Make something up yourself.]

Repeat Exercise 6–5, building on your original phrase with improvised elaborations. Use your body, your intonation and inflection, the sound of your voice, and the manner of your gesture and expression to induce calm, trust, and amusement in your acting partner. Work to make your partner *smile* or *laugh*. As a physicalizer, take one or both of your partner's hands in yours. Try to coax your partner into a genuine rapport with your desires.

Induction tactics (which tend to induce behavior rather than threaten noncompliance) are the common stuff of everyday human interaction, much more common than threats both in life and on the stage. When well played, they give an actor magnetism and charm, just as threatening tactics, when well played, lend an actor a commanding forcefulness.

Both threatening and inductive tactics are efforts on your part to influence the behavior and ideas of the other actor—to interfere with the other actor's state of tranquillity or direction. By playing tactics, the actor creates a character who is trying to shape the scene, the only kind of character that is dramatically interesting. Characters in plays are never merely observers. Even those characters who describe themselves as observers, such as the title character in John Van Druten's *I Am a Camera,* are active in interpersonal engagements. Characters in plays are all interpersonally active: They are always trying to influence, to overthrow, to impress, to seduce, to win over, to suppress, to engage somebody. This is why tactics are so important to the actor: They are the actual "happenings" onstage; they are what is going on between the characters—and therefore between the actors.

Alternating Tactics

Tactics are almost never monolithic onstage; most of the time they alternate—often with mercurial speed—between threats and inducements. Actors who can switch between hair-raising forcefulness and ingratiating charm in an instant—actors such as Sean Penn, for example—are widely admired for encompassing this range of interpersonal effectiveness, which is dramatically thrilling because it suggests an almost explosive unpredictability.

◆ E X E R C I S E   6–6

Mixing Tactics

Pair with a partner. Improvising with phrases from Exercises 6–1 and 6–5 (or similar phrases), create a sequence of varying tactical approaches to your partner. For example:

1. *[threatening]* Get out of here! I said get out of here! *[inductive]* Will you get out of here? Come here. Come on over here. Please? *[threatening again]* Please! Oh, shut up! Shut up! Dammit, John, shut up!

2. *[inductive]* John, come up here. Come on, sit down. I want to talk to you. Will you take off your shoes? Come on, take off your shoes. *[threatening]* I said, take off your shoes. Dammit, John, take off your shoes! *[inductive]* Please? Everything will be OK, I promise. Come on.

Alternate threats and inducements as a way of *increasing the pressure* on your partner. Employ the art of surprise; shift tactics suddenly and without warning.

Try this exercise in three successive stages:

1. With your partner saying the word *no* between each of your phrases.

2. With your partner just nodding *no* each time.

3. With your partner remaining wholly impassive each time—but still not acceding to your demand.

Learn to vary your tactics—and to try harder—not only when your partner specifically turns you down (i.e., says "no"), but when your partner remains impassive. In the latter case, you have to "read in" the obstacle yourself. This will prove important in more complicated acting assignments later on.

The Middle Ranges

Making someone cry and making someone laugh are at the extreme ends of tactical behavior. In the middle there is making somebody listen, making somebody care, making somebody proud, or worried, or happy, or agreeable. These are the middle ranges of acting, and this is where most of an actor's time is spent.

◆ E X E R C I S E   6–7

Eliminating the Extremes

Pair with a partner and designate one of you as A, the other as B. Memorize and play the following scene, escalating steadily from inductive tactics at the beginning to threatening ones at the end.

1. A: I know you will.

    B: No, I won't.

2. A: I know you will.

    B: No, I won't.

3. A: I know you will.

    B: No, I won't!

4. A: I know you will!

    B: No, I won't!

5. A: *[Pulling out all the stops]* I know you will!!

    B: *[Ditto]* No, I won't!!

Repeat several times, each time intensifying the escalation by adding facial expression, gesture, and whole-body movements.

Now, with the pattern of five exchanges fairly set in your mind, repeat but do not escalate the last (fifth) exchange. In other words, hold the last exchange down to the level of the fourth.

The first and fifth exchanges in Exercise 6–7 are the extremities; the second, third, and fourth are the middle ranges where most acting occurs. The extremities must always be there, in the actor's mind at least, for they define what's finally at stake in a scene or play. But most acting exchanges take place at the level of forceful—but not extreme—tactical interaction. Working on the middle levels and on the continuum from powerful induction to electrifying threats, actors explore and develop their tactical range.

The exercises in this lesson should be considered études, or studies, that allow you to explore a mere fraction of acting, but an important fraction: those moments, usually at the climax of a scene, that require you to be deeply committed to succeeding in some cause or other—and trying to succeed by influencing the feelings and behavior of your acting partner. When these études are put into a play, with all your power at their service, they become the key moments in your performance.

Summary

The two basic types of tactics are those that threaten and those that induce. A successful actor learns how to play both types strongly and in rapid alternation. Between the extremities, there is a broad middle range of tactics, which are in process most of the time—although the extremities are always latent in the actor's mind. Tactics are *real* interpersonal behaviors, designed to influence other people; they should be played onstage as intensely as in real life and should aim at creating real reactions (including physiological reactions) in the other actors. Playing tactics forcefully, intensely, and physically brings to the surface human emotions—both from you and from your acting partner—and creates vivid and dynamic acting relationships.

it grows—it becomes a month, a year, a century; it becomes too late! Kiss him, Irma, kiss him while there is still time, or in a moment his hair will be white and there will be another madwoman in Paris." (The Madwoman, in Jean Giraudoux's *The Madwoman of Chaillot*)

7. "My ears have yet not drunk a hundred words
   Of thy tongue's uttering, yet I know the sound;
   Art thou not Romeo, and a Montague?"
   (Juliet, in William Shakespeare's *Romeo and Juliet*)

8. "No/ I don think you was tryin' to tell me I'm some kinda fool/ but/ ya gotta understand/ I ain't never gointa college/ I ain't gonna be no vet or a doctor or a nurse even/ shit/ I probably couldn't even make it as a ad-ministrative assistant's assistant/ but I can ride/ & I wanna be the best I can/ I ain't got much left as a woman/ you right/ I ain't got mucha fami-ly/ do you think that mean I ain't s'posed to want nothin' mo' out my life?" (Cassie, in Ntozake Shange's *Daddy Says*)

9. "That's why I came back here, just to say that I don't do this, come after guys or anything, not like some regular habit or whatever, so I thought you should know that. I think you're really cute and nice and that sort of thing . . . you might have a girlfriend already or not be attracted to me, I would just totally understand that, I would, but I really do hope you call me. Just even to talk on the phone would be fine, because I'd like that, if we were only these phone buddies or whatnot . . . I think I would. Just don't be afraid, Tom, I guess that's why I came back here, to say that. Please do not let yourself be afraid of me or of taking some kind of blind chance, or what people think . . . because this could be so nice. I mean, really, really, really very much so." (Woman, in Neil LaBute's *Fat Pig*)

☐ EXPECTATION

I played a game with myself when I gave that speech that I could really persuade everyone, all the extras, to vote for our slate.

GREGORY PECK, REFERRING TO HIS ROLE
IN THE FILM *OTHER PEOPLE'S MONEY*

Learning to play speeches positively, with expectations of some concrete and specific victory in mind, is a strong step away from grievous actor prob-lems—most particularly self-consciousness and a tendency to play toward self-pity, empty sarcasm, sentimentality, and pious moralizing. No action can be convincing onstage—and no actor can be sufficiently confident in his or her role—without an expectation of success in the action's outcome, without an *excitement* at the prospect of success. Creating that expectation—which the script does not always confirm at the play's conclusion—is the actor's job, and often the actor's most delicate job.

◆ E X E R C I S E   7–3

Try the Impossible

Try to jump twenty feet in the air. (That's right, you can't do it. But try.) Now try to jump twenty feet in the air, expecting to succeed! Think of the prizes you are going to win! Think of the cheering crowds! The adulation! The rewards! The romantic opportunities! You can do it! Do it again! Again! AGAIN!!

What happens in this progressive escalation of expectation in Exercise 7–3? Did the expectation of victory (even of an impossible victory) give you a greater tone, strength, and vivacity? Did you jump even higher? Did you enjoy the exercise more? Did you get more of your body into play? More of your emotions? Were you less self-conscious?

Chances are that you answered "yes" to all those questions. Positive expectation and enthusiasm have brought far more out of you than merely following a stage direction. It was your *imagination* that made you jump higher, act more energetically, feel more deeply, and perform more vividly. And the same process is at work in a subtle and complex performance of a dramatic role.

> ### EXPECTATION
>
> *You can't play a loser, so don't ever do it. You've always got to play it like a winner. You can never give up. That was the lesson to me as an actor in Fargo. The subtext of every scene you do has always to be "I can solve this. There is an answer and I will find it."*
>
> WILLIAM H. MACY

Eye Contact

Where do you look when you act? There is no single answer to this, but in general the best place to look is right at your *acting partner's eyes*. That is because in a strong dramatic scene you are seeking a goal with or from your partner, who is the "other" character with whom you interact. Maintaining direct eye contact with your partner, therefore, is the best way to see if you are on track to win your goal, because it's the surest way to read your partner's innate responses. Eye contact also expresses your confidence—your positive expectation—that you are indeed going to achieve what you seek. It is, moreover, an effective tactic in gaining your partner's trust or respect. The distinguished actor Michael Caine even advises actors to refrain from blinking ("Blinking makes your character seem weak") so as to intensify the acting power that direct eye contact provides.

TWO VIEWS ON EYE CONTACT

Reacting is why one only wants to work with good actors; it's tennis, and you have to react to that ball coming back! And your eye's always got to be on what's coming back to you, and you have to react to that.

EILEEN ATKINS

You never know what [your character's] going to be until the day you walk onto the set and look into the other actor's eyes.

MERYL STREEP

You needn't look at your partner all the time, of course, and sometimes it's wholly appropriate to look at someone or something else—as, for example, to imply to your partner "Stop bothering me with your problems." But you should always look at *something* or *someone* while acting, not just look "away" or study the floor. Looking at the floor, even unconsciously, makes clear you are pursuing no goal, using no tactic, and have no positive expectations. It is, in fact, a nervous acting tic, implying only that you'd rather be anywhere but onstage acting this scene. Looking at the floor between lines, or when you're unsure of yourself, may be a hard habit to break (particularly because you're not always aware when you do it), but you should ask your teacher or fellow classmates to alert you when they see it.

◆ EXERCISE   7–4

Tactics and Expectations

Go back to the exercises in Lesson 6 and repeat them with escalating expectations of victory and full direct eye contact with your partner. You will probably find that the exercises are more fun to do, less "clinical," and less like exercises.

If you have been through the experience of rehearsing plays through to performance, you may recall a director begging the cast for more "energy" in the last days before the play's opening. "Louder! Faster! Funnier!" is the classic (and old-fashioned) directorial plea. But you can't simply pump energy into a play like air into a tire: If a tire leaks, it'll stay flat no matter what's pumped into it, and so will a play. The truest theatrical energy comes not from a director's desperate exhortations but from the actor's eager portrayal of the character's expectations and his or her consequent efforts to bring these expectations to fulfillment.

Summary

Positive expectation lends the actor's portrayal a necessary excitement and energy. Not all characters succeed, of course, but they must be shown to expect success and even to be enthusiastic about their prospects, if their actions are to excite audience interest and empathy. Even the most despairing of dramatic characters must have this quality of positive expectation, for only when their expectations are dashed can their pathos be shared.

8

GOTE

A Basic Method

The foundations of an actor's approach have been set out in the preceding lessons. Admittedly, there's a good deal to keep in mind at one time.

GOTE is an easy-to-remember acronym that stands for and brings together the four basic principles. GOTE, therefore, represents a basic method for approaching an acting assignment. The letters individually stand for

Goal

Other

Tactics

Expectation

Let us go over these terms with an eye to their interdependence and mutual relationship.

Goal is the character's principal quest, which the actor assumes: Everything onstage must be seen, first and foremost, as a character pursuing a goal. Elsewhere the word may be called *victory, objective, want, intention, action,* or *purpose,* and these words may also suffice, when they refer to the same thing.

In brief, the actor becomes the character primarily by pursuing, as vigorously as possible, the character's goal. Moreover, the goal should be something quite specific and outgoing: not just "I want to find self-fulfillment," but "I want to be King of Denmark" or "I want to marry Romeo." If you did the Pledge of Allegiance exercise in Lesson 2, your goal might have been any of the following: to secure freedom, to acquire allies, to win friends, to return and save your sister, to join a republic, to disable the goon squad you left behind, or any variation of each and all of these.

The *other* is the person (or persons) with whom, for whom, or from whom you seek your goal. There is *always* an other in acting; no goal can be achieved simply by yourself. Hamlet cannot simply say, "I want to be King of Denmark," and have a crown appear above his head; nor can Juliet say, "I want to be happily married," and then marry happily. Not in good theatre, anyway. In drama all the victories must be hard-earned and must be achieved through interpersonal struggle. There are simply no good plays about characters learning the multiplication table or developing a personal philosophy without an interpersonal struggle.

The other in a scene, therefore, is what makes achieving goals difficult. Often the other is your chief *obstacle:* another "O" word. The struggle to overcome obstacles—particularly when those obstacles are other persons and other persons' pursuit of *their* goals—creates much of the dynamics of acting, the work of acting. The struggle to overcome obstacles onstage should make you sweat.

So, in acting, the goals that are worth pursuing must be achievable only with the compliance or defeat of other characters. To the extent that these other characters are sympathetic, your character may be seen as inspirational. To the extent that the other characters are obstacles, your character may be seen as heroic. To the extent that the other characters are complex, your character may be seen as profound. The nature of your actions—and of your acting—will be determined by your confrontation with the other who stands between you and your goal.

Putting together the confrontation of goal and other, you will ask the following of every given scene or exercise:

1. What is my goal?

2. Who is/are the other person(s) who affect my gaining it?

   a. How can they help me?

   b. How can they hurt me?

   c. Are they my obstacle?

3. How can I demand/induce/encourage their help?

4. How can I overcome the obstacle they pose?

5. What should my tactics be?

Tactics are the character's means of trying to achieve goals; they are what gives acting its "guts." Tactics—and trying to achieve goals through them—make acting "real" for the actors and make actors indistinguishable from characters, at least from the audience's point of view. In other words, Jane trying to get Jim to fall in love with her is absolutely indistinguishable from Juliet trying to get Romeo to fall in love with her, when Jane is playing Juliet and Jim is playing Romeo. The lines are Shakespeare's, but the tactics are your own. Tactics will come out of your life experience, not out of the script.

As we saw in Lesson 6, tactics can be divided between those that threaten and those that induce, and they can be divided into extreme tactics and a broad middle range of subtler tactics. A good actor is able to move fluidly and purposefully from tactic to tactic in pursuit of victory. Tactical strength and tactical versatility are what make acting, by turns, forceful, seductive, visceral, and dramatic. Actors work all their lives on expanding and developing their tactical range.

Expectation, the last word on the list, gives tone, spring, and excitement to the dramatic pursuit of goals and quest for victory. It also lends every dramatic action at least a touch of enthusiasm, which can prove deliciously infectious. Too often actors choose to pursue goals in a purely academic way. It is not that your character simply "wants" or "desires" something; people have all sorts of petty wants and desires that are rarely worth dramatizing. Look at any fine play, and the chances are that the author created characters who not only desire goals but *crave* them—characters who are excited and enthusiastic about their eventual success; characters who, deep in their hearts, are sure (even mistakenly sure) that they will win in the end. *Expectation, excitement, enthusiasm,* and even *energy* are "E" words that make a memory package: They define characters who have not only wants but passions as well. You are playing one of those characters. The victory you seek is not just an ordinary whim; it is the prime goal of your life, and it is within your reach if you try hard enough. Go for it! NOW!

Get Your Character's GOTE

These first lessons have outlined a method of approaching any role. Approaching the role does not necessarily mean performing the role to everybody's satisfaction—much less to the demands of this highly regarded art—but it is the starting point for professional and beginner alike. Before a role can be played, it must be approached: It must be understood and created in *acting* terms. What makes the character not just an invention of the playwright but a living, breathing, feeling, caring, *acting* person? Characters act. In order to play a character, you must play the character's actions—and in order to play that character brilliantly, you must create those actions in vivid detail and with believable intensity.

GOTE

[Acting is] very clearcut. You have to answer four questions: Who am I speaking to? What do I want from them? How am I going to get it? and What is standing in the way of what I want? But it's not just answering them—you have to answer them incredibly specifically.

JASON ALEXANDER

Getting your character's GOTE—creating those actions in the context of goals, obstacles, tactics, and expectations—is the key to putting yourself into the role and to approaching the character with the full resources of your acting instrument (your voice and body) and your personal history, intelligence, and emotional resourcefulness. How do you get your character's GOTE? Studying the script is, of course, the first step. But using your imagination is the more important second step—more important because most of the "answers" aren't answers at all but, rather, creations. Most of the GOTE aspects are only *implied* by the script, and determining which implications are the correct ones is a highly subjective and imaginative task. Study gives the main lines of a character's desires, but imagination fleshes them out. Indeed, that is one of the particular characteristics of drama, which, unlike narrative fiction, creates action only through spoken words and physical movement rather than thought revelations or extended third-person descriptions.

Often the play is silent about matters crucial to the character. What does Hamlet really want from Ophelia? What are Cordelia's true feelings and desires toward King Lear? The actor's *choices*—governed but not restricted by the actor's research—will determine the character's behavior.

◆ EXERCISE   8–1

The GOTEsheet

The GOTEsheet is a starting point for analyzing any role. Using your imagination, take a blank piece of paper and answer the following questions about a dramatic character from a play you know. Reread the play first, with the questions in mind, and answer *as the character would:*

1. Basic information about the character

    Name:

    Sex:

Age:

Marital status and history:

Educational level:

Economic/social status:

2. **Goal:** What do I really want? When do I want it?

3. **Other:** From whom (in the play) do I want it? Who in the play can help me? Who in the play can hurt me? Who is an obstacle? Why? What are my deepest fears?

4. **Tactics:** How can I get it? How (and whom) should I threaten? How (and whom) should I induce?

5. **Expectation:** Why do I expect to get it? Why does it excite me? What will I do when I get it?

You may answer impressionistically or in lists, but answer vividly, not academically.

Now, memorize, rehearse, and play a scene, trying to implement your answers to the GOTEsheet questions.

Summary

GOTE is an acronym for *goal, other, tactics,* and *expectation*—the four coordinates of the actor's approach to any role. The GOTEsheet is the actor's list of basic questions whose answers will create the foundation for approaching a specific character.

III

The Actor's Tasks

PART III SUGGESTS PRACTICAL METHODS FOR PREPARING AN ACTING role for presentation, either in a scene for class or in a play. Naturally your instructor (in a class) or director (in a play) will provide some specific policies, advice, and guidance in your work; nonetheless, it is finally up to you to develop a fundamental working method for preparing a role on your own.

Scenes are the basic medium of acting. The two-person scene, from three to eight minutes in length, drawn from any play (or adapted from other sources), is the basic exercise for the acting student. It involves, in microcosm, almost all the acting skills a play involves, yet it can be prepared in a relatively short time and with little or no cost.

This section deals primarily with scenes to be presented in class, although some discussion is devoted to scenes in plays, where the method may be somewhat different.

9

Preparing a Role

Finding Your Role

The first step in beginning any kind of scenework, either in class or in performance, is finding a role. Sometimes this may be done for you, as when you are cast in a play or assigned a role (and perhaps a partner) in class. On other occasions you will be in charge of selecting a role yourself—and probably also selecting the play or other material it comes from, as well as an acting partner to play it with. Every class and every instructor has certain rules and limits as to what sorts of scenes you should choose. In general, however, and absent instructions to the contrary,

1. Choose a role of your own sex and close to your own age.

2. Choose a role in which you can clearly see something at stake, emotionally, for the character you will be playing.

3. Choose a role in which something is happening in the scene itself—as opposed to a role in which characters are talking about something that already happened.

4. Choose a role in which you can identify with the character's struggle or dilemma.

5. Choose a role in which the characters and situation interest you personally.

Finding Your "Character"

Do not, for this assignment, try to create "a character" different from yourself. Simply put yourself into the role. "Character," says actress Fiona Shaw, is the "combustion of yourself with events. Put yourself in the situation and you'll discover your character." Her advice is appropriate not only for this lesson but for every exercise in *Acting One*.

You should also try, for exercises in *Acting One*, to choose roles in scenes set in periods and styles that you understand well, with characters whose backgrounds you can identify with. And, given the opportunity, you should try to select scene partners of both sexes over the course of several scene assignments.

Editing a Scene

Sometimes it is necessary to edit a scene, to cut it down in length, or to combine two short scenes into a longer one, or to delete references within the scene that are unrelated to the immediate matters at hand. Sometimes a little rewriting, if permitted by the instructor, may be useful for eliminating a minor character in the scene.

Sometimes you can adapt a scene from a novel or short story by transcribing the dialogue and omitting the narrative. Some outstanding contemporary, realistic scenes for young people can be obtained this way, as many more novels than plays are published in any given year, and novels today tend to include extensive dialogue. In adapting a novel for classroom scene use, you might consider yourself a practicing screenplay adapter, for this is how many films begin.

Once a script is fully edited, you and your partner must obtain exact duplicate copies. You should also agree on the context of the scene: What is the basic relationship of the characters—as they both understand it to be—and what is happening in the scene as both characters understand it? These basic understandings should be just that—basic—one or two sentences that define only the outer boundaries of the scene. For example, "A and B are husband and wife. A is trying to get B to confess her adultery; B is trying to make A get dressed to go to a party." You and your partner should read the scene once or twice together. Then memorization should commence.

Memorization Methods

Memorizing is "donkey work," according to Alec McCowen, who once memorized the Gospel According to Saint Mark for a spectacularly successful one-man presentation. But if pursued diligently and immediately, this donkey work goes hand in glove with the actor's understanding of the role so as to provide the firmest possible basis for richly experimental and emotionally charged acting.

Memorization is sometimes a difficult task, and it invariably gets more difficult as you get older. *You must learn your lines exactly,* however, even for a simple scene performed in class. There are several reasons for this. First, that's the only way your partner can be secure about coming in on cue. Second, learning your lines exactly gives you a confidence in your role that you can never have if you're fishing for the exact way to say something. Third, such rewriting as you do when you paraphrase lines invariably weakens your character, defeats the author's sense of timing, and diminishes the power of the play's builds, climaxes, and rhythmic effects. Fourth, you will look bad in the eyes of those who know the play, who will feel you haven't come up to the level of the character even if they are unaware of the specific line changes you have made. (The slightest paraphrases of Shakespeare, for example, will make the acting seem profoundly "off" even if the source of the deviation is not apparent.) And finally, you are simply insulting the author and the theatre itself by your laziness! So learn the lines verbatim.

GO BEYOND THE LINES

As an actor, I've got to really, really know those lines inside out, so that when I'm performing I'm not spending any energy whatsoever on remembering lines. Most actors in TV shows don't really know what they're about to say next; they're kind of searching for it and so they do all these little pauses and brow scratches and other baloney to cover the fact they don't really know what they're doing. *If I'm not thinking about the lines, I can* behave, *I can go* beyond *the lines.*

ERIC BOGOSIAN

Many actors prefer to learn their lines in rehearsal, going through their parts "on book" (with script in hand) until the lines are embedded in their memory. This common practice invites certain problems. While going through a part on book, you are not acting; you are reacting to the book, not to the situation, and your main contact is not with the actors but with the script. You may pick up patterns and readings in this "running through" that have nothing to do with the interactions between you and your partner but, rather, reflect your immediate idea of what is "theatrical" about your part.

Try sitting down and memorizing your part first. By doing so, you will also be studying your part from your own character's point of view, not jumping to conclusions about what is the most theatrical way to play the scene. You can also develop your GOTEsheet as you memorize, studying the part while you are learning it.

Begin by underlining or highlighting all your lines.

Start reading the text; read aloud for your own part, to yourself for the other character's part. Start with a quarter page or so, and go back to the beginning each time you complete this small section. Soon you will have your first few lines in your memory. Get a postcard and cover up your first line. Read (to yourself) the line before it (your cue line), and recite your line from memory. Move the card down and read (to yourself) the next cue line or lines. Recite your next line from memory. Gradually go through the script, an hour or so at a time, lowering the card as you memorize more and more lines. Eventually, you will have the text committed to memory.

At this point your memorization is still shallow; it will probably not stand up to an intense rehearsal. This is OK; there's no problem with struggling with your lines when your character is struggling to win his or her goals. Your memorization will "lock in," however, as you rehearse the scene, and it will lock in together with the specific goals and tactics of your character as you develop them. But don't stop learning your lines after you first go through the scene off book. Go back to the script and learn them again—learn all of those you haven't mastered exactly. Record your cue lines on a tape recorder, and run your lines with the machine. Or get a friend to run lines with you. Run your lines aloud while driving, cycling, jogging, or showering. Run your lines with your acting partner, without trying to rehearse the actual staging. Write your lines out, by memory, in longhand or at the computer.

Cues: Action Cues and Line Cues

Always learn your lines with your partner's cues. There are actually two cues for each line: the action cue and the line cue. The *action cue* is what prompts you to speak; the *line cue* is the actual line you come in on. Sometimes these cues are simultaneous; sometimes they are not. For example:

EDDIE: You gonna marry him?

CATHERINE: I don't know. We just been . . . goin' around, that's all.
What've you got against him, Eddie? Please, tell me. What?

EDDIE: He don't respect you.

(Arthur Miller, *A View from the Bridge*)

The *action* cue for Eddie's last line is "What've you got against him?" The *line* cue is "What?" Eddie's line is *prepared* in response to the action cue; it is *not delivered,* however, until the line cue.

Sometimes there are certain lines that seem to stick; an actor has memorized the part, but one or two lines don't seem to come when cued. In this case the actor should study the cue (both action cue and line cue) and look for the precise linkage in the character's mind that triggers the response.

Some linkages are obvious and rarely cause problems:

KRISTIN: Government rations are small but sure, and there's a pension for the widow and children.

JEAN: That's all very fine, but it's not in my line to start thinking at once about dying for my wife and children. I must say I had rather bigger ideas.

KRISTIN: You and your ideas! You've got obligations too, and you'd better start thinking about them.

JEAN: Don't you start pestering me about obligations.

(August Strindberg, *Miss Julie*)

That dialogue is easy to memorize, for the action cues contain the germinal words of the responses.

The following dialogue is more difficult to memorize:

NICK: Everybody drinks a lot here in the East. Everybody drinks a lot in the Middle West, too.

GEORGE: We drink a great deal in this country, and I suspect we'll be drinking a great deal more, too . . . if we survive. We should be Arabs or Italians . . . the Arabs don't drink, and the Italians don't get drunk much, except on religious holidays. We should live on Crete, or something.

NICK: And that, of course, would make us cretins.

GEORGE: So it would. Tell me about your wife's money.

(Edward Albee, *Who's Afraid of Virginia Woolf?*)

That is caustic dialogue, representing the half-clever repartee of heavy-drinking faculty colleagues at a late-night party. It is difficult to memorize because it contains elliptical phrases, artificial constructions, and apparent non sequiturs, or illogical jumps. But there are some tricks to help you learn George's part, which is the particularly difficult one here.

George's analysis of the drinking habits of Arabs, Italians, and Cretans may be made simpler by picturing, in your head, a map of the Mediterranean. All of these cultures bound this sea, and George, a history professor, would be thinking of specific locales when he speaks; thus the line has more continuity than may be perceived at first glance. George's apparent out-of-nowhere leap to "Tell me about your wife's money" may be memorized by associating Nick's

> **THREE VIEWS ON LINE LEARNING**
>
> *I think it best to learn the lines before rehearsals start. Actors who like to start from scratch don't even notice what you are doing because they have their faces buried in their scripts. Whereas you, from the start, can look at them, speak to them, listen to them, and be surprised by them, and this element of surprise is one of the most valuable things that can happen.*
>
> PETER BARKWORTH
>
> *I never study lines. I find out in the process of working what my function is in a particular play or movie, who that person is, what they're all about and I learn by reading. I read the script over and over again. I've never really sat down and taken a line and said, "This is the line I have to say."*
>
> CICELY TYSON
>
> *It's sluggish work. I hate it. I always try to synchronize what I'm saying with what I'm doing or not doing; the pattern of movement and words: one prompts the other. . . . I'll write the words out so they become visual, or I'll put difficult speeches on the tape recorder—my own speeches—and listen to them. . . . I'm simply trying to memorize the words, using all the senses I can.*
>
> HUME CRONYN

"that would make us cretins" remark with the fleeting thought "Anybody who would crack a joke like that must be a member of the idle rich." Or simpler yet, the transition may be memorized by picturing a cretin counting out money, an image that henceforth will be triggered by hearing Nick's "cretin" line and will, in turn, trigger George's "money" line. This, by the way, is not merely an acting gimmick. The character of George (inasmuch as we think of him as a real person) would himself go through some sort of mental gymnastic to make the jump. The goal of playing a character like George is to show that these leaps from "out of nowhere" are, in fact, from "out of somewhere": out of his individual and possibly peculiar mind. You are not only playing George's lines; you also are playing George's *thinking* process—his *coming up with* his lines.

Studying the Part

Learning the lines of a role will teach you a great deal about the part that is not immediately apparent. Mainly, it will make clear to you the *logic* of your character's position and how the lines develop not out of an author's whim but, rather, out of a character's thinking process. Learning a long speech—out of George Bernard Shaw, for example, where the speeches can go on for pages—seems at first a formidable task, but as you start to work on it, the structure of the speech begins to assert itself in your mind. By learning the speech you begin to understand the speaker, and to understand why the words are in their particular order, and how the lines of thought, or argument, or reaction, develop in the character's mind. You may be amazed with the speed with which you can learn a long, well-crafted speech and the speed and conviction with which you can deliver it within a short period of time.

While you are memorizing your part, you begin to study it. What are your character's goals? How will other people—particularly the other person or persons in the scene(s) with you—help you to achieve that goal? How are they your obstacles? What sort of tactics can your character use? What sort did he or she grow up with? What is he or she afraid of? Excited by? How vivid are his or her expectations? How wild are his or her fantasies? How can you find the expectations of the character? The enthusiasm? These are questions to be answered first and last by you, the actor. Studying is the private part of actor preparation, and it is important, in a nondirected scene, that you first study your part by yourself and not with your acting partner. Your acting partner, no matter how clever or experienced, is not your acting consultant. Indeed, he or she, in the guise of his or her character, is most likely your *obstacle*. Don't confuse yourself, or diminish yourself, by trying to forge an agreement with your partner as to how your scene should play. The best acting scene will be the result of a dramatic *confrontation* between you and your partner—with both of you seen as individually ambitious (yet vulnerable) characters. Your individualism must be nurtured in private: hence the importance of your private study in approaching your part.

So get your character's GOTE and integrate your memorization of your part with the filling out of your GOTEsheet. Strategize on behalf of your character! Make your character's plans! The GOTEsheet responses, your character's plans, do not come out of rehearsal as much as they come out of you and from your own imagination. Try to prepare a part such as Laura or Jim in the exercise that follows.

◆ E X E R C I S E   9–1

The Gentleman Caller I

Following is the Gentleman Caller scene from Tennessee Williams's modern classic *The Glass Menagerie*. In this play, set in the late 1930s, Laura

Wingfield lives with her mother and brother in an urban tenement apartment. Laura, a young woman, is described by the author as "exquisitely fragile," at least in part because a childhood illness has left her with one leg slightly shorter than the other. The author cautions, however, that Laura's physical defect "need not be more than suggested on the stage." In the play, Laura's mother begs her son—Laura's brother—to invite a coworker to the family home for dinner, in the hope the guest would become a "gentleman caller" for her daughter. And thus Jim O'Connor, an up-and-coming young businessman, arrives one evening for dinner. Laura immediately realizes Jim is a boy she knew and liked in high school, and she can barely speak during the meal. But afterward, Jim follows Laura into the living room, carrying the candelabrum and a glass of dandelion wine, and they have the conversation that follows. In this famous scene (only the first part of which is included in this exercise), the characters' deepest thoughts are expressed mainly indirectly, and dialogue only suggests their profound feelings, fears, and desires.

1. Study the scene and prepare the role of Laura or Jim, depending on your gender. Assume both characters are your actual age (as they could be—their age is unspecified in the play).

2. Underline your actual *lines* in one color. Underline your *line cues* in a second color and your *action cues* (where they are different from the line cues) in a third.

3. Analyze the *logic* of your speeches and imagine the thoughts that connect them. Make notes of the *thought linkages* that connect your lines with each other, and with the other character's lines. Make notes toward a GOTEsheet for your part.

4. *Memorize* your part, using the thought linkages to help you connect the individual lines.

5. Complete your GOTEsheet.

6. In a subsequent class, pair with a partner and play the scene without rehearsal, just as you played the contentless scene (Exercise 5–1). You or your instructor will need to bring to class a pillow, two drinking glasses, and something to represent a candelabrum.

7. Switch partners and play it again. Repeat.

The scene

(Note: All stage directions are by Williams.)

JIM: Hello there, Laura.

LAURA *[Faintly]:*   Hello. *[She clears her throat.]*

JIM: How are you feeling now? Better?

LAURA: Yes. Yes, thank you.

JIM: This is for you. A little dandelion wine. *[He extends the glass toward her with extravagant gallantry.]*

LAURA: Thank you.

JIM: Drink it—but don't get drunk! *[He laughs heartily. Laura takes the glass uncertainly; she laughs shyly.]* Where shall I set the candles?

LAURA: Oh—oh, anywhere . . .

JIM: How about here on the floor? Any objections?

LAURA: No.

JIM: I'll spread a newspaper under to catch the drippings. I like to sit on the floor. Mind if I do?

LAURA: Oh, no.

JIM: Give me a pillow?

LAURA: What?

JIM: A pillow!

LAURA: Oh . . . *[She hands him one quickly.]*

JIM: How about you? Don't you like to sit on the floor?

LAURA: Oh—yes.

JIM: Why don't you, then?

LAURA: I—will.

JIM: Take a pillow! *[Laura does. She sits on the floor on the other side of the candelabrum. Jim crosses his legs and smiles engagingly at her.]* I can't hardly see you sitting way over there.

LAURA: I can—see you.

JIM: I know, but that's not fair, I'm in the limelight. *[Laura moves her pillow closer.]* Good! Now I can see you! Comfortable?

LAURA: Yes.

JIM: So am I. Comfortable as a cow! Will you have some gum?

LAURA: No, thank you.

JIM: I think that I will indulge, with your permission. *[He musingly unwraps a stick of gum and holds it up.]* Think of the fortune made by the guy that invented the first piece of chewing gum. Amazing, huh? The Wrigley Building is one of the sights of Chicago—I saw it summer before last when I went up to the Century of Progress. Did you take in the Century of Progress?

LAURA: No, I didn't.

JIM: Well, it was quite a wonderful exposition. What impressed me most was the Hall of Science. Gives you an idea of what the future will be in America, even more wonderful than the present time is! *[There is a pause. Jim smiles at her.]* Your brother tells me you're shy. Is that right, Laura?

LAURA: I—don't know.

JIM: I judge you to be an old-fashioned type of girl. Well, I think that's a pretty good type to be. Hope you don't think I'm being too personal—do you?

LAURA *[Hastily, out of embarrassment]:*   I believe I *will* take a piece of gum, if you—don't mind. *[Clearing her throat]* Mr. O'Connor, have you—kept up with your singing?

JIM: Singing? Me?

LAURA: Yes. I remember what a beautiful voice you had.

JIM: When did you hear me sing? *[Laura does not answer.]* You say you've heard me sing?

LAURA: Oh, yes! Yes, very often . . . I—don't suppose—you remember me—at all?

JIM *[Smiling doubtfully]:*   You know I have an idea I've seen you before. I had that idea soon as you opened the door. It seemed almost like I was about to remember your name. But the name that I started to call you—wasn't a name! And so I stopped myself before I said it.

LAURA: Wasn't it—Blue Roses?

JIM *[Springing up, grinning]:*   Blue Roses! My gosh, yes—Blue Roses! That's what I had on my tongue when you opened the door! Isn't it funny what tricks your memory plays? I didn't connect you with high school somehow or other. But that's where it was; it was high school.

That scene is famous more for what the characters don't say than what they do. Study how the characters reach out to each other through smiles, physical gestures, and tentative efforts at humor and enthusiasm—"Comfortable as a cow!" Study the author's stage directions and particularly his punctuation: dashes indicating pauses and exclamation points indicating excitement. As you play the scene with different partners, try moving in different ways: As Laura, do you want to hide your physical defect? Or do you want Jim to see it so as to be more sympathetic to you? As Jim, do you want to impress her with your vigor? Or with your sensitivity to her feelings? Do you want to amuse her with your fancy talking—or overcome her shyness by your provocations?

In playing these parts without rehearsal, and with different partners, you will see how your character's thinking, feeling, and behavior are affected by the behavior of the actors playing opposite you. Don't try to simply repeat your part the same way every time; allow yourself to vary your behavior according to what's happening between you and your partner. And, yes, let the scene really "happen" in real time between the two of you. Study your acting partner and his or her reactions to your expressions. Try to get to know your acting partner better, simply by rehearsing the scene together. You may not succeed—but it will make the scene much more interesting.

You will probably want to explore this scene further. Find the play at the library and read it. Learn the entire scene and rehearse it with one or more partners.

Summary

The first step in presenting a scene is to choose, edit, and memorize material. During memorization, you will begin studying the part and preparing your GOTEsheet analysis—as you explore the logic of your character's thinking and the connection of your character's speeches with each other and with the "action cues" that prompt them. A memorized and studied scene can be presented without rehearsal and with different partners, revealing a good deal about the spontaneous behavior that may be part of the scene's situation and interaction.

10

Rehearsing

Rehearsals

Rehearsals are the opportunity to practice and develop the dramatic confrontation between your character and your acting partner's character.

Rehearse originally meant "re-harrow"—that is, to plow the field again. The French word for rehearsal is *répétition*. Thus rehearsal is a process by which you repeat your parts until they are learned—and until the lumps are broken down.

In a play production, rehearsals are under the control of the director. Ordinarily the early rehearsals involve lectures or discussions on the play's meaning, the production concepts, and the development of the play's staging. In preparation for a classroom acting scene, no single individual controls the rehearsal; therefore you and your partner must develop a working method together.

Undirected Rehearsals

Your first task in an "undirected" rehearsal is to exchange contact information and establish a rehearsal schedule. Once scheduled, no rehearsal time should be changed except for reasons of emergency (or mutual convenience). If possible, your schedule should include at least one rehearsal in the space where your scene will be presented. If that is impossible, then rehearse at least once in a similar space. Also, at least one rehearsal should involve all the props you will use and the clothes you will wear in the scene. Ordinarily, this will be the last rehearsal.

Usually you will begin your first rehearsal by "running lines" with your partner. This means sitting or standing apart from others and saying your (memorized or partly memorized) lines to each other as directly as possible.

Don't "try" to act. But don't try to maintain a complete monotone. Inevitably, as you run lines, you will begin to slide into the scene, to slide into acting. This "sliding" will show you the continuity between yourself and your character and help you to discover yourself, quite naturally, in your role.

As soon as you can comfortably run lines without looking at your script, discard it and, without consideration yet of staging the scene, begin to run lines in a variety of imaginary locales. Run your scene while seated at a lunch counter, or while jogging, or while lolling on a sofa. Do the scene while washing the (real) dishes, or while eating a (real) salad, or while changing your (real) outer garments. As you do this, even though the actions may be irrelevant to the content of the scene, the lines will become more natural to you, and you will find yourself, by necessity, studying your partner very freshly each time. As you rehearse in this manner, the relationship between you and your acting partner—as characters in the scene—will grow and deepen of its own accord.

Between rehearsals, you will naturally want to talk about the scene. How much should you discuss or analyze what's happening? The perhaps surprising answer: not much. Analysis may diminish the freshness of the scene and superimpose a director–actor relationship onto your character–character one. Analysis tends to forge a "playing agreement" that may defeat the dramatic confrontation your scene is supposed to portray. Try to find out more about your scene and your characters by rehearsing rather than by analyzing. Do your best thinking about the scene *while it's going on.*

Above all, never try to direct your partner and never ask or allow your partner to direct you. No matter how experienced you feel you are, or how well you think you understand your partner's role, or how well you know "how the scene should play," your job is to act your role to the fullest, not to play both roles at the same time. As an actor, you will shape the scene *from within,* not from the outside. When actors try to direct each other, the scene inevitably becomes self-conscious, and the emotions and rhythms become fixed rather than free-flowing. An acting scene is not a directed performance, and it should not try to look like a directed performance. Its goal is to bring out the most intense, honest, vivid, and dramatic interaction between the two of you. No one will mind, at this stage in your work, if the outward form does not resemble the Royal Shakespeare Company production.

REHEARSALS

Rehearsals are not to get it right straightaway, they're to do it wrong and then find another way of doing it, and see which serves the play better and serves the character better.

JANET SUZMAN

Between rehearsals you should talk about the context of the scene. How old are we (characters)? How long have we known each other? Where did we go to school? Where did we first meet? How rich are our parents? What are we wearing? Where do we work? And so forth.

You can also tell your acting partner which of his or her behaviors stimulate you emotionally: "You really frighten me when you look at me that way," or "I get very charged up when you do that." With such remarks you can encourage your partner to do the kind of things that "get to you" and will, in turn, make your own performance more exciting.

Remember, you want your acting partner to surprise you. You also want your partner to get under your skin, to annoy you, to interest you, to unnerve you, to frighten you, to attract you, or to disgust you. Intellectual analysis, well intentioned and brilliant though it might be, will tend to level out the emotions and eliminate the surprises in your scene. Rehearsal, remember, is "harrowing." It should plow up the field, not smooth it down.

At this point, you can also begin to talk of the staging elements of your eventual presentation. Where should the scene be set? What props should be used? What should you wear? These are decisions you must reach together, preferably after some experimenting during rehearsals. Gradually you will add these elements to the rehearsal process.

Between rehearsal periods—and sometimes during short rehearsal breaks—you should go over your GOTEsheet by yourself, adding to and changing or refining your character's goals as the rehearsals seem to suggest. The rehearsal period is an opportunity for experiment, and nothing that comes out of the study should be treated as sacrosanct—particularly if it does not prove stimulating or effective in rehearsal. During rehearsal you will certainly want to try out various tactics. Which ones work best on your acting partner? If he or she proves impassive to your threats, or immune to your charms, don't simply complain. Try new threats or new charms, and keep trying until you find tactics that actually work. Sure, you can "direct" your partner outside the scene and force him or her to fake the sort of response you want—but how much better it is to find the action that will provoke a real response. If you find your partner difficult, all the better; it will simply make you work harder within the scene, which will translate as acting intensity.

Acting, like life, is not easy; and acting that represents life should not be easy. The most common fault of beginning actors is to try to stage-manage a scene by agreement ("I'll raise my fist and you run toward the door," "I'll smile and you throw your arms around me and give me a kiss") rather than really working hard to make their intended character victories come about. In life, the other guy doesn't always agree—not, at least, without some struggle on your part.

Gradually your rehearsal will take on the form of the finished scene. Some actors feel comfortable only when every gesture, every inflection, and every pause is rehearsed to repeatable perfection. Others like to keep the scene much more fluid and improvisational—particularly insofar as the movement, timing, and emotional levels are concerned. For a fully produced play, repeatability is a crucial factor, since lighting cues, scenery shifts, and special effects must be timed precisely to your actions. In a classroom presentation, in contrast, it is almost always best to keep the scene fairly fluid, concentrating on the vitality and intensity of the character-to-character interaction rather than the fine points of performance finesse.

How much rehearsal do you need? The professional rule of thumb is one hour per minute: an hour of rehearsal for each minute of stage time. A standard two-hour play, therefore, would normally be given three weeks (120 hours) of rehearsal at a professional theatre. Consequently, you might expect to schedule, for your five-minute acting scene, about five hours of rehearsal. But a produced play requires attention to many technical details that are rarely encountered in the classroom scene. It is not unreasonable, therefore, to plan a rehearsal schedule of three one-hour periods for a five-minute scene, provided that the actors do their individual study beforehand and are off book at least midway through the *first* rehearsal.

You should be aware that a great deal of professional film and television acting, some of the highest quality, is performed with practically *no* formal rehearsal. Indeed, in many cases, actors in film/television media are hired for one day only, making any real rehearsal simply impossible. Even in live theatre, understudies frequently perform publicly without any rehearsal. Rehearsal can be most useful to an actor, but there is no absolute minimum length of rehearsal time that must precede performance. Rather, the rehearsals should be used to build the basis for strongly pursued stage interactions and to create the basic structure of a staged acting scene.

Rehearsal Alternatives

Repetitive rehearsals are not, of course, the only means of preparing for your performance.

Improvisation—where you and your partner enact your parts, inventing lines and movement rather than relying on the memorized text—is a time-honored way of immersing yourself in the scene's situation and developing the intensity of the relationship without regard to the precise plotting or character development of the script. You may choose to improvise the situations that precede your scene or follow it. Improvisation takes its own direction and gives you the opportunity to explore the characters in the fullest possible range. Often, particularly in a scene set in a remote period, improvisation unlocks the deepest meaning of a scene's emotional conflict and makes you aware of the depth of feeling your character experiences.

Massage provides an opportunity to get close to your partner physically and lose your natural inhibitions about touching and being touched—inhibitions that can stand in the way of developing a strong relationship onstage. With your partner lying down, gently "stretching" his or her head, limbs, muscle mass, fingers, and toes is an excellent actor massage that helps to align the spine and promote a more relaxed intimacy that can lead to emotionally vivid acting (see Exercise 1–2). Mutual massage can also break down tension and establish trust in its place. Trust is a valuable ingredient in any scene.

Partying, believe it or not, is also a good preparation for acting. Acting is serious business, of course, but it is not necessarily a businesslike business, and establishing personal rapport and sympathy is often critical to a scene's success. Partying cannot replace rehearsals, but getting together just for the fun of it can supplement more serious work perfectly. Sensing your partner's joys and excitements helps you share in his or her idealism and expectations; it helps you to know your partner as a whole person and interact with him or her more effectively and with deeper feeling. Actors, of course, are not necessarily any more gregarious than the rest of the population, but long-lasting professional friendships seem to be particularly characteristic of the acting society.

◆ E X E R C I S E   10–1

The Gentleman Caller II

Before beginning this exercise, you should have read *The Glass Menagerie* and memorized the Gentleman Caller scene in Exercise 9–1.

Select a partner and study and rehearse the scene for class presentation. Between rehearsals, revise your GOTEsheet and make notes on how you feel the scene is developing. Experiment with the concept of shaping the scene from within—that is, try to get the most out of your acting partner while rehearsing, not by telling her or him how to act the other role. After three to five hour-long rehearsals, and one or more "alternative" rehearsals, present the scene. How was it different from the unrehearsed first-time presentation? Was it better in rehearsals than in the class presentation? (The usual answer is *yes*. But you will learn to overcome self-consciousness as you become accustomed to acting in front of an audience.) More important, were you able to use the rehearsals to improve your understanding—and hence your acting—of your role?

Summary

The word *rehearsal,* the public part of scene preparation, comes from a word implying repetition and digging; rehearsals are opportunities to go over your part several times, exploring and experimenting as you go. Rehearsals should enable you to slide into your role rather than jumping into a fully theatrical performance, and your rehearsals should encourage improvisational exploration of your character-to-character relationship. You should make no attempt to direct your partner in rehearsals but should try to shape the scene by acting it. There is no rule governing the number of rehearsals that are necessary, but three to five hours for a five-minute scene is a good starting point. Alternative methods of rehearsing include open improvisation and other person-to-person interactions tangent to the actual material.

11

Staging the Scene

Stage Directions

In a produced play, the director, generally initiates the staging, and the setting is fixed before rehearsals begin. In contrast, in a scene for class, *you* will determine where the scene is set, what sort of furniture and props will come into play, where the doors will be, and what the movement will be like. You also will create the behavior of the action: the laughing, drinking, walking, standing, and sitting that may or may not be particularly specified by the text.

You should know that the published acting editions of most plays contain stage directions that were added by the original stage manager and do not necessarily carry the authority of the playwright. You need not follow them; in fact, you should feel free to disregard *all* stage directions except those that are explicitly required to advance the plot. You are certainly not going to have the Broadway set for your scene, and the original stage directions were chosen for their effectiveness in the context of the original production's scenery, lighting, and overall stylization. In your classroom presentation, the staging should simply liberate and enhance your acting. You should cross out the written stage directions (and stage descriptions), therefore, and start afresh.

Creating the Locale

The tendency among beginners is to have two characters sitting or standing somewhere talking to each other. There may be scenes where this arrangement is the best one possible, but they are rare. In the first place, "somewhere" is just too abstract for the actor's necessary sense of specificity. Where is this somewhere? What's there?

An interior scene can provide a host of locales that provide opportunities and obstacles that will shape your acting. Where are the doors? Where do they lead? Who might be coming in from each? What objects are there? A scene set in a kitchen can, for example, be played at the sink, at a table, by the refrigerator door, at the silverware drawer, on the floor, against the wall, or in various combinations of these locations. Which one or ones make the scene's interaction more intense? More believable? More confrontational?

Look at this kitchen scene from Arthur Miller's *Death of a Salesman*:

WILLY: I hope we didn't get stuck on that machine.

LINDA: They got the biggest ads of any of them!

WILLY: I know, it's a fine machine. What else?

LINDA: Well, there's nine-sixty for the washing machine. And for the vacuum cleaner there's three and a half due on the fifteenth. Then the roof, you got twenty-one dollars remaining.

WILLY: It don't leak, does it?

LINDA: No, they did a wonderful job. Then you owe Frank for the carburetor.

WILLY: I'm not going to pay that man! That goddam Chevrolet, they ought to prohibit the manufacture of that car!

LINDA: Well, you owe him three and a half. And odds and ends, comes to around a hundred and twenty dollars by the fifteenth.

WILLY: A hundred and twenty dollars! My God, if business don't pick up I don't know what I'm gonna do!

LINDA: Well, next week you'll do better.

WILLY: Oh, I'll knock 'em dead next week. I'll go to Hartford. I'm very well liked in Hartford. You know, the trouble is, Linda, people don't seem to take to me.

That lovely scene—seemingly innocuous dialogue culminating in a shocking revelation and reversal—can take on many different colors depending on where in the kitchen the actors choose to play it. Suppose Willy is fixing himself a cup of coffee, or Linda is polishing the knives, or Willy is drinking a glass of milk, or Linda is sitting at the table going over the bills. Suppose there is a drawer to be slammed shut, a drink to be put down a bit too sharply, a knife to be handled a bit too longingly. What happens if Willy is sitting and Linda standing—or the other way around? Suppose Willy kicks the refrigerator (the "machine" he mentions in his first line), hurts his toe, and sits. What response will that stimulate in Linda? If Linda walks out of the room while saying "next week you'll do better," what response will that stimulate in Willy? There are no right or wrong answers to these questions, no right or wrong ways to stage the scene. But there are self-stagings that will encourage stronger acting from both partners.

You should understand, of course, that the architecture and furniture involved in this scene need not be remotely realistic in appearance. The refrigerator can be a wood block or the back of a chair, but Willy can still kick at it and hurt his toe, providing the obstacle that will make his scene vivid and his acting more fully fleshed. Just let the class know, in advance, that "the back of this chair is a refrigerator," and then act as though it were: That's part of acting, too.

Movement and Stage Business

Movement is not essential in any scene, and movement inserted in a scene merely to liven things up does more harm than good. But natural movement that comes out of the scene's situation, and out of the interplay of the characters, can evoke stronger, fuller, and deeper acting from both partners. Movement, because it involves the whole body—muscles, skeleton, internal organs—makes the actor organically active and involves the actor bodily in acting a role and embodying a character.

Moreover, movement creates a general context for the acting of a play's transitions, discoveries, climaxes, and reversals. Learn Willy's last line in the scene above, for example, and give it while jogging. Inevitably, you will stop jogging—or at least change the rhythm of your jogging—as you start to say, "You know, the trouble is, Linda . . ." Jogging would (probably) be inappropriate behavior for Willy in this scene, of course, but drying dishes, playing solitaire, or flipping a coin wouldn't be.

Movement also creates opportunities for physical contact and interaction that would not occur if the actors simply decided to sit down and play the scene "in place." If Willy were jogging with Linda, he would have to reach out and stop her if he decided to stop himself. If Willy were playing solitaire, Linda could help him make a move ("Well, next week you'll do better"), and Willy could grab her arm ("Oh, I'll knock 'em dead next week") and then let go of it ("You know, the trouble is . . ."). The physical interaction will stimulate emotional interaction and give contour to the evolving relationship between the characters.

> 📖 BE HUMAN
>
> *I think very few people are interested in the craft of acting, which is actually to reveal what it is to be human.*
>
> CATE BLANCHETT

Directors have long recognized the importance of finding good stage business; it can prove immensely helpful to actors as well. Stage business—the seemingly minor and unconscious physical actions of the character—provides a pattern of behavior that becomes the baseline of a scene, and usually a baseline that is more interesting than two actors facing each other and talking. Well-chosen stage business has several beneficial functions: It relaxes you because it starts you "doing something"; it tones you up because it keeps you busy; it keeps you mentally alert because it doubles your focus; it intensifies your responses, which are reflected unconsciously in your stage business activity. And it makes you human. If Linda is adding up figures in an account book in the *Death of a Salesman* scene, the way she fingers her pencil will reflect her growing anxiety. If Willy is nursing a cup of coffee, his divided interest between drinking his coffee (something good) and paying his bills (something bad) will keep his feelings jumbled, and his reactions will be far more volatile (and interesting) than if he simply listens to Linda in a stupor.

One of the best things about stage business is that it makes stillness, when it occurs, pay off. When Willy stops jogging, or stops drying dishes, or when Linda puts her pencil down and quietly looks at him, both actors and audience will feel the depth of the moment far more than if both actors were static to begin with. So try to find appropriate and dramatically stimulating stage business possibilities for your scene. How will your acting develop if you play the scene at the piano? At the bar? At the barber shop? In the men's room? At the basketball court? While walking? While exercising? While playing solitaire? While getting dressed?

Interesting Positions

In the earliest days of Greek sculpture—the era art historians call Archaic or Preclassical—statues of humans showed the figure erect, facing forward, one foot about six inches ahead of the other. As sculpture developed, the human form was shown in more and more dynamic positions, until by the late

Renaissance it was depicted in all its writhing, twisted possibilities. The same sort of development happens in acting. The beginning actor is usually stiff and adopts rigid, symmetrical, square-shouldered positions, often sitting or standing primly, facing his or her partner head-on. You must learn to break down this stiffness. Even positions fixed by the situation (a witness in a witness chair, a family at the dinner table, Prometheus chained to his rock) can be explored with an eye to the possible dynamics of your physical positioning.

In an acting class, you are usually limited to the furniture on hand for the staging of your scenes. A sofa is a wonderful luxury for that purpose, for it permits thousands of positions: lying, sitting, flopping on the sofa's arms or back, and innumerable combinations of these. An armchair also offers a great many possibilities. But even without these, you should be able to use furniture, props, and arrangements of your scene locale to create opportunities for positions that are physically interesting and challenging. What happens if your partner's head is in your lap? Or if you are sitting on a chair while your partner lies on the floor (beneath you) and then rises to stand (above you)?

It is almost always effective, in staging a two-person scene, to have the principal targets of your attention on opposite sides of you, at least at key moments; this is so that you can turn from one to the other. Such turning is an action in itself, both a turn *away* from someone or something and a turn *toward* someone or something else. And, as turning also shows the audience more of your face, it also displays your feeling: whether you are turning sadly, happily, angrily, fearfully, or in a state of shock. Having two or more targets of attention, and having them widely spaced around you, leads your acting toward bold physical moves and stimulates an active movement contour for your performance. If your acting partner, the ringing phone, and door offering you escape are all bunched together on your left, you'll be quite limited in choosing where to turn or what to do.

During a class break, if you have one, or after an exercise when your classmates have not yet returned to their seats, look at the positions people take when just talking or lolling around. Aren't they interesting? Generally, their positions are very interesting and much more dynamic (even in repose) than the positions these same people take in their first acting scenes. Our bodies are *naturally* dynamic and interesting, but we naturally stiffen into "sit up straight" positions when we find ourselves on public display. You should learn to transcend this tendency in your own work.

Reaching the Audience

One of the major responsibilities of the stage director is to block (stage) the play in order to make the lines and the plot very clear to the audience. This means taking into account the size of the auditorium, the orientation of the stage to the house, the vocal projection of the actors, the lighting, and myriad other factors. In an acting class, this responsibility is yours. Certainly the class audience must be able to see and hear your scene adequately if they and the instructor are to give you valuable advice. Your job in staging your scene is to make it reach the audience.

Try to ascertain, first of all, what the instructor expects for the physical orientation of the scene. Some instructors like to have scenes performed in the round, others on a proscenium stage or in a proscenium format; still others will permit you to place the audience as you wish. In any event, this factor is your primary consideration. How far away is the audience going to be? In the scene exercise, how important is full projection? If there is a chance that, at this stage of your work, full projection can be achieved only with a loss of honesty and realism, which should you go for? Ask your instructor for guidance.

In a proscenium format—that is, with the audience on one side of you—your staging pattern should keep your face more on the downstage (audience-facing) side than on the upstage side. There are many ways of doing this without being blatant about it. You can enter the scene diagonally from the rear. You can seat yourselves at the upstage sides of a square table placed diagonally to the audience. You can loll about on a sofa placed diagonally toward the audience with your head on the upstage side and your partner sitting on the upstage part of the sofa back and facing you (and then falling into your lap). You can look out an imaginary window facing into the audience. Your partner can come to you, put his or her arms around you as you both look out, first facing straight ahead and then turning to each other. These are all standard directorial techniques that you can adopt to get your scene out to the audience while you are playing very intensely and honestly with each other; they are usually preferable, from an acting point of view, to simply half facing your partner and half "cheating out" to the audience.

◆ E X E R C I S E   11–1

Setting the Stage

Memorize and rehearse either the Gentleman Caller scene from *The Glass Menagerie* or the Willy–Linda scene from *Death of a Salesman*. Arrange your set with an eye to the discussions in this chapter, and prepare the scene accordingly.

Now restage the same scene in a completely different setting—for example:

1. At a piano

2. On beach towels at a beach

3. At an outdoor café

4. At a ballet barre

5. On a living room couch

Begin the staging with Willy or Laura actively doing something with regard to the "set" environment—playing the piano, applying suntan oil, doing exercises at the barre, writing a diary entry—and Linda or Jim doing something quite different and unrelated. Then stage the scene by exploring all possibilities for movement, business, physical positions and dynamics, and projection. Have a friend watch and comment.

Then return to the author's setting and restage the scene in its "proper" environment. Have you learned anything from going outside the standard set that can help you upon your return? Probably so.

Ask yourself: What positions give you the greatest sense of involvement? Of freedom? Of power? Of rapport with your partner? These are the positions you will want to find in your acting scenes. What positions make you feel inhibited? Self-conscious? Tense? Isolated? Stiff? These are positions to avoid.

Summary

Your self-staging should not be an attempt to give a final staging patina to your scene. Rather, it should create a movement pattern that brings out the best acting from you: the most vigorous struggle to achieve your victory, the most provocative tactics, the most enthusiastic pursuit of your character's goals. Staging for your scene should be chosen mainly because it stimulates *you*: It makes you work harder—it requires that you be more forceful, more seductive, more amusing, or more inspirational—to get what your character wants.

LESSON

12

Choices

The Need for Choices

The exciting actor differs from the unexciting actor chiefly because of the quality of her or his acting choices: the choices of goals to pursue and tactics to employ. For these are choices, not givens, and they demand the actor's own imagination as much as they require script analysis and research.

The actor's choices are not always apparent in the lines of a play. In fact, sometimes the choices are not even mentioned in the lines. For example:

VERSHININ: If they are not giving us any tea, let's at least philosophize.

TUSENBACH: Yes, let's. What about?

VERSHININ: What about? Let's dream . . . for example, of the life that will come after us in two or three hundred years.

TUSENBACH: Well? After us they will fly in balloons, styles of coats will change, they will discover the sixth sense, perhaps, and develop it; but life will remain quite the same, a difficult life, mysterious and happy. And after a thousand years, man will be sighing the same: "Ah, how hard it is to live!" and meanwhile, exactly the same as now, he will be afraid of death and not want to die.

VERSHININ: How shall I put it? It seems to me everything on earth must change little by little and is already changing before our eyes. In two or three hundred, eventually a thousand years—it's not a matter of time—a happy life will come. We won't share in that life, of course, but we are living for it now, working, well—suffering; we are creating it—and in that alone lies the purpose of our being and, if you like, our happiness.

(ANTON CHEKHOV, *THREE SISTERS*)

SURPRISE CHOICES

I'm very prone to exploring the unobvious way to do something.
JANET SUZMAN

This conversation between two young military officers seems straightforward enough, but if actors simply played the superficial philosophizing, they would miss the point of the scene entirely—which is that both officers are performing for the women they love, who are listening in the background! Tusenbach is trying to persuade Irina (who is playing cards elsewhere in the room) that his life is terribly hard without her; Vershinin is suggesting to Masha—without saying it in words—that she could find happiness with him. This is, then, a scene not of philosophizing but of romance—even though the romantic partners don't speak to each other.

This understanding should dictate Vershinin's and Tusenbach's tone of voice, deportment, gestures, smiles, enthusiasm, wittiness, bravura, sensitivity, and stage business. Yet none of this appears in Chekhov's stage directions! Thus the actors must choose whether to be sitting, standing, dancing, moving, laughing, singing, joking, moralizing, parodying, pontificating, balancing on one foot, smoking a cigar, looking around the room, or whatever combination of those and other choices will provide the basic *inner and outer* action of the scene, for which the spoken lines are merely a convenient vehicle.

Good Choices

Good choices are bold, scary, and exciting. They are choices you can pursue vigorously and with enthusiasm. They involve other characters as well as yourself. They are both psychological and physical: They involve your mind and body and your partner's mind and body. Good choices stimulate your own emotions when you play them with your partner.

Bad choices are safe, sane, and ordinary. They do not tax your feelings; they provoke in you no joy; they neither frighten nor absorb you. Purely intellectual choices involve neither your feelings nor your body. They are easy and pedestrian. They are self-contained, involving no one but you.

Good choices might be:

I want her to love me.

I want him to cry.

I want him to wet his pants.

She might kill me.

She might kill herself.

I want her to kill herself.

These are not exaggerations. Plays are about moments of crisis, not casual conversations about ordinary day-to-day events. In the theatre, even seemingly casual conversations, such as Vershinin and Tusenbach's, lead in to life-changing decisions. (Because of what happens in that scene, Vershinin will have a life-altering affair with Masha, and Tusenbach will die before the play is over.)

Bad choices might be:

I want to express myself.

I want her to understand my position.

I want to persuade him to agree with me.

I worry that he won't agree with me.

I am afraid of losing.

I want to win.

I want him to admire me.

These are bad choices not because they are wrong but because they are not very provocative—to you, to the actor, or to the audience. They are general rather than specific, intellectual rather than psychological or physical, and self-contained rather than interactive.

As you can see, sex and violence predominate in the good choices, and rational decision making predominates in the bad choices. Because of the perennial furor over sex and violence in film and television, it might seem ironic to focus on them as good choices for the actor. But the furor has obscured the obvious: *All* great plays involve sex or violence—or, more commonly, sex *and* violence. This means not only the great tragedies—*Prometheus Bound, Medea, King Lear,* and so forth—but also great comedies, farces, and melodramas; or, for that matter, bad comedies, farces, and melodramas. Indeed, the theatre was created to help humankind come to terms with life's big mysteries: the ecstasy of sex, the terror of violence—and sometimes the terror of sex, the ecstasy of violence—and for an actor to avoid these mysteries is to miss not only the opportunity of acting but the whole point of the theatre.

When making your acting choices, therefore, *always look for a sexual interest,* and *always look for a potential terror.* Sexual interest includes romance, success, dominance, and even wealth, all of which can have sexual components. Terror includes embarrassment, confusion, humiliation, and pain, all of which have a terrifying component. Make choices that inspire your feelings, that get under your (and your acting partner's) skin. Choices that are merely rational—no matter how rational—will not lead to an exciting performance.

Choose to find your partner interesting. Your partner is an interesting person. Did you know that? Often we don't even notice. We think "He (she) is 'just' my acting partner." But that acting partner is a caring, feeling, fearing, loving person—sometimes frustrated, sometimes beautiful, sometimes explosive. Your partner is capable of violence, brilliance, panic, and schizophrenia; your partner *could* become your lifelong lover or your bitterest enemy or both.

These statements are facts. It is up to you not to dispute them but to work them into your acting relationship. Finding your partner fascinating, or scary, or adorable, or exhilarating is a *choice,* a choice you must learn to make.

You must choose, therefore, to find your partner interesting: to make him or her a worthy opponent if the scene involves opposition, or an alluring sex object if the scene involves sexual attraction, or a frightening menace if the scene involves terror. Only if you give your acting partner the potential for love, for violence, for brilliance, and for explosive *surprise* will you truly get involved with him or her on a personal level.

📝 DO WHATEVER YOU WANT

Don't be afraid to hurt me, you won't, and do whatever you want, go wherever you want with it, I'll go with you. I love to be surprised.

MERYL STREEP, TO KEVIN KLINE ON THE
FIRST DAY OF THEIR SHOOTING *SOPHIE'S CHOICE*

There are many ways to discover how interesting/fascinating/scary your partner really is. Conversation is the most obvious, particularly personal conversation about growing up, about one's plans for the future, that sort of thing. It is important to see your acting partner as an evolving person like yourself, not as a fixed stereotype. Your acting partner has a past and a future, she or he is in flux, is changing, is still an *unfinished* human being. The more you realize this, the easier it will be to play dynamically with your partner, to try to work your magic on him or her and allow his or her magic to work on you.

Study your partner while you rehearse your scene. How does she or he react to your threats in the scene? To your smiles? To your touch on her or his neck? You don't need to come up with answers to these questions. Indeed, they are fundamentally unanswerable in a real relationship. You need only to search them out and to recognize the mystery, complexity, and fascinating profundity of your acting partner. Even in a seemingly commonplace scene, this awareness will prove beneficial.

Choose goals that excite you personally and physically. The audience will never be excited for you if you aren't excited for yourself. Remember, you are not telling or describing a story, you are *embodying* it; and your body must share in the enthusiasm of your pursuit. Imagine winning your goal in the scene: Would winning make you want to jump up and down? No? Then you have made a poor choice.

HITLER AND JESUS

What actors can do without lecturing is show that in each of us there is Hitler and Jesus, and if you are a truly gifted actor you can find that in you, and bring it out, and say, "See, we share this."

RICHARD DREYFUSS

Choose fears that frighten you personally and physically. Does it upset you to think that your partner might turn his back on you? How much? Does it upset you to think that your partner might stick pins under your fingernails? How much?

Which imagined event stimulates the most revulsion in you? The most physical nausea? That is the most powerful image to choose. Using each of these images, play the following line to your partner: "I don't want to see you again." Which image made your voice quiver? Which choice most successfully embodies a touch of fear in the line?

Choose to use everything you've got. In going for your goals, and in challenging your fears, show us every usable thing inside yourself: your capacity for both total love and extreme cruelty, your spiritual hunger, your reckless craziness. Don't hide behind shallow politeness or tentative efforts. Let us see the demon in you, and the child.

Choose to touch your partner. It is equally logical to touch or not to touch your partner; both choices can be defended in a theoretical analysis. But the best acting choice usually is to touch, out of anger or affection or, even better, a mixture of each.

Touching your partner is both physical business and personal contact; it usually intensifies the rapport between actors and deepens the concentration of both partners. More important, it makes *you* feel more involved in the scene. Therefore, when rehearsing a scene, try to find a reason to

rub your partner's shoulders or back

stroke or tousle your partner's hair

playfully poke your partner with your toe

take your partner's hand

grab your partner's wrist

embrace (hug) your partner

cuddle your partner from behind

slap your partner on the shoulder

reach for your partner's neck

All of these touching actions should be noninvasive. You mustn't construe your acting assignment as a blanket permission to take sexual liberties with anyone or to engage in unrehearsed roughhousing. Still, actors must be prepared to be touched, to hug, to kiss, and to engage in staged physical combat (with appropriate training) as part of their artistic work. Your instructor will help you set appropriate boundaries for this touching if you so require.

Touching your partner need not be overtly sexual, and in most scenes not directly connected with sexual overtures (a brother-to-brother scene, for example), touching is obviously a matter of sharing friendship rather than soliciting romance. But touching is so fundamental to intense human relationships that it is invariably useful in acting. There are few acting scenes that cannot be improved simply by directing the actors to touch each other in some way during the crucial exchange. Touching the neck, which is both an erogenous zone and a point of extreme physical vulnerability, can by itself triple the emotional involvement of both actors in a scene representing, for example, a lover's quarrel. Try it.

Choose to make contact. Beginning actors often tend to look away, move away, stare at the floor or ceiling, or turn their backs on their partners at a scene's crucial moments. This behavior comes partly from a mistaken sense of what "looks theatrical" and partly from shyness and uneasiness. It is partly a holdover from adolescence, when major confrontations were avoided by running to your room and slamming the door. In acting, you should never "slam the door."

When someone shouts at you face-to-face, your blood pumps faster, even if you know it's only a scene in acting class. That moment when your blood surges forth is a great acting moment. You mustn't waste it in a meaningless pause while you turn your back and compose your response. Beginning actors continually overrate the effectiveness of long pauses, even-tempered responses, and deeply furrowed brows.

Similarly, when someone smiles engagingly at you, making you feel suffused by human warmth of a sort mere stage directions cannot create, you are in a particularly wonderful emotional state for acting.

It is precisely at these moments—when you are a bit flustered, a bit moved, not entirely sure of yourself—that you should maintain eye contact with your partner and say your line. These moments are fleeting; they may last only a split second. But these moments of deep personal contact provide the human vulnerability that makes acting a lively art. If you retreat from your partner at that moment, by closing your eyes, staring at the floor, or turning your back in heroic defiance (which usually reads as adolescent pique), you are retreating from the most distinctive and exciting part of acting: your raw feelings and your own particular sensitivity. Please don't slam the door on yourself in this way. When someone shouts in your face, shout back, or try to laugh, or cry, or hug the so-and-so, or do all of the above! Don't turn your back. To do so is to turn your back on acting itself.

Choose to try to smile. Most people in most person-to-person situations want to be there, want to be liked by the person they are talking with, want to encourage the other person to be friendly. Consequently, most people smile much of the time. Lovers breaking up, quarreling siblings, labor negotiators, and conspiring executives all smile—or at least try to. To smile while quarreling gives the quarrel a hidden dimension and suggests the possibility that, at the deepest level, both partners seek a reconciliation. This suggestion is both realistic and dramatically effective because it creates sympathy for the characters. Then, when the smile can no longer be maintained—when it struggles against the tears—your scene develops a powerful poignancy. "I want to smile" is one of life's most universal intentions, because it means "I want to be in a situation that pleases me." Everybody wants that, and therefore it should be one of your goal choices.

Choose to hurry your partner. A good pace usually means a rapid pace. When reviewers dislike a play, they usually say that it was "slow" or that it "dragged." But good pace doesn't mean that you have to speak rapidly. What it does mean is that you must be driving hard toward your goal, and that drive means you not only want it but you want it *now.*

"Pacing up a scene" means that you should try to hurry your partner along somewhat, that you should need to win and win quickly. Taking a pause before your speeches—trying to build up feeling before you speak— not only wastes time but shows that you're "only acting." In real life, people don't try to build up their emotions before they speak. They speak and then find that they have built up emotion!

Thus, in your preparation, choose to find time's winged chariot at your back. Your scene should have a sense of urgency. Sweep your partner off his or her feet; leave your partner speechless with your dazzling argument, but don't plod along with the facts, or indulge in your feelings, or pose nobly and thoughtfully in the glow of your own magnificence.

Choose to be loud. Nothing infuriates the audience like not hearing, and you certainly know that it is unwise to infuriate the audience, even for the best of reasons. There are reasons to be loud and reasons to be soft. If you are clever enough, you can always find both. Choose reasons to be loud—at least loud to the point that you can be heard clearly from anywhere in the room.

In scenes where you must be quiet so as not to be overheard by the people upstairs, choose to make the ceiling four feet thick.

In scenes where you tell someone that you love him or her, say it in a way that suggests you don't care if the whole world hears. Indeed, say it so that the whole world *does* hear.

In scenes when your anger can be expressed either coolly or explosively, choose to express it explosively.

Remember, you can justify the opposite choice perfectly well. But in most cases, that would justify bad acting; you would win the battle and lose the war. In addition to being heard by the audience, the "loud" choices stimulate more feeling from your acting partner, which will return more stimulation to you. The cool, quiet, logical choice, eminently justifiable, leads to uninteresting theatre most of the time, yet it is a seductively safe way to play a scene, particularly for the beginning actor. Try the bolder, louder, explosive choices first. They are harder to get out but more liberating. Later, perhaps with a friend acting as a director to guide you, they may be pruned back. Bold choices taken in rehearsal can prove wonderfully enlightening even if toned down by the time of performance.

Choose to do something stupid. This is not facetious advice. Often when I (as a coach) feel a scene is plodding lamely along, I suddenly order the actor to jump up and down, or do a dance step, or sing a song. Or I holler, "Do something stupid!" Though this command seems to have no immediate relevance to the dialogue, and though it always makes the actor acutely uncomfortable, it more often than not stimulates a deeper level of involvement and creativity. Why? Perhaps it reminds the actor that intense human interaction (which is what the scene is about) is always uncomfortable and awkward, though acting may not be, and this instruction brings the awkwardness to the fore—and with it, a level of unplanned reality. Or perhaps "doing something stupid" surprises your acting partner and makes the ensuing interaction more nervy, open-ended, and unpredictable. Or perhaps all great theatre involves an element of the absurd, the awkward, the final chaos of life itself. Probably all three factors come into play, and you can make them come into play in your own scenes if, from time to time, you make the exciting choice to "do something stupid."

◆ E X E R C I S E   12–1

Bold Choices

Study your GOTEsheet for the Laura–Jim scene, the Willy–Linda scene, or any other scene you have prepared. Do your listed goals really stimulate you psychologically and physically? Do your fears make you cringe? Are your tactics boldly chosen? Are your expectations vivid and exciting? Did you, in playing those scenes, work to find your partner fascinating? Did you touch your partner? Was the quest for victory an urgent one? Were you able to smile? Were you able to shout?

> ◪ BOLD CHOICES
>
> *I'm a reasonably calm and quiet-spoken person, until I'm onstage, at which point—to the moon!*
>
> JOHN LITHGOW

Go back to one of those scenes and rewrite your GOTEsheet with bolder choices. Then play the scene with your partner, implementing those choices. Find points in the scene—mere moments—when you can be explosive or desperate, or where you can reach out and touch someone. Making bold choices is something that you will learn to do a small step at a time, but those steps can be very important in your development as an actor.

After playing the scene, ask your partner whether she or he was more stimulated, more frightened, more attracted, more emotionally *involved* with you than before. Chances are the answer will be *yes*. And if your partner was more involved, chances are you were also.

Summary

The quality of your acting is determined by the choices you make, what you choose to play. Good choices, which are bold and interpersonal, stimulate the emotions of both you and your partner. Bad choices may be logical, but they are unstimulating emotionally and psychologically. Good choices usually involve implied sex and violence, which invoke humankind's most urgent lusts and terrors. Choose to find your partner fascinating. Choose goals and terrors that affect you personally. Choose to touch your partner, to quicken the pace of your scene, to confront your partner face-to-face, and to find reasons to be loud rather than quiet or cool and, on occasion, to do something downright stupid.

L E S S O N

13

Performing

Stage Fright

The time comes when the study is complete, the rehearsals are over, the choices are made. Now you perform your scene publicly.

For most actors, tension, nervousness, and stage fright threaten to cancel out the careful preparation. Even veteran actors experience stress in performance, sometimes extreme stress. Fear of the audience, fear of criticism, fear of rejection, fear of forgetting your lines, and fear of looking foolish are the inhibiting factors that may not even surface until the moment of performance, when their appearance can become immediately debilitating.

How can you avoid this fear? First of all, you should recognize that a certain amount of tension is inevitable and may even be desirable. Many actors reach the fullest level of performance only with the added "danger" of a public audience. Even without consciously holding back in rehearsal, many actors find that the presence of a live audience stimulates them to let go. The audience can spur an actor's power and belief, much as the cheering crowd can intensify an athlete's performance or a speechmaker's eloquence. There is nothing wrong with making use of the added edge of excitement that an audience provides.

But stage fright—the numbing fear of evaluation by others—can just as easily dampen your enthusiasm, inhibit your movement, constrict your voice, and paralyze your reflexes. Scenes rehearsed with great passion and fervor can dry up in performance and become mere shadows of their former selves. It is useless to complain that "it was better in rehearsal." Your job is to learn how to make it better in performance.

Classroom Performance

A good classroom performance requires preparation. First, take the time to set your scene properly: Put the furniture in the proper place. Decide where the (imaginary) door is, where the stove is, and what real properties are represented by substitute items. Insofar as necessary, the audience also should be informed of these requirements of the scene. Then your scene should be announced, quite briefly, with any essential details not obvious from the scene itself explained.

Then you and your partner should go to your opening positions and *prepare*. The duration of that preparation varies according to your instructor's guidelines. Some actors like to take a very long time—a minute or more. It is to your advantage, however, to learn to make your preparation in as brief a period as possible—for example, five to ten seconds. Though brief, your preparation should be comprehensive. It should include

♦ A moment of sheer physical release, perhaps by shaking out your arms, kicking your legs, doing a full body bend, or pounding your fist into your hand.

♦ A quick study of your partner, bringing up what you find most fascinating / scary about him or her.

♦ A flash on what excites you in the situation of the scene. What's the best that can happen to your character?

♦ A flash on what terrifies you in the situation of the scene. What's the worst that can happen to your character?

♦ A final GOTEcheck, perhaps in this order: "I'm gonna (EXPECTATION!) win this (GOAL!) by doing this and this (TACTICS) to him/her (OTHER). And I'm gonna win it now!"

Running through this little litany will hurtle you out of your own person (as an acting student) and into the persona of the scene. During this quick run-through, you will enter the play, realize the excitement the situation holds for you, see the potential for joy and pain your character faces, and see your acting partner not as a fellow student but as a character for or with whom you have a deep need or quest.

Concentration on the other character, and on what you (as a character) want that other character to do or to believe, is the best cure for stage fright. That concentration focuses your energy, liberates your resources, organizes your choices. It will help you to forget the audience and to shape the scene from within, not from without. It will help to eliminate your "director's eye" that continually stands outside your role, an eye that can only confuse you and dissipate your character's energy.

WHAT MY MIND'S ON

I'm never thinking about motivation, or family history, or any of that stuff when I'm working. I'm thinking about, "Why is he looking at me like that? Why is his eyebrow standing up? Is he lying to me?" Whatever it is that I'm going through with that character, with that other actor, that's what my mind's on, not style or background or anything else.

MARY STEENBURGEN

Things to ask yourself during the performance are not "How am I doing?" or "What is my next line?" but

◆ Is my partner's face flushed?

◆ Is my partner (my partner's character) telling the truth?

◆ Does he love me?

◆ Will she succumb?

◆ Must I press harder? Softer? Do I have him on the run?

◆ Can I make her listen better? Understand better? Understand me better? Care more? Like me better?

The more you concentrate on your partner's character, the less you will be aware of the audience. The more you ask yourself real questions about your partner's character, the more you will be involved in the scene and the more you will create a real situation.

Play for Results—In the Other Character!

Actors often ask whether, in class work, they should concentrate on results or on the process of acting. The answer might be confusing unless we realize that there are two interpretations of the word *results* in this context.

One is the result as seen by the audience: in other words, theatrical effectiveness. It is almost certainly a mistake for a beginning actor to directly attempt to deliver a sophisticated theatrical result in this sense of the word—that is, to deliver a full-fledged and crisply polished professional performance. Among other reasons, it just can't be done—not without sets, lights, a director, a supporting professional cast, several weeks of rehearsal, and, perhaps most of all, a "real" (and demanding) theatre audience. Better, in class, to concentrate on the process of developing a role through making good choices and through your active involvement with the goals, tactics, and expectations of your character.

THE GIVE AND TAKE

Put all your attention on the other person, which frees you from any self-consciousness. If you can see the experience they're having—What's their face doing? What are they feeling?—that's truly listening and responding. That's the give and take, and the aliveness, that I value.

CHRISTINE LAHTI

But some elements of process include going for certain results seen not in the audience but in the other actor or actors. In your scene, if your goal is to make the other character love you, try during the scene to make the other actor love you. If you are trying to scare the other character, scare the actor. Try to create real, physical results. Try to make the other actor sweat, relax, smile, laugh, cry, or vomit. Try to make his or her heart palpitate or knees weaken, either in fear or in adoration. *Look for results from the other actor, not from the audience.* If you generate a response from your acting partner, you will also create an impact on the audience watching you.

Actors legitimately differ on how much on-the-spot spontaneity should enter into actual performance. Certainly any physical action that is potentially violent—such as slapping or pushing—should be well rehearsed and performed exactly as rehearsed. Sexual advances should be similarly prepared so that both partners agree on what will and won't be done, and that agreement must be honored in the performance. And, certainly, actions in a directed play should be performed as rehearsed, subject to the director's instructions (which may or may not allow for on-the-spot improvisation). But an acting class offers considerable leeway for in-performance improvisation. Frequently, actions taken on impulse will be preferable to those carefully rehearsed. Acting class should be a place for experimentation, and you should give yourself ample room for experimenting in the performance mode itself.

You should end your scene by saying "Scene" or "Curtain" when you finish—allowing a momentary pause after the last line or stage action—and then returning to your seat unless instructed otherwise. This is not the time for grimacing, scowling at your partner, or shrugging as if to say "I guess that wasn't very good, was it?" Learn to respect your work and the work of your partner. Do not offer lame excuses or blame your partner or skulk into the background. If something went horribly wrong in performance, you should certainly be able to ask to repeat the scene. If you are asked whether anything went wrong, you should tell the truth without accusing anyone: It is appropriate to say "We skipped a section of the text" but unwise to say "Joe dropped his lines." Publicly accusing your partner of ruining the scene will make it more difficult to rework the scene effectively and sensitively.

After performing your scene, you should do a quick review in your mind: Were you concentrating? Were you pursuing a goal? Did you move your partner? Surprise him or her? Were you as concentrated, as intense, as free, and as relaxed as you were in your best rehearsal? If not, why not?

Most important, be prepared to learn from your performance. Acting class is a place to learn, not to show off your wares. You have worked hard on your part, memorized your text, developed and studied your GOTEsheet, rehearsed your scene, and performed with eloquence and vigor, and still you are going to receive criticism. Your classmates may be grudging in their approval. Your instructor may talk darkly about your "problems." Your acting partner may stonewall you from across the room. Where did you go wrong?

You didn't. In acting class, you are learning, but you still have a long way to go.

Summary

Stage fright can affect all actors and can destroy the result you thought you had achieved in studying, staging, and rehearsing your scene. Proper preparation and intense concentration will help to lessen the effects of stage fright; so will going for physical results in your stage interactions and keeping your scene improvisational in nonessential matters of blocking and inflection. After a scene, you should leave the stage without apology and review your work in terms of your preparation and choices.

L E S S O N

14

Evaluation and Improvement

Helpful Criticism

It is often said of writing that the best writing is rewriting. So it is with acting. A scene is not "finished" the first time you act it in front of others. A professionally produced play does not reach its finest form until weeks or months into its run; it takes a long time for acting to ripen and mature. As an actor, you will need a chance to prune your excesses, probe your strengths, and polish your rough edges.

Most scenes will improve markedly following judicious critique and reworking if you respond to the criticism positively and engage yourself in the acting process more fully than before.

The first thing to realize after a critique of your scene—particularly after a harsh critique—is that you weren't really *terrible*. Most of us overreact to negative remarks. Rare indeed is the actor who has not quit the profession a hundred times (momentarily, at least) after a waspish review, or a sneering criticism, or even after the damnation of faint praise.

The second thing to realize, however, is that you probably weren't *wonderful* either. Sure, it would have been better with lights and costumes, or with the right props, or if what's-his-name hadn't forgotten his line and blown your first cue. Still, there is work to be done—*your* work—and by doing it you can take giant steps.

YOU NEVER MASTER IT

Acting fascinates me. It's something that you can never get good at. You can never master it. The rules always change. It's a wonderful exercise.

WILLEM DAFOE

The first step is merely listening carefully to the critique, regardless of its source. Certainly there are going to be friends or teachers whose opinions you particularly trust, but the fact is that audiences consist of more strangers than friends and more nonactors than actors or acting teachers. If *anybody* thinks your scene can be improved, then it probably can be, even if that anybody hasn't a notion as to how to go about improving it. Accept the validity of criticism, even if you don't accept the suggested diagnosis or cure.

As you listen to the criticism, try to answer these questions: What didn't they like? Did they understand the story? The relationship? Could they hear? Most important, did they care? That, of course, is the sine qua non of theatre: Remember, nobody pays an audience to care about the characters. Making them care is your job. If they didn't care, you haven't succeeded, no matter how "correct" you were.

Many things get said in a critique, some wise, some foolish, but you can learn from them all. Here are some of the most common criticisms with suggestions for your future improvement.

Indicating and indulging are among the most common problems of beginning actors. Although they are not identical problems, both involve the playing of emotions, rather than actions.

Indicating means that you are trying to show the emotions of the character, rather than playing the intentions of the character, or the GOTE of the scene. For example, if in reading the scene you decide the character should be sad and then you play "being sad," you are simply indicating a feeling to the audience, not experiencing it yourself. If, however, you play "I want him to marry me" and the other character says, "Leave me alone," you will *be* sad, and you don't have to indicate it. Moreover, you might find yourself smiling at that moment (that is, smiling to make him change his mind) rather than "looking sad." Indicating your character's presumed feelings, therefore, is wrong for two separate reasons: (1) It creates only a simulated emotion that the audience sees through. (2) It leads you to make unrealistic and often undramatic choices.*

---

* Although indicating emotions is usually considered an acting fault, indicating *objects* (or people or places) by pointing, nodding, or gesturing toward them is, within limits, perfectly acceptable and, in many cases, desirable. See "Pointing" in Lesson 19.

Indulging means playing an emotion for all it's worth, mainly to show off your ability to emote. In the example above, the indicating actor would try to look sad, and the indulging actor would whoop out great sobs of anguish and despair. Indulging may make you feel good—or at least feel that you're acting up a storm—but it is rarely if ever effective, inasmuch as it calls attention to your acting rather than to the character's plight and feelings.

In the theatre, emotion must always be seen to come out of a character's working through a situation and working through his or her relationships. The best way to generate emotion is to play your GOTEsheet boldly and sensitively—that is, to stimulate your feelings by directly pursuing real goals with and through real people (your scene partners), by using real tactics. The worst way to generate emotion is to decide which emotion to portray and then try to manufacture it on your own.

To rework a scene critiqued as indicated or indulged, restudy the GOTEsheet with an eye particularly to your goal and your interaction with the other actor. For a scene labeled indulgent, you should also rethink the expectation and figure out how you can play the scene more positively. In a scene criticized for indulgence, also consider the time factor. Are you hurrying your partner adequately? Do you want what you want *now*—instead of after having a good cry about it? Remember, the business of the scene is getting what your character wants, not shedding lots of unnecessary tears in the process.

The scene was boring! Chances are no one will ever say directly that your scene was boring, but if the audience was inattentive and the response unduly faint, you can certainly tell that you failed to stimulate the imagination.

Scenes are boring for a variety of reasons—usually because the choices are timid and impersonal and the underlying relationship is too intellectual, too rational, too expository, too polite. No one gets bored at a sexy scene or a violent one, no matter how clumsily played. Rethink your choices, and reexamine the scene for underlying sexual or threatening potential. Get personal with your partner. Strengthen your tactics. Choose to make the scene mean something very vivid to you—something you can get your body into as well as your mind. Intensify your images of victory and your fantasies of defeat.

I couldn't hear! This common criticism should be met in two ways. First, restage your scene so that you open out more to the audience. If it's an intimate scene, put more space between you and your partner so that you aren't tempted to whisper. Then find *reasons* to pick up the scene's volume. If your line is "I love you" and your inclination is to whisper it, change your inclination: Say the line so that the whole world hears!

Every actor has the obligation to make herself or himself heard at all times. In Part V, "The Actor's Technique," there are some specific suggestions that will help you. But at any point in your learning process, you must know that being heard is *your* responsibility—sometimes your first responsibility—as an actor.

An actor inaudible to the audience is likely to be inaudible to the other actors onstage. In other words, the actor is speaking more quietly than he or she would be in the same situation in life (when we are almost never inaudible to the people we're talking to). Stage fright, in any of its many varieties, is the culprit here. Don't ever excuse inaudibility because you were simply "being real." Chances are you were being not only nontheatrical but unreal as well.

That was great! The most devastating criticism of your scene, sometimes, is unmitigated praise. How do you rework a scene that's been praised to the skies? You must take the praise as a challenge to do even better—and to show yourself that you can do even better.

You must remember that in acting, "really great" is not enough, that no amount of praise should stop you from working to get deeper and deeper into the actor's art. Actors who *really* are "really great" are one in a million, perhaps one in a generation. Acting is one of those rare professions that truly achieve the rank of art—which means that practitioners at the very summit of their craft are true immortals who will be remembered centuries beyond their times. Are you there yet? Of course not. Don't ever let praise, no matter how well intended or sincere, stand in the way of reaching your highest potential.

Reworking

When you have brought together the criticisms that can help shape your work and have evaluated your preliminary presentation with your partner, your scene can be rehearsed with an eye to focusing on the specific problems you were able to isolate. You should experience a sense of freedom at this point. You have already done your scene once. Your "first-night" jitters are over, and you can now get on with the work of working on *yourself*. This stage separates the serious student from the casual one, because this is where the hard work begins—work that is not always immediately gratifying, work that does not have the immediate thrill of first-time performance.

Choose a fellow student whom you and your partner trust and ask him or her to observe the reworking rehearsals and judge whether the problems seem to be improving. Sometimes the use of a tape recorder or a videotape recorder (if you are fortunate enough to have such equipment) can be most helpful in spotting what the critics saw and correcting it.

Your work will not always improve; occasionally, in fact, it may go downhill. Sometimes the scene just isn't right for you, or you're not ready for it, or the chemistry between you and your partner is off. Don't fall back on excuses, however, and don't be quick to blame. It is your challenge to make every scene your most fantastic, every partner your best one, and every role your favorite. No one is going to do this for you, either now or in the future. Reworking should be approached with enthusiasm and dedication, which will not always be rewarded by quickly won success but must be relentless nonetheless.

Often you will have a chance to re-present a reworked scene. If you have a choice in the matter, you should do so only after making a serious effort to re-think your approach and after making serious changes in your performance. Don't simply hope for a better mood or a sudden inspiration. Reworking is *working,* and unless you understand that, you will have little improvement to show.

◆ E X E R C I S E   **14–1**

Scene Presentation

Select a partner and a scene. Following all the lessons in Part III, memorize, study, rehearse, stage, and present the scene. Then, guided by a class critique, restudy, restage, re-rehearse, and re-present the same scene in a subsequent class meeting.

Summary

The education of an actor does not end with the first performance; performances are just steps in the learning process. Even good acting can be critiqued, restudied, re-rehearsed, and re-presented to advantage. It is up to you to learn how to take criticism (indeed, how to solicit criticism), how to learn from it, *and* how to grow by it. Growth is not always continuous and not always easy. The best results involve hard work and little glamor, but the finest acting is always accomplished through relentless diligence.

IV

The Actor's Instrument

PARTS II AND III ARE CONCERNED WITH PROCESSES OF ACTING: AP-proaching and preparing dramatic roles. Anyone who has mastered those twelve lessons might be said to have learned "how to act." But becoming an actor means a lot more than learning how to act; it also means becoming a trained and capable acting *instrument.*

The instrument consists of the actor's personal attributes and abilities: appearance, speech and movement capabilities, emotional depths, intelligence, mind–body coordination, sense of timing, sense of drama, and presentational skills. For the actor is both a player and the instrument played; the actor, in other words, plays upon herself or himself in much the same way that a violinist plays upon a violin. Carrying that metaphor one step further, we can say that an actor, like the violinist, can be no better than the instrument—no matter how brilliant his or her approach or dedication to fulfilling tasks. Thus the actor will be rewarded by having a versatile and splendid instrument or held back by possessing an instrument that is unresponsive or undisciplined, making her or him unable to execute commands with passion, subtlety, excitement, or vivacity.

A fundamental goal for every would-be actor is to develop an instrument that can be employed in a wide range of tactics and can bring to life a wide variety of roles. Certainly raw acting talent is a probable factor in an actor's subsequent career, but, now more than ever, a trained acting instrument is every bit as necessary—if not more so. Most often today, the theatre looks for actors who have completed substantial training in actor-training programs, typically an undergraduate drama degree, usually followed by a graduate (M.F.A.) or Professional Actor Training Program degree or by two or three years of apprentice work or experience with a professional theatre company. And this is *intensive* training, not casual classes at odd times. Most professional actor-training programs involve students in thirty to seventy hours a week of classes and rehearsals for about three years.

You will not have a professional actor's instrument, then, in a matter of a few weeks or months; nor will Part IV provide you with more than an outline of what you will be working on if you wish to pursue acting beyond the beginning level. But the time to start developing your instrument is now. For as you learn how to "play" your instrument, you will want to own a better one.

15

The Actor's Voice

Breathing

Most people think of the voice as the most important element of the actor's instrument. Asked to name the three most important aspects of acting, Tommaso Salvini, the great nineteenth-century star said, "Voice, voice, and more voice." We have moved away from the oratorical style of Salvini's era, to be sure, but a supple, commanding, and engaging voice is as important as ever.

Voice is not taught in a day; most successful vocal-training programs last at least two years, usually three. That's three years of weekly or biweekly classes and *daily* drills, lasting about an hour each. Because we have all been using our voices for years, much that must be learned requires unlearning deep-rooted habits. Moreover, we tend to resist that unlearning—deep down, we like the way we speak—and one of the actor's hardest tasks is simply learning to believe in the steps necessary to vocal improvement, beginning with learning to breathe.

Breathing is the basis of voice, as it is the basis for life. To *inspire* means "to breathe in"—as well as to nourish the *spirit* (from the Latin *spiritus*, meaning "breath"). Breathing is as natural as sleeping, except that you cannot do either unselfconsciously when being stared at by an audience. The actor's goal is simply to breathe naturally while under the pressure of performance—and to provide sufficient lung power to support a voice that may be challenged in acting more than in almost any other activity.

The *yawn* is the ideal breath because it comes from a relaxed body and because it takes in a substantial quantity of air in an unforced manner. But the actor cannot yawn continuously during a play—except perhaps in Chekhov. When you yawn, chances are you breathe not from your chest but from your abdomen. And that's where the actor's breathing must originate. The shallow chest breaths that characterize many beginning actors are the result of tension and self-consciousness—the same sort of tension that would cause shallow breathing if we were to come upon a mugger in a dark alley. Deep body breathing, as deep as possible, gives the voice its fullest support and the body its fullest relaxation.

◆ E X E R C I S E   15–1

Breathing from the Abdomen

Breathe deeply from the abdomen. Yawn, stretch your arms, and breathe again. Lie down, knees raised, feet and back on the floor. As you breathe, mark the movement of your abdomen and try to minimize the movement of your chest. Now stand and walk about the room, swinging your arms freely and tasting the air as you breathe it in.

Phonation: Making Sounds

Oddly, nobody knows for certain how sound is made by the human voice. We do know that the sound is caused by air passing through vibrating vocal folds (also called vocal cords), but whether the air vibrates the folds as it does a clarinet reed, or whether the folds, like violin strings, vibrate the air, is a subject of debate among laryngologists (vocal specialists). However it happens, making sounds with your voice (phonation) is a spontaneously learned phenomenon that the actor must cultivate beyond its everyday function.

The easiest sound to make is the vowel *ah*, and the best way to make it is with the most open-throated and relaxed voice possible. *Ah* is the vowel on which singers and actors routinely warm up their voices, practice scales, and learn to develop resonation and vocal power.

◆ E X E R C I S E   15–2

Sounding

Breathing from the abdomen, say *ah* with each exhalation in any of the following ways:

1. ah hah hah hah hah hah hah

2. pah pah pah pah pah pah pah

3. ahhhhhhhhhhhhhhhhhh (sliding down the scale)

Now, turning the body from side to side, walk around the room and make the same series of sounds, gradually increasing the volume toward the end of each breath:

4. ah hah hah Hah Hah HAH HAH HAHH HAHH! *HAHHH!*

5. pah pah Pah Pah PAH PAH PAHH PAHH! *PAHHH!!*

6. ahhhhhhhhhhHHHHHHHHHHHHHH*HHHH!* (sliding down the scale)

What happens when you increase your volume? Do the vocal folds vibrate faster? No, for faster vibrations would simply raise the *pitch* of your voice (make the sounds go higher on the scale). Volume is primarily a function not of phonation but of *resonance*.

Resonance

Resonance is the re-sounding of vocal fold sounds. Re-sounding is a simple phenomenon. Vibration, as of a tuning fork, creates sound, but it also creates other (sympathetic) vibrations, which themselves create sound. Often these secondary sounds, caused by sympathetic vibrations, are louder and fuller than the original tuning-fork sound itself. A tuning fork struck and its stem then placed against an empty cigar box, for example, will create an amplified sound far greater than previously because of the resonation of the air within the cigar box.

Most of the actual sound of the human voice is provided by the resonation of three "cigar boxes" inside the vocal apparatus: the pharyngeal (throat), oral (mouth), and nasal (nose) cavities that lie above the vocal folds. Air that is first vibrated by the vocal folds passes through these three empty cavities and creates sympathetic vibrations in both the tissues and the air within them. What emerges is the rich, full-voiced sound that is characteristic of the peculiar shapes and sizes of each individual's resonating capacities. Much of our resonation is biologically determined; indeed, "voiceprints" identify individuals as clearly as fingerprints do. But we also have a certain degree of control over the amount of resonation we can produce. If properly exercised, this control can favorably alter the power, timbre, tone, and character of our voices.

Almost *all* acting students need to improve resonance, simply because the resonance required of the actor is far greater than that required of most other professionals. The actor must be prepared to be full-voiced continuously for several hours at a stretch on a daily basis, must project with authority, and must be able to "play upon" an instrument with many subtle gradations of resonance—which itself demands a "resonance reserve" that can be called on at an instant. Resonation is one way an actor can increase his or her volume and vocal power without straining the voice. Resonation is a way of making your cavities work for you rather than against you. It is therefore a vocal asset that must be carefully cultivated.

But how do you improve your resonance? *Relaxation* is the first principle. A relaxed throat is an open throat, and an open throat provides deep, mellow resonance. Thus, rolling the head easily about, "floating" it atop the spine, is a standard actor's exercise for relaxing the neck and opening up the pharyngeal cavity.

Posture is the second principle. You would need a movement or vocal coach to work with you to get the best results, but you can get a good start just by developing a comfortably erect posture, with your weight centered, your spine lengthening easily upward, and your head "floating" freely atop your spine. With your muscles then relaxed—particularly in your neck, your jaw, and your face—you will be more generally resonant than before.

Speaking itself is the third principle. An open-jawed, open-mouthed articulation provides greater resonance than a close-lipped, tight-jawed, constricted speech. The vowel *ah* is the standard warm-up vowel for actors and singers because it is made with the jaw fully dropped, providing the greatest oral resonance and thereby the least demand on the vocal folds themselves. *Ee* and the French *uu* are, by contrast, the least resonant vowels because they require a tightening of the jaw, in the first instance, and a closing of the lips in the second—both practices necessarily reducing the amplitude of resonation.

The placement of vowels—that is, the place in the mouth where they are actually formed—determines to some extent how they are resonated. *Ah*, for example, can be fully resonated in the pharynx. Or, by widening the lips, tilting the head backward, and raising the larynx, the actor can shunt *ah* more into the nasal cavity, where it will prove more penetrating but also more strident. Nasal resonance creates a harsher sound than pharyngeal resonance, but on many occasions a harsh sound is desirable, for reasons of either characterization or projection. The actor should learn how to vary resonance by shifts in the placement of vowels.

◆ E X E R C I S E   **15–3**

Exploring Resonance

1. Stand with your feet slightly spread and your arms held loosely at your sides. Say "pah pah pah pah pah" while twisting your arms and torso lightly side to side. Say it again while tilting your head slowly forward, then back. Say it again while yawning and relaxing your throat completely, "letting go" so that your Adam's apple seems to "fall" down into your chest. Form the sound as deep in your throat as you can. Say it again while shunting the air out through your nose. Where do you seem to feel the greatest resonance? The mellowest resonance? The most penetrating?

2. Place one hand on the top of your head and say "pee pah pee pah pee." On which syllable do you feel the most vibration? You should feel it on *pee,* which is formed high in the front of the mouth and thus generates more head and bone (skull) resonance.

3. Place one hand on the bridge of your nose and say "pah pin pah pin pah pin." Which syllable causes the most vibration? *Pin* will, of course, because it has a nasal vowel and thus creates more nasal resonance than *pah.*

4. Put your hands on your cheeks and say "oo ah oo ah oo ah." Which vowel creates the most cheek vibration? *Oo* will, because *oo* is formed high in the back of the mouth, making the cheeks a strong resonator for *oo.*

5. Pair with a partner and place your hands on his or her head, nose bridge, and cheeks, by turns, testing his or her resonance as your partner tests yours.

Exercise 15–3 merely shows you what parts of your body are resonating most strongly on particular vowels. Using different vowels, you can also feel resonating vibrations on the collarbone, shoulder blades, forehead, and other parts of the upper body.

Pitch

Pitch is the highness or lowness of a musical tone. Technically, as we have seen, it is a function of the frequency of the vocal-fold vibrations: the faster the vibrations, the higher the pitch. Most everyday adult speaking takes place within a fairly restricted tonal pitch scale, which we sometimes call "monotoned" (or, more figuratively, "monotonous," meaning, literally, "on one note"). When we are excited (and less inhibited), however, our pitch range is expanded: Listen, for an example, to children hollering on a playground. One of your goals in acting will be to allow yourself the uninhibited excitement that will naturally call into play a broader tonal scale—a larger pitch range.

Your voice is more resonant at different pitches because the resonating tissues are themselves "tuned" to vibrate, sympathetically, with specific notes on the scale. Ordinarily, lower notes develop more pharyngeal (throat) resonance, and higher notes resonate more in the nasal passages. But every voice is different in this respect—which is why you can identify most of the people you know simply by the sound of their voices.

◆ E X E R C I S E   15–4

Exploring Your Pitch Range

- ◆ Repeat Exercise 15–2, using first high notes, then low notes, then a sliding scale of high notes to low notes.
- ◆ Repeat, using a sliding scale of low notes to high notes.
- ◆ Repeat, letting your pitch rise and fall within the same phrase, then fall and rise within the same phrase.

THRILLING WHEN HEARD

Mr. Burton happens to possess a vocal instrument that is exactly what we expect to hear, and almost never do hear, on going to the theatre. Mr. Burton sends out sounds that sweep the walls of the theatre with an apparently effortless power, magnifying the "natural" until we are caught up in its gale, left stunned and breathless. It is thrilling when heard, and the thrill is what playhouses are for.

WALTER KERR, ON THE LATE WELSH ACTOR RICHARD BURTON

A Stageworthy Voice

Speaking is a natural ability, but the actor's voice is cultivated because it must meet certain demands rarely present in everyday life. Stage speaking is to daily conversation what Olympic high hurdling is to the morning jog; it demands training and conditioning as well as above-average gifts. The training is normally carried out under the eye of an accomplished vocal coach, but the conditioning is up to the actor. An hour a day of vocal work-out is to the actor what the daily playing of scales is to the concert pianist and daily calisthenics are to the professional athlete. During that conditioning practice, however, the actor can certainly explore his or her own vocal capacities. Sometimes a tape recorder is helpful in developing stageworthy sound. Exercise 15–5 proves a good starting point for a daily warm-up and exploration.

♦ E X E R C I S E   15–5

Speaking with Resonance

Warm up by repeating Exercises 15–2, 15–3, and 15–4. Then, by memorizing the phrases in the list below, one at a time, recite each phrase twenty times while exploring your own speaking mechanism by taking different postures, deepening your breathing, playing with several "up and down" pitch variations, and seeing how you can develop new areas of resonance. Try to communicate some meaning with your text, but don't worry too much about "interpretation" at this point; the words should mainly serve as a vocalizing exercise. Do this exercise with a tape recorder or ask a friend to check your results.

Recite these phrases in the shower if you like. The bathroom will enlarge your resonance, as if you were speaking inside a violin box, and the steam from the shower will keep your vocal folds moist and fresh.

1. "Roll on, thou deep and dark blue ocean—roll!"

2. "Is this a dagger which I see before me,
   The handle toward my hand? Come, let me clutch thee."

3. "Was this the face that launch'd a thousand ships,
   And burnt the topless towers of Ilium?"

4. "Four score and seven years ago our fathers brought forth on this continent a new nation, conceived in liberty, and dedicated to the proposition that all men are created equal."

5. "O Romeo, Romeo! wherefore art thou Romeo?

   Deny thy father, and refuse thy name;

   Or, if thou wilt not, be but sworn my love,

   And I'll no longer be a Capulet."

6. "Is anybody home?"

7. "Pickle him in pickle sauce!"

8. "You think I'll weep;

   No, I'll not weep.

   I have full cause of weeping; but this heart

   Shall break into a hundred thousand flaws

   Or ere I'll weep. O fool, I shall go mad!"

9. "In the beginning God created the heaven and the earth."

10. "Blasts and fogs upon thee!"

Summary

The actor's voice is primary to her or his acting instrument and must be trained and conditioned to meet the demands of the theatre. Breathing, the making of sounds, resonation, and pitch flexibility and control—the primary tools of the voice—can be cultivated through instruction and exercise.

L E S S O N

16

Stage Speech

Good Diction

Voice produces sound; speech produces language. The process by which raw vocal sound is transformed into speech begins with *articulation*: the shaping of vocal noise into independent and recognizable units of spoken language, or *phonemes*. There are about forty phonemes in spoken English, plus various phonemic combinations, and the fine actor can speak all of them clearly and distinctly.

Good *diction* has long been considered essential to acting, primarily so that the actor can be clearly heard and understood throughout the theatre and can make the most of the author's words and the character's verbal tactics, wit, and persuasive authority. Good diction also means adhering to a standard way of pronouncing words—so that the actors seem to be "all in the same play" and a sense of shared ensemble is created through the play's words.

In some cultures the standard stage pronunciation requires a lofty tone not ordinarily heard in daily life. The British theatre, for example, favors "Received Pronunciation" (you can hear it on the BBC), which has been "received" from schooled elocution rather than from normal social conversation. The German theatre, similarly, uses what is called *Hochdeutsch* (high German) for most classical and modern plays. The standard American stage speech, however, is simply a refinement of middle American pronunciation, emphasizing naturalness rather than elevated elocution. Learning "standard American" requires overcoming speech impediments, such as lisping, and eliminating unwanted regional dialects. Learning standard American, then, requires learning the standard speech sounds of the American English language: how to make them and how to use them.*

Speech Sounds

Formal speech training begins with identifying the forty basic speech sounds and practicing them in various combinations until complete mastery is achieved. This process takes years; it cannot simply be covered as a single part of a beginning acting class. But an elemental understanding of the basic speech sounds can be achieved quickly, and improvement in speech clarity, power, and precision can be developed after short periods of practice.

The *vowel* sounds of English are divided among those that are formed in the front of the mouth, in the back, and in the middle.

Front Vowels

ee as in *beet, heat, feel, see, seize*

ih as in *hit, tin, rift, pill, skit*

ay as in *bake, cane, staple, cradle, straight*

eh as in *bet, sled, when, threat, kept*

aa as in *cad, bat, stab, pal, add*

Back Vowels

ah as in *father, Charles, hard, party*

a as in *wants, pot, God, pollen, bottom*

aw as in *all, bought, cough, walk, trawler*

---

*   I should note here that there are, of course, many plays written to be spoken in *nonstandard* British, German, and American, as well as in other languages, and that there are now an increasing number of directors in this and other countries who do not insist on any standard way of speaking even in plays that represent characters of a single social class. These directors—some of whom use the designations "post-Brechtian" or "postmodern"—prefer to hear each actor's natural dialect, "deconstructing" the theatrical illusion by retaining an emphasis on the theatrical machinery, the acting process itself.

o as in *old, coat, stoke, protest, folk*

ooh as in *foot, look, tootsie, put, good*

oo as in *boot, cool, rude, too, food, true*

Mid Vowels

uh (stressed) as in *cup, rubble, ton, up, none*

uh (unstressed) as in *above, sofa, pencil, amount, unwrap*

ur as in *further, cur, stir, purple, murder*

Diphthongs are glides between vowels—two vowels that are sounded in sequence and seem at first hearing to be one.

Diphthongs

ay-ee as in *hay, say, feign, weigh, play*

eye (ah-ee) as in *I, fly, high, sky, mai tai*

oy (aw-ee) as in *boy, coy, royal, poi, alloy*

you (ee-oo) as in *ewe, few, putrid, puerile, cue*

ow (ah-oo) as in *how, now, brown, cow*

oh (o-oo) as in *slow, throw, go, crow, toe*

Learning to speak vowels clearly and cleanly, and to hear the difference between vowels in similar-sounding words (such as *offal* and *awful*), is particularly important to the actor because the vowel sounds of stage speech carry the tone of the dialogue and convey the nuances of a character's tactical pursuits. Also, the vowel sounds of a person's speech often characterize his or her regional background: A trained ear has no trouble identifying the Virginian, the Wisconsinite, the Texan, and the New Englander simply by hearing their *ahs* and *ows*. Actors practice vowel drills in order to develop clarity and strength in their vowels and also to approximate the norm of standard American rather than their native local dialects.

◆ EXERCISE   16–1

Vowels

Singly or in a group, practice the vowel sounds by reciting the words listed after each vowel on pages 122–123. Notice how the vowel is formed in the mouth. Then speak the diphthongs slowly and see if you can identify which two vowels each diphthong consists of.

◆ E X E R C I S E   16–2

Repeating Syllables

Pair with a partner, and turn back to back. One person will recite as clearly as possible, *in any sequence*, any three of the following syllables. The partner will then try to repeat the syllables exactly. Then reverse roles and repeat the exercise.

poh	pooh
pih	poo
pay	puh
peh	pur
paa	pie
pah	poi
paw	pyu
po	pow

Do the exercise two or three times; then increase the number of syllables recited to five. As you continue the exercise, increase the speed. You may also try using other initial consonants, such as *k* or *d,* which involve other articulators.

The twenty-five *consonants* of English speech are divided into the *plosives* (made by holding the air momentarily before exploding it outward); the *fricatives* (made by blowing air between the articulators—the tongue, teeth, lips, and hard and soft palates); the *nasals* (made by passing air through the nose); the *glides* (made by moving the tongue); and the *blends* (made by combining other consonants).

Plosive Consonants

t as in *tickle, touch, ten*

d as in *dance, delve, dead*

p as in *potato, pill, purpose*

b as in *bombshell, baseball, bed*

k as in *kick, kindred, collection*

g as in *giggle, get, go*

Fricative Consonants

f as in *football, fill, from*

v as in *voter, veil, vigor*

th (unvoiced) as in *think, theatre, thrill*

th (voiced) as in *there, then, they*

s as in *settle, send, century*

z as in *zeal, zoo, zebra*

sh as in *shipshape, shell, sure*

zh as in *leisure, seizure, azure*

h as in *hail, high, hiccup*

Nasal Consonants

m as in *mystery, men, meal*

n as in *needle, nil, nothing*

ng as in *sing, song, kingship*

Glide Consonants

l as in *leader, listen, look*

r as in *real, rotate, roughhouse*

y as in *yellow, yesterday, yolk*

w as in *willow, won't, warrant*

wh as in *which, whippoorwill, where*

Blended Consonants

ch as in *chipmunk, choke, child*

j as in *jump, jail, gentry*

Developing crisp, clean consonants helps the actor convey precise meaning and gives the actor's speech a commanding authority. Consonants punctuate speech sound and are crucial in developing the sharpness of an intellectual argument, a witty retort, or a persuasive demand. Consonants are not as susceptible to regional variation as vowels are (an exception is the Cockney *fing* for *thing*) but they are more prone to impediments. The formation of consonants requires rapid and accurate movement of hundreds of muscle systems in the mouth and perfect placement (at the rate of about ten per second) of tongue, teeth, lips, jaw, glottis, gums, and palates (together, these are called the *articulators*). No actor can afford to have flabby, unresponsive, or lazy articulators. Consonant drills, therefore, aim to make an actor's consonants razor sharp.

◆ E X E R C I S E   16–3

Consonants

Repeat the following consonant drills until you can do them comfortably, rapidly, and, if possible, wittily.

1. Tip it, pippet; tip it, pippet; tip it, pippet.
2. Dab a gak, dab a gak, dab a gak, dab a gak.
3. Azure zoo, azure zoo, azure zoo, azure zoo.
4. Think this fink, think this fink, think this fink.
5. The vase is shaded, the vase is shaded, the vase is shaded.
6. No ming no mong, no ming no mong, no ming no mong.
7. Yell when wending, yell when wending, yell when wending.
8. Jump Chuck, jump Chuck, jump Chuck, jump Chuck.
9. Tapocketa pocketa pocketa pocketa pocketa.
10. Libid ibid libid ibid libid ibid.
11. Rilly billy dilly killy, rilly billy dilly killy.
12. Potato pit, potato pit, potato pit, potato pit.
13. This is it, this is it, this is it, this is it.
14. Calumny, mercantile, exaggerate, elevate, anglophile.
15. Big a pig gig, big a pig gig, big a pig gig.

◆ E X E R C I S E   16–4

Speeches

When you feel comfortable with the simple drills in Exercise 16–3, try reading the following lines from Shakespeare's *Macbeth*.

Reading aloud, repeat the lines until you can read them clearly and accurately. Note the importance of clear articulation in these speeches.

MACBETH: If it were done when 'tis done, then 'twere well
    It were done quickly. If th' assassination
    Could trammel up the consequence, and catch
    With his surcease, success; that but this blow
    Might be the be-all and the end-all—here,
    But here, upon this bank and shoal of time,
    We'd jump the life to come.

LADY MACBETH: Glamis thou art, and Cawdor, and shalt be
    What thou art promised. Yet I do fear thy nature;
    It is too full o' th' milk of human kindness
    To catch the nearest way. Thou wouldst be great;
    Art not without ambition, but without
    The illness should attend it. What thou wouldst highly,
    That wouldst thou holily; wouldst not play false,
    And yet wouldst wrongly win.

No one can say that the speeches in Exercise 16–4 are easy, even for the veteran classical scholar or performer, but you can certainly see that clear articulation is absolutely crucial if any interpretation is to make sense. Only careful speech can distinguish "surcease, success," and "highly . . . holily," yet these are the sorts of verbal problems with which the actor must deal moment by moment in an articulate play.

For more advanced work in speech and diction, you will want to take special classes or individualized training. But running the vowels and consonants, as in the previous exercises, can help you to understand your own manufacture of phonemes, and to learn how to speak them with clarity and distinction. Speech drills also exercise the articulators and the muscles that move them, giving you a greater capacity to be sharp and subtle with your language, and therefore more powerful in your playing of tactics toward a stage victory. Drilling phonemes also helps give you a confidence toward stage speaking and an ear toward correcting your own impediments or regionalisms—particularly if you can work under the guidance of an interested and qualified teacher.

Summary

Each actor must cultivate the ability to articulate the forty-odd English-language phonemes (speech sounds), for this ability underlies powerful, fluid, subtle, and confident stage speaking and therefore tactical interplay. Mastering the phonemes also is the key to eliminating speech impediments, regional mispronunciations, and speaking timidity. Dramatic improvement in your speaking will come about only with concentrated study under a qualified instructor or coach. Speech drills, however, exercise the articulators and help you gain control of your speaking mechanism.

17

Using Your Voice

Liberation

In pursuing your character's goals, getting your character's GOTE, your voice and speech are the primary tools at your disposal. The voice must be free to coax, to bully, to soothe, to inspire, and to explode. The speech must allow you to articulate, persuade, harangue, dazzle, enchant, and entertain. But voice and speech cannot reach these heights if they are inhibited.

The liberated voice is free from socially bred inhibitions: excessive politeness, timidity, deference, or propriety. The actor's liberation is both psychological and technical. The actor needs confidence that absolutely anything can be said onstage so that breathing and speaking mechanisms will be relaxed and supple enough to make speech vibrant and precise.

Self-consciousness is the inhibitor of speaking. The voices of childhood—yelps, squeals, shouts, silliness, and all—are necessarily channeled during long years of social conditioning into acceptable communicative mechanisms—but at what cost! The average adult voice, perhaps still varied and pungent in the privacy of the shower or the fraternity/sorority drinking party, becomes a timid and wary instrument under the close public scrutiny of a gathering of academic peers. *Politeness* (the word has the same root as *politics*) is the necessary lubricant for social interaction, but it stands in the way of vocal and speech development; excessive politeness is the enemy of exciting acting.

The social conditioning we have all passed through (and continue to pass through) produces a fascinating variety of misshapen voices. Psychiatrists often make their initial evaluation of a patient's problem by noting the specific strains in the patient's voice during their first interview. Some young women use the classic "little girl voice," a half octave too high, maintained from childhood in an unconscious attempt to remain "Daddy's little girl," or perhaps to avoid competing too directly with a roughhousing older brother. Some young men have a nasal whine left over from those days when direct confrontation of the parent or teacher was impossible and wheedling was the only way to make an impact.

Sometimes the voices of both sexes suggest that terror underlies every public statement—that even to say "here" in answer to a roll call may result in a crack on the knuckles for some reason or other. If any of these descriptions seems to fit you, don't worry: Everybody experiences, to a degree, these vocal shortcomings. There is almost no one whose voice does not "go dead" at one time or another: when you suddenly see that everybody is looking at you, or when someone asks you a question you cannot answer, or when you suddenly feel that you're inappropriately dressed. The actor's problem is not worrying about a dead or timid voice but, rather, finding the way to counteract these fears and bring life and energy to the art of speaking.

◆ E x e r c i s e   17–1

Rude Chants

Chant, as a group:

1. Kill, kill, kill, kill, kill!

2. Barf, barf, barf, barf, barf!

3. Penis, penis, penis, penis, penis!

4. Urine, urine, urine, urine, urine!

In this impolite exercise, the point is not to giggle or pretend you're saying something else but, rather, to allow your voice the freedom to say, at full volume and with clear speech, the sort of words you don't usually say in public. Try these also:

5. Testicle, testicle, testicle, testicle, testicle!

6. Copulate, copulate, copulate, copulate, copulate!

7. Intercourse, intercourse, intercourse, intercourse, intercourse!

8. Masturbate, masturbate, masturbate, masturbate, masturbate!

As an actor, you should be able to say *anything* boldly on stage. No words, no matter how personally odious to you, should simply stick in your throat.

◆ E X E R C I S E   17–2

Rude Cheering

1. Repeat the chants in Exercise 17–1, exploring your pitch range and resonance possibilities.
2. Chant a "cheer" of "Kill, barf, penis, urine!" Make the cheer *purposeful:* This is the team you are rooting for. Make them win! Make them hear you and know you are cheering them on! Make up gestures and movements for the cheer.
3. Do the same with "Testicle, copulate, intercourse, masturbate!"

This exercise is easy to expand with other words, but keep the doors closed. Your class is a large enough public for this exercise!

Inhibition takes many forms. Another common form is a fear of mispronouncing or misusing large words. In their daily lives, many young people retreat behind a vocabulary of simple language, fad words, and common clichés simply to avoid the possibility of making a mistake. (And how terrified we were, as adolescents, of making a mistake!) Therefore the language they bring to acting is essentially slovenly, immature, and bland. In the theatre, of course, language is created by playwrights, but most young actors have initial (and sometimes continuing) difficulties in rising to the language of the play. Often they consciously or unconsciously rewrite the script into their own words; more often they stumble over or swallow any four-syllable words they find in the text. You can lick this problem. An actor must love words and wordplay. While it is true that many dramatic characters are inarticulate (particularly in plays from the 1950s), a great many more are not. Each actor must rise to the level of verbal dexterity that the character has achieved—and often the characters are verbal dynamos.

◆ E X E R C I S E   17–3

Fancy Talk

Separately, and after checking the meaning and pronunciation of words unfamiliar to you, say these sentences to someone (real or imaginary) with a good deal of *fun:*

1. Throckmorton's in an anomalous predicament!

2. I detest John's egregious braggadocio!

3. What a stentorian denunciation!

4. Her perfidious egalitarianism is obnoxious!

5. Thwart Ellen's obstinacy!

6. Could you correlate the data mellifluously?

7. Long live ubiquitous serendipity!

8. Disambiguate your metaphor!

9. Come to the Christmas colloquium!

10. Restrain your ribald riposting!

11. Cease your antediluvian antics!

12. Your libidinous delusions are tantalizing!

13. I adore elocutionary magnificence!

14. Startling complexities abound!

15. Beware the inevitable consequences!

16. Facilitate copulation!

17. Barf before pontificating!

The last two sentences combine Exercises 17–1 and 17–2. Make up additional combinations of long words and "rude" words, and speak them freely in all ranges of your voice. Here are speeches to say to a (real or imaginary) partner:

1. "I fart at thee!" (Ben Jonson, *The Alchemist*)

2. "The bawdy hand of time is on the prick of noon." (Shakespeare, *Romeo and Juliet*)

3. "Extraordinary how potent cheap music is." (Noel Coward, *Private Lives*)

4. "WEE! WAA! WONDERFUL! I'm stiff! Stiff in the wind! My mane, stiff in the wind! My flanks! My hooves! Mane on my legs, on my flanks, like whips! Raw! Raw! *I'm raw! Raw!*" (Peter Shaffer, *Equus*)

5. "Come down outa dere, yuh yellow, brass-buttoned, Belfast bum, yuh! Come down and I'll knock yer brains out! Yuh lousy, stinkin' yellow mutt of a Catholic-moiderin' bastard!" (Eugene O'Neill, *The Hairy Ape*)

6. "Oh, I should think I was poor and had nothing to bestow if I were reduced to an inglorious ease and freed from the agreeable fatigues of solicitation." (William Congreve, *The Way of the World*)

7. "You see, you piss better when I'm not there." (Samuel Beckett, *Waiting for Godot*)

8. "Detested kite! Thou liest." (Shakespeare, *King Lear*)

9. "I'm a bad publisher because I hate books. Or to be more precise, prose. Or to be even more precise, modern prose, I mean modern novels, first novels and second novels, all that promise and sensibility it falls upon me to judge, to put the firm's money on, and then to push for the third novel, see it done, see the dust jacket done, see the dinner for the national literary editors done, see the signing in Hatchards done, see the lucky author cook himself to death, all in the name of literature. You know what you and Emma have in common? You love literature. I mean you love modern prose literature, I mean you love the new novel by the new Casey or Spinks. It gives you both a thrill." (Harold Pinter, *Betrayal*)

10. "Reaganite heartless macho asshole lawyers." (Tony Kushner, *Millennium Approaches*)

11. "Move your nigger cunt spade faggot lackey ass out of my room." (Tony Kushner, *Perestroika*)

◆ E X E R C I S E   17–4

Address a Group

Thus far you have spoken your lines to a single (real or imaginary) partner. Now address an imaginary group. Using the fanciful sentences, rude chants, and dramatic texts in the previous exercises, deliver them to:

1. A college class

2. A kindergarten class

3. A bar full of people

4. An army battalion

5. A sorority luncheon

6. Your family

Enlarging the audience to your remarks draws forth more vocal power and articulation and makes you use "more voice" than you need when you are simply addressing an intimate friend. Addressing people who are noisy, deaf, deranged, hostile, or unintelligent can add verbal force and articulate distinction to your speech. Practice enlarging your audience for larger speeches by assuming that your character wants to be overheard by people in an adjacent room. This technique can bring your voice and speech to necessary stage levels without sacrificing the directness or honesty of your delivery.

Purposefulness

Purposefulness is what ties the liberated voice to the actor's approach. The actor's voice and speech are not developed as ends in themselves; an instrument, after all, is useful only while you use it. Basically, the actor's speaking mechanism is the prime weapon of the character's tactical pursuits—the prime implement for getting your character's GOTE.

Actors should speak onstage the way people normally do in life, not because they have to but because they *want* to. Every word you speak onstage must be (and seem to be) directed toward your goal; every word must have some tactical service to your cause. As a character, you should not appear to speak simply because the author put words in your mouth but because you have desires, plans, objectives—and because speaking out is the way you expect to get them! Every word spoken onstage, therefore, must be spoken with purposefulness. Words must come from human desire, not mechanical necessity. Purpose, above all else, brings power to your vocal instrument.

These examples illustrate how purposefulness affects the way you use your voice:

◆ You are at a football game as the guest of a friend. The people around you cheer. You do not care who wins the game, but you cheer because you're supposed to.

◆ You are at a football game rooting for your team, for people with whom you identify. You cheer. Your cheers are more vigorous; your voice is fuller and more intense. Why? Because you care. Because you are using your voice to try to help your team. You have a purpose.

◆ You are instructed to say, as distinctly as possible, "Pull up on the door handle." You do so.

◆ Your two-year-old sister is crying in a locked car; nearby a building is on fire. You tell her, "Pull up on the door handle!" You are more distinct, your speech is clearer, more demanding, more penetrating. Why?

> REACHING THE BACK ROW
>
> *All you have to be concerned about is whether or not you've got*
> *something to say; if you've got something to say, they'll hear you.*
>
> SEAN PENN, ON ADVICE HE WAS GIVEN ABOUT HOW TO
>
> REACH THE BACK ROW OF THE THEATRE

Good stage speech results from allying purpose with a liberated and versatile vocal mechanism. It is not sufficient to have a good voice; the actor must *want* to vocalize and must want to demand, cajole, attract, or compel others with the voice as a primary instrument. Even the simplest and most technical vocal exercise—"bah bah bah bah bah," for example—can be enhanced by giving the exercise an interpersonal purpose (to calm someone's nerves, to amuse someone, to solicit someone's sympathy). When your purpose is strong enough, it will override any shyness or timidity or inhibitions you might have. Utterly mild and noncommunicative persons can break through giant psychological sound barriers when they see someone stealing their car, or kissing their sweetheart, or running the wrong way with the football. Create, in your mind, a sufficient goal, and energize your voice and speech in its pursuit.

◆ E X E R C I S E   17–5

Adding Purpose

Go back to Exercise 15–5. Using the same speeches, create a strong situational goal for each speech and speak the words purposefully to a (real or imaginary) partner.

Summary

The actor's voice and stage speech are to be *used,* not merely exhibited. To this end they must be free from inhibiting factors, particularly shyness, excessive politeness, and fear of making verbal mistakes. The actor should develop confidence in his or her verbal dexterity, should become comfortable with both rude language and intricate linguistic construction. *Purpose,* finally, is the motive force of good stage speaking; the actor must ally his or her voice and speaking mechanism with a will to achieve goals in a dramatic situation.

L E S S O N

18

The Actor's Body

Agility

Body training for the actor follows many separate paths. Perhaps surprisingly, *developing strength and stamina* is first on the list. One doesn't always associate athletic functions with artistic endeavors, but the sheer physical work of the actor is often grueling. After all, the demands of the role may involve several hours of onstage time, running up and down stairs, fighting, dueling, changing costume, *all with maximum physical control.* Mere enthusiasm will not accomplish this control. Such famous actors as Jane Fonda and Laurence Olivier have been well known for their demanding physical regimens, developed as a result of their acting careers. Bodybuilding, aerobic exercise, and competitive athletics are now routine activities for actors of all ages.

Develop dexterity and coordination. "Learn the lines and don't bump into the furniture" is the traditional "first lesson" of acting. Physical dexterity means more than merely not bumping into the scenery, however. The actor who is physically coordinated—who can move *with precision and passion at the same time*—can convey meaningful behavior with far more complexity than the actor who merely speaks the words trippingly on the tongue.

Develop physical dynamics. Dynamics means physical force in action. The actor is always either in action or potentially in action, always moving or on the verge of moving. An actor who seems just about to hit out, kiss someone, explode, throw something, or bolt away is an exciting, dynamic actor. The body can be trained toward this dynamic, supple, physical readiness.

Develop specific movement skills. Advanced actor training normally involves learning specific physical patterns, such as ballet, ballroom dancing, period dancing, fencing, hand-to-hand combat, mime, gesture, martial arts, period movement, contact improvisation, and circus technique. These skills are often useful in themselves, and they increase the actor's physical versatility, confidence, and poise. Additionally, they aid an actor's sense of timing and physical aesthetics. Indeed, the relationship between acting and dance has been intimate since the dramas of ancient Greece. Many actor-training programs begin with dance, mime, and stage movement.

Exercise 18–1 gets the blood moving, loosens and stretches the ligaments, flexes several hundred muscles, and makes you feel good. It is only a warm-up, however. After fifteen minutes of sitting in a classroom chair, you're back where you started. Therefore actors need to know how to warm up fast and effectively, for they will do it often.

◆ E X E R C I S E   18–1

Fast Warm-Up

Go back to Exercise 1–1, and repeat that warm-up briskly, adding the following exercises before running in place:

Standing erect, swivel your hips—five times to the left and five to the right.

Drop your chin to your chest, and let the weight of your head slowly bend you over, vertebra by vertebra, until your fingers touch the floor. Bend your knees as necessary.

Tap the floor with your fingers. Make a rhythm of tapping on the floor. Add the fingernails to the tapping. Add the palms.

Rise up slowly, uncurling the spine vertebra by vertebra.

Extend the head upward without straining, allowing it to "float" freely atop the spinal column.

Rotate the head in leftward and rightward spirals, each time spiraling it into a relaxed "floating" position atop the spine.

Bounce ten times, arms at your sides.

Bounce ten times, arms akimbo—going in all directions.

Run in place or jump an imaginary rope while clapping your hands—for fifteen breaths.

TENSION AND ENERGY

To relax does not mean that you should become a bag of bones. A cat or dog at rest are completely relaxed, yet they are still capable of making sudden and definite movements. The purpose of [Alexander] technique is not to get rid of tensions, but to reorganize them into a source of energy and satisfaction.

MATTHIAS ALEXANDER, AS PARAPHRASED BY EDWARD MAISEL

Alignment

The proper alignment of the body—all vital organs poised in a balanced relationship to maximize their healthy functioning—was the primary goal of Australian-born actor–educator F. Matthias Alexander (1869–1955), whose Alexander Technique is the best-known and most effective alignment system for actors. The basic Alexander alignment is a standing position with

1. The head "floating" easily atop the spine

2. The neck free and relaxed

3. The shoulders spread out (not pulled back)

4. The torso lengthened and widened; the rib cage expanded; the vertebrae separated, not crunched together

5. The pelvis freely rotating, the hip joints free and rolling

The Alexander technique produces not a specific posture but an inner alignment of bodily organs. It promotes good posture, but it also promotes relaxed breathing, deep resonance, clear speech, and coordinated whole-body movement. Alexander adherents also add health, longevity, improved appearance, and enhanced self-image to this list.

The Alexander alignment works because it gives the lungs room to function, reduces constriction in the throat and mouth, and gives the diaphragm enough pelvic support to provide a basis of sustained full breathing. The body is poised so that movement springs quite naturally from every limb or digit, or from the trunk itself. Compare this with the hunched-over position of most adults at work or watching television.

The following exercises are necessarily introductory. Enthusiasts of the physical training methods described below devote years to the study of the various potentials of the human mechanism. But all the exercises suggest ways in which the actor can begin physical self-exploration and self-training to develop greater strength, stamina, dexterity, coordination, and physical dynamics.

◆ E X E R C I S E   18–2

Improving Alignment

Stand on the floor, legs comfortably apart. Hunch your shoulders down, squeeze your head down onto your neck, lock your knees, clench your fists, and say, "Hah hah hah hah hah." The sound will be *terrible*. Now try the following.

Relax your arms, open your fists, swing your arms lightly, and let your head "float" upward, keeping your chin level.

Rotate your head one or two times each way, ending in a spiral and "floating" your head as high as you can without straining.

Flex your knees slightly and rotate your hips, coming to rest in a balanced position.

Broaden your shoulders straight out, left and right, and open your rib cage, raising and expanding your ribs outward, forward, and upward. (Imagine a gentle tug from two wires attached to your ribs three inches below your nipples, each pulling upward at a 45-degree angle forward and outward.)

Lengthen your spine without locking it. Say, "Hah hah hah hah hah."

Twist your torso freely; walk and turn and reach while maintaining this alignment. Say, "Hah hah hah hah hah."

Exercise 18–2 will have an immediate short-term result. You will notice greater resonance and freer breathing right away. It is not a simple matter to make this improved alignment a part of your unconscious daily movements, however, nor is it a simple thing to sustain the alignment—at first—without feeling stiff and awkward. Good internal alignment takes a great deal of practice and concentration. You are changing habits of a lifetime, and you cannot expect to do that easily or quickly. But the end result will be greater physical and vocal presence and ability.

Walking

"Cross left," says the director, and the actor knows to walk to her or his left. But how to walk? Fast? Slow? Plodding? Shuffling? Slovenly? Assured?

It's surprising, but you can often tell inexperienced actors simply by the way they walk on the stage. What they have been doing since they were a year old suddenly seems tentative, even clumsy. Maybe this has happened to you. Part of it is self-consciousness, of course; there's nothing like fifty bright lights in your face, and the knowledge that you're wearing splashy makeup for the first time, to make the butterflies dance in your belly. But part of it is not realizing that walking is part of the action of the play—and vitally connected to the goal, or GOTE, of your character.

WALKING AND TALKING

What is acting? It's walking and talking. But it isn't. It's about seeing the possibility or significance of those moments.

FIONA SHAW

Every move onstage must be *purposeful;* it must serve your character's quest to achieve a goal with someone else. Every move is tactical as well. Like speech, walking is tactical: You may walk quickly to accomplish something in a hurry, slowly to sneak up on someone, casually to put someone at ease, or boldly to command authority. There are many different verbs we can use to convey different ways of walking: We can stride, slink, stroll, march, pace, promenade, saunter, tramp, stalk, parade, stomp, skip, tiptoe, run, jog, and sidle, among others. Any of these sixteen verbs can replace "cross" in the director's request to "cross left." But few directors think to use them. Nor should they. That's up to you.

Whatever you do, don't just "cross." What you see, above all, in inexperienced actors is that they are walking because they were told to, not because they *want* to. Remember: The actors may be told what to do, but the *characters they play* must be seen as *wanting* to do it. Choose an *active,* not passive, means of moving. Using one of the sixteen verbs will guarantee that you do so.

◆ EXERCISE   18–3

Sixteen Walks

Explore all of the "sixteen verb" walks. Start by walking in a circle. Then, as the instructor or group leader calls out, stride, slink, stroll, march, pace, promenade, saunter, tramp, stalk, parade, stomp, skip, tiptoe, run, jog, and sidle. Make these walks *your* walks, not stylized "character walks," but for each one invent on-the-spot your own inner story and inner GOTE—for example, "I'll stomp over to my teacher and demand a grade change" or "I'll sidle over to Ashley and ask him/her to join me for lunch." After a while, continue the exercise, but lose the circle and walk in spontaneously chosen directions with each change of verb. Walk toward and away from people designated in your "inner story"—while knowing that they may be walking toward or away from you.

◆ E X E R C I S E   18–4

Walk and Talk

Pair with a partner. Face each other from across the room. Pair one of the following lines with one of the "sixteen verb" walks and "cross left" (or right) to your partner while "walking and talking" *and while maintaining eye contact with your partner at all times.*

1. "How would you like to be my running mate?"

2. "Why don't you want to go to the Ping-Pong match?"

3. "Your roommate's been arrested!"

4. "We've got only five hours before the exam."

5. "I just scored two tickets to the concert. Wanna go?"

6. "Well, I guess I just have to say it wouldn't be fair."

7. "Listen, I think you're terrific; it's just that, well, you know, the other students . . ."

8. "So. You think you're going to win today? Right?"

9. "What's the matter with you today?"

10. "Hey, I got the part!"

11. (sing) "There's a bright golden haze on the meadow . . ."

12. (sing) "Happy birthday to you, happy birthday to you, happy birthday . . ."

Maintaining the eye contact will concentrate your focus on your goal, and on your GOTE, and keep you from "checking out your walk."

What sort of shoes are you wearing? A walk is not only a move; it is also a sound. Depending on the actor's shoes, the composition of the stage floor, and the degree of silence during the cross, an actor's footsteps can be a crucial part of the play's sound design. Actors who seem to "own their own feet" can make a powerful contribution to the play by the assured sound and bearing of their approach. Tadashi Suzuki, a well-known Japanese director and acting teacher, reminds his students (and us) that the feet are primary to the actor's instrument because they are the only parts of the body to touch the ground.[*]

Sitting and Standing

Sitting and standing are also movements we use every day, yet they too can look awkward and timid onstage. Obviously the same rules apply: *All* movements, not just stage crosses, must be seen to come from the character's pursuit of a goal—and active rather than passive movement is crucial in these cases as well. *Sitting* could mean perching or flopping or easing down to a chair. *Standing* could be anything from gently rising to leaping to one's feet.

◆ E X E R C I S E   18–5

Walk, Talk, Sit

Pairing with a partner, and using the same lines as in Exercise 18–4, "cross" to your partner, who is seated, and, while maintaining eye contact all the time, sit in a chair or a couch next to him or her with the last word of the line. (Ideally, the room where this exercise takes place has two chairs and a couch, and the partner is seated in a chair between the second chair and the couch.)

Maintaining eye contact while sitting may be difficult at first, but *keep looking at your partner, not at the chair!* If you are not sure where the chair is, you can touch it, but don't look at it. Of course in real life you may look at a chair when sitting down (to make sure you don't miss the seat), but this is hardly a bold choice (see Lesson 12). The goal you are trying to achieve with your partner must be seen as more important than not missing the seat!

---

[*] Tadashi Suzuki, *The Way of Acting*, trans. J. Thomas Rimer (New York: Theatre Communications Group, 1986).

Vary the exercise by changing your footwear—from hard-sole shoes (including high heels where appropriate) to athletic shoes to flip-flops to barefoot. There should be marked differences with many of these variations. What can you learn from them? And how can you apply it?

Velocity: Accelerating, Decelerating, and Constant

The ability to control acceleration and deceleration is crucial to developing physical dexterity and to creating the dynamics of movement. Accelerating and decelerating movements make clear that you are thinking while moving and that your mind is generating the movements you make. Constant-velocity movements, in contrast, indicate that you are simply executing movements generated by someone else—the director, for example.

Constant-velocity movements may figure in the portrayal of characters "trying to get a grip on themselves," such as a recovering drug addict putting down the bottle of pills. But for beginning actors, constant-velocity movements usually show that the actors are moving only because they have to or are supposed to, not because they want to. Avoid them if you can.

◆ E X E R C I S E   18–6

Acceleration/Deceleration

1. Stand, and extend your arms outward, palms front, elbows slightly flexed.

2. Bring your palms together in a clap, moving your arms at a constant rate of speed.

3. Clap at a constantly *accelerating* rate of speed.

4. Clap at a constantly *decelerating* rate of speed.

Notice the characteristics of the three claps. The first (constant rate of speed) is like perfunctory applause. The second is a gesture of victory— "Eureka!" The third is like bringing the hands together in prayer.

Practice constant, accelerating, and decelerating motions while repeating each of these actions five times:

1. Putting your hand down on a table

2. Moving your hand toward, and seizing, a prop revolver your partner is holding

3. Turning to look at someone behind you
4. Punching a pillow
5. Getting out of a chair
6. Walking to a predetermined spot on the floor
7. Sitting down
8. Lifting a drink (shot-glass size) to your lips and drinking it
9. Touching your partner's neck
10. Touching your partner's hair
11. Taking off your sweater
12. Putting a bottle of pills on a table
13. Lying down on a sofa
14. Pointing your finger at someone; pointing at some *part* of someone

---

Accelerating motions tend to be exciting and enthusiastic. Decelerating motions tend to be graceful and gentle. Constant motions tend to be boring and dutiful. Guess which kinds are most useful in acting. And guess which kinds you most often see with beginning actors.

Counterpoise

Contraposto is an Italian word, used mainly in the analysis of paintings and sculptures, describing counterpoised physical positions in which the body is twisted so that the shoulders and the hips, the arms and the legs, are in different planes. Michelangelo's paintings and sculptures are known for their contraposto and are especially illuminating for actors.

The counterpoised body is both dynamic and balanced; it can be coiled for action even though it seems to be at rest. By contrast, the standing-at-attention, squared-off body—a product of "stand-up-straight" discipline rather than actor training—is static and uninteresting onstage and is impossible to mobilize emotionally or physically.

◆ E X E R C I S E   18–7

Contraposto

1. Feet planted comfortably on the floor, the body aligned as in Exercise 18–2, turn the hips ninety degrees to the left.

2. Extend the right arm up and away. Turn the head another ninety degrees left. Flex the knees.

3. Spring to the reverse position.

4. Relax.

5. Walk, with decelerating velocity, to a point ten yards away, turning as you come to a halt.

6. Walk, with decelerating velocity, to a chair ten yards away; turn and coil as you sit.

7. Toss your head one way, then another.

8. Look one way and point another. Reverse.

9. Get a good sturdy sofa away from a wall. Using the sofa's seat, arms, and back, find ten physically dynamic contraposto positions for yourself, moving from one to the other in a fluid acceleration/deceleration movement. Play a scene or improvisation with someone, moving around the sofa in this fashion.

The body contracts on itself for protection. It extends outward for expression and sometimes for attack. The magnitude of contractions and extensions is one signification of an actor's physical freedom: Children, for example, are usually quite uninhibited in extensions; adults are far more often restrained.

◆ E X E R C I S E   18–8

Contraction/Extension

1. To the sounds of a drumbeat, or a command, CONTRACT! . . . CONTRACT! . . . CONTRACT! . . . CONTRACT!

2. To the sounds of a drumbeat, or a command, EXTEND! . . . EXTEND! . . . EXTEND! . . . EXTEND! . . . LEAP UP! . . . LEAP UP! . . . CONTRACT!

3. Walk with decelerating speed and roll into a tight spiral, knotting yourself up into a little ball. Hold for ten seconds, compressing and compressing, and then EXPLODE!

4. Respond to an imaginary:

Punch in the stomach

Fire in the seat of your pants

Heart attack

Shout to surrender

Cry for help

The Dynamics of Effort

A system of movement analysis invented in the 1940s by Hungarian-born Rudolf Laban is immeasurably helpful in defining, isolating, and developing movement skills in actors. Laban's movement system is laid out in a short book titled *Effort*.* Laban ingeniously described all human movement in terms of three factors—exertion (light or strong moves), space (curving or straight moves), and time (steady or pulsing moves)—and identified eight basic movement types: slashing, pressing, wringing, punching, gliding, flicking, dabbing, and floating.

	Exertion	Space	Time
Slashing	Strong	Curving	Pulsing
Pressing	Strong	Straight	Steady
Wringing	Strong	Curving	Steady
Punching	Strong	Straight	Pulsing
Gliding	Light	Straight	Steady
Flicking	Light	Curving	Pulsing
Dabbing	Light	Straight	Pulsing
Floating	Light	Curving	Steady

A slashing move, for example, requires strong exertion, it curves in space, and it starts and stops suddenly (pulses). A gliding move, by contrast, requires only light exertion, it tends to be straight through space, and it is continuous rather than sudden.

Laban's subsequently expanded the eight categories to twenty-four, depending on which of the three factors dominates, and then to forty-eight, depending on whether the movements are loosely or tightly controlled by the mover. The eight basic categories, however, are useful ways of isolating the major types of movement. Each movement can be practiced in isolation so as to become distinct—that is, distinguished from more generalized moves.

---

* Rudolf Laban, and F. C. Lawrence, *Effort* (London: MacDonald & Evans, 1947).

◆ E X E R C I S E   18–9

Distinct Movements*

Mime all of the props mentioned. In each movement, either the level of exertion (light or strong), the spatial aspect (curving or straight), or the tempo (steady or pulsing) is dominant. Can you tell which by doing the action?

1. *Slashing:* Hit a nail with a hammer, throw coal with a shovel, whip an egg with a whisk.

2. *Pressing:* Crush peppercorns with a mortar and pestle, cut leather with a knife, squeeze a spring between your hands.

3. *Wringing:* Pull a cork with a corkscrew, pluck feathers from a chicken, stretch an elastic band.

4. *Dabbing:* Pat dough with your hands, type on a keyboard, shake seeds through a sieve.

5. *Gliding:* Smooth clay by hand, smear cement with a trowel, smudge putty with a putty knife.

6. *Flicking:* Snap a towel, count the pages of a book by flipping them, break a string with your hand.

7. *Floating:* Scatter seeds by hand, stir oil paint with a stick, polish a tabletop.

8. *Punching:* Thrust a pitchfork into a hay pile, thrust a shovel into dry sand, pierce a thin tabletop with an awl.

◆ E X E R C I S E   18–10

To Be or Not to Be

Repeat Exercise 18–9. With every distinct move, say the first line of Hamlet's great soliloquy: "To be or not to be, that is the question." Imagine on each occasion that you are talking to a group of people who know you, and making it clear to them that you are trying to decide whether you

---

* This exercise is adapted, almost directly, from Laban and Lawrence, *Effort,* pp. 28–31.

should keep on living or embark on a course that may lead you to death or even suicide. See if you can get a response from them. How does your speaking the line vary when you're slashing, or punching, or flicking? How does the imagined response vary? It is easy to picture different Hamlets playing the line while engaging in each of Laban's movement types.

◆ E X E R C I S E   18–11

Walking and Kicking

Walk around a room in a floating manner. A gliding manner. A pressing manner. A slashing manner. What sort of circumstances could lead you, in real life, to do this?

Kick or stamp or push with your foot an imaginary object in each of the eight basic Laban movements. What sort of circumstances could lead you, in real life, to do this?

Move your pelvis in each of the eight basic Laban dynamic patterns. Real-life circumstances?

Distinguishing and isolating movements, Laban-style, is like learning to play the individual notes of a piano. Few sonatas require you to play a single note at a time, at least for any appreciable length of time, and stage movement, like piano music, is a living complex of its various elements. But learning to isolate the dynamics of the body, like learning to play upon the keys of a piano, gives you a vast repertoire of strategies to employ when seeking the goals of your character on the stage.

Summary

The actor's body must be trained into a supple, strong, energetic, dexterous, and dynamic instrument. Physical training programs that may take years encourage the learning of precise movement skills, such as mime and formal dance. Some simple exercises, however, can start you immediately on the road to establishing good physical alignment, integration of onstage speech and movement, control over movement direction and velocity (acceleration and deceleration), dynamic counterpoise and balance, and the potential for bold (explosive) physicalization.

19

Voice and Body Integration

Coordination

"The integration of body and voice—"being able to walk and talk at the same time"–is the acid test of the actor's instrument. If you master this, you will progress accordingly. If you fail, you must go back and try again.

In life we speak and move at the same time naturally, for we initiate both actions. In acting, however, our lines and moves are given to us by others—playwrights, directors, choreographers—and putting them together isn't always easy. The easy fluidity of speaking and moving common to everyday life may be lost. When we concentrate on our lines, we may stiffen physically. When we concentrate on our movements, our speech may become stilted and mechanical.

When your voice and body are well trained, however, your focus on winning your character's goal will integrate speech and movement in your performance. Then your voice and body will no longer be ends in themselves, but will simply be tools you use to try to win the victories your character passionately desires. Like any professional's tools, they may be used naturally, unthinkingly. When performing a concerto, the professional violinist is thinking not about strings and frets and bows but about making great music. And when playing Laura, the actor is thinking not about phonemes or decelerating motions but about making Jim O'Connor want to see her again. The actor's instrument, in performance, is forgotten; the actor has *become* the instrument of—in this case—Laura's quest.

Developing good voice–body integration demands that you are quite clear about what you want in a scene and that you are entirely free to put your whole body (voice and movement) into achieving your goal. If this concentration on victory is your mainspring, both voice and body will serve that concentration: They will be integrated by the strength of your commitment to get what you want.

The following exercise should be a useful first step in integrating voice and body.

◆ E X E R C I S E   **19–1**

Commands

These exercises begin where Exercise 18–5, "Walk, Talk, Sit," left off.

1. Try to make a (real or imaginary) partner come to a specific spot by walking five steps to the spot while saying, "Come right here!" As you reach the spot, pivot around and point to the floor. The movement and speaking should be simultaneous, and you should pivot and point while you are still speaking. Experiment with various timings.

2. Do this exercise with these alternate lines:

   a. "I want you to come right here, please."

   b. "Listen, George, I think it's very important that you come right here before I get any angrier than I already am."

   c. "Come, my friend." (Or "Come, my darling.")

3. Do this exercise while walking to a sofa, or to one of two adjacent chairs, turning and sitting during your last line. Choose lines from items 1 and 2, or write new lines. (But write, don't improvise.)

   You should be able to marry short lines with long moves, and long lines with short moves, and, in fact, to time out any combination of movement and speech in an effective, relaxed, confident manner. Work also on completing your movements with a decelerating turn or sit synchronized with your last word.

◆ E X E R C I S E   **19–2**

Speeches with Business

Study and memorize one of the following speeches, all of them taken from the opening scenes of plays. Or memorize a short speech from the first few pages of any play of your choice. From the context, imagine whom you are speaking to and use your imagination to create a GOTE approach to the speech. Rehearse the speech privately until you feel confident of the lines.

1. "Since the Professor and his wife came to live here, life is off the track. . . . I sleep at odd hours, for lunch and dinner I eat a lot of highly spiced dishes, drink wine . . . all that is not good for your health. We never used to have a free minute. Sonia and I worked—I can tell you that—and now it's only Sonia who works, and I sleep, eat, drink. . . . There's no good in it." (Anton Chekhov, *Uncle Vanya*)

2. ". . . okay. This is how it goes. I mean, went. This is the way it all played out, or is going to. Or *is* . . . right now. Doesn't matter, you'll figure it out. I think. No, you will . . . sure you will! No problem. (*Beat.*) What you need to know for now, I mean, *right* at this moment, is that there was a girl. 'Course there always is, isn't there? I mean, unless there isn't. Then there's not . . . but that's pretty self-explanatory. In this one, there's a girl. There's *definitely* a girl. Huh. I think I'm gonna go talk to her, because . . . well, girls are nice. Basically. And that would be enough, but I need to—talk with her, I mean. To get this started. Or keep it going . . . or whatever. You know what I'm saying! Sort of." (Neil LaBute, *This Is How It Goes*)

3. "Honey, don't *push* with your *fingers*. If you have to push with something, the thing to push with is a crust of bread. And chew—chew! Animals have sections in their stomachs which enable them to digest food without mastication, but human beings are supposed to chew their food before they swallow it down. Eat food leisurely, son, and really enjoy it. A well-cooked meal has lots of delicate flavors that have to be held in the mouth for appreciation. So chew your food and give your salivary glands a chance to function!" (Tennessee Williams, *The Glass Menagerie*)

4. "The street is lined with cars. There's not a breath of fresh air in the neighborhood. The grass don't grow any more, you can't raise a carrot in the back yard. They should've had a law against apartment houses. Remember those two beautiful elm trees out there? When I and Biff hung the swing between them? . . . They should've arrested the builder for cutting those down. They massacred the neighborhood." (Arthur Miller, *Death of a Salesman*)

Now, with the speech learned, practice "delivering" it to a (real or imaginary) partner, using real props—or substitute props—and performing one of the following pieces of stage business at the same time:

1. Changing your clothing

2. Mixing and drinking a Manhattan cocktail

3. Mixing, dressing, and tasting a fruit salad

4. Shuffling a deck of cards and dealing out two hands of gin rummy

5. Peeling and eating a banana, then disposing of the peel

It is, of course, necessary to have the business well in hand. For example, you must know how to mix a Manhattan cocktail in order to do it, and your speech, convincingly. Choose business that is progressive (not simply repetitive) and sufficiently complex so that it involves several parts of your body.

You will probably find that Exercise 19–2 requires a good deal of practice. You will quickly find that there are literally thousands of ways in which your lines and business can be coordinated. How does the behavior affect the speech? How do the speech and the feelings that come with it affect the behavior? Don't try to "interpret" the speech according to the context of the play. Treat the speech simply as an isolated exercise, and let the speech create behavior that supports your delivery. Can you combine certain behaviors with the language so as to charm your partner? To threaten him or her? To beg for pity? To subvert? To frighten? To overwhelm?

◆ E X E R C I S E   19–3

Physical Punctuation

Select any speech that you have memorized, possibly one from the preceding exercise, and deliver it to a (real or imaginary) partner while doing a repetitive physical action, such as

1. Jogging in place

2. Skipping rope

3. Beating egg yolks

4. Doing sit-ups

5. Combing your hair

6. Playing the piano

7. Dribbling a (pretend) basketball

8. Shaving

Talk "over" the physical action; make yourself understood—and your intentions felt—over and above the distraction of your movement.

Now "punctuate" the speech by stopping your movement at a certain point in the text. Experiment with several possible moments. Experiment with stopping one movement, then later in the speech starting another one.

You are your own best teacher of what "works" in Exercise 19–3. Much of the director's work in staging a play is finding the right physical punctuation to drive home significant emotional transitions. You can anticipate this work in your acting by finding out how a change of physical rhythm coordinates with a change in the plot or in a character's intention or understanding of a relationship.

◆ E X E R C I S E   19–4

Physical Rhythms

Memorize one or more of the one-line speeches in Exercise 17–3. Deliver each speech to a (real or imaginary) partner together with an accelerating movement of your hand, such as pointing or slamming your fist on a table.

Deliver each speech with a decelerating movement, such as sitting in a chair, crossing the room and turning, or touching your partner.

◆ E X E R C I S E   19–5

Verbal Rhythms

Give each of the following commands with an accelerating tempo, then with a decelerating tempo.

1. "Get out of this room."
2. "Give me that!"
3. "Go out there and win!"
4. "Kiss me before I explode."
5. "To be or not to be, that is the question."

Combine the accelerating tempo with an accelerating arm/hand movement. Combine the decelerating tempo with a decelerating physical movement.

Pointing

Indicating emotions is usually considered an acting fault (see Lesson 14), but indicating *objects* (or places or people) by physically pointing, nodding, or gesturing toward them is often instrumental in acting performance. In the case of demonstrative pronouns ("that," "those," "these," "this"), some sort of physical indication is often absolutely required, as in "Bring me that book" (when there are several books on the table) or "I'll take one of those" (when there are several groupings of objects in the room). Without a gesture of some sort, it is often impossible to determine the antecedent (referent) of such a pronoun.

More generally, pointing or gesturing, when not overdone, creates a basic and credible opportunity for expressive movement, engaging the body in the actions of the mind and voice. To say "I'm going with her" while turning and pointing to the woman in question clarifies which woman you're referring to and establishes a physical and spatial bond between you and the actor playing that role, almost always augmented with a deeper psychological connection that makes the relationship between you and "her" more vivid—certainly to the audience but usually to yourself as well. It also gets you moving and sharing more of your face and body with the audience on several sides.

Pointing, gesturing, or looking at what you speak of also helps you establish the seeming reality of dramatized places, including divine realms in which your characters believe. To give a toss of your head toward the stage door or window on "He's out there" makes the idea of an "outside" more real, both to an audience and to yourself, though the indicated area is actually nothing but backstage clutter. Looking heavenward when calling upon God's name in Hamlet's "O God! God! How weary, stale, flat and unprofitable seem to me all the uses of this world!" will engage your Hamlet in a dialogue with, or a searching for, this "God," rather than a mere statement or expletive. And if as Saint Joan (in Shakespeare's *I Henry VI*) you glance up on the word *above* when declaring yourself "chosen from above," the gesture will make you more intimidating to the church officers who are persecuting you and will also intensify your feeling—or imagination—that you are indeed communicating directly with a divine presence.

In short, selected and discreet pointing—with your finger, thumb, open hand, both hands, head, eyes, or raised eyebrow—can make your acting clearer, more specific, more physical, more active, and more authentic: spatially and emotionally connected with other actors, surroundings, and the (fictional) places represented in the play.

◆ E X E R C I S E   19–6

Pointing

With a partner, and imagining a simple situation provoking such a line, play each of these sentences first without gesturing, then again with a turn and a pointing gesture on the italicized word—using your finger, thumb, open hand, both hands, head, eyes, or raised eyebrow. Evaluate the differences in your readings. Then try the exercise once more but with a different look or gesture.

1. I want *you* to have this.

2. And what am I supposed to do with *this* one?

3. Quick, go over *there*.

4. Shhhh. Sneak over *there*.

5. Your thoughts come from the devil, but mine come from *God*.

6. She came up from the *train station*.

7. John's *upstairs*.

8. No, you rat, I accuse *you*.

The following speech is too complicated to be used in an exercise, but try to figure out how Shakespeare may have wanted the italicized words in this speech—of a "Stranger" in *Timon of Athens*—to be performed:

Who can call him
His friend that dips in the same dish? for, in
My knowing, Timon has been *this* lord's father,
And kept *his* credit with *his* purse,
Supported *his* estate; nay, Timon's money
Has paid *his* men their wages: *he* ne'er drinks,
But Timon's silver treads upon his lip;
And yet—O, see the monstrousness of man
When he looks out in an ungrateful shape!—
He does deny *him*, in respect of *his*,
What charitable men afford to beggars.

So support your meaning with visual indications; as Shakespeare said, suit the action to the word.

Tempo

The ability to experiment with tempos—both physical and verbal—is an acting asset. There are no intrinsically "right" or "wrong" tempos in the theatre, and rarely do tempos simply accelerate or decelerate in straight-line fashion. A rhythmic variety is characteristic both of fine acting and of life itself. The beginning actor is often stuck in a repetitive, plodding rhythm that is neither dramatic nor lifelike but, rather, is a product of stage fright and dutiful "line reading."

How do the varying rhythms in Exercises 19–5 and 19–6 affect your feelings? Your interactions with your partners? Ask your partners what impact your accelerated deliveries, or your decelerated deliveries, had on them. Get comfortable with these exercises by repeating them several times, varying your text, intention, rhythm, and acting partners.

◆ E x e r c i s e   19–7

Speech/Movement Timing

Select a one-minute speech from any play—such as the speeches in Exercise 19–2. Analyze the GOTE for the character in that speech. Plot out a series of actions that coordinate with the speech, such as crossing the stage, walking around a sofa, picking up a book and tossing it aside, sitting down, smiling, tossing your head, and crossing your legs. Define where the other characters are located. Rehearse the speech very carefully so that you can time the actions to specific words. Create a pattern of accelerating and decelerating movements and verbal tempos. Create two or three punctuations. Let the speech climax at the end so that the crossing of the legs becomes a significant action concluding your line of thought.

When you can do this unconsciously, you will have taken a very long stride toward becoming an actor.

Actors with Disabilities

The emphasis on voice and movement in actor training should not obscure the fact that some actors are disabled in one way or another. There are very fine actors who cannot hear or speak: Witness the Theatre of the Deaf. And there are excellent actors who are paraplegics and amputees. There is certainly nothing superhuman about most actors' instruments, and some indeed transcend serious limitations. Acting is a portrayal of human life and the human condition, and anyone who has a sense of that and can portray a goodly fraction of it will find the opportunity to do so.

Summary

Concentration on goals and on the GOTE of the character integrates the voice and body components of the actor's instrument. Moving and speaking simultaneously and unselfconsciously is difficult for actors to master, but it must be learned if acting is to be fluid, rhythmically dynamic, energetic, lifelike, and properly punctuated. Each actor may have limitations or disabilities, but developing the acting instrument means integrating, as much as possible, all your capacities for dramatically effective speech and movement.

20

Imagination and Creativity

Imagination

Imagination is the wellspring of the acting impulse. It is the source of the actor's goal. "I want to marry Juliet," says Romeo's inner voice, but that inner voice is doing more than stating a character's goal; it must also be reflecting the character's fantasy, the character's dream, the character's *imagined* (and hence *imaginary*) future.

Imagination includes many things: dreams of power or conquest, visions of adventure or revenge, fears of humiliation or isolation, and fantasies of love, ecstasy, adoration, or heavenly ascension: These are not clinical "objectives" or even realistic goals; they are vivid targets of human imagination. The most exciting Romeo will be the one whose romantic and sexual fantasies are the liveliest, most insistent, and most enchanting. The actor who is simply pursuing a marriage certificate (or a Hollywood contract). will be a pedestrian Romeo no matter how brilliantly he phrases Shakespeare's speeches. But where do we get characters' imaginations?

Creativity

When reading and then rereading a role, the actor may come to grips with the character's major goals rather quickly. Subsequent examination, research, and rehearsal will doubtless lead to subtler discoveries of the psychology and social environment of the character, the complexities of his or her relationships, and the arc of the character's individual trajectory through the play. In this way, a character's goals are defined, refined, and sculpted into a detailed composition.

But the defining of goals is only one step toward playing them. The actor still must *bring them to life*. And the life you bring to them is inevitably partly your own. *Your own* life must finally animate—and create—the roles that you play on the stage or on the screen.

Creativity is your personal synthesis of research and imagination. Research gives you the script, the language, the historical background, the dramaturgical shape of the text, and other elements that make the play dramatic. Your own imagination, however, is what gives it life. Combined, research and imagination will *create* your character: making your character a breathing, feeling, fearing, wanting, *imagining* human soul with whom the audience will, at different times, root, care, empathize, and hate.

Creativity and Imagination

Truly creating a character—as contrasted with imitating one—requires unfettered use of your own imagination. But imagination is a notoriously private place. It teems with fantasies of lust, glory, torture, revenge, suicide, and all-but-apocalyptic experiences impossible to describe. Many of these fantasies we never mention to others, even to those we consider our intimates. Some we barely admit even to ourselves, instead *repressing* them (in the psychologist's terms) into the deep denial of our unconscious. Actors, however, must release such fantasies into their work in order to create the human vividness, complexity, and mystery of the roles they play. We want to see Romeo not merely "wanting" to marry/have sex with Juliet but literally *trembling* at the sight of her, and we want to see Juliet barely able to breathe when she realizes it is Romeo beneath her balcony. We want to see the blood rise up in their cheeks; we want to see their lips quiver; we want to see their absolute *terror* of saying the wrong thing. In short, we (the audience) want to see the actors create, *through their own experience*, all of the rapture, confusion, and anxiety of the profoundest love there could ever be—which audience members themselves once experienced or dream of experiencing. Indeed, this is what brings audiences into the theatre. We want to see the fantasies of the human mind straining against the limitations of the physical body and the spoken word.

When the actor truly creates—rather than imitates—the role, the actor creates life itself. And it is in no small measure the actor's life, along with the character's.

Using Your Fantasies

Although the actor's fantasies must be released, they need not be reported. It is not remotely necessary to talk about the inner recesses of your mind. Indeed, doing so will almost always damage the work process by making you self-conscious when you then try to integrate your public revelations into your creative work. Rather simple (and private) imagination exercises can help an actor probe his or her unconscious, inducing a "daydream" state where emotions, memories, and longings commingle just below the surface. These exercises in self-exploration are akin to hypnosis and meditation—both of which are often used by actors to attain what Stanislavsky (see Lesson 21) called the "creative mood."

> **IN DIALOGUE WITH YOUR IMAGINATION**
>
> *Actors have to have a fundamental ability to be in permanent dialogue with their own imaginations, so that when they utter forth something, people hear them.*
>
> FIONA SHAW

◆ E X E R C I S E   20–1

Cold/Hot

For this exercise you need a group leader or instructor and a room whose lighting is controlled by a dimmer.

Lie or sit on the floor. As the light brightens, imagine that the temperature gets warmer, then hotter, then uncomfortably hot, then *painfully* hot.

Imagine that by chanting "ohhhhhhhhhhh," you and the others can appease the gods that control the temperature.

As the light fades, imagine that the temperature cools, that it gets cold and then freezing.

Imagine that you are dying.

Imagine that by chanting "eeeeeeeeeeeee," the group can appease the gods and restore warmth to the world. Imagine that rhythmic stamping reinforces the chant.

The group leader may improvise additional variants for you to imagine.

◆ E X E R C I S E   20–2

Age Regression/Advancement

Look at a partner; study him or her well. Feel your partner's face with your hand. Imagine your partner at half his or her age. At half again that age. Imagine your partner as four years old. As two years old. As a naked infant. As a naked adolescent. Realize that your partner *was* a naked adolescent.

Imagine your partner at double his or her age. At age eighty-five. Look beneath your partner's skin at the skull. Feel your partner's skull. Imagine your partner dead, lying in a shallow grave. Imagine your partner as a skeleton. REALIZE THAT YOUR PARTNER *WILL* BECOME A SKELETON.

Back away from your partner so that several yards separate you. Envision your partner's birth-to-death cycle. Imagine, in fantasy, relationships between your partner and persons in your family, or persons close to you, or you yourself at different ages.

On signal, approach and hug your partner.

The group leader may improvise additional variants for your imagination.

Fantasy is most effective as an individual rather than a class exercise. Fantasizing sexual or violent relationships, for example, may be embarrassing when "performed" at an instructor's command. If given free play within an acting scene, however, such fantasizing can give life to the most pedestrian stage relationship. You are always the master of your own imagination. When you are freed from inhibition and worry over remembering your lines, the creative use of your imagination can give your stage character as much sensitivity and liveliness as you experience in your own dream/nightmare world.

◆ E X E R C I S E   20–3

Facing an Imagined Death

Memorize these lines of Lear's from *King Lear*:

> "No, no, no life!
> Why should a dog, a horse, a rat, have life,
> And thou no breath at all? Thou'lt come no more.
> Never, never, never, never, never!"

In this moment in the play, King Lear grieves over the body of his youngest daughter, Cordelia, who was just hanged. As Lear, you have cut her down, killed the person who hanged her, and carried her dead body onstage.

Make a circle with other members of your group. An object (it could be a person) is placed in the center, on the floor, representing the body of Cordelia. One at a time, deliver the speech. Do not try to imitate the character of King Lear as you might know it. Let the line come from you, just the way you are, but try to make yourself confront the fact of this death that lies in front of you. Try to inquire of the gods—or your God—why this object, your daughter, should lie dead here instead of some dog or rat.

Try again, with the last words of the speech, to come to terms with your daughter's very real death. Try one more time.

As you do the exercise a second and third time, "imagine" the object in the center of the circle is something very specific in your life. A favored pet, perhaps, or a younger sibling, or even an image of yourself. After the exercise (but not during), reflect on how the object you imagined affected your feelings, your vocal delivery, and your general behavior while giving the speech.

◆ E X E R C I S E   20–4

Facing Love

Memorize these lines of Juliet's from *Romeo and Juliet:*

> "My bounty is as boundless as the sea,
> My love as deep—the more I give to thee
> The more I have, for both are infinite."

At this moment in the play, Romeo has just declared "love's faithful vow" to Juliet for the first time, asking for hers in return.

Deliver this line to an imaginary Romeo—and then to another and another, without regard to your or your Romeo's gender. Don't try to imitate what you think Juliet might be like, but deliver the line as you yourself would to a real person you actually love, or would like to love, or to someone you would like to love you. On a subsequent occasion, imagine the object of your love to be a god, or spirit, or animal.

Those last two exercises are very powerful if you imagine them—and experience them—fully. They will undoubtedly engage your deepest emotions (see Lesson 21), if you allow them to do so. Great acting always engages the emotions, and almost always through the medium of imagination. Imagination is what makes a play seem real to you even when you rehearse and perform it night after night. Imagination is what allows you to play both the eighty-year-old man (King Lear) and the thirteen-year-old girl

(Juliet). Imagination also gives you the confidence to speak with conviction and emotional honesty lines written four hundred years ago.

For there's nothing remote or "literary" about facing death or facing love. It's entirely real: Shakespeare did it, we will do it, and our audiences will do it too. And no matter how often we may face death, or face love, we never really understand it fully, we never master it, and we are always awed by it. The same might be said about acting, and about great theatre. It always transcends what we know. Acting is an art that spans the known and the imaginary universes.

Summary

Imagination and discipline are the intangible aspects of an actor's instrument—intangible because they are attitudes rather than skills. The actor's imagination must be liberal, provocative, and lively. Imagination can be practiced, perhaps even taught, but it is an intrinsic aspect of every committed artist in the theatre. It should come into play *now*, not at some vague future in your studies.

L E S S O N

21

Emotion—and Acting
Theory

Many Americans—even those unconnected with the theatre or theatre arts—have heard about something called "Method acting" or simply "the Method." What does this mean?

The method referred to is that of the late Lee Strasberg, who developed it at the Actors Studio in New York during the 1950s and '60s. It, in turn, derives from the acting system developed some forty years previously by the Russian actor and director Konstantin Stanislavsky at his Moscow Art Theatre. The essence of Method acting is that the actors draw deeply on their own emotions and experiences while playing their roles. In Stanislavsky's version of it, the actors "live the life" of their character during the performance. The opposite of this approach is sometimes called "technical acting" or "presentational acting," where the actors are seen as objectively and technically creating their characters and then presenting (rather than representing) those characters to the audience, miming but not necessarily feeling the characters' emotions.

Over the years, these two contrary notions of acting have created a worldwide debate in acting circles. American actors tend to favor the more representational (and Russian) methods. British actors (as well as French and German) tend to favor a more presentational approach.

But the debate is hardly this simple. Most American actors are clearly aware of the necessity of a disciplined and controllable stage technique. And British actors are deeply influenced by the teachings of Stanislavsky, which form, by way of example, the core first-year acting curriculum of the Royal Academy of Dramatic Arts in London.

Nor is the debate strictly a modern one. Indeed, the extent to which actors might be said to feel or not feel the emotions of their characters, and believe or not believe they "are" the characters they play, constitutes what Professor Joseph Roach, in his book *The Player's Passion: Studies in the Science of Acting,*[*] has called "the historic, continuing, and apparently inexhaustible combat between technique and inspiration in performance theory." It is useful to probe at least briefly into this fascinating and important issue.

More than two thousand years before Stanislavsky and Strasberg considered the matter, the Greek philosopher Socrates queried Ion, a rhapsodist (reciter of poems), about the role of real emotion in performance:

SOCRATES: Tell me, Ion, when you produce the greatest effect upon the audience . . . are you in your right mind? Or are you not carried out of yourself? Does not your soul, in ecstasy, seem to be among the persons or the places of which you are speaking?

ION: That strikes home, Socrates. I must frankly confess that at the tale of pity my eyes are filled with tears, and when I speak of horrors, my hair stands on end and my heart throbs.

Obviously, Ion "lived the life" of his characters, feeling the emotions of his roles, and feeling himself to be in the presence of the characters in his tales. But, as Socrates' inquiry soon reveals, Ion was also aware of the powerful effects his acting had on his audience:

SOCRATES: . . . and are you aware that you produce similar effects on most of the spectators?

ION: Only too well; for I look down upon them from the stage, and behold the various emotions of pity, wonder, sternness, stamped upon their countenances when I am speaking.[†]

And so we see that Ion considered his acting both representational (he felt himself among the characters of his story) and presentational (he was checking out the audience all the while). It is a paradox, Socrates realized: Ion was both "in" the fiction of his recitation and, at the same time, outside of it.

Horace, the Roman poet (65–8 B.C.), turned Ion's paradox into a famous maxim of the ancient world: "In order to move the audience, you must first be moved yourself." And this Greco-Roman "Method" belief held near-absolute sway in the theatre for at least the next fifteen hundred years. We are fortunate

---

[*]   (Newark: University of Delaware Press, 1985), pp. 25–26.

[†]   Quoted in *Actors on Acting,* rev. ed., ed. Toby Cole and Helen Krich Chinoy (New York: Crown, 1970), pp. 7–8.

to have some examples of its use in classical times. The Greek actor Aesop, we are told, became so overwrought during a performance of Euripides' *Orestes* that he ran his sword through a stagehand who had chanced to stray into his line of sight. Polus, another ancient Greek actor, placed the ashes of his own dead son onstage in order to inspire himself while giving Electra's speech of lamentation in the Sophocles play. Quintilian, the first-century Roman orator, describes envisioning his wife's and children's imaginary death "with such extreme vividness" that he was "so moved while speaking that I have not merely been wrought upon to tears, but have turned pale and shown all the symptoms of genuine grief." Even in the formally stylized Japanese *kabuki*, actors concentrate on the reality of the dramatic action. As the celebrated seventeenth-century *kabuki* performer Sakata Tojuro explained, "If you wish to be praised, forget the audience and concentrate upon playing the play as if it was really happening."

Yet the same actors also sought to present their characters according to the stage conventions of their times. Quintilian, for all his tears and passion, urged his fellow actors to achieve the "regularity and discipline promised by calculation." He cautioned, for example, that "it is never correct to employ the left hand alone in gesture" and "the hand [may not] be raised above the level of the eyes."

So again we have the paradox: The actor performs with true emotion but also follows a calculated discipline of gestures, phrasings, and deportment. These ideas held sway up to and through the Renaissance, affecting Shakespeare, Molière, and nearly all playwrights and actors until the late eighteenth century. In many of these periods, natural emotion seemed to be favored by commentators; in others, conscious technique. But usually both were considered relatively equal in an alliance of seeming opposites.

In 1773, however, Denis Diderot, the famous French encyclopedist, tackled this issue head-on in a startling book titled *The Paradox of Acting*. Though not published until forty-six years after Diderot's death, this book was widely circulated in Europe from its time of writing. Diderot begins with the radical thesis that "a great actor . . . must [be] an unmoved and disinterested onlooker." He continues: "They say an actor is all the better for being excited, for being angry. I deny it. He is best when he imitates anger. Actors impress the public not when they are furious, but when they play fury well." By contrast, Diderot explained, "Actors who play from the heart . . . are alternately strong and feeble, fiery and cold.. . . Tomorrow they will miss the point they have excelled in today." Thus, Diderot maintains, "The actor who plays from thought . . . will be always at his best; he has considered, combined, learned and arranged the whole thing in his head."

Even those performances that move us deeply, Diderot insisted,

are all planned, . . . they have [all] been practiced a hundred times. . . .
At the moment when [the great actor] touches your heart he is listening

to his own voice; his talent depends not . . . upon feeling, but upon rendering so exactly the outward signs of feeling that you fall into the trap. He has rehearsed . . . every note of his passion. . . . You will see him weep at the word, at the syllable, he has chosen, not a second sooner or later. The broken voice, the half-uttered words, the stifled or prolonged notes [are all just] . . . a magnificent apery.

The actor, Diderot concludes, "is not the person he represents; he plays it, and plays it so well that you think he is the person; the deception is all on your side; he knows well enough he is not the person."*

Diderot's view was rooted in his confidence that all knowledge, including art, was rational and could be categorized, analyzed, alphabetized, and (given his profession) encyclopedized. Diderot's work typifies the Enlightenment era in which he lived, with its demystification of both medieval superstition and Renaissance idealism. The subsequent ages of romanticism and realism, however—particularly in the theatre—brought a strong rebellion against the "objective" rationalism of Enlightenment thinking.

"Put life into all the imagined circumstances and actions," Stanislavsky wrote in *An Actor Prepares,* "until you have completely satisfied your sense of truth, and until you have awakened a sense of faith in the reality of your sensations."† By "life" Stanislavsky meant the ambiguity of emotion, the mystery of love and death, and the confusion of experience. To create this life on stage, Stanislavsky sought to identify the separate steps of the actor's preparation. Absolutely primary to his vision was that the actor seek, in the act of performance, to resolve his or her *character's* problem (in Russian: *zadacha*), as opposed to his or her mere *actor's* problem. Thus the actor playing Juliet concentrates on winning Romeo's love (or her father's respect, or her nurse's complicity), rather than on showing the audience how romantic (or poetic, or young, or pretty) she is. By this means, according to Stanislavsky (and to the author of this book you are reading), the actor represents Juliet as a real and whole person, rather than simply presenting Juliet as a fictional character of the Shakespearean tragic stage. The character's *zadacha* is Stanislavsky's key.

Zadacha was translated as "objective" by Elizabeth Hapgood in the English-language version of *An Actor Prepares,*‡ and that word, along with "goal" and "intention," are used more than "problem" to refer to this concept today. But regardless of the term used ("goal" is used in this book),

---

*   In *Actors on Acting,* pp. 162, 170.

†   Constantin Stanislavski, *An Actor Prepares,* trans. Elizabeth Reynolds Hapgood (New York: Theatre Arts Books, 1936).

‡   For a fuller description of Stanislavsky's Russian terminology see Sharon Marie Carnicke, *Stanislavsky in Focus* (Amsterdam: Harwood Academic Publishers, 1998).

Stanislavsky's basic understanding—that the actor plays a character by active-ly seeking to solve the character's problems, and by pursuing the character's goals—has become fundamental to basic actor instruction almost everywhere in theatre today. It is by pursuing the character's goals, rather than by simply trying to please or entertain the audience, that the actor enters into the full dra-matic and emotional life of the character. And while this method is particular-ly obvious in modern realistic dramas, Stanislavsky and his followers have applied it in historical and more stylized plays as well.

Stanislavsky was one of the first theatre artists to systematically investi-gate the notion of motivation in acting and to advance the concept that every move onstage must be seen to correspond to what the character (and not just the playwright or director) is striving to achieve. He created the notion of "public solitude" to indicate the way in which an actor must focus his or her attention on the events of the play rather than simply on the play's impact on the audience. He established the notion that the play's text was accompanied by a "subtext" of meanings (chiefly unspoken and undescribed character goals) hidden beneath the lines. He hated all forms of empty theatricality, where the actor simply relied on established gim-micks or conceits. He insisted that an "artistic communion" must exist among the actors, in which actors must invest themselves deeply, drawing heavily, therefore, upon their own personal feelings in establishing a rap-port with their characters, their fellow actors, and the fictional events of the play.

And Stanislavsky was profoundly, almost obsessively, concerned with the actor's emotion. Discovering in the writings of the nineteenth-century French psychologist Théodule Armand Ribot that memories of past experiences are recorded by the nervous system and can be stirred by the right stimulus, Stanislavsky began to experiment with recalling his own past emotional states, eventually developing an acting technique known as "emotion memory" (or "emotional recall" or "affective memory"), whereby an actor mentally substi-tutes these remembered situations from his or her own life into the action of the play so as to reach the emotional levels dramatically required. By this sub-stitution of remembered feelings, Stanislavsky sought to make acting natural, truthful, and emotionally vivid for the performer and audience alike.

But Stanislavsky was also quite well versed in external theatrical tech-nique. Born to an affluent, aristocratic family, he had performed in plays, operettas, and operas from the age of six, often in the large, fully equipped theatres in both his family's Moscow home and country estate. A promis-ing singer, he had studied with a major Bolshoi Opera star; Tchaikovsky had proposed writing an opera for him. Like Quintilian, Stanislavsky fully recognized the necessity for rational control in performance. "Feeling . . . does not replace an immense amount of work on the part of our intel-lects," he said. And so he studied elocution, dance, and phrasing as pas-sionately as emotion. At some point in the middle of his career,

Stanislavsky even discarded emotional memory in favor of a more physical approach and devoted most of his later work to the exploration of physical actions as the key to stimulating truthful acting. He began to reproach his actors for excessive wallowing in private emotions. "What's false here? You're playing feelings, your own suffering, that's what's false. I need to see the event and how you react to that event, how you fight people—how you react, not suffer. . . . To take that line . . . is to be passive and sentimental. See everything in terms of action!" he said.* Stanislavsky, too, believed in a paradox of acting.

DOING, NOT SHOWING

You have got to start doing things and not showing them. Don't have any preconceived ideas about how the scene is going to play. Just go on a moment to moment reality level and don't presuppose anything.

JAMES DEAN, ADVISING 18-YEAR-OLD DENNIS HOPPER
ON THE SET OF *REBEL WITHOUT A CAUSE* (1955)

No country—not even Russia—has been as influenced by Stanislavsky's teaching as the United States. By 1920 two of Stanislavsky's disciples, Richard Boleslavsky and Maria Ouspenskaya, had moved to New York and founded the American Laboratory Theatre, bringing Stanislavsky's new "System" to the attention of American actors. Among their converts was an Austrian immigrant, Lee Strasberg, who headed the Actors Studio in New York from 1951 until his death in 1982. Strasberg's ensuing "Method," derived from the early version of Stanislavsky's System and including emotional recall as a principal technique, proved the most influential actor-training theory in America during the 1950s and '60s. Perhaps because it privileged actors over the script, making their own feelings as much the "subject" of the play as their character's actions, serious American actors and not a few celebrities, such as Marilyn Monroe, flocked to his school. Other American acting teachers, some of whom, like Stella Adler and Sonia Moore, had studied with Stanislavsky at a later point in his career, preached the Russian master's later creed of physical actions rather than emotional memory. The result is that great numbers of Americans, including those knowing little about the theatre, are familiar with the name of Stanislavsky and what was originally his "method" of acting.

Of course, there has been a great deal of serious thinking (and writing) about acting since Stanislavsky and the other artists and writers mentioned in this section. Playwright–directors Bertolt Brecht, Antonin Artaud, and

---

* Quoted in Jean Benedetti, *Stanislavski* (London: Methuen, 1988), pp. 77, 271.

Jerzy Grotowski, acting coaches Sanford Meisner and Ann Bogart, drama theorists Joseph Rauch and Michael Goldman, and cognitive psychologists Antonio Damasio and Daniel Schachter are only a small sample of those who have made significant aesthetic and scientific examinations of the infinitely complex relationship of emotion and action in life—examinations that can be applied to the art of acting. But the ongoing debate remains framed by the paradox first posed by Socrates and now symbolized by the Stanislavsky and Strasberg versus Diderot divide. What are your feelings on this issue?

Certainly the teachings and theories of Stanislavsky and Strasberg cannot be ignored. They have revolutionized the modern theatre and reflect, as well, a tradition going back to Socrates and Horace. But the words of Diderot cannot be simply set aside either; they contain undeniable truths, and everyone who works in the theatre knows that great performances (which must, in most cases, be delivered night after night) usually come out of tremendous discipline, planning, calculation, and contrivance. Obviously, acting is a form of Ion's paradox: It is *both* technique and inspiration, head and heart, presentation and representation, calculation and spontaneity. Real emotion is in a tension with rational control. Some exercises might help you to get more of a handle on all of this.

◆ E X E R C I S E   **21–1**

Playing (with) Real Emotion I

This is a modification of emotional memory, blending imaginary dramatic reconstruction with real events and characters drawn from your own life. It also taps in to Stanislavsky's notion of physical actions.

Go back to Exercise 20–3, "Facing an Imagined Death." Rememorize the lines of King Lear and form a circle with your acting group, as in that exercise.

Now think about someone in your own life who has died. The death need not be recent, nor need it necessarily be anyone for whom you remember grieving very deeply. But let yourself think, now, about how wonderful that person (we'll call her "she") was. Think about the wonderful parts of her that you haven't thought about for years. Imagine those wonderful parts you never got to know.

And now imagine her lying with eyes closed, on the verge of death, in the center of the circle. Walking around her, study her labored breathing. Try to breathe "for" her. And now, as you see her approach her dying gasps, imagine that she opens her eyes and looks at you. Imagine her trying, and failing, to reach her arm out to you. Keep trying to breathe "for" her. Now imagine God sending his messenger down to take her breath away for the last time. As this happens, as the messenger approaches her, give Lear's speech, knowing that no matter how quietly you speak, God and God's messenger—and the spirit of your imagined (real) person—are listening.

Pause but don't break out of the exercise when you come to the end of the speech. Think once more about how wonderful the person in your life was, and how much more wonderful she was than you knew while she lived.

Do the speech again. This time, at the second "never," kneel by her hand. And on the last "never," close her eyelids.

Do it again.

EMOTION

The most important thing [in acting], the one thing you can't get away without, is the ability to summon an emotional state to the surface. We, as a population, are conditioned from our early childhood against that: to be strong, not to cry, not to show our feelings in public. Actors have to break through all of that conditioning and be in control of it at the same time. That's the great magic: to be able to summon the demon and then control it.

JAMES CAMERON

Discuss with your fellow students: How truthfully do you think you faced a "real death"? How truthfully did your fellow students feel you faced such a death? In other words, how truthfully did you portray a person facing a real death? The answers might surprise you.

Self-Consciousness

Self-consciousness is, of course, the inhibitor of normal emotion. When we are concentrating on how we're coming across and how we're being perceived, we are highly aware of our appearance, our behavior, and even our feelings. So, when burdened with self-consciousness, we don't really *have* feelings: We restrict or inhibit them. The only way to fully experience these feelings is to release these inhibitions by concentrating on something other than ourselves. Concentrating passionately on an imagined event—including a dramatic event—can free us to experience emotion profoundly and naturally. What helps in such a situation might be that the imagined event

- incorporates something deeply familiar (for example, a real person in your life)
- is inspiring (the person was wonderful)
- is tragic (a real, wonderful person is dying)
- holds the potential for hope (she is trying, with her last breath, to look at you and reach toward you)

Your breathing "for" the dying person is a positive and physical *action*, not merely a meditation on death. It makes you concentrate on—and empathize with—her physiological state, putting you in her place and distracting you from yourself and your own concerns as an actor.

Your kneeling next to her and closing her eyelids gives you a strong physical action that connects you with her, and the earth she's lying on, even more strongly.

The repetition of the exercise also can reduce self-consciousness. Having performed the exercise once, you can plunge even deeper into it a second time, with the confidence that you already proved that you can get through it. And then a third time.

There may come a time when your self-consciousness returns, as you feel—by your repetitions or by others'—that you have explored and experienced the exercise as fully as humanly possible. Even the best actors have their limits. But remember that it's the work of the actor to keep emotions "fresh" and actions "alive" despite weeks, months, or years of continuous rehearsal and performance. Even film actors, who in theory create each moment of their performance only once, in fact have to re-create their performance over and over in "takes" that may have to be matched to each other in the editing studio, each with an identical action and emotional intensity.

◆ E X E R C I S E   21–2

Playing (with) Real Emotion II

Rememorize Juliet's lines from Exercise 20–4. Now think of a person, of either sex (but we'll call this person "he"), whom you were deeply infatuated with some time ago—but never spoke seriously with.

Imagine yourself on a date with him, in a romantic setting with him, in a wildly erotic setting with him.

Play the speech to him as if he were with you in this setting.

Now play it while dancing with him. Snuggling in a hayloft with him. Rescuing him from prison.

Now pair with a partner. Blur the lines between the real person with whom you were infatuated and your present partner. Transfer your infatuation to your partner. Play the line to your partner, convincing him of your passion for him. Play it dancing with him.

In discussing this scene, *don't* discuss the real person you were infatuated with. The emotional substitution will be all the more powerful when it is your secret and yours alone. All the feeling and emotion must be expressed and experienced with and toward your acting partner.

Emotion is a tricky thing. In real life, we're rarely aware of it until it passes: Our knees buckle *after* the train that almost hit us goes by, not *during* the danger. And the moment we start to think "Boy, am I moved," that emotion has already started to fade away. The late French actor Jean-Louis Barrault, in a famous metaphor, compared emotion to perspiration. Like sweat, he said, emotion can't simply be willed into flowing but must arrive naturally and organically when we're deeply engaged in passionate activity. Just as an athlete doesn't "try to sweat" to show how intensely she is competing, so an actor shouldn't "try to emote" to indicate the intensity of her performance. Rather, you, as an actor, should pursue your character's goals—get your character's GOTE—and then the emotions (as well as the sweat) will flow accordingly. Some of the substitutions and techniques described above might help it flow more fully.

> ### EMOTION TAKES US
>
> *In our struggle to control [emotion], we are overcome by tears or laughter, rage or joy, etc. The emotion takes us, we do not take it.*
>
> UTA HAGEN

Summary

Actors—and writers on acting—have argued for more than two thousand years about whether the actor actually experiences or only technically presents genuine emotion onstage. Denis Diderot persuasively propounded the extreme view of "technical" or "presentational" acting, but most who consider the subject consider that genuine emotion is an essential, if paradoxical, component of acting. The techniques of Konstantin Stanislavsky, sometimes transmitted through Lee Strasberg's Method, have had a powerful, if often controversial, impact on bringing emotion into American acting.

V

The Actor's Technique

YOU HAVE STUDIED YOUR GOTE, YOU HAVE WORKED ON DOZENS OF exercises, you have prepared a number of scenes, and, following a critique, you have improved and re-presented them to at least some general satisfaction. Are you an actor now?

Probably not. First, you almost certainly still need work on these same basics: intensifying your pursuit of goals, expanding your tactical ranges, freeing yourself from psychological and social inhibitions (while onstage, anyway), making more exciting acting choices, and creating more inspirational expectations that will draw from you your most powerful and dramatic performing abilities.

And, second, you need to develop expert acting *technique.* Technique is a word most American actors regard with mixed feelings. On the plus side, technique is simply what distinguishes fine artists or craftspersons in any field. On the minus side, an empty technique—technical ability without feeling or person-to-person interplay—is a shallow approximation of acting, bearing little resemblance to the real thing. Acting technique should never be empty. Playwright–director

175

George Bernard Shaw said that "stage technique . . . is the art of making the audience believe that real things are happening to real people,"* and so it is.

TECHNIQUE

It should not for a moment be thought that [acting technique] is something to be coldbloodedly practiced and learned. Not even speech training, which is something that the bulk of actors badly need, can be done coldbloodedly, in a mechanical way.

BERTOLT BRECHT

Technique is not a final gloss or finesse added at the last phase of rehearsal. It is part of life itself; it helps us achieve our goals in life, as well as on the stage. Most of what we know as acting technique is simply effective human behavior: actions that are more economical, gestures that are more pointed, speeches that are more precise and more intense than ineffective ones. Learning to be a more technically proficient actor is also learning to be a more effective person-to-person communicator in daily life.

No element of acting technique is ever wholly artificial or solely theatrical. Even extremely non-naturalistic technique, as in Japanese *noh* or *kabuki* drama, is based on true feeling and effective action toward some sort of victory. Thus every "technical" instruction in Part Five must be regarded as an extension of the life and personality of your character and must be understood in terms of the human reality of your character's situation and GOTE breakdown.

---

* In "The Art of Rehearsal," *Collier's Weekly,* June 24, 1922.

L E S S O N

22

Phrasing

Diction

Diction, emphasis, and inflection are three overlapping aspects of the actor's ability to speak the lines of the text. Together they constitute phrasing.

Diction is the clarity with which words are enunciated and put into action. Think of diction not simply as what is said but as what is *heard*. It is your words ringing in your partner's ear, and ringing with *meaning*, as they seek to encourage, persuade, or even intimidate your partner to act in ways that accomplish your goals.

You might think that in life, when you become emotionally intense, your diction becomes careless. But this is not true: When we are intense our diction actually improves. We speak more clearly, sharply, and penetratingly, and with more precise and communicable meaning. We may even become eloquent and inspirational! The reason is clear: When we care more deeply about things, we try that much harder to communicate, to persuade, to *win* our intensely pursued goals. The more difficult the obstacle, the more taxing the situation, the more ferociously we fight to be heard and understood; consequently, the more powerful and precise our diction becomes. Diction is essentially a tool for pursuing our goals—whether in life or, when onstage, in getting our character's GOTE. The "mumbling" actors of a generation past were in fact quite unlifelike (as well as undramatic) when they affected a slovenly diction to indicate how "emotionally spontaneous" they were. For the most part they appeared only moody, uncaring, and incomprehensible.

So the "technique" of stage diction requires, at the beginning, a solid understanding of using tactics to achieve goals: specifically the tactics of clear, persuasive, and penetrating diction.

Good diction requires, of course, a comprehension of the meaning of your words and of the syntax that holds them together. In complex speech, good diction is essential just for comprehensibility. Hamlet's first line, "A little more than kin, and less than kind," is only the first of many in the play that would be rendered meaningless without clear and distinct diction. But even when the meaning of the speech is not in the actual words at all, diction remains crucial. Communication requires tying your words to your GOTE, specifically to the tactics that your words serve. Look, for example, at Jim's line in Exercise 9–1: "The Wrigley Building is one of the sights of Chicago—I saw it summer before last when I went up to the Century of Progress." The real meaning of this line has nothing to do with midwestern urban architecture or the popular slogan of the era; rather, Jim is trying to impress Laura, and draw her out of her shyness, by demonstrating worldliness, intelligence, and bullish confidence. "I know my way around big cities, and I am fascinated by the future" is what he's really hoping to communicate: He's bragging and flirting, and encouraging Laura to do the same. Confident diction by the actor playing Jim will convey these inner messages; slovenly diction will convey the opposite. And when Laura says, a little while later, "I believe I *will* take a piece of gum, if you—don't mind," Laura's diction (and, consequently, the diction of the actor playing Laura) might seek to emulate the assurance of Jim's, tempered by a little of the elegant deference Laura has learned from her mother. Laura's diction should convey the notion, perhaps, that "I can live comfortably in your world—if you'll just show me how." In this way diction becomes a mark not just of actor technique, but of character goals and tactics.

So analyze what you are doing (or trying to do) with your acting partner—analyze your GOTE—and discover how you must use your words in that task. Are you asking a question? Silencing your partner? Seducing? Begging for approval? Provoking an argument? Making a distinction? Ending a quarrel? Proposing a reconciliation? The *content* of your speech may not always address these goals, but your diction and speaking tone will. Penetrating diction is one of the most potent tools the actor can lend to his or her character. Your instrument must be honed—and your approach focused—to deliver good diction at all times.

Good diction enables the audience to understand the play. If the actor cannot distinguish between "I ask you" and "I asked you," a moment in the play will surely suffer. After several such moments, the audience's attention will surely drift. While the audience puzzles over your meaning, it ceases to care about your emotional truth or about the play's situation and theme. Diction, then, is crucial to the theatre at every level.

Open-Mouthed Speaking

A common barrier to clear stage diction is a tight-lipped, tight-jawed speaking manner, often developed in childhood. This inhibits clear and effective diction, for which a more open-mouthed speaking manner is necessary. There can be many underlying causes for tight-jawed speech: vanity, a desire to look "tough," a distaste for overintellectualizing or overpronouncing words, wearing braces as a child, even prior abuse of various kinds. It's not easy to break these habits, but the following exercise can help liberate any actor.

♦ E X E R C I S E   22–1A

Act with Your Teeth

With a partner, exchange this dialogue:

A: Yes.

B: No.

Repeat four more times.

Do it again, using the actual movements of your mouth—the movement of your lips, teeth, and tongue—as part of your threatening or inductive tactics. Make your acting partner *see* you speak; exaggerate the movements of your teeth and tongue so as to encourage compliance (for the actor saying "Yes") or to threaten retaliation (for the actor saying "No"). I call this "acting with your teeth."

Reverse roles ("yes"-sayers saying "no") and repeat the exercise.

♦ E X E R C I S E   22–1B

Do this short exchange in the same manner: Act it with your teeth. Overpronounce so that you are appealing to your partner or threatening your partner with your mouth movements as well as your words.

A: Come on over here!

B: You just leave me alone!

A: Come on over here!

B: You just leave me alone!

◆ E X E R C I S E   22–1C

Act the Laura–Jim scene with your teeth. Exaggerate the movements of your teeth, lips, and tongue, and overpronounce your words, using your mouth and your diction as part of your overall tactics to achieve your goals.

One can go overboard in this direction, of course. But, in general, actors should be "open-mouthed" when forming words and developing diction, just as they should be "open-throated" when developing good stage voices. In most cases, you should not only speak your words clearly but also *show the other characters* that you are speaking your words clearly. Doing this adds to your comprehensibility, and it enhances your confidence and consequently your stage presence.

Developing Diction

Good stage diction is not something you learn from a book. You learn it from experience, both on the stage and in life. One of the best ways to learn good diction is simply communicating regularly with words—making yourself understood—in active and even hostile situations. Teaching children, addressing rallies, debating politics, and public speaking of any sort will sharpen your diction and train you, almost as a matter of course, in strengthening your capability for oral communication.

◆ E X E R C I S E   22–2

Repeated Sentences

Pair with a partner. Each partner selects a text, such as part of a play script or a narrative page from a book. The first partner begins by reading a sentence from the book. The second partner repeats it exactly, then reads from his or her book another sentence, which the first partner repeats.

Work up to longer and longer sentences. Concentrate on making your partner hear your text precisely and understand it. You have won the victory when your partner repeats the sentence perfectly and with complete comprehension.

Turn back-to-back and continue.

◆ E X E R C I S E   22–3

Shaw Speech

Few playwrights rely on diction as much as George Bernard Shaw, whose plays contain brilliant verbal arguments about a multitude of still-pertinent issues. Memorize any short speech (about five sentences) from one of Shaw's plays and deliver it to your partner. Then ask your partner to paraphrase the content of the speech. Your "success" is indicated not by how well you spoke, but by how well you made your partner hear and understand the speech.

Switch partners and repeat the speech, working harder to make precise points. Act with your teeth, tongue, and lips, not just with your words! Make your partner hear the speech for the first time.

Switch back to your original partner for a final time. Did you improve? Ask your partner.

Emphasis

Emphasis is the stuff of oral interpretation, the decision to make one word or syllable more important than another. Almost any line can be read with a variety of emphases. Look, for example, at Macbeth's line to his wife, after murdering Duncan: "I have done the deed."

I have done the deed. [It was *me!*]

I *have* done the deed. [You thought I wouldn't, didn't you?]

I have *done* the deed. [It's all over now.]

I have done *the* deed. [It's the most *important* deed I've ever done.]

I have done the *deed.* [It's just a "deed," nothing more.]

All of those emphases are justifiable, but you can play only one of them. Which one fits the interpretation, stimulates the action, and best serves your production of the play? Should there be subemphases or equal emphases, such as "I have *done* the *deed*"? Emphasis, in a produced play, may be indicated by the director; more often, however, you will have to make these selections yourself.

Guiding your choice of emphasis should be the question, What do I want the other characters to hear and understand? Like diction, emphasis is a communication device; it should stimulate the right kinds of responses from the other person. What does Macbeth want his wife to understand from his utterance? If he worries that she is taking too much control, he may emphasize *I.* If he thinks she may want to turn back, he may emphasize *done*. If he thinks she may become hysterical, he may emphasize *deed*. Emphasis, then, is closely related to GOTE components, to the goal of your character, and to the tactics you choose to implement that goal.

How do you emphasize a word? The most common way in English is raising its pitch, as (the raised pitch is noted here by a preceding caret [^]): "I have ^done the deed" or "^I have done the deed." Increased volume also emphasizes a word, as does stressing the consonants a bit more precisely, thus "biting off" the syllables. But *coloring the vowels* of the word—giving them an enhanced, elongated, possibly unexpected *tone*—is often an even more effective way of providing special emphasis. Creating emphasis through stress and volume alone can result in strident, mechanical speaking (appropriate for certain characters, of course); adding to that emphasis by carefully shaded tonal variations can create a more evocative, "poetic" speech useful in establishing more subtle relationships.

Movement and gesture are other ways of creating emphasis. Pointing to yourself on the word *I*, or making a fist on the word *done*, can determine what precise message Lady Macbeth (and, through her, the audience) will take from your speech.

◆ E X E R C I S E   22–4

Change of Emphasis

With a partner, and by turns, deliver Macbeth's line "I have done the deed" with each of the five emphases described previously, trying to capture the specific interpersonal meaning of each separate emphasis. Experiment with added *stress*, with *coloring* (elongating or enhancing) the vowels, and with *gestures*. How many of these emphases can you justify to yourself?

Select other lines that lend themselves to experimentation with different emphases, and see how many ways you can play them. Consider this exercise an experiment, however, and don't try to choose a "best" emphasis: That choice can come only from studying the play. Here are some possible lines, all from Shakespeare:

HAMLET: The time is out of joint. O cursed spite,
   That ever I was born to set it right!

KING LEAR: Dost thou call me fool, boy?

OTHELLO: I do not think but Desdemona's honest.

JULIET: You kiss by the book.

CLEOPATRA: O never was there Queen
  So mightily betrayed!

◆ E X E R C I S E   22–5

Punctuate with Emphasis

Using stress and tone emphasis alone, make the meaning of these sentences clear by speaking them to someone:

1. Replace "don't" with "won't."

2. That that is, is; that that is not, is not.

3. She would, would she?

4. Look at "Casanova" over there!

5. What do you mean, "Do my duty"? Duty demands dying!

Act with your teeth!

Inflection

The word *inflection,* which comes from the Latin word for "turn," refers to the voice's rise or fall in pitch, from syllable to syllable. *End-inflection* is the pitch turn at the end of a phrase or sentence. Often pitch turns are the only difference between declarations and questions. Consider the sentence "You're going out"—here unpunctuated. If it is a declaration

  You're going out.

the speaker's pitch would ordinarily drop on the final word. If it is a question

  You're going out?

the pitch would normally rise.
    Inflection is also how we denote sarcasm, substituting a falling pitch for a rising one and unmistakably reversing the meaning of a line. For example, "That's great!" said with a rising inflection means what it says; but "That's great!" said with a falling inflection, particularly when accompanied by a smirk or a raised eyebrow, means "That's terrible!" Needless to say, you must play these inflections with care.

THE ENGLISH SECRET

Ever wonder why American critics and audiences so adore British actors on U.S. stages? Why have Ralph Fiennes, Maggie Smith, Janet McTeer, Diana Rigg, Nigel Hawthorne, Derek Jacobi, Jeremy Irons, Ian McKellen, Roger Rees, Constance Cummings, Jessica Tandy, Stephen Dillane, Jennifer Ehle, Alan Bates, Michael Gambon, Vanessa Redgrave, Roy Dotrice, Lindsey Duncan, and Pauline Collins won coveted Tony acting awards in recent seasons? Perhaps because of "the English secret," the technique of using upward inflections to create a lifelike and exhilarating forward momentum in a dramatic text.* Not always taught in American schools, the upward inflection is well recognized by the Brits:

If we take a downward inflection, we finish the journey. Keep the journey going, keep the inflection buoyantly up, until we reach the end of the trip.

MICHAEL LANGHAM, ENGLISH-BORN STAGE DIRECTOR

Where there is a break within the line . . . [usually] it is simply a poise on a word—i.e., the word holds and lifts for a fraction of a moment before it plunges into the second half of the line. This poise is necessary for the ear of the listener . . . to . . . be ready for the information in the second half of the line . . . Very often, when we do not understand a speech, it is because this shaping has not been attended to.

CICELY BERRY, VOCAL COACH, ROYAL SHAKESPEARE COMPANY

Just remember, there's many an actor sleeping on the embankment tonight, with no soles to his shoes, for lack of an upward inflection.

DONALD SINDEN, ENGLISH CLASSICAL ACTOR

If you listen to ordinary conversations, particularly involved conversations or arguments, you will hear a great variety in pitches and intonations and rapid shifts in the pacing and forcefulness of the spoken words. Similarly, varied inflections and a wide range of pitches and volume levels characterize exciting stage dialogue. The beginning actor, often handicapped by a sketchily memorized text and ample levels of stage fright,

---

* For a fuller discussion see my essay "The English Secret," in Robert Cohen, *More Power to You* (New York: Applause, 2002), pp. 31–43.

frequently speaks in a monotonous tone with steady pitch (poor Johnny One-Note) and falling inflections that dwindle away before the line comes to an end. Continually falling inflections—of the sort you hear when some-one is reading off a laundry list—identify the technically untrained actor and make the play die a slow death. Monotone is as unlifelike as it is unthe-atrical, so you need not worry about learning it—unless your part consists of reading off a laundry list.

In general, rising end-inflections *sustain* the action of a speech, and falling end-inflections *conclude* (or try to conclude) it. A rising inflection demands an answer or a response; a falling inflection suggests an attempt to close off discussion or to have the last word. Thus:

$$\text{Shall we }^{\text{go?}} \nearrow$$

practically demands an answer and suggests that the person so invited can accept or refuse. But

$$\text{Shall we }_{\text{go?}} \searrow$$

though still technically an invitation, suggests that the "going" has already been decided; the person "asked" is merely requested to nod assent and leave. Falling inflections are characteristic of curtain lines:

$$\text{The play is }_{\text{done.}} \searrow$$

and of argument-enders:

$$\text{No more ex}_{\text{cuses!}} \searrow$$

Rising inflections are characteristic of real questions:

$$\text{Are you going}\ ^{\text{out?}} \nearrow$$

or:

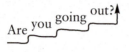

and of statements that imply the question "Don't you agree with me?"

I think she's sad. ("Don't you?")

Similarly, we use rising inflections to point out *opposites* and *antitheses:*

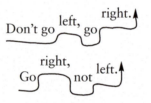

Notice that the two words placed in opposition are both inflected upward, but the preferred word ("right" in this case) is inflected *further* upward, regardless of whether it comes first or second in the sentence. *Operative* or *key words,* such as words new to the current discussion, or highly *unusual* words, or usual words used in *unusual ways,* or words being *quoted* from someone else, are also normally highlighted by upward inflections, regardless of where they appear in a sentence:

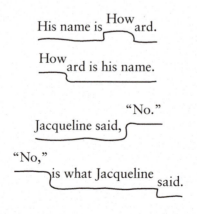

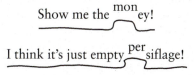

Items in a *list* are likewise lifted in pitch until the last one, if the speaker really intends to communicate that the list is something important:

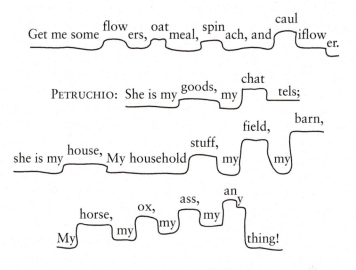

(The Taming of the Shrew)

Notice that the normal inflection of a list rises steadily throughout the speech, until a falling inflection concludes it. In Petruchio's speech, a falling inflection on "chattels" will break up the speech (which restarts by repeating the subject and predicate—"she is"—immediately afterward) so that the actor does not have to reach impossibly high pitch levels.

Notice also that the pitch rise can be very slight in the delivering of this list. The *amount* of rise is not important. What is important is that the rise is steady and perceptible.

Finally, rising inflections create exciting momentum in a speech and distinguish it from flat, droning, rote-memorized recitations. Rising inflections carry and build the basic idea, passion, and *purpose* of a speech through its natural breathing and thinking pauses, as usually marked in the written text by commas. Lifted inflections radiate purposeful, aggressive speech, stimulating your fellow actors and compelling attention from both onstage and offstage audiences. In life as well as theatre, they are the benchmarks of exciting conversation, good argument, and high-spirited interchange.

◆ E X E R C I S E   22–6

Inflections

Study and produce the most vivid and engaging inflections in the following speeches and dialogues:

1. Let's go to the movie, not the play.

2. He's not a genius, he's an idiot.

3. I hate olives, pork, and sea urchins.

4. CLAUDIUS: These words are not mine.

   HAMLET: No, nor mine now.

   (Hamlet)

5. CELIA: Soft, comes he not here?

   ROSALIND: 'Tis he. Slink by and note him.

   (As You Like It)

6. LYSANDER: Not Hermia, but Helena I love!

   (A Midsummer Night's Dream)

7. Estelle is good, but I am better.

   (Note: In this case, "Estelle" and "I" are opposites.)

8. Where would you be without me?

9. (*proposing* to depart) Let's go.

   (*agreeing* to depart) Let's go.

10. HAMLET: To be or not to be, that is the question.

11. JULIET: Romeo, Romeo, wherefore art thou Romeo?

    (The word *wherefore* means "why," not "where." The line asks, "Why does your name have to be Romeo, and you therefore a member of the family my family hates?")

12. TIMON: If thou wert the lion, the fox would
    beguile thee; if thou wert the lamb, the fox would
    eat thee, if thou wert the fox, the lion would
    suspect thee, when peradventure thou wert accused by
    the ass; if thou wert the ass, thy dullness would

torment thee, and still thou livedst but as a
breakfast to the wolf; if thou wert the wolf, thy
greediness would afflict thee, and oft thou shouldst
hazard thy life for thy dinner; wert thou the
unicorn, pride and wrath would confound thee and
make thine own self the conquest of thy fury; wert
thou a bear, thou wouldst be killed by the horse;
wert thou a horse, thou wouldst be seized by the
leopard; wert thou a leopard, thou wert german°; to   °akin
the lion and the spots of thy kindred were jurors on
thy life; What beast couldst thou be, that
were not subject to a beast?

(Timon of Athens)

(This speech will be almost incomprehensible without effective control of speech inflections.)

Inflections are not mere "acting technique." Even Stanislavsky, the patron saint of organic and realistic acting, advised actors to

> give an upward twist to the sound of the last syllable of the last word before the comma . . . [and] leave the high note hanging in the air for a bit. . . . Almost like the warning lift of a hand, [this] causes listeners to wait patiently for the end of the unfinished sentence.

And again,

> Intonations and pauses, in themselves, possess the power to produce a powerful emotional effect.. . . When you need real power in your speech, forget about volume, and remember your rising and falling inflections.*

If inflections rise and fall in everyday speech, why do actors need to *learn* to use rising inflections when they take to the stage? Beginning actors, and sometimes experienced ones, normally read and start memorizing their lines before fully committing to playing their character's goals, and the result is an unconscious tendency to recite, as in the flattened Pledge of Allegiance dutifully spoken in school classrooms (see Lesson 2).

Every speech you say, as a character, should be delivered as *created,* not *recited,* by you. You, not the playwright, should be perceived as the originator of your lines. Inflections are a technical manifestation of the extent to which you create rather than recite your text.

---

* Both quotations are from Constantin Stanislavski, *Building a Character,* trans. Elizabeth Reynolds Hapgood (New York: Theatre Arts Books, 1949), pp. 137, 141.

Phrasing

Considered together, diction, emphasis, and inflection result in phrasing. Phrasing can never be separated from the GOTE principles that give your speeches meaning and give your character the lifeblood to mean them and speak them. But your character's ability to phrase speeches and to pursue goals through words and rhetorical expression is something you, the actor, must supply.

As a first step, you should mark your script with underlines to indicate emphases. Add other notations pertaining to diction, based on the general principles of this lesson.

Which words should be elongated to reach the other character's consciousness? Which words should be stressed? Are there any sarcastic inflections? Argument-enders? Questions demanding answers? Statements begging for agreement? Ideas needing precise clarification?

More generally, how does the character use language, rhetorical expression, and gesture to further his or her cause? How does the character's vocabulary and syntax come into play in the character-to-character relationship? How does the character's phrasing show what kind of a thinker she or he is? What kind of tones does the character use? How much of a poet is he or she? How much of a bureaucrat? How does the character's GOTE translate into the character's phrasing?

Summary

Diction, emphasis, and inflection are ingredients of phrasing, which is the way the character uses words to influence events and other characters. Good phrasing has both real-life similarity and theatrical effectiveness. It clarifies and focuses dialogue, gives specific emphasis to the most important points of a scene or play, and sustains the excitement of the action and the enthusiasm of the characters. Varied and rising pitches are particularly useful as technical adjuncts to the GOTE-determined excitement of good acting.

23

Attack

The First Word

Attack is the delivery of the first word of a speech. The principal rule of attacking a speech is to come in strong—with confidence, vigor, and enthusiasm, and also with substantial volume and pace. The weak attack, common in beginners, is filled with uncertainty, reflecting the beginner's characteristic uneasiness.

There are two reasons why your attack must be strong: a technical reason and a real-life reason. Technically, the actor must attack each speech vigorously in order to get the attention (focus) of the audience immediately at the outset of each speech. Remember, the audience does not know where to look from moment to moment; therefore, it is up to you, the actor, to "pull" its attention every time you have something to say. The timid actor succeeds in doing this only by midsentence; the bold actor captures attention on the first syllable.

In real life a strong attack is even more important: In life, no playwright gives you the "right to speak." People don't automatically fall silent just because it's "your line." In life you must *earn* your opportunity to speak, and by the force of your speaking you must make everybody else stop talking and listen. This process is called *turn-taking* by conversation analysts, and it is as natural to life as it is (or should be) to the stage.

191

Thus the professional actor knows that he or she must "take stage" with both speeches and movement. You must not sink into the artificial comfort of the script with its planned alternation of "my lines and your lines." The professional actor seizes the floor powerfully with the first syllable of each speech. Thus attack defines your presence and earns you the right to speak as a character and to shape the scene you are in.*

Sheer volume is normally a key ingredient of a strong attack. The uncertain actor, worried about making a mistake ("Is that my cue?" "Am I saying the right line?"), often reduces volume to minimize the magnitude of any possible error—committing a graver mistake in the process. In the theatre, it is almost always better to do something wrong boldly than to do something right timidly. So you should learn to give yourself the extra advantage of full projection on each opening syllable.

Volume is not the only attack device, however. Lengthening or coloring the vowel, sighing into an initial vowel, using an unusually high pitch, making a broad physical gesture or a noisy one, or overemphasizing an initial plosive consonant (the *p* in *perhaps,* perhaps) will also intensify your attack. So will opening your eyes wider, taking in a big gulp of air, rising from your chair, bouncing up on your toes, or taking a step forward. So will "acting with your teeth."

Remember, these "technical" actions are taken from ordinary life. Observe two people in an involved conversation or an argument and you will see most if not all of these turn-taking techniques coming into play—quite unconsciously and, more important, quite unselfconsciously. See whether you can put each of these attack devices into a patch of dialogue you and your partner have already memorized.

The *pace* of your attack is another major consideration. Normally your attack should be fast rather than slow, despite the beginner's tendency to be slow rather than fast.

Why should your attack be fast? Technically, to speed up the action of the play. In the final rehearsals, most directors admonish the actors to "pick up your cues!" Elapsed time between lines—the pauses of slow attacks—is

---

* How about Laura's "Hello" at the beginning of the Gentleman Caller scene (Exercise 9–1), which the playwright specifically indicates should be delivered "faintly"? Obviously, this line should not be spoken loudly, but actors err if they simply "try to be faint" in attacking it. Laura is, in fact, trying to be bold—and, for her, actually *is* being bold. The author's stage direction that immediately follows says "She clears her throat," indicating that Laura is trying to be bolder still. The actor playing Laura must therefore try to be bold, as Laura does, but come somewhat short of the mark. It would do little good to whimper the line: Laura wants to make an impression with Jim right from the beginning; she just doesn't yet know how.

wasted time as far as the audience is concerned. The audience gets no information and has no idea what you are thinking about during your pregnant pause. Indeed, audience members don't even know where to look, for they have no idea whose line is coming next.

> ### INTERRUPT YOUR PARTNER
>
> *In everyday life we often would have gone on talking if someone hadn't interrupted us. In your play, what would you have said if the other character hadn't interrupted you? Similarly, what launches you into interrupting the other character?*
>
> PETER BARKWORTH

In real life, people do not simply trade lines in alternation. They break into conversations and interrupt each other. They are eager to speak rather than simply obliged to say lines. To re-create that sort of high-intensity conversation, directors ask actors to pick up their cues, to portray a vivid discussion rather than a listless one.

When you attack a speech with pace, you are responding much more directly to your partner's line. Your emotions, stimulated by your partner, will be in full flush only for a split second. If you respond at that moment, your response will be filled with feeling; if you wait a second or two, that feeling will be dissipated. In acting, your most intense feelings should occur *while you're speaking,* not before or after, and you must seize the moment when you are most moved, not the moment a half second later, to attack your speech.

Physical Attack

Speech is an action, and your attack on any single speech is physical as well as verbal. As an actor, you should learn to "move into" your speeches, not just utter them passively. This can mean a strong gesture on or right before your first word, or a stage move (standing up, sitting down, stepping forward), or just a toss of your head. It almost always means "acting with your teeth" and making it clear, from your head and mouth movements, that you *intend* to speak and intend to be *seen speaking.* Remember, you have to *work* to seize the floor and to "interrupt" your partner. Remember also that it is your *goal* (and your GOTE) that makes you speak and that physical action by you is often needed to make that speech work toward—and not against—your character's goals. So be reasonably aggressive in "taking stage" when you begin your character's speeches.

Turn-Taking

A strong attack does not mean that you cannot pause during your speech, of course, or that you must race through your lines. Far from it. A strong attack means that you cannot pause unnecessarily *before* your speech, but that you seize the stage first—and then develop your nuances afterward. A good playwright will help you by providing strong "turn-taking" attack words at the beginning of speeches.

◆ E X E R C I S E   23–1

Turn-Taking Dialogue

Read to yourself, and then aloud with a partner, this scene between two teenagers. The "she" in the first line refers to Eva's mother. Read the scene aloud several times with attention to making strong attacks.

ROBERT: Where does she think we go?

EVA: Oh, I tell her we just go walking in the woods, talking. She knows that but she thinks we do other things too.

ROBERT: Like what?

EVA: You know.

ROBERT: Like what?

EVA: You know. Dirty things.

ROBERT: What does she think that for?

EVA: I don't tell her, though.

ROBERT: What would you tell her?

EVA: About that. About when I have to pee and things.

ROBERT: Well, there's nothing dirty about that.

EVA: Well, don't you think I know!

ROBERT: She means other things.

EVA: What?

ROBERT: Never mind.

EVA: Well, don't you think I know?

(Lanford Wilson, *The Rimers of Eldritch*)

The scene in Exercise 23–1, fraught with repressed sexual curiosity and suspense (it will lead to a clumsy attempted rape and a shooting), is filled with awkwardness and hesitancy. The dialogue clearly is not meant for racing through. Nonetheless, the scene develops its anxious intensity only if the attacks are continuously strong. Notice how Wilson, the playwright, has placed attack words such as *oh* and *well,* which can be attacked on cue and then followed by a pause. Each character speaks quickly in order to seize the conversation from the other—and then pauses to figure out what to say. Notice also how Eva uses "You know" as a temporizing answer to respond in a noncommittal way and make Robert stop asking embarrassing questions.

All characters in dialogue try to control the conversation—even when they wish to cease conversing or cease answering questions. The only way to take control is with a strong attack, not a weak one.

Study the following dialogue from Shakespeare's *Hamlet,* which provides a more forceful argument than the Wilson scene. In the scene, Prince Hamlet confronts his mother while Polonius is hiding behind a curtain.

HAMLET: Now, mother, what's the matter?

QUEEN: Hamlet, thou hast thy father much offended.

HAMLET: Mother, you have my father much offended.

QUEEN: Come, come, you answer with an idle tongue.

HAMLET: Go, go, you question with a wicked tongue.

QUEEN: Why, how now, Hamlet!

HAMLET: What's the matter now?

QUEEN: Have you forgot me?

HAMLET: No, by the rood, not so;
You are the queen, your husband's brother's wife,
And—would it were not so—you are my mother.

QUEEN: Nay, then I'll set those to you that can speak.

HAMLET: Come, come, and sit you down; you shall not budge;
You go not till I set you up a glass
Where you may see the inmost part of you.

QUEEN: What wilt thou do? Thou wilt not murder me?
Help, help, ho!

POLONIUS *[Behind a curtain]:*   What, ho! help, help, help!

HAMLET *[Drawing his sword]:*   How now! A rat? *[Stabbing through the curtain]* Dead, for a ducat, dead!

POLONIUS *[Behind]:*   O, I am slain!

QUEEN: O me, what hast thou done?

HAMLET: Nay, I know not: Is it the king?

QUEEN: O, what a rash and bloody deed is this!

HAMLET: A bloody deed! Almost as bad, good mother,
  As kill a king, and marry with his brother.

QUEEN: As kill a king!

HAMLET: Ay, lady, 'twas my word.

(William Shakespeare, *Hamlet*)

Shakespeare's dialogue, in general, displays masterful turn-taking. Shakespeare was an actor as well as a playwright, and consequently his verse is the most "actable" in the English language. The vast majority of Shakespearean speeches—perhaps 90 percent or more—begin with one-syllable words, which are the easiest to attack, particularly in a verse form (iambic pentameter) that stresses the second, not the first, syllable. And in Shakespeare, polysyllabic opening words are usually commands, interjections, the names of the characters addressed, or repeated words from the previous line, all of which are easy to attack strongly.

In the scene from *Hamlet,* all possible turn-taking devices are in play: repeated attention-getters ("Come, come"), characters' names ("Hamlet," "Mother"), interjections ("O"), temporizers ("Why," "How now!"), and monosyllables, often in combination. Read that scene with a partner, finding how you can make strong attacks and still leave some room for pauses within several of the lines.

Preparing Strong Attacks

Understanding the dramatic need for the strong attack, how do you go about creating it onstage? Confidence in your lines, and in your character's tactics and intentions, is paramount. Weak attacks almost never come from conscious decision but rather derive from actor trepidation. (Remember when you were in your elementary school choir and were shy about singing your first notes until you could confirm that everyone else was singing with you?)

Preparation, however, is a specific key to delivering strong attacks. Remember: The line cue is the actual word you come in after; the action cue

is the word or phrase, often earlier in the cue line, that prompts you to prepare your own speech. Thus:

QUEEN: Have you forgot me?

HAMLET: No, . . .

Me is the line cue; *forgot* is the action cue. When the Queen has said, "Have
you forgot . . .", Hamlet already knows what she's asking and is preparing
his reply before she has finished her sentence. Thus when she completes her
question, the word *no* is already on the tip of his tongue, ready to fly out.

Go through your script and underline all the *action* cues in your partner's
lines—the words that tell you what you need to know before you really
want to speak up. If you become aware of action cues, you will be able to
understand—and portray—your character by picking up your partner's
cues and delivering your lines with a strong attack, rather than merely following a technical command of the director.

◆ E X E R C I S E   23–2

Action Cues

Pair with a partner and select a short, intense, two-person scene made up of
very short speeches. Underline all the action cues. Analyze all the turn-taking devices. Then read the scene aloud, emphasizing the attack points as
much as possible without racing the lines.

Memorize, rehearse, and play the scene as you have studied it.

Summary

Attack, which is the delivery of the first word of your line, is a crucial technical element of the stage because it focuses attention on the speaking person and conveys the idea that your character *wants* to speak—and not that
you are speaking only because the playwright has ordered you to. In the
theatre, as in life, you must earn your right to speak. You must take the
stage by the forcefulness of your speaking, and your vocal and physical attacks are the principal ways by which you do this. Strong attacks require
substantial volume, energy, clarity, and pace, as well, many times, as an aggressive physical presence. You can prepare for strong attacks by studying

your cue lines for action cues that spur your response shortly before it actually comes so that you will be fully ready to speak on your line cue. Picking up cues, via the strong attack, does not mean rushing or racing your lines. Pauses taken after a strong attack—within the body of your line rather than before your line—can be even more effective if the attacks in the scene are uniformly strong ones.

24

Follow-Through

The Hook

As it is important to pick up your cues, so it is important not to drop the end of your sentences. The last word of each speech must be audible and intelligible. So directors have urged beginning actors since time immemorial.

Beginning actors often drop the ends of their sentences or their speeches. When they come to the end of their scripted words, they sort of glide to a stop in the manner of a newly licensed driver gently pulling into a parking place.

Your character's goals, however, must be pursued *beyond* the end of the line. The end of the speech is the moment when you are trying to compel your partner—the other character in your scene—to agree with you, or yield to you, or do your bidding in one fashion or another.

In acting, every line you speak must stimulate a reaction or a response from the other characters. Metaphorically, your line must hook the attention of your acting partner and demand that your partner react in some way or other. A weak follow-through has no hook and consequently will catch no fish, no matter how beautifully cast.

Questions as Questions

The easiest lines to follow through are questions—simply because a question forces your partner to respond. When you ask, "Where are you going?" the question mark (which resembles a hook!) demands an answer and by so doing pulls your partner *and the audience* into your situation. When asked with real interrogative compulsion, questions create immediate drama; for that reason, they are used as the opening lines in a great number of dramatic masterpieces:

"When shall we three meet again?"—*Macbeth*

"What is it, children?"—*Oedipus the King*

"What's the matter?"—*Major Barbara*

"Now what's got into you?"—*The Misanthrope*

"Who's there?"—*Hamlet*

Because of their immediacy and their focus on the other person (the askee), questions can be played forcefully and followed through with rising—not falling—excitement. Yet beginning actors tend to play questions as statements and with falling inflections rather than the rising inflection that is both more dramatic and more true to real-life questioning. Many beginning actors will tend to ask

"Where are you going?"

rather than

"Where are you going?"

or

"Where are you go. ing?"

or

"Where are you go. ing?"

To the beginner, such a falling inflection may seem sophisticated. It certainly conveys a superior attitude, a disdain for the askee, and it can be useful when this is part of the play. But the falling inflection is both unlifelike and uninvolving—a flat statement rather than a demand for information. Try asking the question to a partner both ways, and notice how your partner responds to the various inflections.

The first rule of follow-through is to ask real questions. Give rising end-inflections as you look your partner—the askee—in the eye: *Demand an answer* with your inflection and your expression. Reach your hand out to your partner, encouraging a response. *Care* what that answer is. If you do this, everyone will hear the ends of your sentences, and you will create intense interaction onstage as you yield the floor—for the moment—to your acting partner.

Statements as Questions

Although it is unwise, most of the time, to turn your questions into statements, it is usually quite desirable to turn your statements into questions. Most statements are, in fact, invocations if not direct questions: Most statements "ask" the other person to agree, or to praise the speaker, or to accept the speaker's wishes, plans, or definitions. "I'm going out" is a statement responding to the previous question, but it also can be inflected to ask a variety of implicit questions:

I'm going out. (Do you want to come?)

I'm going out. (Would you rather I'd stay?)

I'm going out. (Are you going to ask me where?)

I'm going out. (Do you want to make plans for my return?)

Again, the upward inflection of the last word, the gaze and expression of the actor speaking, and the intentions played between actors can make the line an effective stage communication, not just a flat statement of fact. Follow-through is crucial here. The line must *lead* somewhere, must demand a reaction or a response. If you can find the hidden question in the otherwise declarative speech, you can hook the other actor—and through him or her, the audience—with the parting word or syllable.

◆ E X E R C I S E   24–1

Making Questions

Play the following lines to hook your partner by ending them with an upward inflection. Make each line into either a question or an implicit question (a request for a favorable response or confirmation). Put pressure on your partner: Play for the goal of your partner's favorable response.

1. Are you sure you won't have some oatmeal?

2. How long have I been back? Six months? Seven?

3. May one still speak of time?

4. It's time for me to go!

5. What are you thinking of?

6. How comest thou hither, tell me, and wherefore?

7. I hope you're not going to make a nuisance of yourself.

8. I said, go answer the door. What are you, deaf?

9. Seems to me you were staring through the window at me.

10. I believe my attitude must be deemed the proper one.

These are all lines from well-known plays. Number 4 is Vershinin's attempted leave-taking from Olga at the end of Chekhov's *Three Sisters*. As he is waiting for Masha to arrive, he doesn't leave. His line is a request for Olga to say "Wait, don't go."

Find reasons to make all these lines similar requests.

Statements as Statements

Some statements are intended to close a discussion or end a relationship. "I am going out!" spoken very firmly, with a downward inflection on the last syllable and perhaps a gesture of finality (pointing to the floor, shaking the fist), conveys the message that "as far as I am concerned, there is no more to be said on this subject!" The most powerful lines, said in this fashion, can literally leave the other character speechless:

LADY BRITOMART: Charles Lomax: if you can behave yourself, behave yourself. If not, leave the room. *[Lomax sits on the settee . . . quite overcome.]*

(GEORGE BERNARD SHAW, *MAJOR BARBARA*)

TOM: You'll go up, up on a broomstick, over Blue Mountain with seventeen gentlemen callers! You ugly—babbling old—*witch! [Amanda is . . . stunned and stupefied . . .]*

(TENNESSEE WILLIAMS, *THE GLASS MENAGERIE*)

LINDA: You're a pair of animals! Not one, not another living soul would have had the cruelty to walk out on that man in a restaurant!

BIFF *[Not looking at her]*:   Is that what he said?

LINDA: He didn't have to say anything. He was so humiliated he nearly limped when he came in.

HAPPY: But, Mom, he had a great time with us—

BIFF [*Cutting him off violently*]:   Shut up! [*Without another word, Happy goes upstairs.*]

(ARTHUR MILLER, *DEATH OF A SALESMAN*)

Those strong declarations provoke momentary speechlessness, as the original stage directions make clear. But you can use many such lines to attempt to "win going away." One of the differences between a scripted argument and a real one is that, in life, you are not trying to sustain dialogue; you are trying to win—and thereby end—the argument each and every time you speak. You are always trying to create "the last word." Strong follow-throughs create that lifelike situation; in an argument, the last word of your speech is played as what you hope will be the last word on the subject. Notice that Linda's "Shut up!" in the *Death of a Salesman* scene has both a strong attack and a strong follow-through, as mandated by the author's stage directions. It is a particularly powerful climactic moment of theatre for that reason.

Invocations to "shut up"—that is, speeches intended to leave the others speechless—generally conclude with a highly stressed and downwardly inflected terminal syllable, usually integrated with an authoritative physical action. The speeches need not be shouted (notice Lady Britomart's elegant tone). And they need not be successful. (Tom's denunciation of his mother actually fails, as he exits the room clumsily, breaking some of his sister's glass figurines as he goes.) Nevertheless, these lines should be played as your character's attempt to achieve victory: to make the disagreeing characters be quiet, recognize your character's correctness (or authority), and yield to your character's point of view or leadership. The hook of the last word should be intense, accompanied by continued eye contact (are they obeying?) and physical assurance.

◆ E X E R C I S E   24–2

Argument-Enders

Give the following speeches to a partner, foreclosing all discussion. Use downward inflections to close each speech. Try to make any reply almost impossible.

1. Get out!

2. The matter is closed!

3. I'll see you in court.

4. We shall never surrender.

5. Honor thy father and thy mother.

6. I may vomit.

Trail-Offs

Not all speeches have a hook at the end. Some speeches just trail off. Tennessee Williams wrote a play (*In the Bar of a Tokyo Hotel*) in which more than three-quarters of the speeches end in midsentence. Sometimes characters realize they've said all they really mean before they've completed their sentence. Sometimes they forget what they were saying while speaking; sometimes they just lapse into dreamland. Sometimes characters trail off in their speeches simply because they understand only too well that they needn't complete their words in order to communicate their thoughts.*

Playing trail-offs is dangerous for the beginner because the communication must be sustained on deeper and subtler levels, without the support of the follow-through hook. But the actor should be prepared for the occasional speech that winds into one's own reflections rather than hooking into the partner for a response.

Summary

Effective follow-through on the last words of your speech is a hook demanding a reaction from the other character. Questions hook your partner when they are asked with a rising inflection and direct eye contact. Statements can be used like questions to provoke a response. Statements calculated to provoke silence from the partner can be used as attempts to end arguments and force agreement. Expression, gaze, inflection (generally upward for questions, downward for statements), and appropriate physical actions or gestures are the ingredients of the successful hook.

---

* For a fuller discussion see my essay "Spoken Dialogue in Written Drama," in Robert Cohen, *More Power to You* (New York: Applause, 2002), pp. 78–81.

25

Line Linkage

Analyzing Dialogue

Attack and follow-through are not just isolated parts of your speeches; they are integrated elements of free-flowing dialogue. The link between lines of dialogue—between your partner's follow-through and your attack and vice versa—is a primary technical key to building a scene's intensity.

Study the following dialogue between Tom and his mother in *The Glass Menagerie*. (This is the Tennessee Williams play you may remember from Exercise 9–1. Tom is Laura's brother, and Amanda is their mother.)

AMANDA: . . . What are you looking at?

TOM: The moon.

AMANDA: Is there a moon this evening?

TOM: It's rising over Garfinkel's Delicatessen.

AMANDA: So it is! A little silver slipper of a moon. Have you made a wish on it yet?

TOM: Um-hum.

AMANDA: What did you wish for?

> ◫ LINKS
>
> *It's always through the mental links between one thought and another that an actor needs to find his way in order to achieve the consistency of the journey.*
>
> JANET SUZMAN

TOM: That's a secret.

AMANDA: A secret, huh? Well, I won't tell mine either. I will be just as mysterious as you.

TOM: I bet I can guess what yours is.

AMANDA: Is my head so transparent?

TOM: You're not a sphinx.

AMANDA: No, I don't have secrets. I'll tell you what I wished for on the moon. Success and happiness for my precious children! I wish for that whenever there's a moon, and when there isn't a moon, I wish for it, too.

TOM: I thought perhaps you wished for a gentleman caller.

AMANDA: Why do you say that?

TOM: Don't you remember asking me to fetch one?

AMANDA: I remember suggesting that it would be nice for your sister if you brought home some nice young man from the warehouse. I think that I've made that suggestion more than once.

TOM: Yes, you have made it repeatedly.

AMANDA: Well?

TOM: We are going to have one.

AMANDA: *What?*

TOM: A gentleman caller!

AMANDA: You mean you have asked some nice young man to come over?

TOM: Yep. I've asked him to dinner.

AMANDA: You really did?

TOM: I did!

AMANDA: You did, and did he—*accept?*

TOM: He did!

AMANDA: Well, well—well, well! That's—lovely!

TOM: I thought that you would be pleased.

AMANDA: It's definite, then?

TOM: Very definite.

AMANDA: Soon?

TOM: Very soon.

AMANDA: For heaven's sake, stop putting on and tell me some things, will you?

TOM: What things do you want me to tell you?

AMANDA: *Naturally* I would like to know when he's *coming!*

TOM: He's coming tomorrow.

AMANDA: *Tomorrow?*

TOM: Yep. Tomorrow.

AMANDA: But, Tom!

TOM: Yes, Mother?

AMANDA: Tomorrow gives me no time!

TOM: Time for what?

AMANDA: Preparations!

What actually transpires here? Very little, if you are looking only for plot or for strictly narrative information. You could write the events of this scene in one or two sentences. But Williams has written forty-six speeches. Why? To build a relationship. What transpires is an exchange of feelings between a son and a mother; it is a carefully arranged interchange of strokings, put-downs, requests for attention, attempts to charm, attempts to outwit, attempts to achieve dominance, attempts to surprise. The goals and tactics are more subtle than in many of the previous exercises, but they are nonetheless evident to the sensitive reader–actor. These speeches demonstrate the artistry of superbly crafted *dramatic* dialogue, as contrasted with narrative story-telling: The relationships are expressed through verbal interaction, not by description. Through GOTE.

You can analyze this interchange of dialogue for line-linkage characteristics. First, study the particular attack and follow-through techniques. Notice that the writing is peppered with questions (twenty of them), even questions that answer questions: ". . . tell me some things, will you?" "What things do you want me to tell you?" Words repeated from line to line develop the impact of a musical refrain: "You really did?" "I did!"

"You did, and did he—*accept?*" "He did!" Notice how Williams stresses attack and follow-through words in "*Naturally* I would like to know when he's *coming!*" Finally, notice how Williams uses pauses within the dialogue without interfering with the attacks or follow-throughs:

AMANDA: . . . and did he—*accept?*

TOM: He did!

AMANDA: Well, well—well, well! That's—lovely!

The three pauses, marked by dashes in the original, give Amanda time to reflect, to relish her victory, and to formulate her considered opinion of Tom's act, without slowing the attacks or trailing off the follow-throughs.

Rising End-Inflections

The key to linkage is that the follow-through of one speech sets up the attack of the next speech, much like a springboard sets up a dive. Attacking from a weak cue is like diving from a broken springboard.

Look at the first four lines of Williams's dialogue quoted at the beginning of this lesson: two questions and two answers. If the questions are posed and inflected as questions, the following speeches will be dramatically easy to attack. If they are simply stated with falling inflections, however, the following lines will be off to a deadly start. Witness

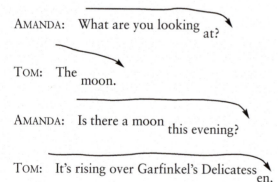

AMANDA: What are you looking at?

TOM: The moon.

AMANDA: Is there a moon this evening?

TOM: It's rising over Garfinkel's Delicatessen.

This is laundry-list acting. The speeches are simply read off as lines on a list; the inflections create no pressure on Tom, no interaction between him and his mother at the emotional level, and no compulsion for the audience to care. Compare with

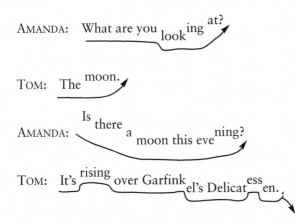

No attempt should be made to specify the "best" inflection of those speeches. Both ways of playing the lines are valid, in the sense that people can and do talk that way some of the time. The second way, however, is brighter, more energetic, more interactive, and builds more momentum. The rising inflections give a lift to the interchange and a life to the feelings that pass between the actors. The goals are clearer, the tactics more compelling, and the character's expectations are more lively (and lifelike).

In general, rising end-inflections are the technical key to keeping a scene alive and to developing the momentum of line linkage. They are crucial in *building* a scene because they lead somewhere. Rising inflections are lifelike as well as dramatic: In real life, if you are asking questions, arguing points, responding playfully, teasing, challenging, demanding, amusing, or persuading, you are probably using a preponderance of rising inflections in your speech. Conversely, if you are dutifully rote-reciting, you are probably using mostly falling (and weakly falling) inflections. Actors have a term for weak downwardly inflected cues: "He handed me a dead fish." Better to give your fellow actor a springboard: It is more lifelike, more stimulating, and more dramatic all at the same time.

Falling End-Inflections

Falling end-inflections can be used to create transitions: to end an argument, to change the subject or the mood, all without creating an unneeded pause.

AMANDA: So ^{on?}

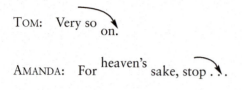

TOM: Very so on.

AMANDA: For heaven's sake, stop .

Tom's falling end-inflection on *soon* makes clear to Amanda that she'll get no further with him in that line of questioning, so she has to try another tack. Her "for heaven's sake" is a temporizing phrase, one that she can attack strongly and right on cue—but one that's noncommital enough to suggest she doesn't know exactly what she's going to say next. Noncommital phrases, such as interjections, give the character (and the actor) thinking time; they permit a rapid superficial attack while you are simultaneously summoning up your reserves for the stronger attack that immediately follows.

Attack Inflections

Attack inflections, or "front inflections," are the dive you make off the end-inflection springboard. The most exciting attack inflections come in at a *higher pitch* than the preceding end-inflection. Study this linkage:

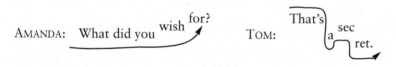

AMANDA: What did you wish for?   TOM: That's a secret.

Compare with this reading, common among beginning actors:

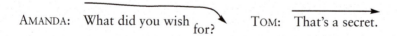

AMANDA: What did you wish for?   TOM: That's a secret.

An answer that "comes in on top of" (at a higher pitch than) an upward-inflected question shows a character seizing control of a scene rather than dutifully responding to an investigation. Attacks that come in low (in pitch, not in energy) can show something else. For example:

TOM: He's coming to morrow.

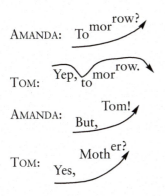

Tom's "Yep" suggests his excitement at having fulfilled her command, forcing her to deal with the immediacy of his action, forcing her to deal with him on his own terms. (Williams's use of the slang *yep* also suggests this.) Tom's "Yes," however, in response to her implied criticism ("But, Tom!") might begin on a low-pitched attack, perhaps in conscious self-mockery of his subservience.

Sometimes the lines call for a playful attack in your follow-through. For example:

AMANDA: Tomorrow gives me no time!

TOM: Time for what?

Tom's repetition of Amanda's follow-through words in his attack gives him an opportunity to repronounce her word, perhaps mocking her inflection (or accent, or note of hysteria) as he rephrases the issue. Note, of course, that Tom knows exactly what Amanda means by "no time." His line is only a rhetorical ploy—thus emphasizing the relationship between technical aspects of line linkage and real-life aspects of person-to-person (including child-to-parent) interaction.

Pauses

Pauses play an important role in dialogue. The plays of Samuel Beckett and Harold Pinter, for example, have become famous for their pauses. Look at the following scene from Pinter's *Betrayal:*

ROBERT: Speak.

JERRY: Yes.
    [Pause]

ROBERT: You look quite rough.
   [Pause]
     What's the trouble?
   [Pause]
     It's not about you and Emma, is it?
   [Pause]
     I know all about that.

JERRY: Yes. So I've . . . been told.

ROBERT: Ah.
   [Pause]
     Well, it's not very important, is it?

Five stipulated pauses, plus one ellipsis (. . .) indicating a sixth, in a scene of less than three dozen words, clearly demonstrate unusual line linkage. The pauses, however, can be integrated in the scene because of the intense interest each character has in the other's thoughts. The action continues through the silences with the intensity of each character's investigation of the other. Robert still must ask his questions so as to demand answers—that is, with rising inflections—and then Jerry's silences will be answer enough. The pauses that follow are nearly deafening. Even Robert's "Ah" is an invitation for Jerry to speak, and when he doesn't, we know Jerry's extreme discomfort by what he *doesn't* do.

Pauses serve as line linkage when they are not mere lapses or when they are not just a comfortable rest stop that the actor needs to collect his or her thoughts and feelings. "Rest stop" pauses, even momentary ones, become holes in the dialogue where the actor's energy falls out of the scene and the audience's attention begins to wander. In order to be effective, for both actor and audience, pauses must be part of the linkage between lines: They must betoken *something that does not happen* instead of just *nothing happening.*

Long Speeches

A long speech in a play also requires good line linkage, but here the linkage is between your first clause or sentence and your second, and so on until the end. A long speech is not simply a series of sentences; it is an integrated expression. If it is to have a lifelike vitality, the components of that expression must develop an integrated momentum.

Rising inflections are generally the means of sustaining a long speech. A rising inflection means that you have something more to say; it allows you to hold the stage and discourage other characters from contradicting or interrupting you while you're taking a quick breath.

Look at the following speech from Shaw's *Man and Superman:*

RAMSDEN: I will not allow you or any man to treat me as if I were a mere member of the British public. I detest its prejudices; I scorn its narrowness: I demand the right to think for myself. You pose as an advanced man. Let me tell you that I was an advanced man before you were born.

Were you to give that speech simply as a series of flat declarations, with your inflections falling at each period or semicolon (as most beginning actors would read it), your tirade would develop no momentum. It would be something like running a hundred-yard dash in stop-and-start bursts of ten yards each. Try reading it continuously, but with rising inflections on *public, prejudices, narrowness, myself,* and *man,* and end it with a dramatically falling inflection on *born.* The speech will be easier to sustain and will have a far greater impact on anyone—either on the stage with you or in the audience—who hears and watches it.

◆ E X E R C I S E   25–1

Line Linking

Select a six- or seven-line sequence from the Tom–Amanda scene. With a partner, analyze the sequence for line-linkage possibilities. Read through the lines, concentrating on finding the best possible linkings. Don't be afraid to devote your thinking to pure technical analysis. But as you grow comfortable repeating the sequence, try to understand how the inflections relate to the victories sought by your character, and to the tactics used. Make the inflections "real" by trying to be yourself. Are these inflections *yours?* They should become yours.

◆ E X E R C I S E   25–2

The Long Speech

Select any long speech from any prose play, preferably a speech that contains a sustained argument or explanation. In your study, try to find clauses or sentences that call for a rising end-inflection. Mark these in the text of the speech. Memorize and practice the speech until you feel comfortable with it. Deliver it. Are you able to sustain the argument or explanation?

Line Linking in Practice

Line linking, like any acting technique, should be learned in the classroom or studio to the point that it becomes an integral part of your acting instrument. During an acting performance, you should not be thinking about attacks, or follow-throughs, or inflections. You should be thinking solely about your goal and your GOTE. By that time, the technique of linking your lines to others should be unconscious and automatic. The better you understand the relationship between line linking onstage and line linking in daily life, the easier this technique will be.

Line linking is rarely addressed in American acting schools, although it is considered a rudiment of actor training in Great Britain. It has obvious dangers: Nothing will make your acting seem more artificial than concentrating on line linking to the exclusion of all other techniques. Expert line linking is the result of the stage intuition and sense of timing that come from experience. The technique is extremely important in the finest acting you will *see,* and it should become part of the finest acting you will *do* as well.

Summary

Line linking is not easily mastered, but some general principles can be understood and put into practice by the beginner: (1) Pauses are generally ineffective line links unless they indicate specific questions not answered or roads not taken. (2) Rising end-inflections provide a springboard for your partner's next line and stimulate energetic dialogue exchanges. Rising inflections sustain long speeches by acting as springboards for subsequent sentences. (3) Strong attacks that come in at a higher pitch ("on top of" a cue—particularly a cue that is itself upwardly inflected) are extremely powerful dramatically. (4) Line linkages that are theatrically effective ordinarily reflect the liveliness of real-life conversation or argument; they are rhetorical features of dialogue if the play's *characters* use rhetorical devices themselves.

LESSON

26

Scene Structure

Breaking Down a Script

Plays, when you see them in print or in manuscript, are customarily divided into acts and scenes, with the acts separated by intermissions and the scenes by brief pauses in the action. But in acting you must divide a play into even smaller units.

French scenes begin with the entrance or exit of each named character. They are called French scenes because in traditional French scripts they are actually so identified and numbered. Even when not so identified in print, however, they are useful in defining a two-person or three-person "scene" to do in acting class.

Subscenes are even more important for actors: They are units of action within a scene, or French scene, in which each character pursues, to some sort of conclusion, one primary goal. The subscene ends when that goal is accomplished, or abandoned, or (as is more common) reassessed and revised. Subscenes can run from a few seconds to several minutes.

Beats were defined first by Stanislavsky as single units of action within a scene or subscene. Persons initially understood Stanislavsky's term as corresponding to beats in a musical measure—although it has subsequently been suggested that Stanislavsky's Russian term was something more like "bits" and took its present English form only as spoken in his heavy Polish accent by the actor Richard Boleslavsky, who first brought Stanislavsky's teachings to America. In any event, the term *beats* has entered the actor's lexicon as representing individual units of action, which, in our terms, means those short units in which the actor employs a single tactic. In a subscene in which you are pursuing one goal, you might play several—or several dozen—individual beats.

Moments are usually construed as silent beats: moments of reflection when your character sizes up a situation before proceeding. "Take a moment here" is a direction not simply to pause but to plan your next active beat.

These terms are not precisely defined, of course, but they are useful in helping you divide any segment of dramatic material into workable units of varying meaning, intensity, and emotional charge.

Choosing a Scene to Do in Class

When you are choosing a scene for preparation and class presentation, the key criteria should be:

- Does the scene contain compelling *goals for each character?*

- Does the scene permit (or, better, does it stimulate) varied *tactics* for each character? Tactics that you can do? Tactics that will expand your range?

- Does the scene provide a reasonably intense and important *interaction* between all the characters in it? Involvement with *other* people?

- Does the scene have a clear *structure* of subscenes and beats?

In order to answer that last question, you will have to study elementary dramatic structure.

Structural Characteristics

The basic structure of dramatic action is usually described as an inverted V listing to starboard (to the right). A conflict begins with some sort of incitement, escalates slowly to a peak of intensity, and breaks suddenly into some sort of release. The peak of the intensity—the top of the inverted V—is called the climax, the incitement is called the inciting action, and the release is called the resolution or denouement. The inverted V leans to the right because the buildup to climax is slower than the collapse to resolution—and because building to climax sustains audience interest almost indefinitely, whereas climax and resolution provide an aesthetic and emotional jolt that are immensely satisfying but essentially short-lived.

This basic structure is characteristic of plays and scenes and of subscenes as well: It is absolutely fundamental to the drama. Thus a play leads up to a climax, but so does every scene and subscene, albeit in a more restrained fashion. You can graph the action of a play thus:

But if you look more closely at the lines in that graph, they are more accurately drawn as:

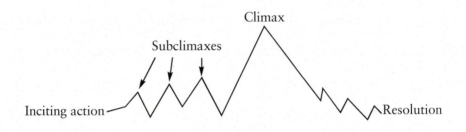

The climax of a play, or of a scene, is of primary importance to the actor: It is the moment of maximum dramatic tension, and it is the moment when the issues of the play are most clearly defined and the emotions of the characters are most nakedly exposed. In classical dramaturgy (the study of dramatic form), the climax may bring about *recognition* (of higher truth or truths), *reversal* (of fortunes or thinking), and a *catharsis* (a profusion of feelings leading finally to their purification or "cleansing"). Climaxes in tragedies have been awesome: Oedipus gouging out his eyes, Hamlet slaying his uncle, Phaedra taking a fatal poison. Climaxes of comedies are more subtle, but they are inevitably present in well-written and well-produced plays.

You must understand that dramatic structure is not merely a creation of the theatre, nor is it an artifice of dramatic writing. It is fundamental to life itself. It can be seen in explicit acts, such as sexual orgasm; in ritual enactments, such as the bullfight; in other aesthetic forms, such as the symphony; and in many public events, such as boxing matches, horse races, and auctions. In the long range the pattern can be seen in the cycle of life, in Shakespeare's "seven ages of man," and T. S. Eliot's "birth, and copulation, and death." That the pattern of life-rhythms can be represented by the aesthetic pattern of drama is one of the reasons the theatre has been such a satisfying art for more than twenty-five hundred years.

Transitions

Transitions are the imaginary lines between scenes, between subscenes, and between the beats of an actor's performance. Transitions are changes: of attitudes, of actions, of understandings. Nothing communicates information about your character so effectively as your transitions, because change is inherently noticeable and meaningful. Frowning conveys concern, for example, but not so vividly, nor so precisely, as a smile that suddenly *turns into* a frown. That process of turning into, or turning, signals what a character is thinking. Frowning, by itself, is merely the exhibition of an attitude. A smile turning into a frown is an action that can be construed as motivated, intended (if not intentional), and meaningful.

Sharp transitions, as a rule, are more dramatically effective than muddy ones, partly because of the theatre's demand for compression and clarity and partly because of the desirability of dramatic variety. The closer you can define the moment in a scene when love turns to hate or the desire to conquer turns to the desire to escape, the more precisely and vividly you can play the actions on either side of the transition and the more exciting you can make the transition itself. Thus defining transitions closely in your performance, and playing them sharply and boldly, is an important aspect of acting technique.

Scene Breakdown

We can study the elements of scene structure by looking at another passage from Williams's *Glass Menagerie*: the French scene in Scene 3 between Tom and Amanda in which Tom argues with his mother about his lack of independence.

Subscene 1

TOM: What in Christ's name am I—

AMANDA *[Shrilly]*:   Don't you use that—

TOM: Supposed to do!

AMANDA: Expression! Not in my—

TOM: Ohhh!

AMANDA: Presence! Have you gone out of your senses?

TOM: I have, that's true, *driven* out!

AMANDA: What is the matter with you, you—big—big—IDIOT!

Subscene 2

TOM: Look!—I've got *no thing*, no single thing—

AMANDA: Lower your voice!

TOM: In my life here that I can call my OWN! Everything is—

AMANDA: Stop that shouting!

TOM: Yesterday you confiscated my books! You had the nerve to—

AMANDA: I took that horrible novel back to the library—yes! That hideous book by that insane Mr. Lawrence. *[Tom laughs wildly.]* I cannot control the output of diseased minds or people who cater to them— *[Tom laughs still more wildly.]* BUT I WON'T ALLOW SUCH FILTH BROUGHT INTO MY HOUSE! No, no, no, no, no!

Subscene 3

TOM: House, house! Who pays rent on it, who makes a slave of himself to—

AMANDA *[Fairly screeching]:*   Don't you DARE to—

TOM: No, no, I mustn't say things! *I've* got to just—

AMANDA: Let me tell you—

TOM: I don't want to hear any more! *[He tears the portieres open and goes out, Amanda following.]*

Subscene 4

AMANDA: You *will* hear more, you—

TOM: No, I won't hear more, I'm going out!

AMANDA: You come right back in—

TOM: Out, out, out! Because I'm—

AMANDA: Come back here, Tom Wingfield! I'm not through talking to you!

TOM: Oh, go—*[He is interrupted by Laura's cry from the other room, beginning a new subscene—and French scene.]*

The French scene between Tom and Amanda is divided here into four subscenes. The primary goals for each character in each subscene might be described as follows:

Tom

Subscene 1: Shame Amanda for "expelling" him.

Subscene 2: Get control of his personal property.

Subscene 3: Get credit (and with it, control) for paying the rent.

Subscene 4: Hurt her deeply, so that he can win next time.

Amanda

Subscene 1: Clean up Tom's language.

Subscene 2: Clean up Tom's behavior.

Subscene 3: Get control of her house.

Subscene 4: Get control of her son.

Note that the goals described here are positive and highly interactional. Tom's goal in subscene 4 is not just "to leave." If all he wants is to leave, he would just leave. To say "I'm going out!" is itself an action, independent of going out, and it has a goal beyond merely self-describing one's behavior. If we remember that Tom's father also left Amanda, we realize how threatening and painful his words are to her—wholly apart from his actual departure. Similarly, Amanda's goal in subscene 2 is not "to justify herself," or "to get angry at Tom." She doesn't need justice, and she doesn't want to be angry. What she wants is for her son to be obedient and chaste. You might even say her goal is to make her son an innocent baby.

Each of the subscenes has several beats, approximately two per subscene per character, which can be described by rough identification and a quote or paraphrase of the relevant lines (some of which never get spoken) or actions:

Tom

1. Rhetorical question: What am I supposed to do?

2. Accusation: You're driving me crazy!

3. Abject irony: Nothing here is mine.

4. Mocking *(laughing wildly):* You are ridiculous!

5. Heroic martyrdom: I pay for this house! I am a slave!

6. Pretend rage *(tearing the portieres):* I'll destroy this house!

7. Threat of abandonment: I'm going out!

8. Curse: Go to Hell!

Amanda

1. Elegant chiding: Don't use that expression!

2. Rhetorical question: Have you lost your mind?

3. Maternal command: Lower your voice! Stop that shouting!

4. Frighten Tom with ugliness: horrible . . . hideous

5. Frighten Tom with illness: insane . . . diseased

6. Frighten Tom with immorality: Filth!

7. Shame Tom as usurper: Don't you dare!

8. Regain rational authority: You will hear more!

9. Regain maternal authority: Come back here, Tom Wingfield!

A well-orchestrated pattern of beats creates the variety of actions, tactics, and interactions that characterize a good scene or subscene. In such a scene, the acting of each character evolves and changes from moment to moment; it doesn't simply pour out in a single, monolithic (and monotonous) rant or in a tedious whining complaint. Finding, distinguishing, and playing the scene's individual beats, and the structure that organizes them into a dramatic pattern, makes your acting specific rather than generalized and compelling rather than melodramatic.

As to the structure of this scene, notice how Williams has carefully provided each actor with climactic expressions, sometimes with intentionally incorrect grammar, sometimes with capitalized insults, sometimes with a rapid stage cross, and finally with Tom about to swear at his mother, and Laura—a character new to the scene—desperately entering the conflict and raising the level of tension by one full psyche. Each of these climaxes tops the previous one; this is the way arguments—and scenes—are built.

Notice also how Williams, one of the most skilled writers of American stage dialogue, builds the rising intensity within the subscenes. Tom first laughs "wildly" and then "still more wildly," thus increasing the level of tension during his mother's speech. Repetitions are used to escalate effect rather than to convey added content. Sometimes the escalation is in the words themselves. Reverse Amanda's "hideous book" with her previous "horrible novel" and you will see that the line loses punch: "Hideous book" is a stronger pejorative because *hideous* is more specific and extreme and *book* has harsh consonants. This intensification is not accidental. More often, however, the escalating repetitions such as Tom's "I'm going out! . . . Out, out out!" and Amanda's "No, no, no, no, no!" demand a buildup in the actor's delivery. The buildup in these repeated words can be developed in many ways, but they must build. Monotonous delivery of any of these lines would defeat the dramatic impact of the argument and destroy its realism.

Transitions occur quite naturally between subscenes. They do not necessarily require pauses, or "moments," but pauses are often effective. In the transition between the first two subscenes, for example:

AMANDA: . . . you—big—big—IDIOT!

TOM: Look!—I've got *no thing* . . .

Amanda's climax, built by the escalating repetition of *big* and the all-capitalized and exclamation-pointed *idiot,* is a terrifying insult when delivered from mother to son. It forces Tom to assess just how deeply he has alienated his mother. He might well take a moment to collect himself, because when he speaks, he introduces a new argument, one perhaps he has not raised before but has ruminated about. Clearly, the pause after "Look!" is an opportunity for Tom to cut back his intensity, to try to speak calmly instead of shouting. That his mother then accuses him of shouting becomes all the more revealing, and poignant, and counterproductive, and soon he is back up there, shouting as before.

Building to a climax, sharpening transitions, and playing beats and moments to their fullest potential is the technical side of good dramatic acting. Technique echoes reality, and it provides a good shape for dramatic dialogue: It brings out the structure of well-written plays and even gives a sense of structure to poorly written ones. Finding the structure in a scene is not an easy task, but the ingredients are known and their outline can be traced. Being able to define how a scene is put together is a necessary first step to making the scene *work*. It is necessary, in acting, not merely to know what a scene is about, or what a character is about, but how a scene or a character can be made to reveal what it's about.

◆ E X E R C I S E   26–1

Scene Structure in Action

Learn the *Glass Menagerie* scene with a partner. Follow the breakdown of the scene closely. Subsequently, in class, do the scene in unison: half the class playing Tom, the other half playing Amanda. Try to blend in with the majority in terms of rising and falling intensities, the duration of pauses, and the rising/falling inflections. Repeat three times. Then, with a new partner, play the scene "cold."

Did new structural elements assert themselves from the unison experience? Don't try to copy anyone; do try, however, to come to grips with what seem to be universal structural elements in the dialogue.

Summary

Scenes are not monolithic; they are structured dramatic material, and defining the structure is part of the actor's task. Scenes can be divided into French scenes, subscenes, beats, and moments, with transitions defining the beginning and end of each. The orchestration of these into a building and climaxing pattern creates dramatic form, builds and sustains audience interest, and delivers an aesthetic "jolt" that is always satisfying and often cathartic. This structure is inherent in a good dramatic text, but much of it is supported by the actor, and much is created by the actor.

27

Building a Scene

Building and Topping

A scene is built both by the depth of the interplay between actors and by the incorporation of good structural builds in that playing.

The climax of a scene—and the subclimaxes that precede it—are the focal points of the scene. These are the *highs,* in actor parlance, and it is your job to make the most of them.

But structure demands more than climaxes, and a scene that is simply a series of highs becomes a shouting match and little else. In order to have highs you must have lows, and in order to get from lows to highs and back again you must have builds and cutbacks.

Much of the structuring of a scene will come through improvisation and spontaneous rehearsal. But some of it will come through conscious effort. You must be prepared to make that effort.

A *build* means rising intensity, usually signified by increased volume, increased pitch range (particularly on the high side), and more vigorous physical activity. Building is simply a function of active goal-pursuit and GOTE-pursuit: When you are trying to win, you try harder and harder as the action continues; you escalate your efforts. *Topping* is line-by-line building. A line that tops the previous one is stronger in delivery: usually louder, sharper, angrier (in an argument), and more physical. In a standard build, one line tops another in serial fashion. Actors should feel very comfortable with standard builds, for they are the basic building blocks of most dramatic scenes.

◆ E X E R C I S E   27–1

Standard Build I

Play this scene: You are a boxing referee counting out the champion who has just been knocked out by the challenger. Imagine a crowd cheering you on and the challenger dancing excitedly beside you as you count: "One, two, three, four, five, six, seven, eight, nine, ten—and the winner is [use your own name here]!" Make each number more excited than the last.

◆ E X E R C I S E   27–2

Standard Build II

Play this scene with your partner. You and a partner are bidding at an auction for something you both dearly want. With each bid, you feel you are getting closer to clinching the sale. Try to top your partner with each bid, and try to win the auction each time.

YOU: Ten dollars.

YOUR PARTNER: Twenty dollars!

YOU: Thirty dollars!

YOUR PARTNER: Forty dollars!

Keep bidding to one hundred dollars, topping each line. Try bidding to two hundred dollars.

◆ E X E R C I S E   27–3

Standard Build III

You and a partner exchange the following dialogue, topping each other every time.

YOU: Be quiet.

YOUR PARTNER: You be quiet.

YOU: You be quiet.

YOUR PARTNER: You be quiet.

YOU: You be quiet.

YOUR PARTNER: You be quiet!

Try eight exchanges, then ten, then twelve. How far can you go? (But don't destroy your voice!) You can play variations on this build, such as "You will!" "I won't!" or "Yes!" "No!"

In doing those exercises, you quickly see that a straight build cannot go on very long; you quickly reach the top of your vocal range (and in scene acting you would reach the top of an emotional/verbalizing range as well). No further building is possible. There are two techniques to prevent that. The first is to develop more subtle gradations of topping; well-trained actors can "go up the ladder with smaller steps" and can sustain a straight build in finely modulated ways. That ability, of course, requires considerable training and experience. The second technique you can put into practice immediately: cutting back.

Cutting Back

A cutback is a sudden drop in intensity—at least in expressed intensity—that allows you to start building again. The cutback cannot be arbitrary, however; it must come from some change of approach, and usually from some minor subclimax in the action or argument. The four subscenes of *The Glass Menagerie* studied in Lesson 26 show four builds followed by cutbacks, each build reaching a bit higher than the last. On a larger scale, this is the ordinary pattern of drama.

Each cutback must be tied to some sort of realization, or reconsideration, within the scene itself. In the auction exercise, for example, imagine that after "eighty dollars," you stop bidding, pull out your wallet, check the "secret compartment," and then with a smile whisper "ninety dollars." You have de-escalated the intensity in a classic cutback, from which you and your partner can start the build all over again, climaxing at a final sale of "two hundred dollars" without losing the overall build or losing your voices.

Getting on Top

Topping the other actor's line—and topping it while leaving both yourself and your partner with somewhere yet to go—is one of the great skills of acting, as it exemplifies your goal orientation and fulfills, momentarily at least, some of your character's expectations.

Volume and pitch are the first ingredients of getting on top. You can hear this in music, where a composer builds excitement into a score by adding voices, adding instruments, and raising the volume and pitch. Physicalizing is another way: In an American musical, the classic build progresses from solo to chorus to solo plus chorus, to "Everybody dance." Listen to some of the great musical builds in music literature: The "Dies Irae" from Verdi's *Requiem* for its rising and apocalyptic exhilaration; Ravel's *Bolero* for its steadily growing sensuality. An actor who could master such builds would be able to achieve near-miracles onstage.

As an actor you can build an argument by becoming more precise, by lengthening the vowels, by getting more reckless, by risking more tactically, by showing more feeling, by loosening your tie, by grabbing a knife, by standing up, by standing on your toes, by stepping forward, by making a noise, by slamming your fist on the table, by "biting" your words, by turning over a piece of furniture, by smashing your glass in the fireplace. Conversely, you can build a seduction scene by getting sultrier and sultrier, by letting your voice grow more and more liquid, your body more sensual and evocative, and your actions more and more fetching and charming.

Pacing a Build

Line linking is crucial in building, since lines that build *must* be springboards for each other. Look at the exchanges between Tom and Amanda in both Lesson 25 and Lesson 26. See how the builds—fairly obvious in each case—evolved from closely linked lines—indeed, from overlapping lines in the second of those scenes. In general, pauses kill builds, and therefore pauses, again in general, should be reserved for transitions and cutbacks.

Accelerating tempos are characteristic of a build; this occasionally means speeding up line delivery, but more often it means speeding up cue pickups. A scene reaching its climax is like an argument reaching its breaking point: Both people are simply *dying* to speak; they can't wait to be *let* into the conversation—they *break in* instead. This accelerated tempo speeds up the blood and induces a recklessness that is also characteristic of the emotional exuberance of climactic confrontations. Think of a bullfight, which reaches its peak of excitement as the bull gets closer and closer to the matador and passes in shorter and shorter (faster and faster) lunges. So does a scene build to its highest level of intensity.

Cutting back—on pacing, on volume—is, as we have seen, usually necessary between subscenes, following climaxes and subclimaxes, and between some beats. But cutting back too quickly and too often is a trap for the beginning actor. Cutting back is (unfortunately) a comfortable thing to do: It gives you some breathing space and thinking time; it takes the pressure off. But we say "unfortunately" because too much cutting back slackens the dramatic tension of a scene, undercutting its dramatic structure. It may be easy for you, but it's bad for your scene and for your character's goal-oriented attack. So *cut back only for aggressive (goal-oriented, GOTE-oriented) reasons*. Not because you're tired, or under too much pressure from the scene, but because it will help you to win your goal.

Please don't try to "justify" cutting back because "you do it in life." You can find plenty of reasons to be an uninteresting actor if you look hard enough. Remember, if a bull doesn't escalate its anger and intensity during the bullfight, sharpening its tactics and speeding up its charges, the promoter gets a new bull. If an actor fails in the same way—in the professional theatre, at least—the director gets a new actor.

Complex Builds

Straight builds—with escalating volume, rising pitch, and accelerating tempos—cannot be sustained indefinitely, and they cannot simply follow each other like a string of sausages, not even like an ascending string of sausages. In addition to straight builds, the theatre has much more subtle builds that could be called complex.

Complex builds require a change of *tactics* within a build.

◆ E X E R C I S E   27–4

I Detest Monday

Build the following line: "I detest Monday, Tuesday, Wednesday, Thursday, Friday, Saturday, and Sunday!"

Now build this line: "I adore Monday, Tuesday, Wednesday, Thursday, Friday, Saturday, Sunday."

Notice that building the first line requires a growing sense of displeasure, whereas building the second requires an increased sensitivity and enjoyment. Each line heads toward a different climax or end point. As an actor, you should work to differentiate all seven steps—in both directions—by degree of intensity.

◆ E X E R C I S E   27–5

I Detest January

Substitute months of the year for days of the week, increasing the steps of Exercise 27–4 from seven to twelve.

◆ E X E R C I S E   27–6

Come Here

With a partner, build the following exchange:

YOU: Come here.

YOUR PARTNER: No.

YOU: Come here.

YOUR PARTNER: No.

YOU: Come here.

YOUR PARTNER: No.

YOU: Come here.

YOUR PARTNER: No.

You can play the "Come here" dialogue as a straight build, or you can vary the tactics. In this case, varying the tactics is the best solution if the tactics build—that is, you first invite, then command, then wheedle, then threaten. Or you could invite, wheedle, threaten, and seduce. In either event, the change of tactics permits a varied approach within a straight and continuous build.

Building can also employ a change of rhetoric or tone of voice. A parent arguing with a child will frequently escalate the argument by talking in a louder and lower voice, and by employing the child's full name: "Jonathan Mark Spencer, you come right in here!" Increasing formality, with rising emotional drive, builds a scene. Molière, the French comic dramatist of the seventeenth century (and one of the best dramatic craftsmen of all time), used this device frequently. Look at this straight build of a lovers' quarrel from *The Bourgeois Gentleman* as it shifts from simple banter to the more formal to the overinflated:

BANTER: Well, then explain.

No, I've said enough.

Tell me.

No, I have nothing to tell.

MORE FORMAL: Have a heart.

No.

I beg you.

Leave me alone.

I implore you.

Go away from me.

OVERINFLATED: Speak to me!

Absolutely not!

Enlighten my suspicions!

I can't be bothered.

Ameliorate my anxiety!

I have no wish to do so.

◆ E X E R C I S E   27–7

Building Molière

Use the speeches from *The Bourgeois Gentleman* to practice building dialogue exchanges. Involve your movements and expression, not merely your voice.

Once again, building is something that happens in life, not just in the theatre. If you are pursuing a goal, and you find obstacles in your way, you have to work harder to win what you want. If at first you don't succeed—and you won't, or the play will be over after the first line—then you have to not only try, try again but try *harder*. Try *better*. Arguments escalate precisely because the other person doesn't agree with you. Seductions intensify because the object of your desire doesn't immediately run into your arms.

Whatever you strive for in the theatre, you are bound to encounter resistance (in dramaturgy it's called conflict). Your efforts to overcome the resistance are akin to your efforts to top your partner and thereby build your scenes. Building a scene, then, shows most of all that you *care*. A scene that doesn't build not only seems dramatically flat but seems to be about someone (you, if you're the culprit) who doesn't care whether she or he wins or loses, who doesn't care about the outcome or achieving a goal. The person who cares *will* escalate the arguments and actions, *will* top all objection and counter all resistance, *will* explode right to the climax and catharsis if necessary to get what he or she wants. This intensification is what building requires and what building is; it is not simply a mechanical fact of good dramaturgy but a reflection of deeply felt human interaction.

GET THAT PERSON

The only thing you can bring to the stage is your will to get that other person to do your bidding.

WILLIAM H. MACY

Summary

Scenes don't just happen—they are built. Building means finding the structure of the scene and playing the builds up to the subclimaxes and climaxes. Scenes build by increased volume, raised pitch, increased commitment and concern, and accelerated tempos. Experienced actors can make straight builds of infinitely subtle gradations; beginning actors should start the process of learning how to make those small steps toward climactic heights. No builds can be sustained indefinitely, however, so actors must also learn to cut back from time to time, usually between subscenes, after subclimaxes, or both, to give themselves room to build again. Builds can also be varied and complex, building on tactics and tones and rhetorical formulation rather than straight volume, pitch, and intensity. In addition to matching mechanical matters of dramaturgy, building is lifelike. It conveys the impression of characters who care deeply and are committed to the winning of deeply desired goals.

LESSON

28

Creating a Monologue

Going It Alone

There will come a time when you are asked to prepare and present a dramatic monologue. This is a speech from a play, or a collection of dramatic speeches that you can effectively link together, that is performed with nobody else onstage. Sometimes this speech will be an excerpt from a play that, if fully staged, would have other characters onstage at that point. In other cases, the speech was originally meant to be spoken directly to the audience, with no other characters onstage at the time. In this situation it is also called a soliloquy.

Why do actors perform monologues? For one reason, it is a simple way to create an acting exercise without having to involve anyone else. For another, the monologue is the most frequently used form of audition piece, either for actors seeking a role in a play or admission to an acting school. Most graduate acting schools, for example, require at least two contrasting monologues (ordinarily one from a classical play and one from a modern play) as part of the application procedure. And so acting classes often assign monologues as part of the basic training. But monologues are particularly difficult and raise some fundamental acting problems.

The basic problem of the monologue is: To whom is it addressed? Put another way, who is the Other of your character's GOTE; of your Goal-Other-Tactics-Expectation formula?

The answer is that in every monologue you *must* identify an Other person or persons to whom you are speaking, and you must then play your monologue to that person or persons. Monologues can never be simply or wholly self-addressed. Even when you are "thinking out loud," you must be thinking out loud "to" or "for" someone else.

The Monologue to Someone Else

In most cases in which you perform, as a monologue, a speech from a play, you should be speaking to persons whose presence you imagine. In this case, it is first necessary to physically "place" the imaginary person or persons in the scene with you as though they were, indeed, "in the scene (scenery) with you." In other words, locate them on the "set."

Second, it is necessary to devise and create specific tactics that you will play to these imaginary people and also to "create," again through your imagination, their reaction to your tactics—so that you will be able to adjust your evolving goals and tactics to their "reactions."

Third, it is necessary, when performing a monologue, to "really try" to win your goals through these imaginary people. To perform your tactics as vigorously, and as passionately, as you would if there were a "real" acting partner responding to you. To look your imaginary partners in the eye, and to stare them down, or to beckon them forward. This, of course, takes sort of a "double imagination," and it requires that you not only act your part but imagine your partner's part. But all of this is completely in line with the nature of acting.

The Soliloquy

A soliloquy, in contrast, does not have any identifiable "other person" to whom you are clearly speaking. Don't think that this is only a problem in Shakespearean acting. The soliloquy has a long history reaching right up to the most modern theatre. Sophocles, Molière, Chekhov, Brecht, Miller, Williams, Beckett, O'Neill, (Lanford) Wilson, Kushner, LaBute, and a probable majority of present-day American playwrights employ soliloquies. So you will inevitably have to face the question of whom the soliloquy is addressed to.

In the works of Shakespeare, Brecht, Wilson, and many contemporary authors, the soliloquy may often be addressed directly to the audience, thereby making the audience the other. In these soliloquies, you can look the audience (singly and collectively) in the eye and employ tactics (charm, threaten, seduce) directly on them just as you would on an acting partner or partners. In these cases the soliloquy may be called a *direct address*. Iago's soliloquies in *Othello* and Richard's in *Richard III,* for example, are clearly meant to be spoken directly to a live audience, and the characters' obvious goals are to solicit audience admiration and support. It is my personal (if admittedly debatable) opinion that *all* of Shakespeare's soliloquies may be so addressed and that Hamlet, for example, is seeking a certain audience feedback in his soliloquies: "To be or not to be, that is the question [don't you think?]."* This position, at the least, can make for very active and engaging soliloquies, as the actor can simply play the GOTE directly to the audience and engage in a full range of tactical interactions with audience members.

In more realistic plays like Chekhov's, however, characters are usually not expected to look the audience directly in the eye, and the soliloquies are generally thought of as "thinking out loud." It might be useful in these works to ponder what reasons people have for thinking out loud—why *you* ever think out loud, if you do.

Sometimes thinking out loud is a form of prayer. In these cases you might be described as speaking to God or to God's representative. Some characters—Konstantine, for example, in Chekhov's *Seagull*—could be said to be soliloquizing to their literary muse. Others could be speaking to ghosts or spirits: to one of their parents in heaven or to their "guardian angel." Most people—and most dramatic characters—can be said to feel themselves at times in the presence of a set of characters from somewhat spiritual worlds: divinities, deceased ancestors, momentarily absent role models and loved ones. Soliloquies can be addressed to these spiritual creatures.

Sometimes thinking out loud is a form of rehearsal. You might be preparing a speech you hope to give to someone sometime: an invitation to a date or the climax of a yet unspoken argument. In this case you are speaking to a real person—who is simply not present.

Sometimes thinking out loud is a trial musing-over of possibilities to see "how they sound." Putting vaguely formed ideas into words, and then into spoken words, can be the process by which we organize our thoughts. In these cases the walls—the environment—can be a sounding board that helps focus your mind. (In Willy Russell's one-woman play *Shirley Valentine,* the sole character directly addresses "wall" in the first act, which takes place in a kitchen, and "rock" in the second act, which takes place on a beach.)

A character's "musings" may be addressed to a pseudo-audience. Chekhov frequently allows characters to soliloquize in the presence of deaf or sleeping characters. Do they hear and understand? We—and the soliloquizing characters—don't know exactly. So the soliloquy is a working-out of ideas, posing as a kind of nonsense lullaby to a less than fully perceptive character.

---

* Given that an actor at the front of the stage in Shakespeare's Globe Theatre was surrounded by audience by a full 270 degrees left to right, and from the third gallery down to his feet top to bottom, there would be almost no place he could look *without* facing members of the audience. See *Acting Two,* page 367, for more on this.

In all cases, however, the soliloquy will take on resonance and dramatic meaning to the extent that it is played *to someone else* (a god, a muse, a wall, a nonpresent loved one, as a rehearsal to a nonpresent enemy) than just "to yourself." That outside presence will engage your GOTE: It will create an Other, an expectation and a goal for the speech, and it will induce you to employ tactics in the goal's pursuit. No soliloquy or monologue should be simply a meditation or be self-absorbing.

MONOLOGUES

There is really no such thing as soliloquy. For example, you can't talk to yourself: you talk to the people next to you intensely, and when you've exhausted them you burst into passionate discourse with the audience and worry them silly with the state of mind you're in.

IAN JUDGE

Playing a Monologue or Soliloquy

Choose a monologue in which you can define at least one "other" person or persons to whom you are speaking: persons whose opinions you *care* about; persons whose actions can help you achieve specific goals.

"Place" those persons in specific locations. If you are staging your monologue before an audience, locate the persons between you and the audience, or in the audience, or behind the audience. Make the location very specific; have an exact sight-mark for each character and imagine the sight-mark (an "exit" sign, say) as being (looking like, acting like) the character.

Distinguish the "placed" persons by locating each on a different side of the room. If you are speaking both to the (present) Dauphin and to your (spiritual) God (as, for example, in a monologue from *St. Joan*), place "the prince" as seated to your left and place "God" above to your right.

Use the audience as a character only in a soliloquy where you are addressing the audience as themselves. Do not, for example, use members of the audience as actual named characters in the play.

Divide the monologue or soliloquy into subscenes, beats, and transitions, paying attention to rising action and climaxes, just as in the scene preparation in the last lesson.

Prepare and perform your monologue or soliloquy as you would a scene, building your tactics, arguments, and appeals as you would with a two-person dialogue. Plan to "top" the imagined reactions of your imaginary acting "partners." Don't just act: Interact. The authority of your monologue presentation will, in good measure, be a function of how well you can make us believe you are really talking with and listening to "other" people (or gods, or ghosts) and are trying to put real pressure on them.

◆ E X E R C I S E   28–1

Prepare a Monologue

Go back to Exercise 7–2. Choose one of the longer speeches, read the play (or at least the scene) the speech comes from, and prepare it as a class monologue. Follow the principles described above.

Choose a monologue (long speech) from any play: prepare and present it. Choose a soliloquy from any play; prepare and present it.

Summary

Monologues and soliloquies are important acting exercises. In both, it is necessary to identify and create—through your imaginative resources—the "other" person or persons directly or indirectly addressed in the speech. Soliloquies should be interactions with these imaginary "others"; they should convey your character's goals, tactics, and expectations; they should not be merely meditations, no matter how eloquent or articulate.

L'Envoi

L'envoi is a rather quaint literary term for the author's last words—sort of like saying "The ball is now in *your* court." It is also an opportunity for the author to return to the first person, which I now choose to do.

The problems of acting transcend culture, theatrical experience, and educational background; they surface in all actors almost all the time. Good actors lick their problems by training, by craft, by instinct, and by dedication. They put their time where it belongs: in their work. I have never known harder-working actors than veteran professionals. The more experienced they are, the more time and effort they put into their acting, and the more serious they are about matters of craft and technique.

The lessons in *Acting One* can be covered in a one-year course. Better, they can be explored in some depth in a one-and-a-half or a two-year course, interspersed with scenework. There are some lessons that actors could return to well into their flourishing careers; without question, areas touched on here will remain problems for some actors throughout their lives.

To study acting as a humanistic activity, as a means of self-expression and of developing self-confidence, to study the art of theatre as exemplified by the actor and by the acting process: These are laudable goals. To a great extent, they are *my* goals. To study acting with the idea of making your livelihood as an actor—an artist of the theatre—is an equally laudable goal but an infinitely more difficult one.

My l'envoi is addressed primarily to those actors who want to go on, beyond *Acting One,* to the possibilities of a professional career. This career requires great dedication and sacrifice. The hours are long, the working conditions dreary, the life perplexing, the opportunities few, and the rewards seemingly always around the corner. The pay is bad (when there is pay), and the work is irregular (when there is work). The politics are often pervasive and unfair.

REALLY TRY

Your work should be like a light bulb. You're on your tippy toes trying to screw it into the socket on the ceiling but you can't quite get it all the way. I think it's the same in acting. You've got to be reaching. And it's always got to be imperfect.

DUSTIN HOFFMAN

To overcome these conditions you will need a solid acting approach that you can "turn on" in an instant at an audition, a cold reading, an interview, a rehearsal, or as a hurriedly summoned understudy.

You will need working habits that are concentrated and efficient, and you will need the freedom to employ them twenty-four hours a day—*any* day—when necessary.

You will need an instrument that is the world's best: Lacking that, you need one that is very close to being the world's best. There are only a few hundred career actors, after all; there are hundreds of *thousands* of acting students, community actors, and retired football players and rock stars.

You will need a technique that is fully developed, that goes into operation silently and unconsciously and seems unforced, and that clings to your approach like skin to a snake.

You will need to feel comfortable in periods other than your own, and with styles of speaking, moving, gesturing, and behaving that at first sight seem strange, even ridiculous. You will need to feel comfortable performing in forums quite unlike your acting classroom: in big open amphitheatres, cramped television studios, in-the-round experimental theatres, and in a casting director's office. Certainly, if you want to be a stage actor, performing in a varied repertoire of characters and styles, you will need training of the sort explored in my text following this one, *Acting Two*.

You will need to understand different sorts of characters: fat people, thin people, scared people, proud people, rulers, slaves, winners, losers, mutes, mutants. And you will have to learn how much of *you* is in them—and how much of them is in you. And you must learn how to show all this without fear of discovery, but rather with joy in the freedom of your fearlessness.

You will also have to know how to manage a career and build an art at the same time; how to stay fed and intellectually satisfied on a day-to-day and year-to-year basis.

You will need a love for the theatre: for plays as well as playing, for ideas, for words, for deeply drawn characters and feelings, for the rhythm of dialog, for physical expression, for the human body, for poetry, for nuance, for imagery, and for life itself and all that it can teach us.

You will need the most demanding and most exacting standards—for *yourself*—and a willingness to reach for them always.

If you have these things, and also the ineffables of talent and luck, you may have a chance. If you have them in prodigious quantity, you may have a good chance. I certainly wish you well. This book is dedicated to your success.

ACTING TWO

Introduction

Acting Two is, as the overall introduction to this volume explains, a continuation of the lessons in *Acting One*. But while *Acting One* is devoted to basic acting—how to act and interact with others in modern plays, set within your own general area of life experience and using speech patterns comparable to your own—*Acting Two* is devoted to how to act in *any* play, including works set in different eras, written in different theatrical styles, and employing wholly different modes of speech and types of characters than you have ever experienced in your everyday life.

How do you do all this without sacrificing the truth and authenticity in interactions that you learned to create in *Acting One?* That is the overriding concern of *Acting Two.*

Characters in stylized plays, as in realistic ones, are driven by goals, which they seek to achieve through interactions with others. And in so doing they use tactics and develop expectations that make them humanly unique. And even though Aeschylus's Prometheus, Shakespeare's Puck and Pyramus, and Barrie's Peter Pan are creatures of worlds other than our own, playing them requires getting their GOTE—the basic principles of Goal, Other, Tactics and Expectation explored in *Acting One*—just as if they were envisioned as wholly human characters like Tom Wingfield and Linda Loman. *Acting Two,* therefore, does not simply ask you to put on the artificial styles of playwrights from other eras or inclinations, or the outward form of a character radically unlike yourself. Rather, it asks you to *make an extension of yourself* into worlds unlike your own, and into characters who inhabit these worlds differently, perhaps, than you would.

Doing this is not as hard as it might at first appear. Imagine taking a trip to a different country where people are speaking a different language or a different dialect of your own language. They have different customs, obey different laws, are paid by and buy goods in a different economy. They may also drive on a different side of the street, laugh at different sorts of jokes, and get enraged at different provocations. You are still you; indeed, you are still completely "the real you," but you *by necessity* start to adjust to these new situations—if only to survive, eat, make friends, and stay out of trouble.

Playing style is no different. In playing style, you (the real you) simply enter a different world, which may be in a different century, where people wear different clothes, worship different gods, marry and ally with others for different reasons, and speak a different language or style (such as blank verse, rhyming couplets, operatic arias) in order to get what they want. Perhaps this new world even exists in a completely different plane of reality, one where people fly out of windows (*Peter Pan*), are visited by ghosts (*Hamlet)*, or are punished by lightning-throwing gods (*Prometheus Bound*). Still, if you, in your imagination, could extend yourself into these worlds, you would *still be yourself* but in a new world. It may be a dream world, but it's still you who lives in it. This is how you integrate style—no matter how fanciful, artificial, or otherworldy—yet retain your own core of being.

Or suppose you were born into your own world but to parents quite unlike your own. Suppose you lived your life in a wholly unfamiliar political, economic, social, cultural, and religious environment. Imagine extending yourself—your mind, your identity, or perhaps your "soul" (if that word has meaning for you)—into the current life of such a "character." You would almost certainly think, speak, dress, move, believe, behave, and perform in manners quite unlike your present ones, but you would still be you.

Acting Two seeks to lead you into these different worlds. It is mainly concerned with how actors approach dramatic styles, both those developed throughout the theatre's long history and those that are created in the present day, and in human characterizations, in their vast range from dominating to submissive, gregarious to paranoid, explosive to serene. Above all, it is concerned with *how these styles and roles can be completely faithful to the theatrical worlds their authors have inhabited and/or invented, but also with complete authenticity to the humanness of their cores.*

Is this a hard task? Absolutely. That is why there's a very short list of actors in any generation who truly become great masters across the dramatic repertoire. But it is unquestionably an approachable subject, and it can become an inexhaustibly fascinating challenge.

It is certainly a necessary one for the would-be professional actor. Creating compelling realistic interactions with contemporary characters like yourself can provide you with the foundation blocks of acting, and with a basis for attaining professional roles in American film and television and, though to a lesser extent, in current theatre. But it will prepare you for only a small fraction of what actors are asked to do in any of these media in the twenty-first century. Today, actors are expected to play gods, demons, animals, machines, kings, gangsters, and witches. They must seem to behave authentically in different centuries, in different millennia, or even in the future; to appear as half their age or four times older (sometimes even in the same work); to demonstrate expertise in professions they know nothing of; to perform acts and think thoughts in ways utterly different from anything they have ever experienced in their real-world lives.

None of this is easy to learn. And if you are an actor, you have to learn it fast. The real Henry V had twenty-eight years to prepare to lead his troops into battle at Agincourt. The actor playing Henry will probably have only four weeks of rehearsal to look, sound, and act "every inch a king."

The task of extending yourself into an age, sex, personality, or belief system different from your own—and doing so with the authenticity and truthfulness that you have previously achieved (and that is the hallmark of contemporary American acting)—is no easy challenge. But it is crucial to the creation of theatre that transcends mere realism: to playing great dramatic works throughout the ages that reach beyond the narrow dimensions of our daily life and carry us—actors and audiences alike—into the realms of myth, history, heroics, high comedy, brilliant argument, and unforgettable archetype that makes for truly memorable theatre experiences. Learning to make these very extensions, with unaffected assurance and genuine passion, is the goal of this book.

Terminology: Style, Character, and Performance

All books use words in unique ways. The words *style* and *character* are long known in theatre discourse but have been defined quite differently by authors and teachers over the centuries. I would like to introduce the three key words as I use them in this book, which I hope will provide a consistent and meaningful basis for discussions that follow.

Style refers to the ways *a specific group of characters* behave within a play. This includes their *collective* behavior—for example, that they speak in blank verse or eat with chopsticks, or that the young men show off their wigs to attract women and the young women their bustles to attract men. Such collective behavior might also include their collective thinking—that they worship Zeus, hate Jews, think fornication bestial, or believe witty discourse to be the height of female eroticism. Style is the thinking and behavior that all persons within a group of characters (and there may be many groups within a play, such as the aristocrats, workmen, and fairies of Shakespeare's *Midsummer Night's Dream*) would have learned as children and are expected to master before becoming adults.

Character, however, is essentially the opposite. Character is how each *individual* member of the social group *separates and becomes distinct* from it. When, in the royal court, Prince Hamlet chooses black garments where others wear red and gold, and speaks sarcastically when others are intoning pleasantries, the Prince is defining his character by its *dissimilarity* to the accepted "style" of courtly behavior. Such dissimilarity can be by choice, in which case it is seen as conscious rebellion, or by unconscious reaction to events beyond the character's control, in which case it is viewed as part of the character's psychological makeup. Usually, in drama, it can be seen as a combination of the two, as it invariably is in Hamlet's case. Most great dramatic characters—Molière's Alceste, Ibsen's Hedda, Shakespeare's Iago, Shaw's Barbara, Miller's Willy, Kushner's Roy Cohn—are known by their refusal (or inability) to accommodate themselves to the collective behavior of the society in which they find themselves.

A third key term is raised later in the book. *Performance* is the way we *perform for public audiences* in everyday life, seeking to present a public image of ourselves to whomever may cross our paths or arrive, seen or unseen, into our presence—as do, for example, passersby on a crowded sidewalk, classmates in our high school cafeteria, people in the stands with us at a basketball game. At certain times our public performance becomes particularly conscious, as when we answer questions in class, participate in a wedding ceremony, give a political speech, or engage in an emergency rescue effort. But much of the time our public performance is as unconscious as the confident image we try to maintain while walking to class—knowing all the while that persons are observing us do so.

In the theatre, all actors publicly perform the roles of characters in front of an audience, of course, and this book considers that. But we also shall be speaking of *characters* who publicly perform—in front of other characters in the play, and for other characters who are *not* specifically in the play but, like passersby in our own everyday lives, may be presumed as possibly in the vicinity of the characters we enact and in their minds as well. From time to time, I shall call this public level of performance a character's *performative* behavior.

Acting Two's Structure

This book is written in two parts. Part I is a series of exercises and discussions that all have one goal: to explore how you can be completely yourself and at the same time extend yourself into a different theatrical world—in style, character, and performance. Where actual dramatic dialogue is used in Part I, it is solely directed to this goal and not to establishing acting styles for specific dramatic periods or authors. Much of the dramatic material is from fifteenth-century English drama—the first recorded plays we have in our language. This is mainly because you probably have never seen or read these works (though you will probably recognize the stories), and because the original actors of these plays never took an acting class and thus had to figure out how to play their parts just as you will. They are also, in my opinion, very fine pieces of theatre that can be brought to vivid dramatic life in ways that address all the issues of style, character, and performance.

Part II is a series of dramatic fragments—individual speeches and two-person scenes—from different periods in the theatre's history, including the present. This sampling is not an exhaustive list of the world's great dramatic styles, of course, but it presents the main lines of theatrical stylizations and nearly all the major ingredients of stylization. Each dramatic fragment is presented and "coached" in a different manner, so that the actor can explore mystical transcendence in Sophoclean tragedy; intellectual brashness and comic pratfalls in Machiavellian *commedia;* the interweaving of verse, action, and emotion in Shakespeare; the marrying of amorous and rhyming competition in Molière; the banking of sexual fires with super-refined wit in Aphra Behn; the emergence of subtle subtext in Chekhov and vigorous rhetoric in Shaw; the hypertheatrical text manipulations of Ionesco and Brecht; and the varying stylistic creations of a sampling of today's best American playwrights.

The lessons to be learned in studying each era, however, are not limited to the scenes or practices under immediate discussion: There are subtexts and comic pratfalls in Shakespeare and Molière, sexual fires in Sophocles and Ionesco, dramatic manipulations in Machiavelli and Behn. Each fragment is an exemplar of almost every lesson in Part I; each will lead to discoveries in every fragment in Part II.

So study, rehearse, and perform as many of these fragments as your instructor thinks would be worthwhile. And, if you wish to be a great actor someday, do the other ones—or ones like them from another source—on your own time, with like-minded friends.

A Word About Gender

Most of the scenes selected for this book are written as taking place between a man and a woman, but any of these roles may be played—in acting class, anyway—by students of any gender. Indeed, cross-gender casting has been more the rule than the exception throughout history, even in professional theatre. Classic Greek, Roman, traditional Asian, and Shakespearean plays were performed in their own time by all-male (or in a few cases all-female) companies, and many are still so performed today. And in recent years, audiences throughout America and Europe have seen dozens of female Hamlets and Lears, male Cleopatras and Olivias, and hundreds of cases where actors have alternately performed male and female roles within the same play—including *I Am My Own Wife,* featured in Lesson 16. So you should welcome the opportunity, in the exercises in *Acting Two,* to make at least one acting extension of yourself into a character of the opposite sex.

PART

I

Extensions of Yourself

IN PART I, A NUMBER OF EXERCISES AND, TOWARD THE END, THREE SHORT scenes introduce fundamental principles in nine acting lessons. All of these exercises are intended to lead students into worlds or characters unlike their own—to be "extensions" into behaviors (such as speaking in rhyme or walking as God) quite different from those students normally experience in daily life. These exercises provide the foundation for approaching style and character without asking the actor to sacrifice the principles of playing goals or interacting tactically with others—the foundations of *Acting One* and of acting realistically.

These exercises and short scenes should be considered as simple études, or practice pieces. There is no attempt in Part I (though there is in Part II) to seriously describe, much less analyze, individual plays, historical periods, or styles of individual dramatists.

Consequently, the études in this section can be fully explored simply as what they are and without reference to play or period. In Part I, basic principles of acting in style and character are the entire subject, and discussions of verse structure, period deportment, and the author's larger intent are presented only to the extent they serve to encourage the student to learn these principles from a guided practicing of the étude.

L E S S O N

1

Style

◆ E X E R C I S E   1–1

Baby Talk

Sit in a chair. Imagine you have suddenly experienced total paralysis from the neck down—you cannot control any part of your body except your head. Terrified, you want to call for help. But there is no one within earshot, and you cannot reach the phone on the table next to you.

Suddenly, you become aware that there is in fact *one* person nearby, a little girl about two or three years old and, though curious, she is very frightened. If you could get her to bring you the phone and hold it up to your face, you could punch in 911 with your tongue.

So speak to the imaginary girl in words of your choosing, asking her to pick up the phone and bring it to you.

But *watch out!* If you speak too loudly, or do anything the little girl thinks is scary, she will run away and never come back.

In a class situation, everyone in the class should try this exercise, one at a time.

After the first go-round, have one class member play the role of the adult and another—squatting or kneeling—the child, and then switch parts.

Measure your success in this exercise by how tempted the "child" was to pick up the phone.

How did you approach that problem? Before discussing it, try this variation on the same exercise.

◆ E X E R C I S E   1–2

Baby Moves

You're in a situation similar to that of Exercise 1–1, but this time you are standing near a wall. You are not paralyzed, but for reasons you don't understand, every time you move more than one foot from the wall you experience incapacitating pain. You need help, fast. And there's the little girl again, across from you as before. You cannot go over to her, for you'll collapse in agony if you move away from the wall. Once again, try to talk the imaginary girl into bringing you the phone so you can summon help.

This time you can move, kneel, squat, sit, or lie down—as long as you stay within one foot of the wall.

But *watch out! Don't frighten her!*

In a class situation, everyone may try this, one at a time.

Afterward, try Exercise 1–2 as a group exercise with all the actors having their backs to as many walls of the room as are available, and with an imaginary child in the middle of the room. Or have one actor, or the instructor, play the role of the child.

Now that you've tried both of these exercises, what did you find yourself doing? Did you use your regular everyday voice in Exercise 1–1, or did you use a different one? In Exercise 1–2, did you remain standing, or did you lower yourself in some way?

If you are like most people, you began to "baby talk," adopting a baby vocabulary and a baby voice to get what you wanted. Your voice went higher, softer, and more musical; you chose the friendliest possible words, such as "sweetie" and "honey"; you may even have invented words or expressions, like "tickle tickle!" or "hoppy here!" And you probably changed your facial expression as well, smiling rather than frowning. Maybe you also winked your eyes, waggled your eyebrows, or made funny faces. In general, you probably coaxed rather than explained and did your best to entertain the child while persuading her to do what you needed done.

In Exercise 1–2 you probably did all this but also made yourself appear smaller: perhaps by kneeling, squatting, bending over, or lying down. This would be natural, of course—you were trying to make the little girl less afraid and were seeking to win her trust by becoming more little-girl-like yourself.

In all this you were performing "in style," for this is what style is in real life: *a behavior you adopt to assimilate with a particular person or group of persons.* And assimilating with other people is often a useful, even essential, means of getting what you want, or need, from those persons.

In *Acting One* terms, your GOTE is intact: You are still playing a goal (to get the phone), and seeking to achieve that Goal through the aid of an Other (the small child). However, your Tactics have become quite different from what you would use were you speaking to an adult, and your Expectations now include your rarely experienced fear of frightening away the person whose help you are seeking. The style of your communication, then, has shifted drastically from your normal, everyday behavior, but it is *pure situational necessity,* not theatrical decoration, that has evoked this change.

Style, therefore, is not so much what you *are* as what you *do* to gain the trust (or the admiration, or the confidence) of other people in a given situation. It is an *action,* not an affectation. It has a purpose and is used to achieve goals. Speaking baby talk in this exercise does not mean that you're a baby, or that you're a smiley, eyebrow-waggling sort of person. It means only that you have *adopted these behaviors* for a few moments in order to get what you need.

What is significant about this? Four things:

1. *Style is not primarily decorative; rather, it is useful—sometimes it is necessary.* Talk baby talk, and a baby will approach you. Talk adult talk, and you'll scare the child away (and, in this exercise, starve—or worse).

2. *Style is not automatic behavior; it is chosen behavior.* You have a choice to make here: Talk baby talk and live, or talk adult talk and die. You choose to talk baby talk in order to get help, not because you're a baby-like person.

3. *Style is a function of the person addressed as much as or more than it is a function of the person who is doing the addressing.* You talk baby talk not because *you're* a baby but because *the person you're talking to* is and will respond to you better if you speak her language.

4. *Style is something we learn, not something we are born into.* Baby talk may not come naturally or immediately to you; you may have to improvise and practice it a bit before you get good at it.

The first style we learn is our family's: how to get along with our parents and how to compete successfully with our siblings. When we go to school, we learn how to be popular within a social set: how to fit in, how to wear the right clothes and use the right expressions, how to be cool.

Of course, we may not succeed in fitting in. This lack of success may be the result of external factors—our race, religion, dialect, social or economic class, physical or intellectual defects (as we perceive them). Or it may be because of an incompatibility, as we see it, between our now-ingrained family style and the perceived school style. But if, in our early school years, we fail to fit in to what we see as an in-group, we then almost certainly seek to fit in to an out-group; the pressure to conform to *some* group is all but overwhelming in those years.

And later, as we start to differentiate ourselves as adults, we will assimilate the styles of many groups. We develop ways of speaking and behaving appropriate for interacting with family, friends, colleagues, and hoped-for romantic partners. We develop professional styles: the attorney's deferential courtroom decorum ("May it please the court" rather than "Listen here, Judge"), or the new car salesperson's hearty greeting with a right hand briskly extended ("Hey, how ya doin' today?" rather than the arched-eyebrow inquiry, "May I help you?"). Doctors, morticians, teaching assistants, building contractors, and rock singers each have (and continually refine) their distinctive on-the-job styles—which include their dress, posture, grooming, language, and manners of both speaking and moving—and each of these styles might be quite different from the ones they use with friends, family, or romantic partners.

Furthermore, all these styles are essentially *learned*. No one is born cool, or a lawyer or a rock singer; one learns the style of various subcultures or professions—both consciously, by instruction from mentors, and unconsciously, by aping role models. We aggressively acquire the styles by which we dress, move, and frame our discourse and appearance.

So, to quote T. S. Eliot, you "prepare a face to meet the faces that you meet." We are *all* stylized actors, and good ones, too.

Mastering a *dramatic* style is roughly the same process—though it ordinarily must happen more quickly and more as a result of imagination and research than actual real-world experience.

Think back to Exercises 1–1 and 1–2. Did you feel that some people in the room were better at baby talk than you were? Maybe they have had more little children to practice on over the past few years. Maybe they have bolder imaginations or fewer inhibitions than you do. And maybe you were too worried about looking foolish. All of these factors are important in the art of developing an acting style: the *experience* to prepare you for employing a style with confidence, the *imagination* to be creative in languages and manners not normally your own, and the *playfulness* to express yourself fully, enthusiastically, and (by common standards) outrageously. No one can master style without taking the chance of looking like a fool.

Master these exercises, and you have taken the first—but giant—step toward playing in style. You have left your own style behind and adopted another, not because you found it prettier or cleverer (or just because you were told to) but because you found it *useful*.

Summary

Style is not only something one performs in the theatre; it is something we all do in life. It is a behavior we purposefully adopt to address different sorts of people. Style is, therefore, something we do, not something we are: It is something we can both learn and choose as suits our purposes.

LESSON

2

Stylized Exchanges

◆ EXERCISE 2–1

Pig Latin

With a partner, memorize the following "scene." Make up your own situation (for example: B has asked her roommate A to turn off the music so she can study, but A has just come to the best part of the CD and wants to hear it to the end), and play the scene as truthfully as possible.

A: No.

B: Yes.

A: No!

B: Yes!

A: NO!

B: YES!

We will assume that the argument naturally escalates in intensity—in volume as well as in precision—as it goes through the three paired exchanges, as indicated by the use of exclamation points and capital letters.

Now, assume that your partner does not speak English, only pig Latin. *You* can speak either language, but in order for your partner to understand you, you must speak in his or her language.

Now, using the same situation, play the scene just as truthfully as you did before. But speak in pig Latin instead of English so that you can be understood (as will your partner). Thus:

A: Ohnay.

B: Essyay.

A: Ohnay!

B: Essyay!

A: OHNAY!

B: ESSYAY!

Do you feel a bit silly doing this? That wouldn't be surprising—but if you do, it's only because you're not yet acting truthfully. Do the scene again, and do it *entirely seriously*. You *really* want her to turn off the music, or, in the other part, you really want to hear to the end of the CD, but can make her understand this only by speaking pig Latin to her.

What you and your partner are doing in this exercise is, just as in Lesson 1, *creating a style*. You are acting truthfully—trying to achieve a real goal with and through another person—and you are wholly "in the moment" as you perform this, but you are speaking in an invented, artificial language rather than the one you use in daily life. And that is what acting "style" is all about.

So do whatever you can, short of physical contact, to get what you want in this exchange. (Understand that removing physical contact from your list of options allows you and your partner to throw everything else you've got—voice, gesture, and emotion—into the exercise without having to be concerned with causing or receiving physical harm. By avoiding the physical contact, and knowing your partner will as well, you can really let yourselves go vocally and emotionally.)

Repeat the exchange, but make up a more intense argument this time. Suppose you are each trying to get your hands on the lottery ticket you believe to be the million-dollar winner. Or to be the one let into an invitation-only audition for an upcoming feature film. Repeat two or three times, letting the argument escalate further each time.

◆ E X E R C I S E   2–2

Speaking in (Foreign) Tongues

Now vary the exercise by using *real* languages—for example:

Spanish (or Italian)

A: No.

B: Sí. *(pronounced "see")*

A: No!

B: Sí!

A: NO!

B: SÍ!

German

A: Nein. *(pronounced "nine")*

B: Ja. *(pronounced "ya")*

A: Nein!

B: Ja!

A: NEIN!

B: JA!

Russian

A: Nyet. *(pronounced "nee-YET")*

B: Da. *(pronounced "dah")*

A: Nyet!

B: Da!

A: NYET!

B: DA!

French

A: Non. *(pronounced something like "nawhh")*

B: Oui. *(pronounced something like "weehh")*

A: Non!

B: Oui!

A: NON!

B: OUI!

Hungarian

A: Nem. *(pronounced "nehm")*

B: Igen. *(pronounced "EE-gehn")*

A: Nem!

B: Igen!

A: NEM!

B: IGEN!

Japanese

A: Hai *(pronounced "HAH-ee")*

B: Ie. *(pronounced "ee-EH")*

A: Hai!

B: Ie!

A: HAI!

B: IE!

Turkish

A: Evet. *(pronounced "eh-vet")*

B: Hayir. *(pronounced "hah-yurh")*

A: Evet!

B: Hayir!

A: EVET!

B: HAYIR!

If you can, get someone in your group who speaks the language—or even better, a native speaker—to help you with the exact pronunciation, and try to use this as precisely as you can.

Remember your acting assumption: that *you* speak both English and the second language with equal fluency, but *the person you are speaking to* speaks only the second. You are not using the second in order to be pretty, or fancy, or clever, or "dramatic," but only as a tactic to achieve your goal: to get the other person out of the room—or whatever other goal your situation creates for you.

Again, with this exercise you are creating a style, in this case not with an artificial language but a real one. And you are speaking it not because you *want* to, but because you *have* to: because it's the only way you can communicate effectively. We adopt "stylized" speech, therefore, for only one reason: to be understood. Thus, stylized speech is a *winning strategy*.

Style, of course, is a matter not merely of language—baby talk, pig Latin, or foreign tongues—but of a wide range of vocal, physical, emotional, and associational factors, including body language, gesture, proxemics (how close you get to people), vocal tone, and facial expressions. Indeed, without thinking about it, you and your partner probably introduced some of these stylistic factors into your performance of the Spanish, German, Russian, French, Hungarian, Japanese, and Turkish versions of these exercises, just from whatever unconscious associations with these cultures you may have developed over the years. It is almost automatic, for example, for some people to become a little more bombastic when speaking German, more unctuous when speaking French, or more physically animated when speaking Italian—even if they don't know half a dozen words of those languages. That these characteristics are stereotypes doesn't mean natives don't exhibit them, and foreigners often pick them up when they are immersed in a culture where they're commonly practiced.

Now repeat Exercise 2–2 in pig Latin. Do you find that you have added a little body language and vocal expression to this as well—something more than you did when you just exchanged "yes" and "no" in English? Perhaps these additions come from your early associations of pig Latin: speaking it in elementary school, for example, or speaking it to your little sister, or to children in the neighborhood. Something in the language kicks off a slightly different "you" from the one you "play" at other times. Or perhaps it is just an extra oomph you use to make yourself understood in a second language.

Or, even more interesting, perhaps you are unconsciously trying to *out-do* your acting partner (and, in this case, your adversary—the one you want to win your goal from) by *speaking pig Latin better* and more forcefully than he or she does.

The fact is that speaking to achieve a goal carries with it the desire not merely to adopt a style but to *excel* at it. You not only want to speak pig Latin, but you want to speak *great* pig Latin (or great Spanish, German, Russian, French, Hungarian, Japanese, or Turkish), even if it's your second or third language. You want to speak great pig Latin not because it's an inherently better language than English but simply because you want to out-do your opponent—through your greater eloquence and forcefulness. And in order to be forceful, to be compelling, to be eloquent, you must master the style that the situation requires.

You must *own* that style as well, and that's not easy. As children, we assume that the style of speech we are growing up with is the only one on earth; speech styles we encounter for the first time in later life, therefore, seem "strange," "affected," or "weird." We are surprised when we find English people telling us we have "American accents," even though we unquestioningly accept that they have "English" ones. We unconsciously prioritize our learned behaviors: It is the English who drive on the "wrong" side of the road. These feelings, known as egocentrism—seeing ourselves as if at the center of the world—usually linger in our unconscious for a lifetime. If you're going to perform in pig Latin (or in any other style), therefore, you must not only learn it but also seize and own it. You must be as comfortable in your newly acquired "style" as in your five-year-old jeans. You must make style as *real* for yourself, and as necessary, as the skin on your body. Then not only will you employ it, but you will want to enjoy it. And want to *excel* at it.

◆ E X E R C I S E   2–3

Contemporary Greetings

With a partner, come together as if with a friend on the street and shake hands, saying:

A: Hey, how ya doin'?

B: Fine, how're you?

How did you shake hands? In the conventional fashion, with hands extended thumbs-up, straight from the body's midsection? Or with the 1960s "hippie shake," with hands extended fingers-up, grasping around your partner's thumb? Or with the athlete's high-five slap? If conventional, was your (or your partner's) handshake firm, like a politician's, or painfully aggressive, like an enraged rival's, or limp, like a reluctant accomplice's? Is it correct to associate personality traits with different styles of handshake?

With the same or another partner, cast yourselves as a doctor and a patient. Come together as if in the doctor's office and shake hands, saying (and using your partner's actual name):

PATIENT: Good morning, Doctor [last name].

DOCTOR: Good to see you, [first name].

Or as a student and professor, saying:

STUDENT: Professor [last name]!

PROFESSOR: [first name]?

Or as a cheerleader and a basketball player, saying:

CHEERLEADER: Great game, [first name].

PLAYER: Thanks, [first name].

Make up other greetings appropriate to persons known to you and your partner, and rehearse these with appropriate handshakes and language. Greetings, in both word and deed, establish and define social, professional, age, and gender relationships by the manner in which they are (consciously or unconsciously) executed.

Varied Salutations

Of course there are dozens of different kinds of greetings. Besides those mentioned above are the knuckle-rap, the cheek kiss, the air kiss, the bear hug, the sudden ("surprised") head-cock and grin, and the outstretched, splayed arms.

Handshakes of any sort, as a common form of greeting, date only to the first part of the nineteenth century—and even then only in Western, or Westernized, cultures.* What is common to all eras, however, are conventionalized greetings, which we may call salutations. People have "saluted" each other in some recognized fashion since the beginning of human civilization. And "recognized fashion" is a vital ingredient of this salutation because

---

* Desmond Morris, *Bodytalk: A World Guide to Gestures* (London: Jonathan Cape, 1994), p. 124. Although most greetings today propose little more than pleasure at meeting others, there are times we see the ancient roots of such practices of greeting and obeisance. The handclasps between Menachem Begin and Anwar Sadat in 1979, and Yitzak Rabin and Yassar Arafat in 1993, both brokered by U.S. presidents during formal ceremonies, were long-sought and hard-won representations of peace efforts between bitter Middle Eastern enemies. And the kneeling and curtsying of actors and state officers before the English queen at public receptions or knighting ceremonies is a reminder of the social authority—at least symbolic—retained by hereditary monarchs in class-conscious societies.

A Renaissance bow Wearing his traditional multicolored costume and black eye-mask, Arlecchino, a rascally character from the Italian *commedia dell'arte,* takes a bow in the sixteenth century. Arlecchino's right hand proffers his hat, while his left hand holds at the ready a traditional "slapstick"—a trick baton that makes a comically loud slapping sound when hitting a victim on the buttocks.

it assures that the greetee will recognize that the greeter's intentions are, at minimum, peaceful. The modern handshake, for example, evolved from the male greeter's desire to show that his fighting (right) hand was not holding a dagger; it was, therefore, not merely a courteous gesture but a survival tactic.

Beyond survival, greetings are used to show (or perhaps to feign) respect, appreciation, or subservience. Lowering the body implies fealty, a medieval term acknowledging the obedience required of those of lower social rank. In a society that believed in the divine right of kings, such self-lowering even suggested a greater distance from God. And the actor's deep bow or curtsy at play's end originally signaled, to a royal patron, "If I failed to amuse you, please feel free to chop off my head immediately!"

Such salutations vary enormously by culture and period. In Japan, for example, the handshake is never employed (except in Western or international business contexts); rather, the bow is universal, with the depth of the bow dependent on the status of its user. In China, the *kowtow*—a full-body prostration—was current through many dynasties, and in Ottoman cultures a nine-point kneel (feet, knees, elbows, hands, forehead touching the ground) was mandatory before the sultan and remains the primary submissive pose during Islamic prayer. Kisses are common in American and European society, often between men and women, or women and women, and sometimes, particularly on the European continent, between men and men. In America and England, this is usually a peck on the cheek, or air kiss, but in France, kisses on both cheeks are mandatory, and in Poland, three kisses—on one cheek, then the other, then the first again. In military cultures around the world, a variety of crisp salutes serve the purposes of both greeting and rank recognition.

This great variety of greetings existed as well in former times. There is, therefore, no single "Elizabethan bow" or "Restoration curtsy" but, rather, a wide menu of dips and bobs that have been used in every period and every culture. Few of these were formally standardized, and all would have varied according to the personality and athleticism of the individuals employing them; nonetheless, some basic patterns of such salutations are characteristic of most periods. Some of these are outlined and described in the "Medieval and Elizabethan Salutations" box and elsewhere in this book.*

⬦ MEDIEVAL AND ELIZABETHAN SALUTATIONS

Hundreds of different salutations and acknowledgments of deference are known to have existed during the late medieval and succeeding Elizabethan and Jacobean eras.

Kneeling, ordinarily on one knee, was universal for servants before their masters or superiors. And petitioners to royalty or high officers (as well as convicted criminals or captured warriors) knelt on both knees: "Lend me your knees," says the kneeling Mariana, employing the plural, to Isabella in Shakespeare's *Measure for Measure* when urging her friend to kneel beside her before the duke.

The modern handshake didn't exist in these times, but most researchers believe that military men, from the Roman era forward, grasped each other right hand to right wrist, with the greeter's left

(Continued)

---

* More can be found on this subject in Isabel Chisman and Hester E. Raven-Hart, *Manners and Movements in Costume Plays* (London: Kenyon-Deane, 1934), and Bari Rolfe, *Movement for Period Plays* (Oakland, CA: Personabooks, 1985).

(*Continued*)

Kneeling in supplication   The crowned Queen Tamara kneels before the victorious Titus, begging him to spare her two sons—also kneeling—in what is believed to be the only existing sketch of an actual Shakespearean performance (of Titus Andronicus) during the dramatist's lifetime.

hand following to grasp the other's left forearm just below the elbow, thereby signaling that neither had warlike intentions.

Bowing and curtsying were the standard greetings and shows of deference among most cultured and courtly persons (those about whom most plays of the time were written). These salutations could be anything from a simple bending of the knees and tipping of the head, for persons of either sex, to the more elaborate bows (for men) and curtsies (for women) described below. Mastering these salutations is one of the basic tasks of actors in any traditionally staged play of medieval or Shakespearean times.

MALE BOWS

By a courtier: With the feet comfortably apart and at right angles or a bit more (the dancer's fourth position), the left leg is drawn directly back in a sweeping motion, with the left foot landing anywhere from fifteen to twenty-four inches directly behind the right one. At the same time, the upper body angles forward, while the right hand sweeps upward in a large circle, removing the hat and sweeping it toward the person greeted, before circling back down to a resting place at the front of the left hip, with the hat dangling below, its inner lining facing the body. The left hand, meanwhile, rests on the back of the left hip (at the sword hilt) or is swept to that position by a more modest circle in the opposite direction of the right hand—a move helpful for balance.

The same bow may be used by a hatless courtier, but the right hand sweeps by the person greeted in a gesture of pleasantry before landing, palm inward, on the left hipbone, sometimes joining the left hand in a tight clasp.

A messenger's obeisance A messenger or servant bows before two ladies, one standing and one seated, in a detail of the famous drawing of London's Swan Theatre, originally made about 1596 by one Johannes de Witt and subsequently redrawn by one of his friends. Although the drawing is best known for its uniquely detailed view of a Shakespearean-era theatre interior, it also shows three actors of that time in what appears to be a realistic depiction of a stage action, either in performance or in dress rehearsal.

By a country servant: A quick bend of both knees and a downward tip of the head, while the right hand removes the cap and brings it to the chest, where it is held by both hands. (The hatless servant may keep the hands to the sides or bring them to the chest.)

By a court messenger or officious servant: The courtier's bow, but much deeper and often reversed. In the famous Johannes de Witt drawing dating from 1596 of what seems to be a rehearsal, or perhaps a performance, in London's Swan Theatre, a servant, holding an angled staff in his left hand, is shown executing such a bow.

Rising from all such bows is basically a matter of simply reversing the movements.

Whereas the petitioner "lends a knee" in ancient parlance, the bow, in an Elizabethan court or manor, was called "making a leg," and the point of making an especially good leg was to show off the fine flex and contour of one's calf, as well as the expensive silk hose dressing it. That is why the feet are always turned out (at approximately right angles) in such bows. In addition, a confident pursed smile, cock of the head, and gaze of the eye, along with the vigor and sprightliness of the attack and the graceful coordination of all the movements into a single, seemingly effortless ballet, were required attributes of a dazzling courtier.

FEMALE CURTSIES

The woman's curtsy begins with one foot swept directly behind and to right angles to the other, with the swept-back heel landing directly

(*Continued*)

(*Continued*)

behind and at right angles to the forward instep (the dancer's "open third" position). Both knees are then bent simultaneously, and the upper body slightly inclined forward, with the hands brought demurely together below the belly button, palms and (modestly curled) fingers facing inward.

For a more ostentatious curtsy, as to royalty, the same basic foot movement is used, but it ends with the legs farther apart and further crossed (the left foot to the right of the right one); then, the body's weight is placed solidly on the back foot, and the woman sinks to a near-seated position, with the forward thigh "sitting" on the back one. This can go as deeply as can be managed, depending on the dress, the status of the person being curtsied to, and (very important) the woman's athleticism. With this curtsy, the arms may be stretched outward and may in fact hold the skirt, raising it gracefully an inch or two as the body sinks. (Be sure, in practicing this curtsy, that you can also rise to your feet when it concludes!)

A woman's curtsy is generally much less assertive than the male bow (the word *curtsy* is simply a variant of *courtesy*), and the legs, completely hidden by the skirt, cannot even be seen. A demure expression, with eyes down and head inclined gracefully to the side, completes the submissive salutation.

◆ E X E R C I S E   2–4

Making Elizabethan Greetings

Learn bows (for men) or curtsies (for women); practice them with one or more partners. Then rehearse and play one or more of the following short greetings with a partner, varying the depth of your bow or curtsy with the perceived rank of your partner and the particular impression you want to convey to him or her. Men will want to get a floppy hat, and perhaps a "sword" to slip into a belt loop for this exercise; women should wear a long rehearsal skirt.

1. HASTINGS: Good time of day unto my gracious lord!

    RICHARD: As much unto my good Lord Chamberlain!

    (Richard III, Act 1, Scene 1)

    (Richard, the duke of Gloucester, angling to become king, has helped rescue Lord Chamberlain Hastings from prison—though he will later, as Richard III, have him executed.)

2. DON JOHN: My lord and brother, God save you!

    DON PEDRO: Good den, ° brother.   ° *afternoon*

    (Much Ado About Nothing, Act 3, Scene 2)

    (Though half-brothers, Don John, a bastard, is consumed with envy of his brother's higher rank and fortune.)

3. TIMON: I am joyful of your sights. Most welcome, sir!

    ALCIBIADES: Sir, you have saved my longing, and I feed
        Most hungerly on your sight.

    TIMON: Right welcome, sir!

    (Timon of Athens, Act 1, Scene 1)

    (Timon, a rich man, welcomes General Alcibiades and his entourage to a party at his home; Alcibiades responds with an even more flowery greeting. "Saved my longing" means "Your appearance has saved me the anguish of missing your company.")

4. FIRST LORD: The good time of day to you, sir.

    SECOND LORD: I also wish it to you.

    (Timon of Athens, Act 3, Scene 6)

    (Two nobles meet in the Athenian equivalent of a Senate.)

5. DUKE: Good morning to you, fair and gracious daughter.

    ISABELLA: The better, given me by so holy a man.

    (Measure for Measure, Act 4, Scene 3)

    (Vincentio, the duke of Vienna, posing as a Franciscan friar, meets Isabella, a nun-in-training. The two characters, while restrained by their religious garb, are also quite possibly in love, thus making every action inwardly complex.)

6. OTHELLO: O my fair warrior!

    DESDEMONA: My dear Othello!

    (Othello, Act 2, Scene 1)

    (A great general greets his new bride shortly after she debarks from a sea voyage on which they have had to travel separately.)

7. KING OF NAVARRE: Fair Princess, welcome to the court of Navarre.

   PRINCESS OF FRANCE: "Fair" I give you back again, and "welcome"
   I have not yet.

   (Love's Labor's Lost, Act 2, Scene 2)

   (The characters, both royal, are in love but playfully quarreling. The
   princess may well not respond to the king's bow, since she doesn't accept
   his greeting. Or she may curtsy mockingly, with obvious exaggeration,
   to emphasize her repudiation of his welcome.)

8. HERO: Good morrow, coz.

   BEATRICE: Good morrow, sweet Hero.

   (Much Ado About Nothing, Act 3, Scene 4)

   (Two female cousins, and best of friends, meet; *coz* is an affectionate
   nickname for *cousin* and can even be used between nonrelatives. No
   curtsy would be employed at this point, since the women are simply
   best friends, and nonroyal, so an appropriate Elizabethan embrace
   must be invented.)

9. SIR TOBY: 'Save you, gentleman.

   VIOLA: And you, sir.

   (Twelfth Night, Act 3, Scene 1)

   (Sir Toby, dissolute uncle of the rich homeowner Olivia, welcomes
   Viola, who is in man's disguise, to Olivia's home. In this greeting,
   Toby has to mask his inebriation, while Viola has to mask her femi-
   ninity.)

10. WILLIAM: Good ev'n, Audrey.

    AUDREY: God ye °good ev'n, William.   °*give you*

    (As You Like It, Act 5, Scene 1)

    (Young country people once in love. Now, however, with aristocrats
    visiting nearby, Audrey's eyes have opened to new possibilities, includ-
    ing the witty court jester, Touchstone, who is wooing her and stands be-
    side her during this exchange. William must recapture Audrey's love
    without embarrassing himself in front of the court-savvy Touchstone;
    Audrey must be polite to her ex-boyfriend without dismaying her new
    romantic interest.)

11. THIRD CITIZEN: Neighbors, God speed!

    FIRST CITIZEN: Give you good morrow, sir.

    (*Richard III*, Act 2, Scene 3)

    (Citizens meet hurriedly in the street just after hearing about the king's death and the accession of a new king. They need information fast and, as these are dangerous times, don't want to reveal their own political leanings.)

12. PISTOL: God save you, Sir John!

    FALSTAFF: Welcome, ancient Pistol.

    (*Henry IV, Part II*, Act 2, Scene 4)

    (In a tavern, these heavy drinkers and carousers meet again, each trying to impress their fellow barflies with their bravado and good fellowship.)

13. NURSE: God ye good morrow, gentlemen.

    MERCUTIO: God ye good den, fair gentlewoman.

    (*Romeo and Juliet*, Act 2, Scene 4)

    (Juliet's nurse, looking for Romeo, meets him on a street in Verona. But it is Romeo's friend Mercutio who replies, jesting—by calling her a gentlewoman, which she is not, being of humble birth—at the nurse's mistaking of afternoon for morning.)

14. MISTRESS QUICKLY: Give your worship good morrow.

    FALSTAFF: Good morrow, goodwife.

    MISTRESS QUICKLY: Not so, an't °please your worship.   °*if it*

    FALSTAFF: Good maid, then.

    (*The Merry Wives of Windsor*, Act 2, Scene 2)

    (Mistress Quickly mockingly inflates Falstaff's title to "your worship." Falstaff mocks Quickly's marital/sexual status—she is an unmarried barkeep with a reputation for promiscuity. She agrees, making the point to all around them that Falstaff hasn't married her yet. Falstaff mocks her as a "good maid"—a virgin, which, since she is not one, becomes his rationalization for not marrying her.)

◆ E X E R C I S E   2–5

Ad-libbing Elizabethan Greetings

Make up some paper crowns, and bring in hats, rehearsal skirts, and walking sticks and staffs; distribute around the class so that each participant fashions a character of obvious status (such as royal, noble, peasant). Moving about the room, with classmates, engage in impromptu greetings with people of different ranks, using the appropriate physical greeting and any number of the lines below, all drawn from Shakespeare's plays. Your goal, in every case, is *at minimum* to convince the person you're addressing that you are comfortable in your own skin, conversant with the appropriate behaviors of your society, and *a person worth knowing better.* Do it! And keep doing it until you feel good doing it. Until you *enjoy* doing it!

All hail, my lords!

All health unto my gracious sovereign!

All health, my sovereign lord!

Brother, good day.

Faith, sir, God save you!

Gentleman, God save thee!

God give you good morrow, master Parson.

God make your Majesty joyful, as you have been!

God save you gentlemen!

God save you, Madam!

'Save your honor!

God speed fair Helena!

Good dawning to thee, friend.

Good day and happiness, dear Rosalind!

Good even, Varro.

Good morrow and God save your Majesty!

Good morrow to your worship.

Good morrow, fair ones!

Good morrow, gallants.

Good morrow, gentle mistress.

Good morrow, good Sir Hugh.

Good morrow, noble sir.

Good Signior Angelo.

Good time of day unto your royal Grace!

Hail to your lordship!

Hail, noble Prince!

Hail, you anointed deputies of heaven!

Happily met, my lady and my wife!

Happy return be to your royal grace!

How does my good Lord Hamlet?

How now, brother Edmond?

How now, spirit?

How now, fair maid?

How now, how now?

How now, master Parson?

How now, my hardy, stout, resolvèd mates!

How now, my Lord of Worcester?

How now, my noble lord?

How now, Signior Launce?

Long live Lord Titus, my beloved brother.

Many good morrows to my noble lord!

Many good morrows to your Majesty!

My cousin Vernon, welcome, by my soul!

My excellent good friends! How dost thou?

My gracious prince, and honorable peers.

My gracious sovereign.

My honorable lords, health to you all!

My ladies both, good day to you.

My lovely Aaron.

My most dear lord!

My noble lords and cousins all, good morrow.

My very worthy cousin, fairly met!

O thou good Kent.

O worthiest cousin!

Our old and faithful friend, we are glad to see you.

Sir Proteus! 'save you!

Sir Toby Belch! How now, Sir Toby Belch!

Welcome, dear Rosencrantz and Guildenstern!

Welcome, good Messala.

Welcome, my good friends!

Welcome, pure wit.

Welcome, sweet Prince!

Well be with you, gentlemen!

Well met, honest gentlemen.

Well met, Mistress Page.

Why, how now, Dromio!

◆ EXERCISE   2–6

Ad-libbing Elizabethan Insults

Just so we don't get too touchy-feely in these greetings, let's repeat Exercise 2–5, but instead of responding with a greeting, respond with your choice of Shakespearean insults. Really try to frighten your partner! Get him or her to fear crossing you again. Be really rude with any of the following:

A plague on thee!

A pox o' your throats!

Beetle-headed, flap-ear'd knave!

Blasts and fogs upon thee!

Comb your noddle with a three-legg'd stool.

Foul wrinkled witch!

Go thou and fill another room in hell.

Go, ye giddy goose!

Gross lout!

Hence, rotten thing!

Idol of idiot-worshippers.

Out, dog!

Pernicious blood-sucker!

Take thy face hence!

Thou art a boil, a plague-sore, an embossed carbuncle!

Thou art a wickedness!

Thou disease of a friend!

Thou full dish of fool!

Thou mongrel, beef-witted lord!

Thou rag of honor!

Vanish like hailstones; go!

Vengeance rot you all!

Were I like thee I'd throw away myself.

You mad-headed ape!

Your misery increase with your age!

◆ EXERCISE   2-7

Hamlet's Greeting to the Players

Learn and play Hamlet's very special greeting to the Players in Act 2 of *Hamlet*. Shakespeare never wrote another greeting like this one; Hamlet's words are profoundly simple yet almost clumsy: He uses *well* and *welcome* no less than four times, and *friend/friends* twice, overdoing his greeting like Timon in Exercise 2-4, but with greater sincerity of friendship—as perhaps befits a prince who believes himself to be living in a prison, betrayed by those closest to him.

Greeting them with Hamlet's line, see if you can convince the Players of your profound joy at their arrival—and make them want to help you (even if it means defying the king).

HAMLET: You are welcome, masters, welcome all. I am glad to see thee
well. Welcome, good friends. O, old friend!

Summary

Style—in life as well as in the theatre—describes real, not fake, behavior: that which is purposeful and not just showy. Both foreign languages and older versions of our own language are—and must appear—as real to their speakers as ours is to us. Likewise, foreign and ancient gestures, such as bows and curtsies, must seem to emanate from a desire to please or impress—not merely to imitate. Even wholly imaginary or manufactured languages, such as pig Latin, must be played, in acting, as if your life depended on it—which, by the way, it *could*.

3

Roses Are Red

Rhyme and Verse

We sometimes think of verse drama as something of a curiosity—a relatively minor form of theatre popular in "olden times." This perception is quite inaccurate: Verse has actually been the *major* form of dramatic language throughout history, including, in much of the world, the present day. All ancient drama, from the Egyptian to the Roman, was in verse (often sung or chanted), often in rhyme as well, as was most medieval, Renaissance, and later European drama, including most of Shakespeare, Racine, Molière, Goethe, Calderón, and their contemporaries, right up to the eighteenth century. Most Asian and African drama, from ancient to modern, is in verse and is quite often sung or chanted. And a significant proportion of modern European and American theatre contains verse or song or both. Indeed, it is prose drama that is, historically at least, the curiosity, having appeared just occasionally from the Renaissance on, and dominating drama only during the past two centuries—and then only in the West.

But *playing* verse drama nonetheless seems foreign to American actors, generally raised on the notion (fostered by television and film as much as by theatre) that acting should be "true to life." Since verse is artificially contrived, does it follow that verse acting must be artificial?

The answer is emphatically "No!"

Verse simply indicates a theatrical framework, like a proscenium (or an audience) surrounding a stage, or like the houselights going down at the start of the performance. It says "We're playing now," but it doesn't make the playing any less emotionally vivid or situationally intense. Indeed, emotions and situations can be made *more* dramatically powerful by the skillful use of verse, and rhyme as well, by both playwright and performer.

◆ E X E R C I S E   3–1

Roses Are Red

With a partner, quickly learn the following dialogue:

A: Roses are red.

B: Violets are blue.

A: I'd like some bread.

B: I'd like some too!

Now imagine that you and your partner are playing two people sitting down at a coffee shop for lunch. Without discussing it beforehand, and without agreeing on any specific "situation" between the two of you, play the dialogue as an ice-breaking conversation, looking each other in the eye most of the time and miming any props you may wish to introduce.

Now play it again, inventing a specific goal for your character: perhaps to set the stage to invite your partner to join your club, or to go to a party later that evening.

This "scene" is a bit of sheer nonsense, of course, but it introduces, at a very simple level, the near-magical charm of verse. For in playing the scene, which is nearly empty of practical content, a relationship will emerge between you and your acting partner: possibly seductive, possibly argumentative or competitive, and almost surely probing playfully into your partner's mind and feelings. It is hard to play this scene without one or both partners cracking a smile at some point.

This is the power—and attraction—of verse. Verse is not spontaneous chatter; it is not ordinary daily discourse. Rather, it is a deliberately *contrived* language: thought-out, crafted, and controlled. To speak in verse is to announce that you have *designed the shape* of what you want to say and that you have chosen your words for their sounds as well as for their meanings. And for persons to *exchange* lines with each other in verse means that they seek to match each other in sharing sounds as well as ideas.

Two people exchanging lines with each other in the *same verse pattern* suggests they want to have and, more important, want to *perform* some sort of interpersonal relationship. So when two characters exchange lines in the "roses are red" pattern (or any other pattern), they are making an effort to "speak the same language," or to "be on the same page" with each other, regardless of the specific literal meaning of the lines.

The "roses are red" verse, of course, is extremely simple: four lines (a quatrain) in which each line has four syllables (as long as *violets* is pronounced "vi-lets" rather than "vi-o-lets"). And the stresses (the accents, or emphases) fall on the first and fourth syllables of each line:

RO-ses are RED.
VI(O)-lets are BLUE.
I'D like some BREAD.
I'D like some TOO!

The lines rhyme in an *ABAB* pattern: The last syllables of the first and third lines rhyme, as do those of the second and fourth.

The regular pattern of verse, with its alternation of stressed and unstressed syllables, creates a steady pulse that may be thought of as the heartbeat of speech. It provides a sense of drive and momentum, as well as composure and completion, to any spoken text. If you stop this verse in the middle of a line—

RO-ses are RED.
VI(O)-lets are BLUE.
I'D like some BREAD.
I'D like . . .

— the effect is unsettling, as though the speaker has had a heart attack. The absence of closure is so unnerving, in fact, that hearers often shout out the missing words, even if they have to invent them, to fill the gap.

And rhyme creates, in the verse pattern, a ringing double-pulse, adding to the rhythm of stresses a rhythm of matching sounds. This emphasizes further the contrivance of verse: that the spoken words are deliberately composed.

◆ E X E R C I S E   3–2

Roses Are Redder—Take One

Play the "roses are red" scene a few more times, switching partners with others in your group and varying the situation. Look into your partner's eyes most of the time, but if you shift your focus, look at something else (that you imagine), not just "away." Here are some possible situations:

In a candle-lit restaurant: as a romantic overture

In a concentration camp: between starving inmates

At a gangster meeting: planning a heist

Contestants at a poetry-reading competition

Contestants at a bread-baking competition

At an English-as-a-second-language class competition

At a basketball game: as a romantic overture

In a candle-lit restaurant: planning a heist

Now repeat the exercise with a situation you and your partner create. Come up with simple goals—and subtle communications that might achieve them—that can be expressed by intonations, smiles, laughs, gestures, winks, muscle flexes, head tosses, touching your partner on the hand or shoulder, or anything that comes to mind but falls within the rules of decorum.

Remember to maintain eye contact with your partner most of the time and to try to see what lies behind your partner's eyes. The forcefulness and magnetism of your acting will be a function not so much of how inventively you say your lines but how well you draw your partner out while saying them.

Eye Contact—And Looking Elsewhere

Eye contact—looking your partner directly in the eye—is a powerful acting tool. It makes clear, to your acting partner but also to an audience, that you are *really seeking your goal*, because you are studying your partner's responses to your speeches and actions for specific clues as to how you might proceed. If, for example, you are speaking with someone whom you plan to ask out on a date, you will generally be looking at his or her eyes to check the reaction to what you're saying, so as to determine the best time to pop the question or to adjust your tone and pace if you sense things aren't going as well as you'd hoped.

Maintaining eye contact is also a good way to let your partner know you're serious about something that involves him or her, that you're genuinely inquiring, not just making a rote remark like "How ya doin'?"

But this doesn't mean you must *always* look your partner in the eye. It's an effective tactic to look elsewhere from time to time, toward, say, other people to whom, in the example suggested, you might turn if your partner doesn't respond. Showing that you have other fish to fry puts pressure on your partner and may help you achieve your goal.

What you generally should *not* do, however, is simply look away. Looking at the floor, for example, is not an active acting choice; it is just an unconscious avoidance of deep situational involvement. Inexperienced actors glance at the floor mainly out of stage fright: fear of forgetting their lines, or embarrassment about looking foolish. Whatever your acting goal is, you can rarely achieve it by staring at the floor or, for that matter, off into the flies. Look at your partner, look at other people who might be useful to achieving your goal, look *for* other people who might be useful, look at or for God, look for a critical prop (such as a gun) or at the set (such as the opulence of a room you want to rob), look out the window at people who might serve as role models, but please don't look at the floor—unless you're playing a carpet salesman.

◆ E X E R C I S E   3–3

Roses Are Redder—Take Two

Repeat the exercise, using any of these variant quatrains, again with a situation of your choosing and a specific environment (law office, bedroom, barroom, city park) for that situation. Maintain constant eye contact with your partner and the useful persons or items in the environment of your situation.

A: Roses are red.

B: Violets are blue.

A: Honesty's dead!

B: What else is new?

A: Roses are red.

B: Violets are blue.

A: You look well fed!

B: What's that to you?

A: Roses are red.

B: Violets are blue.

A: What's that you said?

B: I'm teasing you.

A: Roses are red.

B: Violets are blue.

A: I'm off to bed.

B: Can I come too?

A: Roses are red.

B: Violets are blue.

A: Heard you were wed . . . ?

B: No, that's not true!

A: Roses are red.

B: Violets are blue.

A: What lies ahead?

B: I'll rhyme with you!

◆ E X E R C I S E   3–4

Roses Are Redder—Take Three

Starting with the opening gambit ("Roses are red / Violets are blue") and a situation and goal in your head, make up the final two lines, keeping them strictly within the pattern: four syllables, stressed on the first and fourth, the "A" lines and "B" lines rhymed with their counterparts. Remember, again, to maintain eye contact with your partner or useful persons and items in the environment, all the time, even when (*particularly* when) you are searching for your own line.

Take your time and don't feel rushed; this is not a cleverness contest. And don't judge the appropriateness of the content of your line after you say it! Even if what you've come out with seems like total nonsense, the sound of your words conveys its own authority and will move you toward your goal. This is the power of style: Even sheer nonsense works if the style is confidently asserted.

Thinking Your Character's Thoughts

Choosing your own words makes this a more difficult assignment, but your skill at throwing yourself into this task, while still maintaining eye contact with your partner and environment, is a measure of your potential as an actor in a stylized play. The greatest difficulty of acting is to make the people watching believe that you are not only saying your character's words but *thinking them up*. The best acting always persuades us—the audience—that you the actor are the *creator* of your character's words, not just their interpreter (or, worse, their reciter).

For that matter, we like to believe that you are spontaneously creating your character's stage movements and personally chose your character's clothing. Of course we know that, normally at least, a playwright wrote the words, a director arranged the moves, and a designer designed the costume. But at the moment of performance we like to think that you, the character (which is also you, the actor, for you're the person we see in the role), are *initiating,* and not merely repeating, your part. This is why we are captivated, not just entertained, by great acting.

Of course this illusion is generally more difficult to achieve when you are speaking in (and moving in, and dressing in) styles other than your own. But in the following exercise, you *are* coming up with your character's lines, so you can directly apply them to the goal (seductive? competitive? aggressive?) you seek to achieve with and through your acting partner. And your intonations, smiles, winks, and flexes will all be part of your integrated and goal-directed acting package in this mini verse drama, *Roses Are Red.*

◆ E X E R C I S E   3–5

Roses Are Redder—Take Four

Bring a funny (or funky) costume, or simply a funny (or funky) hat, and an appropriate prop to class and repeat Exercise 3–4, folding them into the exercise—trying, all the while, to make the relationship interaction real within the context of the funny or funky accoutrements.

Playing the Play

You might think of the "Roses are red/Violets are blue" opening gambit, like "Knock, knock," as an invitation to *play*. But play is also work. And it is real. Remember that the original English word for acting was *playing* and that we still call a single drama a *play* and a theatre a *playhouse*. The simple versification of "Roses are red" suggests a "playful" (childlike) environment as well as a "play" (dramatic) environment; verse suggests an invitation to child's play much as a rising curtain announces that a dramatic play is about to begin. What child's play and dramatic play have in common is that both are intensely engaged; the shouts of children playing tag are as bloodcurdling as anything cried on the stage by Medea or Othello. In both child's play and "a play," participants can become *emotionally* real. Since the circumstances are imaginary—it's "only a play"—they can lead to no real-world consequences. The stage Romeo dies in the fifth act—yet plays again tomorrow night. *Play* provides imaginary contexts so that the engagement of its actors may be total. In play, real blood is not shed so that real tears may be.

Summary

Verse—the contrived patterning of stressed and unstressed syllables in speech, often augmented by a regular rhyme scheme—creates a sort of steady heartbeat in speech, which conveys a regular momentum and sense of closure to the language and, when two or more characters exchange it, the sense that the characters live, or wish to live, in the same "world." Verse is also the mark of a deliberately "styled" language that implies playfulness, and playing, and has therefore been fundamental to theatre through the ages, permitting actors to act with total emotional authenticity while remaining within the framework of "playing" in "a play."

4

Playing God

Now it's time to work on an actual play, one that happens to be among the very first plays in the English language. Let's look at a dramatic character who, while appearing in human form,* is as far from a normal human being such as ourselves as we can possibly imagine.

◆ E X E R C I S E   4–1

Playing God

Memorize and practice speaking the following lines. (Please note that while God is referred to as "he" in this play, both sexes may play this speech. No one—in acting class, anyway—should have a monopoly on "playing God.")

> Here 'neath me now a new isle I neven°   °*name*
> The island of Earth. . . .

This is the beginning of a speech by God in *The Creation of the Universe,* a play from the fifteenth century. It is written in Middle English (from which

---

* Medieval theology held that God literally created Adam in his own image; hence God was played, in medieval drama, as outwardly human.

it is here slightly adapted); the author is unknown. In this fragment, God creates the Earth, which he calls an island; he is speaking to a group of surrounding angels as he does so.

Standing on a low stool or bench, play God. Perform the line to your classmates, who are your surrounding angels. As you say the words, imagine you are in the process of creating Earth, giving it the name of your choosing.

At the same time, try to impress the angels with your divine power: your ability to create such a place and your authority to name it. This is not merely vanity; you are about to give them a code of ethics, and you want them to heed your authority. So your goal is not merely to convey the information of the line but to make the angels *tremble*.

This is, obviously, a superhuman challenge. See the extent to which, in your own human imagination, you can rise to it.

As you play the line, notice how the playwright has, in the phrasing of the words, helped you achieve your goals.

First, well-chosen words reflect your authority and dignity: words like *isle* and *neven* (rhymes with *heaven*) and the poetic contraction *'neath* (for *beneath*) lend the line a melodious and awe-inspiring tone. (Note: The single apostrophe ['] indicates a contraction, or a letter or letters missing, as in *e'er* for *ever* and *'tis* for *it is*.)

You will doubtless also notice the striking *alliteration* (repeated initial consonant sounds) in the line, which includes no less than four words beginning with the letter *n*. There is also marked *assonance* (the close juxtaposition of similar vowel sounds), as in the phrases "'neath me" and "isle I." These repeated sounds create a sense of harmony in the language, a pleasing and otherworldly pattern, appropriate for God.

There is also a deliberate and definite rhythm to these words:

DAH dah dah DAH, d'DAH DAH dah DAH dah
d'DAH DAH dah DAH!

This pattern of stressed and unstressed syllables, while not as regular as "Roses are red/Violets are blue," sets up a throbbing beat that continues through the entire line.

Moreover, the normal order of subject, object, predicate, and adverb is reversed. Instead of "I neven . . . a new isle . . . here," the author has written "Here . . . a new isle I neven." And a figure of speech is used: specifically, a *metaphor* (an implied comparison), whereby the Earth is described as an isle. Both the reversal of syntactical units and use of metaphor imply a formal and rehearsed declaration, rather than a spontaneous remark.

These word choices, sound patterns, images, rhythms, and syntactical variations radiate a very special sense of grace, authority, and intelligence for the character of God, whose words would thereby have seemed—certainly to a medieval audience—divinely inspired. Indeed, the formality of the language allows the audience to see the actor, who is in reality someone like themselves, *as* God, and even in some ways "godlike."

Thus the exalted style of the language creates a speech more persuasive than would everyday phrasings. Compare it, for example, with "I've made a planet down there, see? It's called . . . uhhh . . . Earth!" or "Hey! That new rock looks kinda like an island down there, duhdn' it? I'm namin' it Earth." Colloquial phrasing can convey the *content* of the original line but not the *character* (grace, authority, intelligence) of its speaker.

And what's wrong with that? Simply that the content isn't what makes the angels tremble—and thus doesn't deliver the totality of your line, which must convince the angels (and through them the audience) that you are capable of creating and naming the human planet and therefore have godlike power. This, is what *acting* requires. It's one thing to say you're creating the Earth; it's another to convince people you're actually doing it. The written line stipulates a fact—that you have created Earth—but the acted line creates an identity: you as God. Without the latter, we cannot be thrilled by the former. *We* want to tremble a bit too.

In other words God must not only make pronouncements but exude an aura of godliness—of divine power and moral authority. It is through the *style* of your assertions, not merely their content, that you will "play God" and propel the angels to follow your divine leadership.

Thus poetic images, alliterations, rolling assonance, formal syntactical structures, and rhythmic speech will all, if convincingly performed, indicate to the angels (and through them the audience) that your words were not arbitrarily summoned from the chaos of a human mind but were instead composed by the force of divinity itself. That the lines were in fact written by a human author and are now spoken by a human (indeed, a student) actor only indicates the tremendous challenge of making these characters come to life onstage.

So play this opening of God's speech again, and again, and yet again, seeking to do two things at the same time:

1. Convey the content (the meaning) of the line, which is the easy part.

2. Convey the "godliness" of your character—the grace and authority and divine leadership—that will make the angels want to do what you will soon be asking them to do.

How might you go about all this? How can you play God? Fortunately, you need obey no mere stereotype: God has been imagined in many guises throughout world history—as saintly, brutish, spiritual, intellectual, and poetic; alternatively as compassionate and ferocious, beneficent and terrible.

So concentrate not on the *character* of God but on the *situation* of God that the playwright has created with his words in this scene.

Here . . .

You start the line with a declaration of absolute centrality, calling the attention of all the angels to yourself (the center of "Here") and the action you are about to do. This word is a "grabber"—it implies "Don't look elsewhere. Look *here,* look at me."

. . . 'neath me . . .

You must be "on high" if what you are about to describe is beneath you, so *revel* in your height. And by squeezing a syllable out of *beneath* to make the contraction *'neath,* you are (in addition to creating alliteration and regularizing the rhythm of the line) slighting the lower space, emphasizing that it isn't worth two whole syllables to explain its position.

. . . now . . .

Coupled with the initial "Here," you are defining not just spatial centrality but temporal immediacy, the "here and now" that lets the angels know that something is on the verge of happening—right at this instant, right in their midst.

. . . a new . . .

This conveys excitement, for we are always astounded—and frightened—by the new. So *electrify* your angels, who presumably have been hanging around for most of eternity up to this point, with an entirely novel creation.

. . . isle . . .

The word is deliberately poetic, suggesting a magical place, but it is also homonymic (sounds identical) with *I'll,* providing a subliminal suggestion of your (God's) instrumental role in the Creation.

. . . I neven . . .

Here you move to a formal, almost legalistic term, making it thereby clear that this is an important action you're engaged in, not a whim, not a brief experiment, but a cosmos-changing creation.

. . . The island . . .

Your words now repeat, and expand upon, your creation of an *isle.* It's not just the doubling to two syllables; the new homonym expands to *I-land,* subliminally suggesting your identification with, and protection of, your new creation. The original English audience, of course, knowing that as an island itself, England was protected from invasion by sea, would be reassured by this image that the Earth would be protected by its creator, who considers the Earth an "I-land," that is, part of himself.

. . . of Earth.

Here you complete the naming action predicted by *neven,* fulfilling the action you have promised with the "here and now" opening. But note that the word is—to the angels—a surprise. And one question for you: *When* did you decide what it should be called? In acting, it is almost always more powerful and captivating if that decision is *fresh:* something you *do onstage,* in the moment, rather than a past decision you merely report on at the time we see you.

Well, how then do you "play" these thirteen words, words so fraught with meaning that it takes several pages to gloss them?

No one can (or should) tell you exactly, since this is part of the actor's job, and each actor will (and should) do it a bit differently. But you certainly want to

◆ Grab focus and attention with "Here"

◆ Emphasize the immediacy of the situation with "now"

◆ Encourage delight and excitement with "new isle"

◆ Indicate the importance and gravity of your action with "neven"

◆ Decide on a name for this new planet in real time, at the present moment, with your angels watching (and fearing, and admiring)

Try it!

Playing a Character

Playing a "character" is a tricky business, because characters generally see themselves not as "characters" but as normal people. They think of *other* people as characters. A miser, for instance, doesn't think of himself as a miser; he simply thinks that other people are greedy. A paranoid doesn't think she's paranoid; she simply thinks other people are out to get her. So if you're asked to play God, you shouldn't start by saying to yourself "I'm God!" Instead, start by saying, "These people around me are my angels." And you will become godlike without even thinking about it.

You play character by seeing *other* people as characters. You become a character by characterizing others. You enter a character's mind-set not by transforming yourself but by *transforming the way you see others around you.* This process, *reciprocal characterization,* has the great advantage of being exactly how we become seen as characters in our everyday lives. For example, the teacher in your acting class is not thinking "I am a professor" when she teaches; instead, she is thinking, "These are my students." And because she sees them as students, she acts "professorial"—standing tall, nodding sagely, and writing things on the blackboard so "her students" will better understand "their lesson." So as God, look down at your surrounding "angels" and make them focus on the new tasks you are giving them. Inspire them to become your ministers on a new and challenging planet. Awe them. Put the fear of God in them. This is not arrogance on your part: Help them understand that to be led by a magnificent God like yourself will dignify them. Become the God that they desire of you; give them the divine leadership you can see they crave.

Take charge. Don't simply "walk," but stride, swirl, point, stand tall. Don't simply "talk," but thunder, bellow, whisper, resonate, command. Find the voice inside yourself that will inspire your angels with your godliness and will make them fear your displeasure. Find a face that doesn't just smile but beams, that doesn't just frown but glares. Earn their adoration and respect. And start looking for the angel who will betray you. (For one will.)

If you've had a chance to prepare this, you can do it in costume. Be entirely creative here. A giant robe and sandals? A colorful blanket draped over you? An African dashiki? A towering staff? No one can know what "God" looks like, so you can't be wrong in your choices—*as long as you try to inspire* "your" angels.

If you feel unsuited to this task, don't worry: You *are* unsuited to it. Remember: You are *playing* God, but you *aren't* God. You're only *acting* (thank God!). Which is as far as you can go in this exercise.

But act up a storm: The role requires it. Acting is doing your best to live up to a character, or style, that is not entirely your own. There will always be a tension between the character and yourself, between the style of the play and your own style of life. You are not God, and you aren't Oedipus or Amanda Wingfield, either. No one is. But you can try your hardest, using the tools the playwright (and, later, the director and costume designer) have given you. It is the *effort* to play God that is what, in the theatre, is godlike.

Summary

Playing God means not only delivering God's lines but persuading your onstage hearers (the angels in this case) that you are godlike and carry the authority and dignity of God. If you don't, the lines will be out of context and meaningless. But, fortunately for you, everyone has a different notion of the authority and dignity of God, and your ideas are as valid as anyone else's. Moreover, you don't have to embody everybody's notion of God (and you won't in any case). You only have to try, which is all you can do.

5

Characterization

Reciprocal Characterization

The preceding lesson described a primary process of playing character, *reciprocal characterization*, whereby your character is determined chiefly by how you view other characters, and how you react in character to the way you view them. Acting a character is not merely imitating the outward behavior of a certain kind of person but *thinking like* that person, and making the resulting actions that person would make. Your character behavior is then an *action*, not a demonstration of certain traits. To ourselves, we are personality-neutral.*

---

* There's a classic experiment demonstrating this: When asked to rate themselves and others according to various personality scales, subjects invariably gave specific traits, such as stinginess, arrogance, happiness, to other people, while mostly rating themselves as "depends on situation," a category they rarely used to describe others. See my *Acting Power* (Palo Alto, CA: Mayfield, 1978), p. 18.

◆ E X E R C I S E   5–1

Reciprocal Characterization: Richard and Hastings

Let's go back to one of the Elizabethan greetings from Lesson 2. In this and subsequent cases in this chapter, in addition to bowing and curtsying, try to see the person you're greeting through the eyes of the person you're playing.

HASTINGS: Good time of day unto my gracious lord!

RICHARD: As much unto my good Lord Chamberlain!

Lord Hastings believes himself rescued from prison by Richard, whom he sees as his savior. He's also aware that Richard is aggressive, imaginative, and royal; clearly he hopes for further advancement from this distinguished patron.

Richard, by contrast, sees Hastings as a man of high status and title but, in reality, a weak, stupid sycophant.

With a partner, play the exchange, bowing deeply to each other as in Lesson 2. (Hastings, bowing to royalty, should bow the more deeply.) If a woman plays either role, she may be greeted as "gracious lady" or "Lady Chamberlain" if you wish, and she should then curtsy instead of bowing.

Allow the goals you play with each other, and the way you view each other, to affect your bows or curtsies. Also, recognize that the exchange takes place *in public*. So *perform* this exchange, and your bodily inclinations of (real or pretended) respect, to publicly announce your relationship with the other person in this greeting.

Intrinsic Characterization

Now let's take another step in characterization.

In addition to the characterizing that occurs by seeing other people differently from the way you see yourself, your own physical and psychological makeup obviously comes into play as well. We can call these the *intrinsic* aspects of character because they seem to exist whether other people are around or not. (Indeed, many beginning actors—and beginning directors—assume that these intrinsic aspects of character are all that characterization consists of.)

We can find intrinsic aspects of character from descriptions in the text, including stage directions by the author, verbal descriptions by other characters, the character's own self-reflections, or inferences we can draw from the lines or action of the play.

For example: When Hastings enters in an early scene of *Richard III,* another character remarks, "Here comes the sweating lord." This might suggest Hastings is fat or at least out of shape.

And the action of the play indicates that Hastings several times fails to recognize the danger he is in, even when other characters warn him. "I know he loves me well," Hastings says of Richard when almost everyone else realizes that Richard is about to have him executed. This might suggest that Hastings is naive.

We know that Hastings boasts of having a mistress, which might suggest he is lascivious and foolhardy. He describes himself in the play as "triumphant," which might suggest that he is arrogant. He jests that other men are wimpy ("Where is your boar-spear, man? Fear you the boar?" he gibes), suggesting that he is pompous, hollowly heroic.

It is from the perspectives of his own intrinsic characteristics—physically unfit, naive, foolhardy, arrogant, and pompous—that Hastings perceives Richard as his savior. The contrast between what we see in Hastings and how Hastings sees himself creates the dynamic tension—and human poignancy—of his character and role.

Richard, for his part, is repeatedly described as misshapen: History reports him "crook-backed" and "hard-favored of visage." He admits in the play to being "deformed, unfinished," and the play's other characters describe him in even more grotesque terms: a "poisonous bunch-backed toad," a "bottled spider," an "abortive, rooting hog." Specifically, he is described as having a withered arm, an ugly face, a humped back, and one leg shorter than the other, and you may wish to incorporate all of these into your "intrinsic" portrayal of the character. And then you would want to fold in his persistent drive to power and his psychopathic lust for evil ("I am determined to be a villain"), which will animate these physical deformities into a Richard that will terrify, perplex, and thrill his allies and adversaries alike.

From this misshapen and intentionally villainous persona, Richard looks upon the fawning, pompous Hastings, and they exchange pleasantries. And we can sense what is going to happen.

◆ EXERCISE   5–2

Intrinsic Characterization: Richard and Hastings

Play the simple exchange again, with a variety of partners, switching back and forth between the roles. Create the intrinsic characters by letting your imagination take off from any of the above-mentioned points. Give each role a costume: a cape for Richard, perhaps, which could (for class purposes) be a blanket draped over your shoulders; a sword in your belt; a crutch under your arm (or arms: Anthony Sher made a famous choice of giving Richard two crutches with which he hopped about the stage); and perhaps shoes of unequal sizes. And for Hastings, a pillow under your shirt, perhaps; a blanket or a sheet draped over you; a floppy hat, say; and perhaps a staff of office. (If this two-line exchange intrigues you, you might want to work up the entire scene, still a short one: which is Act 1, Scene 1, lines 122–144; or even the more murderous "Off with his head!" final scene between the two: Act 3, Scene 4, lines 59–79.)

Intrinsic Characterizations: Extensions and Stereotypes

There are many ways in which actors can create an intrinsic characterization—developing character voices, character walks, character tics, for example—but these methods are also a minefield. Extending yourself into behaviors you cannot convincingly perform, particularly in a realistic play, can result in mere stereotypes and caricatures. That's one reason for looking at reciprocal characterization first.

But you certainly can explore intrinsic characterization, subtly in realistic plays and more aggressively in comic plays that include farcical or stock characters, such as those derived from Roman comedies (Italian *commedia* and certain works of Molière and Shakespeare) or modern farces, musical comedies, and TV sitcoms. Here are exercises and discussions to get you started.

Centering

The Russian teacher Michael Chekhov (nephew of the famed playwright and disciple of Stanislavsky) popularized the teaching of "finding your center" in the 1930s and '40s; it is one way of extending your body into at least the image of another. Using Chekhov's technique, an actor playing Hastings might choose to mentally center his body in his chest, puffing himself up with the pride of his position as Lord Chamberlain, while the actor playing Richard might choose to mentally find his body's center in the sour pit of his stomach, longing for power and recognition, or perhaps in his twisted arm, which has so forced a reorganization of his life's goals. In any case, the place where the actor chooses to center his or her movement will affect that movement—and the implicit character that is observed by both the other characters and the audience.

◆ E X E R C I S E   5–3

Centering

Stride about the room, concentrating on the fullness and grandness of your chest. Greet people you see with Hastings's line ("Good time of day . . .") and a more modest bow but always concentrating on *showing off your magnificent chest*.

Stride about the room, concentrating on the sour pain in the pit of your stomach. Greet people who greet you with Richard's line ("As much unto . . .") and a commensurately reduced or distorted bow.

Play these characters, and play other Elizabethan greetings from Lesson 2, while striding around the room and concentrating on various other parts of your body: your loins, your fingertips, your knees, your sinuses, your belly, your anus, your chin.

See how this affects your speaking, your breathing, your walking, your posture, and your general attitude.

Our bodies are not all alike. Chances are, if you could magically inhabit someone else's body, you would start thinking, moving, and acting differently. Well, acting a role *is* inhabiting someone else's body, even if a fictitious one, and the opportunity to recenter your body, through your creative imagination, can extend you into a different aspect of yourself.

Character Postures and Walks

People stand and move in different ways—for all sorts of reasons unassociated with a psychological center. Physical realities (height, weight, strength, health, injury) are invariably factors, as are certain psychological traits (confidence, recklessness, timidity, specific phobias). Occupational identities play a role in, say, the cowboy's lope, the gambler's stealth, the pimp's swagger, the nurse's stride. And cultural codes probably induce the surfer's shuffle, the party girl's sashay, the jock's guffaw, and the scholar's scowl—all of which, at least at the unconscious level, we use to signal like-minded souls.

◆ E X E R C I S E   5–4

Character Walks

Imagine that you are applying for a job as a professor at your own college or university and are walking across your campus to a job interview. Walk around the room as though it were the route to the interview, greeting people you know and silently acknowledging others that you assume know you, while at the same time imagining that you

1. Are much taller than you are

2. Are much shorter than you are

3. Are much fatter than you are

4. Are much leaner than you are

5. Have one leg shorter than another

6. Have a pain in one hip

7. Are always sore from riding horseback all day

8. Always carry large sums of cash on your person

9. Are blind

10. Are afraid of people

11. Are extremely pigeon-toed

12. Have just had a sex-change operation resulting in your becoming a man (even if, in real life, you are a man)

13. Have just had a sex-change operation resulting in your becoming a woman (even if, in real life, you are a woman)

14. Have an extreme need to find a bathroom

15. Are extremely afraid of spiders, which are known to be present around you

16. Have just had a nose job

Try to project whatever image you think will help you get the job.

Character Voices

In Lesson 4 you were asked to find God's voice within yourself. Of course, no one knows what God's voice sounds like. Nor do we know what Hamlet's voice, Jocasta's voice, or Stanley Kowalski's voice sounds like either. These are all fictional characters, even if based on real people, and your voice is going to be delivering the character's voice no matter what happens.

But *which* of your voices? You have many: one you use with your parents, another with small children, another with your closest friends, perhaps another with the officer who stops and questions you. And then there are the voices you can create and employ for special occasions: football games, nightclubs, church services, parties, council meetings, special prayers. And surely you have rehearsed, in your mind at least, a few voices you have never yet used in public: addressing a political rally on behalf of your cause, telling someone you love her, demanding the overthrow of an intolerant regime, energizing your teammates before the final quarter, giving your Academy Award acceptance speech.

So by finding, and sometimes then extending, your varied voices, you will find your version of God's voice, and maybe Hamlet's or Jocasta's voice as well.

How do you extend your voice? Experiment—with an instructor's help if possible—by varying your normal placement of vowels, or formation of consonants, or vocal resonance. What happens, for example, if your character has a "heavy tongue" that insists on lying on the floor of your mouth? Or a jaw that continually pulls to the left? Or an upper lip that bunches up toward your nose? Try changing your resonance by elevating your head a half inch and tilting it forward, while forming your vowels deeper in your throat, giving a more hollow and perhaps obsequious sound. Or cock your head to the right and throw your vowels up into your sinuses for a nasal twang. Such "character voices" are more usually heard in cartoons, radio shows, and impersonation acts (listen to Tim Russell on *A Prairie Home Companion*) than in straight drama, but actors such as Dustin Hoffman and Lily Tomlin have created brilliant characters on the stage and in film using these techniques.

◆ E X E R C I S E   5–5

Finding Your Voices

These exercises require you not to extend your voice artificially but to find the voice within you specific to the situation, and expand it in its own direction.

1. Face a (real or imaginary) ocean and speak to it in Byron's famous apostrophe:

     Roll on, thou deep and dark blue ocean—roll!

   Repeat until you feel you are commanding the waves.

2. Face a (real or imaginary) thunderstorm and challenge it in Lear's cry:

     Blow, winds, and crack your cheeks! Rage! Blow!

   Repeat, challenging the heavens to topple you—if they dare.

3. Look out into an imaginary night and, hoping that your loved one might be there, speak to him in Juliet's words,

> Romeo, doff thy name,
> And for that name, which is no part of thee,
> Take all myself.

Repeat, inducing Romeo, should he magically be there, to literally take *all* of you and fall as deeply in love with you as you are with him.

4. Dance around a cauldron and make it bubble with the witch's words from *Macbeth:*

> Double, double toil and trouble;
> Fire burn, and cauldron bubble.

Repeat three times (as the witches do), letting your voice and movements be the fire that makes the cauldron heat and boil over.

5. Drop to the floor and summon vengeance from hell in Othello's oath:

> Arise, black vengeance, from thy hollow hell!

Repeat, seeking to catch the devil's ear with your voice, your roaring vowels, the resonance of your own name, hidden in a near anagram in this speech: Othello as o - the - hell - o)

6. Kneel before your aging, dying, deeply confused father and seek his blessing using Cordelia's words from *King Lear:*

> O look upon me, sir,
> And hold your hands in benediction o'er me.

Repeat, seeking to penetrate the old man's confusion and relieve his guilt for disowning you.

7. Protect yourself from the blows of your master in Dromio's words from *The Comedy of Errors:*

> What mean you, sir? For God's sake, hold your hands!

Repeat, pleading—with voice and gestures—to induce your master to stop beating you.

Character Descriptions

Since the late nineteenth century, dramatists have often included in the texts of their plays descriptions of the characters, giving them specific appearances, voices, and behaviors in stage directions, usually at the point of the charac-ter's first entrance. The following exercise contains several such stage direc-tions, followed by a line or two of dialogue from characters in well-known plays.

♦ E X E R C I S E   5–6

Playing Out Character Descriptions

Find clothing from your own wardrobe, or borrow some from friends, or rummage through thrift shops that might have what you need, and costume yourself as best you can for the following parts. Then find the most appro-priate voice within yourself, and, consulting a full-length mirror where pos-sible, create the silhouette and movement pattern matching the following characters in their opening lines and movements. Then perform them.

1. Eddie, in Sam Shepard's *Fool for Love*, is talking to May (his girlfriend and half sister) whom he has previously abandoned.

[Stark, low-rent motel room on the edge of the Mojave Desert. Eddie wears muddy, broken-down cowboy boots with silver gaffer's tape wrapped around them at the toe and instep, well-worn, faded, dirty jeans that smell like horse sweat. Brown western shirt with snaps. A pair of spurs dangles from his belt. When he walks, he limps slightly and gives the impression he's rarely off a horse. There's a peculiar broken-down quality about his body in general, as though he's aged long before his time. He's in his late thirties. He wears a bucking glove on his right hand and works resin into the glove from a small white bag. He pulls his hand out and removes gloves.]

EDDIE: *[seated, tossing glove on the table]:* May, look. May? I'm not goin' anywhere. See? I'm right here.

2. Margaret (Maggie), in Tennessee Williams's *Cat on a Hot Tin Roof*, is talking to her husband, Brick, who is offstage showering.

[A bed-sitting-room of a plantation home in the Mississippi Delta (c. 1955). A pretty young woman, with anxious lines in her face, enters. Margaret's voice is both rapid and drawling. In her long speeches she has the vocal tricks of a priest delivering a liturgical chant, the lines are almost sung, always continuing a little beyond her breath so she has to gasp for another. Sometimes she intersperses the lines with a little wordless singing, such as "Da-da-daaaa!"]

MARGARET: *[shouting above the roar of water]:* One of those no-neck monsters hit me with a hot buttered biscuit so I have t'change. It's too bad you can't wring their necks if they've got no necks to wring! Isn't that right, honey? Yep, they're no-neck monsters, all no-neck people are monsters. Hear them? Hear them screaming? I don't know where their voice-boxes are located since they don't have necks.

3. Brick is responding to Margaret in item 2.

[He stands there in the bathroom doorway drying his hair with a towel and hanging onto the towel rack because one ankle is broken, plastered and bound. He is still slim and firm as a boy. His liquor hasn't started tearing him down outside. He has the additional charm of that cool air of detachment that people have who have given up the struggle. But now and then, when disturbed, something flashes behind it, like lightning in a fair sky, which shows that at some deeper level he is far from peaceful. Perhaps in a stronger light he would show some signs of deliquescence, but the fading, still warm, light from the gallery treats him gently. A tone of politely feigned interest, masking indifference, or worse, is characteristic of his speech with Margaret.]

Jason Patrick and Ashley Judd play Brick and Maggie in the 2004 Broadway revival of *Cat on a Hot Tin Roof.* (Photo © Joan Marcus)

BRICK: Wha'd you say, Maggie? Water was on s'loud I couldn't hearya. . . .
Why d'ya call Gooper's kiddies no-neck monsters?

4. Herald Loomis, in August Wilson's *Joe Turner's Come and Gone*

*[August 1911. A boardinghouse in Pittsburgh. From the deep and near
South the sons and daughters of newly freed African slaves wander into
the city. Isolated, cut off from memory, having forgotten the names of
the gods and only guessing at their faces, they arrive dazed and stunned,
their heart kicking in their chest with a song worth singing. Enter
Herald Loomis and his eleven-year-old daughter, Zonia. Herald Loomis
is thirty-two years old. He is at times possessed. A man driven not by the
hellhounds that seemingly bay at his heels, but by his search for a world
that speaks to something about himself. He is unable to harmonize the
forces that swirl around him, and seeks to recreate the world into one
that contains his image. He wears a hat and a long wool coat.]*

LOOMIS: Me and my daughter looking for a place to stay, mister. You got
a sign say you got rooms. *[pause]* Mister, if you ain't got no rooms we
can go somewhere else.

5. Mattie Campbell, in August Wilson's *Joe Turner's Come and Gone*

*[Enter Mattie Campbell. She is a young woman of twenty-six whose
attractiveness is hidden under the weight and concerns of a dissatisfied
life. She is a woman in an honest search for love and companionship.
She has suffered many defeats in her search, and though not always
uncompromising, still believes in the possibility of love.]*

MATTIE: I'm looking for a man named Bynum. Lady told me to come
back later. Are you the man they call Bynum? The man folks say can fix
things? Can you fix it so my man come back to me?

6. Lawrence Garfinkle, in Jerry Sterner's *Other People's Money*

*[Andrew Jorgenson's office. The present (1987). Lights up on Garfinkle.
He is an immense man of forty, though he looks older. He is always
elegantly dressed, surprisingly graceful for his bulk. He is, in some way,
larger than life. His deep, rich voice fills the stage. He speaks in a New
York rhythm. He looks about.]*

GARFINKLE: Haven't seen a place this shitty since I left the Bronx.

7. Laura Wingfield, in Tennessee Williams's *The Glass Menagerie*

*[The Wingfield apartment. Laura is seated at the table. Laura's
situation is even graver (than her mother's). A childhood illness has left
her crippled, one leg slightly shorter than the other, and held in a brace.*

This defect need not be more than suggested on the stage. Stemming from this, Laura's separation increases till she is like a piece of her own glass collection, too exquisitely fragile to move from the shelf.]

LAURA: *[rising]* I'll bring in the blanc mange.*

8. Maxine, in Tennessee Williams's *Night of the Iguana*

[The play takes place in the summer of 1940 in a rather rustic and very Bohemian hotel in Puerto Barrio in Mexico. Mrs. Maxine Faulk, the proprietor of the hotel, comes around the turn of the verandah. She is a stout, swarthy woman in her middle forties—affable and rapaciously lusty. She is wearing a pair of Levi's and a blouse that is half unbuttoned. Mrs. Faulk looks down the hill and is pleased by the sight of someone coming up from the tourist bus below.]

MAXINE: *[calling out]* Shannon! *[A man's voice from below answers: "Hi!"]* Hah! *[Maxine always laughs with a single harsh, loud bark, opening her mouth like a seal expecting a fish to be thrown to it.]* My spies told me that you were back under the border!

9. Miss Roj (a man) in George C. Wolfe's *The Colored Museum*

[Electronic music. A neon sign which spells out THE BOTTOMLESS PIT. There is a blast of smoke and, from the haze, Miss Roj appears. He is dressed in striped patio pants, white go-go boots, a halter, and cat-shaped sunglasses. What would seem ridiculous on anyone else, Miss Roj wears as if it were high fashion. He carries himself with total elegance and absolute arrogance.]

MISS ROJ: God created black people and black people created style. The name's Miss Roj . . . that's R.O.J. thank you and you can find me every Wednesday, Friday and Saturday nights at "The Bottomless Pit," the watering hole for the wild and weary which asks the question, "Is there life after Jherri-curl?"

10. Esther, in Lynn Nottage's *Intimate Apparel*

[Lower Manhattan, 1905. A bedroom. A clumsy ragtime melody bleeds in from the parlor. In the distance the sound of laughter and general merriment. Esther, a rather plain African-American woman (35), sits at a sewing machine table diligently trimming a camisole with lace. She is all focus and determination.]

---

* A custard dessert, pronounced "blaw mawnj."

Shané Williams (at sewing machine) plays Esther in the 2003 South Coast Repertory co-premiere of *Intimate Apparel*. Brenda Pressley plays Mrs. Dickson, her landlady. (Photo © Ken Howard)

ESTHER: Mr. Charles is overly generous. But he's been coming to these parties for near two years and if he ain't met a woman, I'd bet it ain't a woman he after.

11. Blanche du Bois, in Tennessee Williams's *A Streetcar Named Desire*

[New Orleans, c. 1947. Blanche comes around the corner, carrying a valise. She looks at a slip of paper, then at the building, then at the slip and again at the building. Her expression is one of shocked disbelief. Her appearance is incongruous to this setting. She is daintily dressed in a white suit with a fluffy bodice, necklace and earrings of pearl, white

gloves and hat, looking as if she were arriving at a summer tea or cocktail party in the garden district. She is about (thirty). Her delicate beauty must avoid a strong light. There is something about her uncertain manner, as well as her white clothes, that suggests a moth.]

BLANCHE: *[with faintly hysterical humor]* They told me to take a streetcar named Desire, and then transfer to one called Cemeteries and ride six blocks and get off at—Elysian Fields!

12. Stanley Kowalski, in Tennessee Williams's *A Streetcar Named Desire*

[Stanley throws the screen door of the kitchen open and comes in. He is of medium height, about five feet eight or nine, and strongly, compactly built. Animal joy in his being is implicit in all his movements and attitudes. Since earliest manhood the center of his life has been pleasure with women, the giving and taking of it, not with weak indulgence, dependently, but with the power and pride of a richly feathered male bird among hens. Branching out from this complete and satisfying center are all the auxiliary channels of his life, such as his heartiness with men, his appreciation of rough humor, his love of good drink and food and games, his car, his radio, everything that is his, that bears his emblem of the gaudy seed-bearer.]

STANLEY: H'lo. Where's the little woman?

Animal Imagery

In the previous two stage directions, dramatist Tennessee Williams writes that the manner of Blanche du Bois "suggests a moth" and that Stanley has the power of a "richly feathered male bird" and expresses "animal joy in his being." Williams continued this animal imagery in *Cat on a Hot Tin Roof*, where the character of Maggie is the title feline, her mother-in-law is "an old bulldog" rushing onstage like a "charging rhino," and her father-in-law "smiles wolfishly." Such imagery makes us "see" the characters vividly, even if we know nothing else about the play.

Williams is not alone in using such images to make characters come to life. In Shakespeare's *King Lear*, the King calls Goneril a "detested kite" (bird of prey), "serpent-like," and one of his "pelican daughters." Shakespeare's Othello, to Iago, is likewise an "old black ram," and the wicked Duke of Gloucester, to his enemies, becomes a "toad," a "rooting hog," a "crab," and a "bottled spider."

If playwrights can make use of animal imagery to describe their characters, so can you in playing them. By doing so, you "animate" these characters, extending yourself into a feral vitality that is specific to a species different from your own as well as into a powerful archetype of superhuman (or at least nonhuman) behavior—as represented by such idealized animals throughout history as the sacred Egyptian Cat, the ferocious British Lion, the sturdy Russian Bear, and the fearsome Tamil Tiger.

Using animal imagery can be as simple as going to a zoo and imagining the animals your character might identify with. Robert de Niro imagined his Travis Bickle, in *Taxi Driver,* as a crab, moving sideways and back rather than straight ahead, to create the sense of a deranged and awkward predator.* British actor Anthony Sher extended himself into the "bottled spider" image of Gloucester by making his first entrance supported by two crutches, and scuttling around the stage spider-like; American actor James Newcomb went for the praying mantis in the same role, darting his arms about to capture his prey. Actors should be careful not to let animal imagery substitute for full-fledged characterizations, but when the "animal in you" can be brought out by extending yourself into a different species of mammal or reptile, powerful, vivid, and specific characters can erupt brilliantly onto the stage.

♦ E X E R C I S E   5–7

Animate (Animalize) Your Character

Replay the Hastings–Richard greeting from Exercise 5–1 with Hastings as a peacock and Richard a spider. You needn't give a literal impression of the animal—just your impression of the animal's essence, hybridized onto your own.

Try it with different animals. A lion and a serpent. An ostrich and a hyena. A walrus and a fox. A giraffe and a warthog.

Take any of the speeches from Exercise 5–6 and animate it with an animal of your choice. Don't rely on your memory of animals. Do what many actors do, go to the zoo!

Intrinsic and Reciprocal Characterization

Intrinsic and reciprocal characterization work as a team, as two sides of the same coin. But they are seen from two different perspectives: Intrinsic character is that which we gather from reading the play; reciprocal is that which we

---

* Doug Tomlinson, *Actors on Acting for the Screen* (New York: Garland, 1994), p. 143.

gather from playing the part. Critics, who read the plays but don't usually act them, write mainly about intrinsic characteristics. And since the actor reads the play before playing it, intrinsic characterization generally comes to the actor's mind first. You read the play and make conclusions about what sort of person you are about to portray. Many beginning actors simply stop there and go no further.

But reciprocal characterization—the way your character perceives other characters—is what drives the role *during the performance itself*; it is what evokes characteristics *from* you. It is not the reader's view, nor the critic's; it is the actor's view in the real time of the play. So if these two aspects of characterization are to function as a team, teamwork is required. You will create the intrinsic character through studying the way the part is described and appears on the page. And you will create the reciprocal characterization through your imagination: by getting *inside* that character to see other people not as you do in your own life, but as you do with your character's eyes. Put these aspects of character together and you will have the kernel of characterization. A few more exercises will get you started.

◆ E X E R C I S E   5–8

Character Greetings

Let's replay some of the greetings in Exercise 2–4 aided by our discussions of characterization. Comments below each dialogue will guide you to possible text considerations (refer to Exercise 2–4 for basic descriptions of the situations), and you can flesh these out, now, with extensions: You might try bodily recenterings, animal imagery, or other intrinsic characterizing techniques.

Don John/Don Pedro

DON JOHN: My lord and brother, God save you!

DON PEDRO: Good den, brother.

Don Pedro is a prince of Arragon, recently returned from a victorious military battle. He sees his half-brother as an embarrassment to his family name. Don John is a bastard, resentful of the legitimate and more noble Pedro, and admits to villainy ("I am a plain-dealing villain," he tells a friend). Don John sees his brother as an obstacle to his advancement, though at this point he is trying to lure him into a trap. Both actors may imagine themselves wearing formal garb, either as military officers (with Don Pedro the more distinguished) or as party guests.

If you want to extend this exchange to a fuller scene, it's *Much Ado About Nothing,* Act 3, Scene 2, lines 80–91.

Duke/Isabella

DUKE: Good morning to you, fair and gracious daughter.

ISABELLA: The better, given me by so holy a man.

The text indicates that the duke, disguised as a friar, is attracted to Isabella (to whom he will propose marriage) and preoccupied with profound moral and religious questions. Isabella, a young woman, having begun training as a nun, now finds herself in a deeply compromised moral position with her brother and the duke's deputy. The duke sees her as a beautiful and endangered young woman; she sees him as a potential savior for her desperate situation. Both actors could imagine themselves in religious vestments.

The scene, which is intense, continues at *Measure for Measure,* Act 4, Scene 3, lines 112–148.

Othello/Desdemona

OTHELLO: O my fair warrior!

DESDEMONA: My dear Othello!

Othello is an African general flush with great victories and a new bride. From the text we gather that he sees Desdemona as a beautiful and sainted woman ("my soul's joy" he calls her moments after this), brave enough to follow him, against her father's direst warnings, into an interracial marriage. Desdemona, a virtuous but naive Venetian socialite, clearly adores her magnificent husband. They both see the crowd of soldiers surrounding them as loyal supporters of what they foresee as a long and illustrious life together. The actors should imagine Othello garbed as an officer—the text describes him as holding a sword—and Desdemona as a discreet bride forced to travel separately from her husband aboard a ship, from which she has only recently debarked. Their greeting would presumably be some form of embrace.

The scene continues at *Othello,* Act 2, Scene 1, lines 181–198.

Mistress Quickly/Falstaff

MISTRESS QUICKLY: Give your worship good morrow.

FALSTAFF: Good morrow, goodwife.

Lester Purry, as Othello, greets Cheyenne Casebier as Desdemona in the 2004 Guthrie production of *Othello* in Minneapolis. (Photo © Michal Daniel)

MISTRESS QUICKLY: Not so, an't please your worship.

FALSTAFF: Good maid, then.

Sir John Falstaff, who appears in three of Shakespeare's plays, is famously outsized. He is middle-aged or older, fat, and long fallen into drinking and womanizing. The text shows him to be garrulous, amoral, whimsical, a leader among his drinking buddies, and brilliant at avoiding commitment. Mistress Quickly, his steady woman friend and eventually his wife, is his true counterpart, somewhere between a barkeep and a brothel madam. Each sees the other as a formidable challenge, and the gender difference, with all it implies socially and politically, ignites fireworks.

If you'd like to continue the scene, it's at *The Merry Wives of Windsor*, Act 2, Scene 2, lines 33–136.

William/Audrey

WILLIAM: Good ev'n, Audrey.

AUDREY: God ye good ev'n, William.

They are a shepherd and shepherdess in *As You Like It*, neither educated, both presumably fit and hardy from working in the fields. He sees her as a

Mistress Quickly (Libby George) and Sir John Falstaff (Dennis Robertson) greeting each other in the 2000 Utah Shakespearean Festival production of *The Merry Wives of Windsor*. (© 2000 Utah Shakespeare Festival; photo by Karl Hugh)

beautiful princess; she sees him as a rustic ignoramus; both of them see the court jester, Touchstone, who is watching this encounter, as a distinguished and admirably learned celebrity.

Nurse/Mercutio

NURSE: God ye good morrow, gentlemen.

MERCUTIO: God ye good den, fair gentlewoman.

She was Juliet's wet nurse, having lost her own daughter shortly after childbirth; we know from the text that she is gabby, affectionate, and loves to laugh and joke. We infer that she is heavyset because, like the "sweating" Hastings, she is out of breath when she returns to the Capulet home after this scene. Mercutio is an unattached young nobleman, quick to jest and pun with his friends and to fight with his enemies. Clearly she sees him as one of a group of thoughtless young aristocrats—the sort she deals with only when necessary—and he sees her as a bulky, servant-class woman useful only as a target for his playfulness and showing off.

Country rustics William (Gregory Derelian, left) and Audrey (Vanessa Aspillaga) greet each other, with the contrastingly sophisticated Touchstone (Richard Thomas) between them, in the 2005 New York Public Theatre production of *As You Like It*. (Photo © Michal Daniel)

You might like to continue the exchange for three more lines, until Romeo interrupts it:

NURSE: God ye good morrow, gentlemen.

MERCUTIO: God ye good den, fair gentlewoman.

NURSE: Is it good den?

MERCUTIO: 'Tis no less, I tell ye, for the bawdy hand of the dial is now upon the prick of noon.

NURSE: Out upon you, what a man art you?

Mercutio (Jeffrey Binder) and the Nurse (Anne F. Butler) parry words in the 1997 production of *Romeo and Juliet* at the Colorado Shakespeare Festival. (Courtesy Colorado Shakespeare Festival; photo © P. Switzer)

Sir Toby Belch/Viola

SIR TOBY: 'Save you, gentleman.

VIOLA: And you, sir.

Sir Toby is not unlike Falstaff; enamored of his "cakes and ale" (and therefore presumably fat and somewhat addled), he spends much of his time drinking with his men friends, cavorting with the housemaid (whom he eventually marries), and playing practical jokes on his adversary in his niece Olivia's household, where he lives as a family retainer. Viola is a young woman who, stranded in a foreign country, has taken on the disguise and name (Cesario) of a man. Toby regards "him" as a lower-class servant; Viola perceives Toby as a man just unorthodox enough, as a man's man, to see through her disguise.

You could continue this scene, if you wish, with lines that follow almost immediately at *Twelfth Night*, Act 3, Scene 1, lines 74–83.

Summary

Character is composed of two fundamental aspects: the *intrinsic* aspects that we infer from the dialogue and the stage directions, and the *reciprocal* aspects that the actor plays while performing the character and seeing other people in the play as characters. By blending these two interrelated aspects, you can actively play, not merely demonstrate, a character's personality, and you can look through the eyes of the character.

6

More God

Here's more of the speech you worked on in Lesson 4.

Here 'neath me now a new isle I neven,
The island of Earth. And see: Now it starts—
Earth, wholly, and Hell; this highest be Heaven,
And those wielding wealth° shall dwell in these parts.   °*enjoying well-being*
This grant I ye, ministers mine°   °*my angels*
To-whiles° ye are stable in thought.   °*as long as*
But to them that are nought°:   °*not (stable)*
Be put to my prison—and pine°!   °*suffer*

This is not an easy text; it includes now-unfamiliar words (*neven, to-whiles*), familiar but archaic words (*ye*), and tricky phrasing ("those wielding wealth"). But some of this language and phrasing was archaic even in the fifteenth century. The medieval authors and actors who wrestled with this material (as you do) were seeking to depict a world they thought to be four thousand years before their own time. Thus they used words that were archaic even to them, and phrasings that imposed a certain distance between the dialogue and daily speech. So don't be discouraged: Difficult tasks generate hard work but often spectacular results.

In the continuation of the speech, you (as God) now create Hell and Heaven; then you tell the angels (here called your "ministers") that they may live happily ("wielding wealth") in Heaven, so long as they remain level-headed ("stable in thought"). But, you then warn them, they will be sent to Hell to endure endless suffering (to "pine") if they wander from the straight and narrow path you have ordained.

Now we see the larger design of God's speech. There is a continuation of the alliteration in line 1; now we have several series of words beginning with the same consonant: "wholly/Hell/highest/heaven," "wielding/wealth/ (d)well," and "put/prison/pine." But we can also see that the speech is composed in a verse form, with repeated patterns of vocal stress (for example, "but to them that are nought"—dah dah DAH dah dah DAH) and of rhyme (ABAB—"neven, starts, Heaven, parts"—as well as ABBA—"mine, thought, nought, pine"). The dramatist's complex verse patterns provide a firm sense of carefully *composed* language, appearing not as spontaneous chatter but as measured, almost *musical* thought.

And the rhyme makes the language particularly *entertaining*—as we saw in the "roses are red" exercise—which is why rhyme continues to play such an important role in popular music, light verse, and advertising jingles. Rhymes also convey an appealing sense of harmony, wholeness, finality, and, in the medieval mind, something approaching magic or divinity. Rhyme is a fundamental strategy for convincing an audience that a character's words are, if not divinely created, then at least divinely inspired.

◆ E X E R C I S E   6–1

A Stanza, by God

Study and memorize the longer speech. Now—play the speech to the angels.

This time, you have multiple goals to achieve during the course of the speech. During the first lines, as before, you want to impress the angels that you are qualified to give them rules of moral instruction—and that these rules are more important, and more central to their future existence, than, say, advice in a newspaper column. Try to show them that your words are backed by *divinity,* by the universe itself, not just by an ordinary person or committee.

Then make your charge to the angels: If they remain levelheaded, they can live as your personal assistants in Heaven, enjoying the full wealth of your divine spirit. Should they reject that stability, you will make them suffer in Hell.

Using the language of the author, and your own tactics and skills in speaking it, *encourage* the angels to accept your authority and to keep to the path you have shown them. And, conversely, *discourage* them from veering off the path and landing in Hell. Indeed, *scare* the Hell out of them.

⬚ THE CHARACTER OF GOD

Exercise 6–1 is an acting, not a religious, exercise, nor is it meant to
be a sacrilegious one. The "God" referred to is not necessarily your
God, nor your teacher's God, nor the author's God, nor, for that
matter, any living person's God. Rather, he—or she—is a dramatic
character conceived by an anonymous medieval writer six hundred
years ago. Your task—which would be fundamentally no different
if you were playing Zeus in a Greek tragedy—is to understand
what this specific character of God is trying to achieve and *how*
you can try to achieve it. Don't confuse your character's behavior
with your own religious beliefs, or your disbeliefs.

Why did the dramatist choose the particular words in this speech? Or, to
put it another way, why didn't he use simpler language? Why didn't he (if it
was a he) simply "say what he meant"?

Words are not merely the sum of their semantic content (their "meaning"). They also transmit sound, imagery, feeling, and, through these, the
intelligence and seriousness of the speaker. Well-turned phrases become
calls to action that can live on long after they were first uttered. If Lincoln
had begun his Gettysburg address in the simplest possible way, "Eighty-
seven years ago, the constitutional drafters declared that a portion of North
America would become an independent country," no one would have remembered his speech by the following morning. But "Fourscore and seven
years ago, our fathers brought forth, on this continent, a new nation" will
live in the hearts of Americans for centuries to come.

Look at how the medieval dramatist chose words that gave richer meaning, and denser texture, to the speech you have learned.

"Earth, wholly, and Hell" introduces a fascinating intervening adverb:
The word *wholly* is homonymic with *holy* and also *hole-y,* which suggests
on the front end that the Earth is not only whole (complete and contained,
as an island) but holy (tied to Heaven); while, on the back end, Hell is a
"hole" (or even a "Hell-hole").

"[T]hose wielding wealth shall dwell in these parts" is a complex phrase
basically suggesting that persons selected for Heaven will enjoy happiness
and well-being (the original meaning of *wealth*). But it also suggests that
such persons will also have riches and prosperity—the more modern meaning of *wealth*. The phrase is deliberately ambivalent as to which comes first:
whether those wielding earthly wealth will go to Heaven, or those who go

to Heaven will wield wealth when they get there. But both meanings are put forward as God's gift to humankind.

"This grant I ye" is formal, almost legal phrasing. Compare the word order and word choice with the more common "I give you this," or, more simply, "Here, take this!" "This grant I" is *ritualizing* language, which sanctifies what it pronounces; it is similar to the traditional line in wedding ceremonies, "With this ring I thee wed," conveying content (information) in a format used to solemnize (and therefore make unbreakable) sacred covenants.

In "ministers mine," you reverse the normal order of noun and modifier, placing yourself in the line-ending, climactic position, which emphasizes your authority over your angels (as does the scansion: "MIN-is-ters MINE"); while at the same time your alliteration on those two words emphasizes your shared friendship with those well beneath you in the celestial hierarchy. And by thus taking the angels into your bosom as your personal ministers, you are providing them with something very special: your love and trust.

The stipulation "stable in thought," however, includes a hidden warning: "Don't let this Earth give you any new ideas." Since "stable" also refers to a place where animals are kept, your implication is that your angels, like domesticated animals, are not to think for themselves. (One of them, Lucifer, will disobey this command and suffer grave consequences.)

With "But" at the start of line 7, you make a sharp tactical turn, shifting from blessing to threatening the angels. Having secured their attention by your beneficence, you now seek to ensure their obedience.

The phrase "them that are nought" is a euphemism: You don't define the sins they might commit (so as not to give them ideas); you merely promise punishment to those who take a negative attitude toward your instructions. Boldly distinguish the word *naught* (pronounced "nawt" and meaning "nothing") from *not*. Both meanings are implicit in the line—you will consider the straying angels both "unstable" and "nothing"—but the latter is by far the more punishing. Make it clear that you intend not just to criticize but to *obliterate* those angels who "leave your stable."

"My prison" refers to Hell, of course, which you mentioned in the first quatrain. *Prison* also carries the meaning of capture (from the Latin *prehension*, "apprehension, seizure"); you are suggesting you will personally grab them—in a grip so fierce they will never escape.

To the medieval mind, the word *pine*, which originally meant "to suffer," had immediate resonance with the wooden cross (from a Jerusalem pine tree) on which Jesus was crucified. So the suggestion is not merely "longing," as we use it today, but excruciating pain.

See how many of these notions you can play effectively to your listeners, who are the angels, played by your classmates. Try to inspire them with trust—while at the same time putting "the fear of God" into them.

Go back to what you did (or the discussion) in Lesson 4: Find your "voice of God." Create "God's costume."

And stage yourself as God.

◆ *Point to* the places you are naming and/or creating: Point out the island of Earth, and then Hell, and then "this highest," which is Heaven, as you name them. Let the angels know precisely what you are talking about—"'neath me" is a pretty big place; you can, with a gesture, be more specific as to what you're identifying. And the word *this* is what grammarians call a demonstrative pronoun (along with *that, these,* and *those*). Such pronouns almost *require* some sort of visual indication; otherwise, your listener will say "*Which* highest?"

INDICATING

This is a good time to clear up a misunderstanding about the word *indicating*. Most acting teachers (including this author) urge actors not to indicate a character's emotion but rather to play the action of the scene (try to win the character's goal) with energy, focus, and intensity, by which actions you will *experience* the emotion. The audience will sense your emotion more authentically if they don't see you trying to "indicate" or "push" that emotion out in a technical fashion.

But that doesn't mean you should avoid physically gesturing to *objects* in order to explain what you mean. You cannot, for example, say "Sit in this chair" without somehow pointing out the specific chair you mean: The word *this* doesn't explain "which," and an indicative gesture of some sort is necessary to successfully complete the speech act. Not only is there nothing wrong with this form of indicating, but it is essential. It is also helpful in supporting the actor's sense that artificial props represent the real thing. When you say "this highest be Heaven," merely pointing, at the same time, to a wooden scaffold or to whatever the scene designer has fashioned will make the fake Heaven much more real to you as well.

So don't indicate emotion, but *do* feel free to indicate the objects—the people, places, things—that support your point, clarify your argument, and help you win your character's goals.

◆ *Look* in the direction of "those wielding wealth." As *those* is a demonstrative pronoun, demonstrate to the angels those whom you expect to be their role models.

◆ *Gesture* on the phrase "This grant I ye," supporting the future granting of "this" (another demonstrative pronoun, referring to Heaven but also to God's—your—love) by a symbolic handing over. What sort of gesture? It could be specific, to "this highest . . . Heaven," but you've already made that part clear. So try a ritualized, open-handed gesture of emphatic affection, referring simply to "everything you see here." Ritualized gestures solemnize important transitions: a tap of the queen's sword to award knighthood, the placing of a wedding ring on a bride's finger, the handing over of the America's Cup to the yachting champion.

◆ *Move to* your angels, circling or touching them or both, on "ministers mine" to show them the warmth of your love.

◆ *Glare at* any angel of whom you may be suspicious (and know that Lucifer is among this crowd).

◆ *Emphasize,* with a swift and sudden gesture or posture of absolute conviction, that you are disciplined enough to mete out any punishment necessary, on "pine."

Let whatever costume you have chosen for this role (see Lesson 4) flow with these moves and gestures; indeed, choose your costume so that its movements extend your own.

Is all this hokey? Yes it is, if you don't do it with conviction, or if you do it simply because you are told to do it. No it isn't, if you are an actor and convince us that you *want* to do it—and, in fact, *need* to do it. This, once again, is what acting is: It's getting inside a presumably fictional being—a character—and playing his or her part to the hilt. Obviously, lighting, scenery, sound enhancement, special effects, and a real costume and wig will help a lot, but no amount of technical support will make you God, and no fabric or fog machine will be necessary for the other actors or audience to accept you as God.

Playing "God" is an inexhaustible exercise; you can play it many times and make it better each time. Rising to the challenge of this role helps you deliver qualities we rarely explore outside of the stage: grandiosity, unlimited authority, charisma. Merely exploring them—if you can do so without inhibition—can extend your personality as well as your acting ability.

Summary

Playing a character requires mastering not merely the *meaning* of your words and actions but also the *nature* of the language the playwright has given you, its sounds and shapes and natural progressions. And mastery includes both vocal and physical expressiveness, which you can draw from yourself by seeking to meet the challenges of the role. The role of God, in particular, poses more challenges than most of us rise to in a lifetime.

7

The Battle of the Sexes:
Noah and His Wife

It's time to play some human beings. Since this is a book on style and character, they aren't exactly going to be the human beings next door, but they are certainly going to have things in common with all humanity.

Let's look at a scene from one of the first masterpieces of English drama: the Noah play in the Wakefield cycle of the fourteenth century, an expansion of the Bible story written by an author who, though anonymous, is known to us as the "Wakefield Master," a title honoring the Yorkshire city where he (presumably) lived and the excellence of his craftsmanship.

As you will quickly see, the scene—an argument between Noah and his wife—owes far less to Genesis than to the eternally humorous "battle of the sexes" we see in comedies from all ages. Furious marital disputes and lovers' quarrels, comic while bordering dangerously on the abusive, are familiar in the Old and New Comedies of ancient Greece, and subsequently in Roman, medieval, Renaissance, and modern drama. They were standard in *commedia dell'arte* and early English Punch and Judy puppet shows; they surface in Shakespeare's *Taming of the Shrew,* Molière's *Bourgeois Gentleman,* as well as in modern TV sitcoms (*Everybody Loves Raymond*), Broadway comedies (*Barefoot in the Park*), and musicals (*Guys and Dolls*).

The medieval era, however, an age when the status of women was rapidly rising (owing to increased literacy and urbanization), was particularly attuned to the plight of women seeking their independent voices in a world of men trying to retain their historic prerogatives. Thus, in this scene where

Otto Coehelo and Mehr Mansouri play Noah and his wife in a production by the Focused Program in Medieval Drama at the University of California, Irvine. (Photo © Phil Channing)

Noah is struggling to get his wife to board the ark as the rain begins, Noah's wife is cockily asserting her independence. I have added stage directions so that you can readily follow the action.*

NOAH: Now are we there as we should be.
   Do get in our gear, our cattle and fee°,   °possessions
   Into this vessel here, my children free.

[Noah's children—his three sons and their wives—enter the ark. Noah's wife remains outside.]

NOAH'S WIFE *[looking at the ark]*:
   I was ne'er barred up before—as ever might I thee—
   In such a hostelry as this!
   In faith, I cannot find
   Which is the front, which the behind.
   But shall we here be impined°,   °imprisoned
   Noah, as thou have bliss°?   °if you want to be happy

NOAH: Dame, if we have skill, here must we abide grace.
   Therefore, wife, with good will come into this place.

---

*   Adapted from the original and edited by Robert Cohen and Edgar Schell.

NOAH'S WIFE [*standing her ground, outside the ark*]:
    Sir, for Jack nor for Jill will I turn my face
    Till I have on this hill spun a space
    On my rock°.   °*tool for spinning thread*
    Well were he that might get me!
    Now will I down set me;
    And reck° I no man stop me   °*reckon*
    For dread of a knock°!   °*a hit on the head*

[*She sits down on a hill and spins.*]

NOAH [*within the ark, hearing thunder and seeing rain*]:
    Behold to the heavens! The cataracts all,
    They are open full even, great and small,
    And the planets all seven have left their stall.
    These thunders and lightnings down here fall
    Full stout
    On both halls and bowers,
    Castles and towers.
    Full sharp are these showers
    That rain hereabout.

    Therefore, wife, have done; come into ship fast.

NOAH'S WIFE [*still sitting on her hill and spinning*]:
    Yea, Noah—Go clout thy shoon°!   °*go fix your shoes*
    The better will they last.

                  ·   ·   ·

NOAH: Peter°! I trow we dote°.   °*St. Peter* °*I think we'll go mad*
Without any more note°,   °*if we keep quarreling*
Come in if ye will.

NOAH'S WIFE [*seeing the water rising near her*]:
    Yipes! Water nighs so near that I sit not dry!
    Into ship with my gear, therefore will I hie
    For dread that I drown here!

[*She struggles onto the ark but stays right by the door.*]

NOAH: Dame, surely
    It be'est brought full dear° ye abode so long by   °*It's too bad*
    Out of ship.

NOAH'S WIFE: I will not for thy bidding
    Go from door to the midding°.   °*center of the boat*

Medieval wear   A man and woman in the late thirteenth century. These are probably the sort of clothes Noah and his wife—as well as members of the audience—would be wearing in the plays of that period: for the men, a knee-length tunic with overlong sleeves gathered at the wrists, and hose and boots beneath; for the women, a floor-length, long-sleeved, loose-fitting woolen gown or robe. Both men and women wore hoods or caps. The voluminous costumes do not restrict bold movements but may limit the effectiveness of subtle or delicate gestures.

NOAH: In faith, and for your long tarrying,
   Ye shall have a lick of the whip.

NOAH'S WIFE: Spare me not, I pray thee, but e'en as thou think;
   These great words shall not flay me.

NOAH: Abide, dame, and drink°:   °*listen to my response*
   For beaten shalt thou be with this staff till thou stink.

[He strikes her with his "staff," a harmless baton.]
   Are my strokes good? Say me.

NOAH'S WIFE: What say ye, Fred Fink°?   °*a made-up name*

NOAH *[striking her]*:
   Speak! Cry me mercy, I say.

NOAH'S WIFE: Thereto say I, *nay!*

NOAH: If thou don't, by this day,
   Thy head shall I break!

NOAH'S WIFE: Lord, I were at ease, and heartily I'd heal,
   Might I once have a mess of honest widow's meal,
   For thy soul, no less, a mass penny should I deal

[pointing to, and addressing, the women in the audience]

And so would all of these, here in the commonweal°,   °*village*
These wives that are here,
For the lives they have led,
Wish their husbands dead.
For, as ever I ate bread,
So wish I our sire were.

NOAH *[addressing the men in the audience]*:
Ye men that have wives, while they are young,
If ye love your lives, chastise their tongue.
Me thinks my heart rives°, both liver and lung,   °*breaks*
To see such strives°, wed-men among   °*arguments*
But I,
As have I bliss,
Shall chastise this.

[He strikes at her; she dodges.]

NOAH'S WIFE: Yet may ye miss,
Simple Si°!   °*a made-up name, possibly a reference to the Simple Simon
of the nursery rhyme*
NOAH: I shall make thee still as stone, beginner of blunder°!°*first sinner*
I shall beat thy back and bone, and break all in sunder.

NOAH'S WIFE *[as they resume fighting]*:
Out, alas, I am gone! Out upon thee, man's wonder!

[She rolls on top of him in victory.]

NOAH: See how she can groan, and I lie under!
But wife,
Let us halt this ado,
For my back is near in two.

NOAH'S WIFE: And I'm so black and blue
That I may lose my life.

Clearly the scene, though biblically inspired and from a play with deeply reverential passages, is a farce. Its wife-beating theme would be appalling—except that it's the husband who begs for mercy and we know nobody has really been hurt. The language is far more fluid and informal than in *The Creation of the Universe*, with comic names and homely invectives ("Go clout thy shoon!"), verse lines from as few as two to as many as thirteen syllables, a wide range of rhyme schemes (including the rare AAAA), and alliteration, which is present only in spurts, invariably indicating failed pomposity.

◆ E X E R C I S E 7–1

Noah and His Wife

Play the scene with the following suggestions:

◆ Use a stool or a chair for the hill on which Noah's wife sits, and simply mime the ark and the entrance to the ark.

◆ Use a mat or carpeted floor for the fight between Noah and his wife, and use a harmless baton (such as a toy plastic baseball bat) for the staff with which Noah hits his wife. Use another plastic baton for the wife's spindle, as she will use this for her weapon. Use imaginary string and an imaginary rock for the spinning of the wool.

◆ Stage the fight in a very simple way, emphasizing the reactions to the blows rather than the force of the blows themselves and working out how Noah's wife ends up sitting on top of him.

◆ Stage the scene with the audience around it, in a circle or semicircle, and with the men and women in the audience grouped separately. Each gender can cheer on their own representative.

◆ Imagine your three sons and three daughters-in-law have gone into the ark and are watching you both.

◆ Here's the kicker: Play the scene with the goal of *convincing your three sons and three daughters-in-law that your gender is the smarter one!*

If you can do this, you will enjoy the liberating experience of medieval comedy, which is essentially a mass public spectacle, not a drama for an elite-only audience.

Notice that everything in the text of the scene is your tool to demonstrate how smart you are. The rhymes, which in Lesson 6 could be construed as demonstrating the character's divinity, now demonstrate your cleverness at matching words. See how the wife trumps Noah with this rhyme:

NOAH: Speak! Cry me mercy, I say.

NOAH'S WIFE: Thereto say I, *Nay!*

Her "I, Nay!" both repeats his "I" and counteracts his "say," giving her a double victory: absorbing his word and turning it around on him. Noah's earlier rhyme

Abide, dame, and drink

For beaten shall thou be with this staff till thou stink

pairs a five-syllable line with a twelve-syllable one (a technique revived by American poet Ogden Nash five centuries later). It is a delightfully comic insult. The wife's made-up names for her husband, Fred Fink and Simple Si, show her mastery of the art of the insult, deploying both alliteration and rhyme.

Noah's alliteration ("I shall beat thy back and bone") shows his unyielding stamina in assault. His employment of gratuitous facts ("the planets all seven") seeks to establish that he is graced with vast knowledge, while the wife's metaphoric epithets ("Go clout thy shoon!") show her a woman of inventive linguistic imagination. These are combatants who love the battle and are well practiced at it. Playing these roles challenges you, the actor, to let loose a barrage of medieval verbal flourishes—all in the service of humiliating your spouse and convincing your children that yours is the superior sex.

And your blows—let them appear to be ferocious! (This is the reason to use a harmless, featherweight plastic baton.) Flex your muscles: Show that you are not to be made a fool of!

In all this, speaking and moving, *be a role model for your same-sex children!* Noah, show your boys how to handle their wives! Wife, show your daughters-in-law how to stand up to their husbands! And both of you: Never think that you are trying to win this fight just for yourself. Rather, understand that you are trying to win to better influence your same-sex children. You are trying to show them how to have a happier life.

Now let's go one step further: Play the scene with the goal of convincing the surrounding *audience* that your gender is the smarter one. Be a role model for all the men, or all the women, in the audience. In fact, try to convince *both* sexes that your ways are the best. Wife: Try to make all the men stop abusing their women. Noah: Try to make all the women stop defying their men. *Entertain* them with the vivacity of your argument.

How a play entertains its audience (using the word *entertain* in its original sense of "capture attention"[*] as well as its modern sense) is, however, an issue complicated enough to have a lesson of its own. Indeed, this may be the thorniest puzzle in acting theory; even Stanislavsky was stumped by it. For while the Russian master realized that pleasing the audience was the "super-super-objective" of the actor, he also admitted that he "could not yet define" how this notion fit in with his other discoveries. We'll take our own crack at this in the next lesson.

---

[*] From the French *entre*, "between," and *tenir*, "to hold," or something like "to bring together."

L E S S O N

8

Performance: Being Public in Public

In a famous paradox, Russian director Konstantin Stanislavsky declared that acting was "doing something private in public." By the 1950s, this maxim had become a central principle of the Actors Studio in America, where Lee Strasberg, the Studio's director, developed his signature "private moment" exercise in which Studio members would perform, onstage, moments of their own personal, private behavior—actions they would never dream of doing outside of class if observed by others. An entire generation of actors was surprised to discover that these private moments, while not at all intended to be "theatrical," would turn out to be intensely compelling when executed faithfully. Strasberg demonstrated that the *authenticity* of actors who could perform their own private experiences from their own emotional core could become more theatrically engaging than authenticity achieved by simply following a director's instructions. An actor's ability to touch his or her private feelings, fears, and fantasies can make his or her stage interactions—a romance, an argument, a shared experience—affecting, convincing, and memorable.

But acting is also a *public* interaction—and not just because it is performed before a theatre audience. Acting is public because real life is lived mainly in public. As sociologist Erving Goffman persuasively demonstrated,[*] we "perform roles"—and quite different ones—in most of our waking

---

[*] In *The Presentation of Self in Everyday Life* (Garden City, NY: Doubleday, 1959), among other works.

moments. We perform these roles to our friends, our families, our employers, our lovers, and to the world of strangers around us. Some of us also perform to God or to saints or spirits or devils. If the characters we play onstage are to be truly authentic, they must be not only private in public but public in public as well.

Let's see this in practice. In Lessons 4 and 6, God, in *The Creation of the Universe,* is speaking publicly to a group of angels. Immediately afterward, he turns and addresses one of them individually:

> Of all the mights I have made, most next after me
> I make thee as master and mirror of my might.
> I build thee here boonly° in bliss for to be   °*happily*
> I name thee for Lucifer, bearer of light.

Here, God is addressing the angel Lucifer directly, but he is also "naming" Lucifer to the other angels, who are overhearing his remarks. Thus God's speech may be described as both a *private interaction* with Lucifer and, simultaneously, a *performed public pronouncement* to the angels. God is speaking both privately and publicly at the same time.

We can then say that God has two levels of audience for these remarks: Lucifer is his primary audience; the angels are his secondary audience. These audiences exist simultaneously, but God is speaking to them on different levels: He is speaking directly to his primary audience (Lucifer) and indirectly (by their overhearing him) to his secondary one (the angels). The *performative* aspects of his behavior (such as the versification and rhyme pattern of his thoughts) come into play with his indirect performance to the secondary audience.

We can also identify God's third, or tertiary, level of audience: those other angels who, though not in sight, may be presumed elsewhere in Heaven and therefore still within range of an all-powerful (and thus universally heard) God.

◆ E x e r c i s e   8–1

A Performative God

Play this speech, referring back to the commentary in Lessons 4 and 6, but now in the context of these three different levels of audience. Speak directly to Lucifer, looking him straight in the eye, but be certain that the angels around you (your second audience) are also paying close attention. And *project* your message to all the angels everywhere in Heaven, so that they receive your message as well. Let your words resound throughout the cosmos. Find inside yourself the voice, cadences, and gestures that will command the attention, admiration, and respect of the entire divine universe.

Performative Aspects of Dramatic Scenes

◆ E X E R C I S E   8–2

Performing Your Greetings and Insults

Return to Exercises 2–4, 2–5, and 2–6: the Elizabethan greetings and insults. Replay these exercises with a partner but in an actual crowded courtyard or city plaza. Play them with your partner, as before, but at the same time *perform* them to the crowd. Show everybody how warm, and welcoming, and eloquent, and noble you can be in greeting your partner, and how terrifying you can be in insulting him or her. Make a public statement about *yourself* with your greeting or insult. Make passersby admire you, or fear you, as the case may be. Make your greeting or insult a *public* performance.

When we experience these exercises, we soon realize that personal communication almost always includes a performative element. To hail someone graciously is not merely to interact graciously with that person but to demonstrate to anyone who might be within earshot that you are a gracious person. And to insult someone is not merely to inflict a measure of pain upon him but to let the world know you are not a person with whom to be trifled. We are always, in our interactions with a particular individual, projecting an image of ourselves to everyone who may happen to be watching or listening. We may even be *seeking*—consciously or unconsciously—to induce these bystanders to pay attention to us. This is at the heart of performance in life—and in the theatre.

In the scene from the Noah play in Lesson 7, Noah and his wife are, at the primary level, interacting with each other (trying to change each other's behavior), while at the secondary level they're performing for their children (trying to teach them how to treat the opposite sex). And at the tertiary level Noah is hoping that God will hear that his effort to get the ark under way is proceeding apace, as God instructed.

Noah and his wife are also performing for a *fourth* level of audience, the imagined community of their fellow citizens—some doubters, some admirers—who have gathered around them. But of course this community is represented, in the theatre, by the live theatre audience! And here is the major linking between the private and public levels of acting—interacting with your partner *and* giving a performance to an audience—that Stanislavsky was thinking about.

The Audience in the Theatre

Theatre was a more openly public event in ages past, and the audience was more openly evident in the theatrical event. Ancient Greek theatre, which was performed to audiences numbering in the several thousands (seventeen thousand at Athens and Epidaurus), featured a chorus, representing citizens or demigods, who would both witness and comment on the actions of the principal characters. The physical design of the Greek theatre placed the chorus between the principal characters and the audience, so that characters speaking to the chorus were also speaking directly to the audience immediately behind them. In medieval theatre, audiences gathered freely around the action on at least three sides of the stage—sometimes all four—and actors would and could talk directly to them (as Noah and his wife do), sometimes walking among them while speaking. Most of this mingling was carried over into Renaissance theatres as well: In Italian plazas and gardens where *commedia* was performed, in Spanish *corrales,* and in English innyards and aptly named public theatres during the time of Shakespeare, spectators not only surrounded the stage but sometimes sat right on it. And since these theatres operated outdoors, in full daylight, actors and audiences could see each other equally.* For two thousand years, therefore, the theatre audience was clearly a major part of the overall stage picture.

Moreover, most of the interactions dramatized onstage in earlier eras were assumed to take place in public, not private environments. We tend to forget that the privacy we treasure today—the free-standing home, the sound-insulated apartment, the closed-in car—is a relatively recent development.

---

* Even after theatre moved indoors during the seventeenth century, the audience area was not at first darkened but was illuminated as brightly as the stage. Only since the late nineteenth century has the audience sat, voyeur-like, in a dark space watching spotlighted actors.

Prior to the 1850s, and the advent of central heating, air conditioning, indoor plumbing, telephones, and television, waking life took place mainly in public environments. City dwellers lived in warrens of tiny, interconnected rooms, where beds were normally shared among entire families, and the family business (as in the case of Shakespeare's father's glove factory) was often on the ground floor. Country people boarded their children, parents, farmhands, and even animals in their houses. Even the rich maintained estates that teemed with servants, relatives, and family retainers. Before Stanislavsky's time, therefore, doing something "in private" was a rather rare event. Even taking a bath or using the toilet were ordinarily done in the company of others.

It should not be surprising, therefore, that the dramas of past eras are largely set in public places: not in kitchens or living rooms, as modern realistic drama tends to be, but in palaces, plazas, public parlors, battlefields, banquet halls, and ballrooms. Castles were practically cities. When Hamlet, famously, says, "Now I am alone," it is a rare theatrical event—and he is shortly burst in upon by friends who do not even bother to knock.

Today, actors are expected to explore the public as well as the private interactions of their characters. The revivals of pre-naturalistic plays, both on the stage and in films; the growing popularity of post-naturalistic, directly performative theatrical techniques, exemplified by the plays of Bertolt Brecht, musical theatre, dance theatre, and other popular dramas and dramatic forms; the sociological studies of Goffman and newer postmodern theorists; and the development of globalized entertainment and communications through film, television, and the Internet have led to a fresh study of the nature of the role that *audience* plays in the behavior of dramatic characters and in the acting of the actors that play them.

Let's experiment further with this notion, using excerpts from three great dramatists (with whom you will work further in later lessons): Sophocles, Shakespeare, and Chekhov.

◆ SCENE 8–1

The Performative Context: Oedipus and Creon

Here is a portion of a scene from Sophocles' *Oedipus Tyrannus* (also known as *Oedipus Rex* and *Oedipus the King*), first performed around 430 B.C. Oedipus, the mythical tenth-century B.C. ruler of Thebes, is arguing with his brother-in-law, Creon. Memorize and, with a partner, perform this exchange, which takes place in or in front of the palace. Oedipus has accused Creon of trying to undermine his authority, and Creon has defended himself.*

CREON: Do you intend to banish me?

OEDIPUS: No. No, not banish you. I want to see you *dead*—to make you an example for all aspiring to my throne.

CREON: Then you won't do as I suggest? You won't believe me?

OEDIPUS: You have not shown that you deserve belief.

CREON: No, because I see that you are mad.

OEDIPUS: In my own eyes, I am sane.

CREON: You should be sane in mine as well.

OEDIPUS: No. You are a traitor!

CREON: And what if you are wrong?

OEDIPUS: Still—*I* will rule.

CREON: Not when you rule treacherously.

OEDIPUS: O Thebes! My city! Listen to him!

CREON: My city too!

It is easy to see that this scene, like all Greek drama, occurs in a public context: When Oedipus cries "My city! Listen to him!" he is appealing to the chorus—a representing group of Theban citizens—to take his side. And Creon's response, though directed to Oedipus, is likewise an appeal to those same citizens, reminding them that he, too, is a member of Theban society. Indeed, as the play makes clear, Creon has lived in Thebes all his life, and Oedipus arrived there only after he had grown to maturity.

This exchange, though framed as an argument between two characters, is in fact a public debate between two political rivals. Each is trying to gain the chorus's sympathy and respect for his own position. When Creon calls Oedipus mad, he is seeking to make the chorus accept this definition of Oedipus's behavior in order to weaken Oedipus's authority. When Oedipus

---

* The *Oedipus* scenes here and in Lesson 9 are from the translation by Luci Berkowitz and Theodore F. Brunner, published in the Norton Critical Edition, 1970. They are slightly edited and abridged. I have added stage directions.

says "*I* will rule," he is trying to demonstrate such fierce authority that Creon will back down.

Moreover, Oedipus is also trying to forestall any further uprisings. When he says he wants to make Creon "an example for all aspiring to my throne," the "all" is specifically directed to anyone in the chorus who might be thinking of supporting Creon or his allegations.

So, while the characters are arguing with each other (interacting at the primary level), they are also performing for the chorus of citizens of tenth-century B.C. Thebes (the secondary level), seeking to win approval of their positions and righteous authority. And, as this scene plays in the Theatre of Dionysus in Athens, they are also performing for a theatre audience (the tertiary level) of fifth-century B.C. Athenians. One can easily draw the analogy of a televised debate between presidential candidates who are simultaneously arguing with each other's positions, performing for the applause of the studio audience, and, at the tertiary level, seeking the votes of the television audience.

Play the scene in front of a "chorus" of your classmates. Try to *humiliate* your rival and *impress* the citizenry. Try to persuade the chorus to believe that you are the most authoritative and righteous leader in all Greece. Try to win their vote, and the votes of imagined observers you cannot see, as though you were competing in a forthcoming election. Try to win their applause—or even shouts of approval! And chorus: Feel free to murmur sounds of encouragement to these competitors. Inspire them to work for your vote—and your applause.

Multiple Audiences

To recapitulate: Persons in real life interact with each other yet also perform for multiple audiences. Such audiences include persons who they know are observing their interaction (persons within their line of sight), persons who they believe *may* be observing it (such as unseen passersby and servants in adjacent rooms), and those (including gods, ghosts, and other spiritual presences) whom they can only *imagine* to be listening in to what they say. Because characters in plays, if they are like persons in real life, perform for multiple audiences, it is an easy stretch to say that by this process the actors playing those characters do so as well and thus also perform to the theatre audiences that come to see them. In short, performing for others, including unseen and unknown others, is a normal real-life activity, not something we do only when acting on a stage.

◆ E X E R C I S E   8–3

The Performative Context: Shakespeare

Memorize one of the following speeches from Shakespeare's *Hamlet*. Each of the two characters, Queen Gertrude and King Claudius, is trying to persuade Prince Hamlet (who is Gertrude's son and Claudius's nephew and stepson) not to go back to school. Each speech takes place at the Danish court not long after King Hamlet, Prince Hamlet's father, died suddenly.

QUEEN: Good Hamlet, cast thy nighted° color off,   °*gloomy*
And let thine eye look like a friend on Denmark.
Do not for ever with thy vailed° lids   °*half-closed*
Seek for thy noble father in the dust.
Thou know'st 'tis common; all that lives must die,
Passing through nature to eternity.

.   .   .

CLAUDIUS: For your intent

In going back to school in Wittenberg,
It is most retrograde to our desire:
And we beseech you, bend you to remain
Here, in the cheer and comfort of our eye,
Our chiefest courtier, cousin, and our son.

Now play the speech you have chosen to someone playing Prince Hamlet, surrounded by a host of other nobles and attendants. Your goals are twofold: On the primary level, you must appeal to your son/nephew to stay by your side. On the secondary level, you, as a ruler, must show your court that you have the authority to command your own family (otherwise, how can you command a kingdom?).

Note that the situation for both of you, Gertrude and Claudius, is very perilous. King Hamlet has just died under somewhat mysterious circumstances, and because you—his widow and brother—married with "unseemly haste" immediately thereafter, a foreign prince now holds "a weak supposal" of your "worth" and thinks your kingdom may be "disjoint[ed]." He is openly planning a military attack. So it is essential, since your reign is beginning with an international crisis, that you assure the court of your capacity for strong leadership and the solidarity of your marriage. Neither of you can afford to publicly kowtow to your son/nephew's wishes.

Combining the appeal to your son/nephew with the show of political and marital strength, however, is a tricky task. Your appeal is based on loving concern, expressed in your words "good Hamlet," "friend," "we beseech you," "cheer and comfort," "cousin," "son." But beneath these kindnesses you must convey to the court the capacity for effective rule. Your tone and body language under the phrases "it is most retrograde to our desire" and "all that lives must die" must suggest the iron fist beneath the velvet glove. Indeed, Claudius's "our son" contains strong elements of both affection and authority, for by publicly assuming the parental role, Claudius emasculates Hamlet's own adulthood, and by using the royal "we" to indicate himself, he also reinforces his bond with Gertrude—while at the same time asserting parental authority over his new stepson.

Try your speech several times, seeking to influence both audiences simultaneously: encouraging Hamlet (your primary audience) to stay in your home, while at the same time assuring the court (your secondary audience) to accept your authority on all upcoming political and military matters.

There is a tertiary audience as well. Although Hamlet doesn't yet know it, Claudius murdered Hamlet's father; moreover, he feels guilty about it. And Gertrude, though perhaps unaware of her first husband's murder by her second, is almost certainly guilty of the earlier adultery of which she is later accused. Both of these characters are, though not yet openly, seeking to make their peace with God and perhaps hoping that they can do so by the "love" they show their son/nephew.

Playing at these three levels at the same time is not easy, but it's essential if you are to capture what's really happening in these moments of the play. All these communications would be going on simultaneously if the situation were experienced by real people, so they must be seen as going on among characters who are played by real people. This is how acting reaches into the complexity of human personalities. The ability to speak effectively and at different levels to multiple audiences is a skill that all trained actors have—and all successful public figures (such as Gertrude and Claudius) have as well.

And finally: Playing to the onstage onlookers is the link with which the actor—without arbitrarily pushing "projection"—connects with the theatre audience as well. In speaking to the nobles in the room, and to those listening in from (hypothetical) adjacent rooms as well, and to God even beyond that, the actors playing Claudius and Gertrude will authentically and convincingly reach the farther audience: the one watching the play in the theatre. They will be not merely private in public but public in public.

◆ SCENE 8−2

The Performative Context: Chekhov

With a partner, memorize the following brief scene from Chekhov's *Three Sisters,* between Kuligin, a schoolteacher, and his younger wife, Masha. The scene takes place in the midst of a crowded birthday party for one of Masha's sisters.*

KULIGIN *[to everyone, with his arm around Masha]*:   Today I feel cheerful and in the best of spirits. *[turning to Masha]* Masha, at four o'clock this afternoon we have to be at the headmaster's. An excursion has been arranged for the teachers and their families.

MASHA: I am not going.

KULIGIN: Dear Masha, why not?

MASHA: We'll talk about it afterwards. *[pause]* Very well, I will go, only let me alone, please. *[walks away]*

KULIGIN: And then we shall spend the evening at the headmaster's. In spite of the delicate state of his health, that man tries before all things to be sociable. He is an excellent, noble personality. A splendid man. Yesterday, after the meeting, he said to me, "I am tired, Fyodor Ilyitch, I am tired." *[looks at the clock, then at his watch. Turns to one of Masha's sisters]* Your clock is seven minutes fast. "Yes," he said, "I am tired."

Here the dissonance between the performative and private voices is particularly glaring, creating discomfort for both characters and for the family members and friends at the party as well. It is a classic awkwardness: a spousal quarrel in public.

Play this scene with the rest of your class playing the surrounding party guests. Try to win over your spouse (your primary audience), while at the same time projecting a good image to the guests (your secondary audience). If you are Kuligin, that image is probably that of the well-spoken, locally respected schoolteacher. If you are Masha, that image might well be that of the artistic, passionate, restless wife—for indeed, Masha has already begun to fall in love with one of the other guests, with whom she will have an affair before long.

---

* This and Scene 14–1 are from Constance Garnett's translation, first published in 1916.

Play the scene again, reaching to be heard, and understood, by your public audience in every corner of the room—and any people who might be outside the room as well. Play to everyone in the house and therefore to everyone in the theatre house as well. Imagine that there are eavesdropping servants everywhere! You desperately want to win the respect and admiration of *all* of them, even as you truthfully address your remarks to each other.

II

The Scenes

THE SECOND HALF OF *ACTING TWO* PRESENTS A VARIETY OF SCENES FROM eight major periods—Greek, *commedia,* Elizabethan, neoclassic, Restoration, Belle Epoque (1890–1914), mid-twentieth-century "hypertheatre," and contemporary—each of which has made a profound contribution to Western theatrical history. These periods are presented in chronological order and with attention to the cultural and theatrical patterns that are reflected in the writing of the scenes.

It is essential for the actor to understand what sort of world the dramatist was imagining when writing the play. That world includes discrete aspects such as clothing, manners, social etiquette, prevailing religions and philosophies, and attitudes toward sexuality, money, politics, morality, social class, and lifestyle issues: urban versus rural, for example. But the actor should have absolutely no thought of concretizing any specific or universally accepted "period style" for any period play. The reasons for this constraint are multiple and various:

◆ Culture and style evolve rapidly within every historical period. Significant changes in English clothing, for example, can be identified almost *annually*

335

from the reign of Edward III (1327–1377). Thus there can hardly be a set notion of what constituted a "medieval sleeve" or an "Elizabethan bonnet," for there would have been dozens of sleeves and bonnets during those periods.

◆ Stylistic differences among individual authors writing at the same time are vast in nearly every historical period. No Athenian theatregoer would ever mistake a play of Sophocles for one of Euripides, though both were Greek tragedians of the same era. The same is true of later contemporaries, such as Shakespeare and Ben Jonson, George Bernard Shaw and Oscar Wilde, Margaret Edson and David Mamet.

◆ We know far less about actual production methods prior to 1650 than is generally admitted. History provides only tantalizing hints as to the staging, costuming, and acting of plays in Greek, medieval, Renaissance, and Elizabethan times. Stage directions are rare, theatregoing descriptions rarer, and contemporary visual reproductions almost nonexistent (or of doubtful reliability). Contemporary reconstructions (including my own) of early drama are educated guesses, and while they provide a general overview, they cannot be construed as authoritative with regard to details.

◆ Styles from the past are taken both from daily life and from the theatre, but these are not the same. The clothing of a period is not identical with its costuming, nor does daily speech correspond with the stage speech of the era. So in trying to conjure the world of a dramatist's imagination, we must look at both the daily world in which the dramatist ate and slept and the theatrical one in which he or she worked.

◆ Authors in the past often set their plays in periods different from those in which they were written. Most Greek tragedies written in the fifth century B.C. concerned characters and events from a much earlier mythic history, perhaps five to seven hundred years in the Attic past. Medieval mystery plays were set in biblical times, and Shakespeare's plays were set in ancient

Rome, early Britain, and Renaissance Italy, among other ages and locales. So today's producers must consider at least two "period styles" for any such dramatic work: the style of the author and that of the author's characters.

◆ Dramatists are not historians and have never sought to present to their audiences historic documents or dioramas. Rather, they interpret the period they have chosen, and often they deliberately incorporate elements from other periods (including their own), or no period at all, in order to provide a critique of the historical characters or actions they portray.

◆ Contemporary directors rarely stage plays from past eras with external fidelity to their perceived period style. Indeed, in the current theatre, classic plays are more often than not staged in periods radically different from the ones in which they were written or set. Or such plays are set in no historical period at all, or periods that change during the course of the play.

The outward manifestations of historical styles, therefore, are subject to radical reexamination and revision in contemporary performance. Nonetheless, these historical styles remain embedded in dramatic texts of every period and resonate through the play's action and language. Historical foundations will continue to serve as a key to understanding—and exploiting—how the play can be effectively performed on today's stage, no matter how or where it is "set" by the contemporary director or designers.

The scenes in Part II are presented with suggestions as to how a contemporary actor might capture the essence—*from the inside* more than from mere mimicry of superficial details—of their stylistic and character elements. Suggestions, therefore, come from possibilities of movement, voice and speech production, costume, staging, and—particularly in those plays that have come down to us in their original English rather than translation—text analysis.

LESSON

9

Greek Tragedy

The Greeks did not actually invent drama. A full twenty-five centuries before the Greeks donned their masks in Athens, Egyptians were staging plays on the banks of the Nile, which means that Egyptian drama was as ancient to the Greeks as Greek drama is to us.

Still, Greek drama is the earliest from which we actually have scripts. And those surviving plays include several dozen that are produced today in nearly every language of the theatrical world. Many of them also serve as the jumping-off point for later dramas, from Roman (Seneca's *Oedipus*) and neoclassic (Jean Racine's *Phèdre*) to modern (Eugene O'Neill's *Mourning Becomes Electra,* Jean-Paul Sartre's *The Flies,* Jean Anouilh's *Antigone*) and contemporary (Neil LaBute's *Medea Redux,* John Barton's *Tantalus*). In addition, we have a body of criticism (chiefly from Aristotle), various theatrical anecdotes (from Athenaeus, Plato, and others), hundreds of sculptures and vase paintings, and the actual ruins of dozens of Greek theatres. The classical Greek theatre, therefore, is a vast, rich treasure from which we steadily draw scripts, source material, and inspiration.*

Delving into Greek drama, however, means that we must move into a world radically different from our own—different in its culture, its performance spaces, and its drama.

---

* Actually, when we say "Greek" in most of these contexts, we really should be saying "Athenian" because almost all the playwrights, philosophers, artists, and architects we are referring to, wherever they may have hailed from, plied their trade in the independent city-state of Athens.

Greek ladies   Three ladies of classic Greece, as drawn from a Greek vase. The Greek *himation,* a long tunic worn by both men and women, went all the way to the ground; often, for women, an overgarment was also wrapped around the upper body, held in place by two clasps. This drapery, which was also the style of classical Greek stage costumes, required skilled moment-to-moment management by the actor, who had to continually adjust the hang and sway of the garments.

As to culture, the ancient Greeks worshipped gods of fiery passions and uncertain morality, whom they balanced with a philosophy that valued self-knowledge ("Know thyself") and the golden mean ("Nothing to excess"). Athenian citizens operated a slave society at home and engaged in widespread trade abroad. Politically, they alternated among democracy (which they invented), oligarchy, and empire. Militarily, they were aggressive and often exploitative. They made giant leaps in mathematics, medicine, history, and astronomy. They revered music, dancing, the human body, vivid illustration, and grandiose architecture.

By the middle of the fifth century B.C., Greek plays were performed in and around a circular *orchestra,* which contained a chanting and dancing chorus (ranging from twelve to fifty members), a raised stage for the principal actors, and behind the stage a building (*skēnē*) whose doors provided entrances and exits for the principals. The actors, all male, wore long gowns (*himatia*), elevated shoes (*kothornoi*), tall head/hairpieces (*onkoi*), and full-face masks. No more than three actors played all the parts, changing masks offstage. The audience, seated in a circular stone *theatron,* was by today's standards gigantic.

A Greek philosopher   Greek men who prided themselves on their austerity would merely drape their naked bodies in a simple cloak, gathered over the left shoulder, concealing the left arm and hand. This garment, severely restricted athleticism, and actors, particularly in tragedies, would gesture with the right hand only.

The tragic dramas were written in unrhymed verse, sung or chanted rather than spoken. Each play was formally divided into a series of episodes between principal characters that alternated with choral odes addressed to the audience. There was also a prologue, generally spoken by an actor playing a god or demigod, and an epilogue, chanted by the chorus. Such tragedies were normally presented in groups of three on related themes (a *trilogy*) in a single day; the trilogy was normally followed by a briefer "satyr play," which mocked the concerns of what preceded it.

None of this adds up to a single "Greek style" or even "Greek tragic style," for reasons described in the introduction to Part II. But every one of these factors—culture, theatre, and drama—influences the nature of acting in these masterpieces.

◆ S C E N E   9–1

Politician vs. Prophet: Oedipus and Teiresias

This scene from *Oedipus Tyrannus* follows the excerpt in Lesson 8. Thebes has been visited by a plague, and Creon has been sent to the oracle at Delphi

Classical gesture   Characters were more animated in comedies than in tragedies, gesturing more vigorously, though still largely with the right hand. These four are from an ancient production of Terence's *Phormio*, a Roman comedy modeled after a Greek original. From a drawing in the Vatican Museum.

to find a cure. He returns and announces that the plague has been sent by the gods because the murderer of Laius, the previous king, has not yet been found and punished. Creon suggests that Oedipus send for the blind prophet, Teiresias, for advice. The seer, we soon find, knows a terrible secret: Oedipus, who believes he was the child of distant parents, is actually the long-abandoned son of Laius. Moreover, Oedipus murdered Laius—whom he of course did not recognize—in a long-forgotten quarrel and subsequently came to Thebes and took his father's throne. Worst, he then married Laius's widow, Jocasta—Oedipus's own mother. Naturally, Teiresias does not want to speak about these things.

With a partner, memorize, stage, and perform for your class this masterful scene between these two legendary figures in Greek mythic history. Consider your classmates (the scene's audience) to be its chorus of ancient Theban citizens. Find a large chair to use for Oedipus's throne (which he will almost certainly leave during the scene, but may return to), and let Teiresias enter with a walking stick and wearing a blindfold, led, perhaps, by another actor playing a servant who leads the prophet to and from this meeting.

[Oedipus sits or stands before a chorus of Theban citizens. The blind Teiresias, whom he has summoned, arrives, led by a servant.]

OEDIPUS: Teiresias, all things are known to you—the secrets of heaven and earth, the sacred and profane. Though you are blind, you surely see the plague that rakes our city. My Lord Teiresias, we turn to you as our only hope. We must find Laius' murderers and drive them out. Then, only then, will we find release from our suffering. I ask you not to spare your gifts of prophecy. Look to the voices of prophetic birds or the answers written in the flames. Spare nothing. Save all of us—yourself, your city, your king, and all that is touched by this deathly pollution.

TEIRESIAS: O God! How horrible wisdom is! How horrible when it does not help the wise. *[turns to leave]* I should not have come. *[He starts away.]*

OEDIPUS: Why? *[restraining him]* What's wrong?

TEIRESIAS: Let me go! It will be better if you bear your own distress and I bear mine.

OEDIPUS: This city gave you life and yet you refuse her an answer? You speak as if you were her enemy!

TEIRESIAS: No! No! It is because I see the danger in your words. And mine would add still more.

OEDIPUS: For God's sake, if you know, don't turn away from us! We are pleading, we are begging you!

TEIRESIAS: Because you are blind! No! I shall not reveal my secrets. And I shall not reveal yours!

OEDIPUS: What? You know, and yet you refuse to speak? Would you betray us and watch our city fall helplessly to her death?

TEIRESIAS: I will not cause you further grief. I will not grieve myself. Stop asking me: I will tell you nothing!

OEDIPUS: You monster! You could stir the stones of earth to a burning rage! You will not tell? What will it take?

TEIRESIAS: Know thyself, Oedipus! You denounce me, but you do not yet know yourself!

OEDIPUS: Ah, yes! You disgrace your city, and then you expect us to control our rage!

TEIRESIAS: It does not matter if I speak; the future has already been determined.

OEDIPUS: And if it has, then it is for you to tell me, *prophet!*

TEIRESIAS: I shall say no more. Rage if you wish.

OEDIPUS: I *am* enraged. And now I will tell you what *I* think. I think this was *your* doing. *You* plotted the crime, *you* saw it carried out, it was *your* doing. All but the actual killing. And had you not been blind, you would have done *that*, too!

TEIRESIAS: Do you believe what you have said? Then accept your own decree. From this day on, deny yourself the right to speak to anyone. For you, Oedipus, are the desecrator, the polluter of this land!

OEDIPUS: Traitor! Do you think that you can get away with this?

Ken Ruta as the masked Teiresias in *Oedipus Rex,* led onstage by a young boy. (Courtesy American Conservatory Theatre.)

TEIRESIAS: The truth is my protection.

OEDIPUS: Who taught you this? It did not come from prophecy.

TEIRESIAS: *You* taught me. *You* drove me, *you* forced me to say it against my will.

OEDIPUS: Say it again. I want to make sure I understand you.

TEIRESIAS: Understand me? Or are you trying to provoke me?

OEDIPUS: No, I want to be sure, I want to know. Say it again!

TEIRESIAS: I say that you, Oedipus Tyrannus, are the murderer you seek.

OEDIPUS: So! A second time! Now twice you will regret what you have said!

TEIRESIAS: Shall I tell you more? Shall I fan your flames of anger?

OEDIPUS: Yes. Tell me more. Tell me whatever suits you. It will be in vain.

TEIRESIAS: I say you live in shame with the woman you love, blind to your own calamity.

OEDIPUS: Do you think you can speak like this forever?

TEIRESIAS: I do, if there is any strength in truth.

OEDIPUS: There is—for everyone but you. You—you cripple! Your ears are deaf, your eyes are blind, your mind—your *mind* is crippled!

TEIRESIAS: You fool! You slander me when one day you will hear the same . . .

OEDIPUS [*interrupting*]:   You live in night, Teiresias, in night that never turns to day. And so, you cannot hurt me—or any man who sees the light.

TEIRESIAS: No, it is not I who will cause your fall. No, Oedipus, you are destroying yourself.

OEDIPUS: How much of this am I to bear? Leave! Now! Leave my house!

TEIRESIAS: I would not be here had you not sent for me.

OEDIPUS: I would never have sent for you had I known the madness I would hear.

TEIRESIAS: To you, I am mad; but not to your parents . . .

OEDIPUS: Wait! My parents? Who are my parents?

TEIRESIAS: This day shall bring you birth *and* death.

OEDIPUS: Why must you persist with riddles?

TEIRESIAS: Are you not the best of men when it comes to riddles?*

OEDIPUS: You mock the very skill that proves me great.

TEIRESIAS: A great misfortune—which will destroy you.

OEDIPUS: I don't care. If I have saved this land, I do not care.

TEIRESIAS: Then I shall go.

OEDIPUS: Go. You won't be missed.

TEIRESIAS: I am not afraid of you. You cannot hurt me. And I tell you this: The man you seek—the man whose death or banishment you ordered, the man who murdered Laius—that man is here, living in our midst. Soon it will be known to all of you—he is a native Theban. And he will

---

* The citizens of Thebes chose Oedipus as their king because he had solved the riddle of the Sphinx, thus saving the city from destruction.

find no joy in that discovery. His eyes see now, but soon they will be blind: rich now, but soon a beggar. Holding a scepter now, but soon a cane, he will grope for the earth beneath him—in a foreign land. Both brother and father to the children that he loves. Both son and husband to the woman who bore him. Both heir and spoiler of his father's bed and the one who took his life. Go, think on this. And if you find the words I speak are lies, *then* say that I am blind. *[Teiresias leaves, and Oedipus goes into the palace.]*

Here, as in the *Oedipus* scene in Lesson 8, each character is playing for the opinion of the chorus, trying with each reference to "this city" and "our city" and "your city" and "this land" to discredit the other (e.g., "Would you betray us and watch *our city* fall helplessly to her death?") in front of the very citizens who constitute the city and land they all share. But their appeals, their tactics, and their performative behaviors are quite different. Oedipus's argument with Creon in Lesson 8 is essentially political; it is a power struggle between two would-be rulers. (The Greek word *creon*, in fact, means "ruler," and Creon will succeed Oedipus as king by the end of the play.) So here, as in the excerpt in Lesson 8, Creon performs the public role of a *professional* politician, impressing his hearers (the chorus) with his authority, wisdom, logic, control of the agenda, political courage, determination, and capacity to employ military force that will get them—and through them Teiresias—on his side. Imagine yourself in a presidential debate, as you did in the Creon–Oedipus scene. While responding to the charges of your opponent (Teiresias in this case), you must exert every effort to win the public's support for your candidacy.

But Teiresias is not a politician, and his appeal to the chorus is quite different from Creon's. To win their respect, he must inspire them not with political might but with his divine wisdom and gift of prophecy. How do you, a mere earth-bound actor, do *that*? It's hard enough to perform the role of national dictator, and it's twice as hard to convincingly perform that of a future-knowing prophet with direct access to divine wisdom.

Or is it? Here's where imagination joins with your acting instrument: You must find *the voice within you* that convinces others your words come directly from the gods. You must find and develop, as you did in Lessons 4 and 6, a voice that suggests to all observers that you are divinely inspired and that you bring truthful and irrevocable messages from a supernatural world. (You will need this voice in many other parts: Shaw's Saint Joan, Pirandello's Stepfather, Kushner's Angel, and any of Shakespeare's witches, ghosts, and soothsayers, for example.)

Do you have such a voice? Of course you do—but it's not the one you use every day. In fact, it's not the one evangelical preachers or tribal shamans use every day. Rather, it's the professional *job* of prophets, as well as preachers and shamans, to find, refine, and then employ the voice in their work that will successfully relay the (assumed or real) supernatural forces that they believe, or at least wish others to believe, are latent in their words. And you must find and develop not merely the voice but the physical behavior—the bearing, movement, and gestures—that will also reflect your oneness with the divine world.

You should know that Teiresias—though this is not manifest in this play—is a transsexual: born as a man but now sporting a woman's breasts. This information can stimulate your most surreal imagination to create the supernatural world from which seers emanate.

Without the otherworldly voice and behavior, Teiresias would be seen not as a prophet but simply as an educated guesser, and he would be no match for Oedipus, the king. You can confront Oedipus successfully only if your *spiritual* power matches (or even tops) his *political* might.

Think of Teiresias, then, as a *professional* prophet. Prophecy is your job, and you must perform your job convincingly. It is not enough merely to know the future; you must convince the chorus that you're the kind of person who, unlike them, *could* know the future. Otherwise, they will laugh you off.

Imagine, then, that you've been training yourself in delivering such prophetic speeches for many years. That you have studied prophetic speaking does not mean that your prophecies are insincere. Theological and rabbinical seminaries give courses in preaching theory and practice, and beginning preachers rehearse to perfect their deliveries. The stirring cadences of Martin Luther King Jr. were learned and long practiced at his father's knee for years before he mesmerized millions at the Lincoln Memorial.

As Teiresias, convince the chorus that your words are stronger than those of Oedipus because they *come from another world:* a world of gods and prophecy, a world where the future is as clear as the past, and where the truth is absolute and irrevocable. Because this feat can't be achieved with words alone, create and develop the reverential tones, cadences, movements, gestures, and godlike bearing that will shock and awe the chorus, silencing the powerful (but woefully human) leader who opposes you. A supernatural text requires supernatural delivery: Find your deepest resonance, your most forthright builds and crescendos. In movement, extend your arms, whirl about, wave your walking staff, and enter a conjurer's state of rapture, of magical fascination. Call upon the gods, the clouds, the sky. Summon the thunder! And know that you can do it because you speak and move with the inspiration of Apollo, Zeus, Athena, and Dionysus.

Is this silly? Well, of course it would be if we were in a rational, skeptical, empirical world, such as a science classroom or a coffee shop. But it's not at all silly in an ancient Greek hillside theatre, where *Oedipus* was first performed, and it's not silly in a modern theatre when we have been effectively transported to that earlier and more mystical world. Your commitment to the power of Teiresias's actions will transport us to a world where prophets spoke confidently of the future and with the force of what they fully believed (and/or persuaded others to believe) to have been divine inspiration.

So you must assume the mantle of prophecy to play this role and not worry about how outlandish it might seem on the campus quad. Assume the mantle literally: Fashion yourself one with an ordinary blanket and safety pin and use this "cape of divination" to accentuate your rapturous, Dionysian movements as you deliver Teiresias's words.

Remember: A professional prophet could never take his audience for granted even in ancient times. There were skeptics aplenty in Athens; indeed, Sophocles' colleague Euripides was one. So you have to believe in the strength of your prophecy (or as Jean Giraudoux said, you have to "believe that you believe" in it) for the duration of the scene. That belief, *if you fully engage it,* will transport us, the audience beyond the chorus, to a world where prophets could stun to silence any merely mortal king.

Create the battle between Oedipus's political muscle and Teiresias's spiritual authority. Each of you must try your hardest to get the chorus on your character's side. Then switch parts and try it again.

More Greek Scenes

Is that all there is to Greek tragedy? Hardly. We have looked only at one scene and at little in the way of Greek costumes, props, or staging effects. But the public and political arena represented by the chorus, and the cosmos of ancient gods that you will have to find in your imagination, are the key ingredients of this seminal dramatic form. If you master these, you will be prepared for the theatrical worlds that ancient Greek drama can propel onto the contemporary stage.

Other Greek scenes you might explore are:

Ismene–Antigone in *Antigone* by Sophocles

Hecuba–Menelaus in *The Trojan Women* by Euripides

Creon–Haemon in *Antigone*

Prometheus–Hermes in *Prometheus Bound* by Aeschylus

10

Commedia

Greek and Roman drama all but disappeared with the fall of the Roman Empire in A.D. 476 and the consequent rise of the Catholic church as the pre-eminent intellectual and cultural force throughout Europe. Then, about a thousand years later, classical theatre was reborn, during what we now call the Renaissance. Long-forgotten classic plays of the Greeks and Romans were rediscovered and, thanks to the invention of movable type in the mid-1400s, published for general readers, first in their original tongues, then in translation, and finally in modernized adaptations. By the early 1500s, emerging troupes of professional actors were performing both these and new plays in the public squares and royal courts of Europe, starting in Italy, the home base of the old Roman Empire and the medieval Holy Roman Empire.

Commedia Styles and Scripts

One of the most exciting of the new emergent styles was the Italian *commedia,* comic drama based on the plays of Roman-era dramatists, chiefly Plautus. We now recognize two forms of *commedia: commedia erudita,* which was an adaptation of a Roman comedy (written by a dramatist "erudite" enough to read Latin), and the subsequent *commedia dell'arte,* which, starting from the same stories, embroidered them with improvised dialogue and recurring characters, most of them masked, who have since become famous: Arlecchino (Harlequin), the scamp; Pantalone, the rich old codger; Dottore (Doctor), the pretentious intellectual; Capitano, the bragging soldier; Zanni, the clown; and Colombina (Columbine), the lovely damsel.

Scapino.   *Cap.* *Zerbino*

A *commedia* greeting   The scamplike Scapino and the pompous Capitano Zerbino meeting on the street in a 1618 *commedia* illustration by Jacques Callot. Notice the out-turned legs, the expressive finger gestures, the swords, and the angled postures.

Because *commedia dell'arte* was largely improvised, no complete *commedia dell'arte* scripts survive, although we have many fragments, illustrations, derivations, and descriptions. But we do have several plays of the earlier *commedia erudita* type, from which *commedia dell'arte* was directly derived.

Commedia Performances

Commedia performances of both sorts almost always took place outdoors, with both men and women actors, on a simple trestle stage with the audience gathered around on at least three sides. Like the Roman comic playwrights before them, *commedia* dramatists limited themselves to simplistic and universal comic themes (superheated lust, marital discord, social climbing), stock characters (the wily servant, the audacious maid, the bombastic soldier, the sweet young girl, the foolishly amorous old geezer), and conventional plot devices (mistaken identity, hiding and spying, the reunion of long-lost relatives). Characters and plot were predictable, so the plays succeeded mainly through the skill of the actors: their comic imagination, verbal and physical dexterity, charm, and timing.

The legendary *commedia* actor Ferruccio Soleri plays the scamp Arlecchino (left, in his traditional patchwork costume), arguing with a stuttering waiter, in the Teatro Piccolo di Milano's celebrated adaptation of Carlo Goldoni's *Servant of Two Masters,* playing its farewell tour of the United States in 2005. (Photo courtesy of Teatro Piccolo)

Indeed, the necessity for acting genius is built into *commedia dell'arte,* which brags of performance mastery in its very name. The *arte* must be lived up to at every moment—even at the expense of other theatrical values (plot credibility, human sensitivity, thematic profundity, poetic beauty) that earlier and later ages would consider more important.

Though there is no chorus in either form of *commedia,* the characters often address the audience directly, giving the audience the role of chorus and asking them for their judgment of key issues. The setting is almost always presumed to be a public one, generally a street or plaza, facilitating this form of direct audience address. Characters in *commedia* often break into song, or comic bits of business (called *lazzi*), or independent speeches that bear little relationship to the plot.

Commedia and Renaissance Ideals

The Renaissance was a rebirth not merely of secular literature but of many classical ideals, of which the most important was doubtless the one uttered by Protagoras, a pre-Socratic philosopher: "Man is the measure of all things." After a thousand years of medieval Christianity, this humanist culture brought the return of paintings, sculptures, and plays drawn from contemporary life—and not just biblical history—along with a fascination with human scheming, intrigue, and debate.

Acting *Commedia*: Machiavelli's *Clizia*

The two speeches in Exercise 10–1 are from Niccolò Machiavelli's *commedia erudita* called *Clizia*, written about 1524. This play has characteristically ancient roots. It began as a Greek comedy, now lost, by Diphilus, from the fourth century B.C., and was subsequently adapted into Latin by Plautus, the Roman comic dramatist, a century later. Machiavelli's version comes seventeen centuries later yet, with the author translating Plautus's version into contemporary Italian, setting the play in Florence, and making many plot and character changes.

The author is the same Niccolò Machiavelli who wrote *The Prince*, which is considered the world's greatest textbook on political power. But Machiavelli is also regarded as one of Italy's greatest playwrights—perhaps, in fact, the greatest until Luigi Pirandello. In both his political and his dramatic writings, Machiavelli had the Renaissance gift of looking clearly and closely at human interactions, unfiltered by mythic fantasy, religious moralizing, or gothic obscurities and sentimentalism.

◆ E X E R C I S E   10–1

Commedia: Direct Address

The two speeches that follow, which are from different parts of *Clizia,* are monologues addressed directly to the theatre audience. Cleandro, a young man, is telling us how much he loves a pretty girl named Clizia, who has been a lodger in his home since childhood. Sofronia, Cleandro's mother, is complaining that her husband, Nicomaco, loves Clizia as well, and he is indeed going crazy over her. The setting is a city street. The translation is my own.

Memorize, prepare, and present either speech.

CLEANDRO: Who was it said that lovers are like soldiers? He sure was speaking the truth! The general wants his men young and sturdy; so do women. Old soldiers are a dirty joke; so are old lovers. Soldiers get chewed out by their sergeants; lovers by their ladies. Soldiers sleep out in the rain on the battlefields; so do would-be Romeos, who get sopping wet under the balconies of their Juliets. Soldiers pursue their enemies with total ferocity, just as lovers attack their rivals. Secrecy, faith, and courage are the emblems of both the soldier and the lover: neither blackest night, nor iciest cold, nor driving-est wind, nor rain, sleet nor hail shall halt either one on their road to conquest! So that, at the end of his lonely struggle, the soldier dies dismembered in a ditch: and the lover dies strung out in despair! And so it is with me: Clizia lives in my house. I see her, I eat with her. The closer she gets, the more I want her; the more I want her, the less I have her; the less I have her, the more I am overwhelmed by the agony of passion! But where is my servant Eustachio? Oh, wait, there he is! Eustachio! Eustachio!

.   .   .

SOFRONIA: *[speaking about Nicomaco, her husband]* It's amazing, the change in this man! Why, right up through last year, he was serious, consistent, respectful, honorable! He woke up early, got dressed, went to church, and went about his work! In the morning he'd make his rounds: to the market, city hall; maybe a business call or two; then to a quiet lunch with a few friends, perhaps a visit with his son, to give the boy a few words of advice—worthwhile lessons from history, you know, sage observations on current affairs—and then he'd come home for his afternoon chores, evening prayers, and a quick visit to his study to plan the next day's events. Then, at nine o'clock, we'd have a big family dinner in front of the fireplace. He was a model husband, father, and citizen; an exemplar of family values. But now look at him! All of a sudden, he's lost in fantasy: All he thinks about is this girl, Clizia! He ignores his business, neglects his properties, and forgets his friends! Instead, all he does is yell and scream! About what, nobody knows; most of the time he doesn't even know himself! A thousand times a day he comes home and then goes right out again, for no reason at all! He's never here at mealtime: If you talk to him he doesn't respond—or if he does, he doesn't make any sense! The servants laugh at him, his son's completely written him off, and everyone in the house now feels they can do whatever they want! Well, I'm going to church and pray things get better. Hey: There's Eustachio!

First question: Was your monologue funny?
Second question: Should it have been?

It's obvious that anything labeled *commedia* would be expected to be funny. And it certainly is. But what does this have to do with playing the goal of the character? How is playing *commedia,* or playing comedy, consistent with basic acting technique, which teaches you above all else to try to achieve your character's goals?

The best answer is this: Since these speeches take place in a public setting—a street with presumed passersby—both Cleandro and Sofronia want the passersby, who (conveniently) also include the theatre audience, to support their arguments. That way, the passersby, or audience, can help them achieve their individual goals. It's always easier to win an argument with someone if the people who happen to be around you are on your side. It's even easier if they are openly rooting for you: cheering your remarks and laughing at your jokes. The other person is almost bound to give in.

So you can simply make the presumed passersby and theatre audience into characters in your play—that is, into sixteenth-century Florentines—and then do whatever you can to get them to see things your way. Persuade them to *support* you in winning Clizia's love (if you are playing Cleandro) or shaming Nicomaco into giving up his absurd quest (if you are playing Sofronia). Inspire them to *laugh at your jokes* and *cheer your insights.* You know your goal; let the audience help you win it. If an analogy would help, imagine you are arguing with someone who has cut in line ahead of you to buy one of the last available tickets to a rock concert. Let all the other people in line hear—and believe—your explanation of who's first in line! Get them to send the interloper to the back!

Why must you be "entertaining"? Why can't you simply state your case and expect us to agree? Because your case—as an objective legal argument—isn't by itself all that interesting! Why should we, the audience, care whether you get Clizia or someone else does? Or whether your husband behaves properly or improperly? Indeed, young men fall in love all the time, husbands stray all the time, and there's no particular reason why we should care about your problems rather than our own. So you have to make us care, and the only way you can do that is by capturing our imagination—by *entertaining* us—both in the normal sense (amusing us) and in the original one (grabbing our attention). Think of your speech as a sales pitch—and yourself as a street performer selling a product. Convince us your situation deserves our highest respect. Make us forget our own goals and, instead, think about yours and how we might help you win them.

Acrobatics and pratfalls   Physical comedy is a prominent feature of all *commedia,* and the handstand by Arlecchino mocks the tumbled comic servant Cornetto in this drawing of the period.

How? Look for clues in the dialogue. Italian comedy is filled with puns and wordplays, quotations and misquotations of famous lines, mini-poems of alliterations, assonance, and rhymes, and an entire repertoire of nonverbal utterances: stutters, blusters, bawdy innuendo, linguistic indecencies, mispronunciations (particularly of foreign languages), pseudomelodramatic posturing, gasps, wheezes, and inventive throat-gaggings (hence the word *gag* for "joke").

Try the bits of comic business suggested in the stage directions, provided by me, in the versions of the two speeches that follow, perhaps augmenting them with a study of the illustrations in this chapter—which, though idealized by their draftsmen, date from the sixteenth and seventeenth centuries. Or invent better ones! *Commedia* is famed for its *lazzi* (singular: *lazzo*), a nearinfinite assemblage of pratfalls, double takes, exaggerated trembles (such as knocking knees and chattering teeth), rowdy (yet harmless) battles, sexual gropings and gestures, and elaborate comic miming (for example, Arlecchino swats and stuns an imaginary fly on his forehead, then carefully plucks off its wings and eats it—with great fanfare). The *commedia dell'arte* "slapstick"— a trick baton made of two wooden slats, hinged together to make a sharp sound when struck on an object, such as Zanni's bottom—has indeed become the word we use to describe all such physical stage buffooneries. Many of these comic *lazzi* have found their way directly into contemporary stage comedies and farces; many more are seen nightly on television sitcoms.

Granted, the humor of such *lazzi* can be viewed as merely *stupido,* which is in a sense inevitable, for they are hundreds of years old and originally designed for an illiterate audience. But the greatest comic actors reinvent classic *lazzi* all the time, making them original and particular to themselves.

So act out these speeches and get the audience to laugh with you—and at your adversaries!

CLEANDRO: *[looking the audience right in the eyes, looking for someone to accuse]* Who was it said that lovers are like soldiers? *[finding the person, and smiling at her or him]* He sure was speaking the truth! *[puffing himself up as a pompous Italian general, perhaps Mussolini]* The general wants his men young and sturdy; *[suddenly going goo-goo-eyed; his version of an infatuated young girl]* so do women. *[tottering about with an imaginary rifle on his shoulder]* Old soldiers are a dirty joke; *[tottering about making limp sexual overtures]* so are old lovers. *[cowering in mock fear]* Soldiers get chewed out by their sergeants; *[cowering further in mock terror, hands across his nether regions]* lovers by their ladies. *[falling to the floor with his imaginary rifle, as a soldier in a rainstorm]* Soldiers sleep out in the rain on the battlefields; *[rolling over in the rain trying to serenade a girl on a balcony, the "rifle" now becoming a "guitar," batting off the raindrops falling in his eyes]* so do would-be Romeos, who get sopping wet under the balconies of their Juliets. *[responding to a sudden downpour, then rising ferociously]* Soldiers pursue their enemies with total ferocity, *[roars to his left]* just as lovers attack their rivals. *[roars even more fiercely to his right, and then to his rear, and then to the audience. Catches himself up short, as if stopping himself before getting too carried away. Then, miming the nouns as he says them]* Secrecy, faith, and courage are the emblems of both the soldier and the lover: neither *[miming nouns as before]* blackest night, nor iciest cold, nor driving-est wind, nor rain, sleet nor hail shall halt either one *[exaggerated heroic bravado]* on their road to conquest! *[directly to the audience, as if summing up philosophically]* So that, at the end of his lonely struggle, the soldier *["dying" vaingloriously, hand on head wound]* dies dismembered in a ditch: *[rolling over, hand on heart wound]* and the lover dies strung out in despair! *[up and charming]* And so it is with me: Clizia lives *[points to his house]* in my house. *[starts to house, quickly returns]* I see her, I eat with her. *[starts further to house, quickly returns]* The closer she gets, the more I want her; *[starts even further to house, quickly returns]* the more I want her, the less I have her; *[starts even further to house, quickly returns]* the less I have her, the more I am overwhelmed by the agony of passion! *[glances in opposite direction, returns]* But where is my servant Eustachio? *[glances in opposite direction, returns, glances back—a double take]* Oh, wait, there he is! *[hollering in his direction]* Eustachio! Eustachio!

SOFRONIA: *[advancing directly toward the audience, while pointing back to her left to where her husband has just run away from her]* It's amazing, the change in this man! *[turning back toward her husband, and, leaping in the air, pretending to spit at him with a loud "Ptooooie!" Then turning back to the audience, indicating him with her thumb as in an umpire's gesture for "Out!"]* Why, right up through last year, he was *[showing her thumb as in "one"]* serious, *[showing her index finger as in "two"]* consistent, *[showing her middle finger as in "three"]* respectful, *[starting to show her fourth finger, but instead re-raising her middle— indecent—one again]* honorable! He woke up early, got dressed, went to church, and went about his work! In the morning *[suddenly speaking rapidly, while miming all this in exaggerated imitation of an old man]* he'd make his rounds: to the market, city hall; maybe a business call or two; then to a quiet lunch with a few friends, perhaps a visit with his son, to give the boy a few words of advice— *[employing a pretentiously sanctimonious voice]* worthwhile lessons from history, you know, sage observations on current affairs— *[back to exaggerated miming and fast speaking]* and then he'd come home for his afternoon chores, evening prayers, and a quick visit to his study to plan the next day's events. *[miming exhaustion, sitting on a bench and spreading out]* Then, at nine o'clock, we'd have a big family dinner in front of the fireplace. *[exaggerated eating noises and miming]* He was a model husband, father, and citizen; an exemplar of family values. *[rising in presumed anger, and pointing over the audience's heads at her "husband," who is presumed walking about town]* But now look at him! All of a sudden, he's lost in fantasy: All he thinks about is this girl, *[sashaying around like a dim-witted, sex-crazed girl, and stuttering her name]* Clizia! *[building this sentence in intensity with each verb]* He *ignores* his business, NEGLECTS his properties, and *FORGETS HIS FRIENDS!* *[now yelling and screaming]* Instead, all he does is YELL AND SCREAM! *[suddenly realizing she should modify her own behavior; quieting down]* About what, nobody knows; most of the time he doesn't even know himself! *[miming this, tiptoeing home and turning around]* A thousand times a day he comes home and then goes right out again, for no reason at all! He's never here at mealtime: If you talk to him he doesn't respond—or if he does, he doesn't make any sense! *[leaping into the air spitting, "Ptooooie!" "Ptooooie!"]* The servants laugh at him *[laughing uproariously, then suddenly stopping]*, his son's completely written him off *[miming huge Xs on a page]*, and everyone in the house now feels they can do whatever they want! *[one more "Ptooooie!"; gathering her things and heading off to the left]* Well, I'm going to church and pray things get better. *[looking back at the audience, seeing her servant to her right and swinging back to him]* Hey: There's Eustachio!

In all this behavior, understand that you are putting on a performance for your fellow citizens, inciting them to side with you. Win them over with your humor, your self-assurance, your witty descriptions, your physical and vocal elaborations of your case. If you can do this, you are beginning to appreciate the style of old Italian comedy: You are a "commedia-n."

Commedia Lazzi

In his wonderful book *Lazzi: The Comic Routines of the Commedia Dell'Arte,** Mel Gordon describes two hundred *lazzi* known to have been used in *commedia* performances between 1550 and 1750. These are usually performed by the Zanni characters (clowns—this is where we get our word *zany*), most usually potbellied Pulcinella, or Arlecchino, the cunning and acrobatic rascal eternally familiar in his black mask and multicolored, diamond-patterned costume.

Some of the simpler ones are

◆ *Lazzo of the Hands Behind the Back* Arlecchino, attempting to hide behind Scaramuccia, places his arms around him, making all the hand gestures for him. In this way, Arlecchino torments Scaramuccia by slapping his face, pinching his nose, and so forth.

◆ *Lazzo of Eating the Cherries* While Scapino is speaking, Arlecchino shows his indifference by taking imaginary cherries out of his hat, eating them, and throwing the pits at Scapino.

◆ *Lazzo of Imitating a Dog* To frighten Scaramuccia, Arlecchino snarls and snaps at him like a dog.

Here are some of the more complex:

◆ *Lazzo of the Rope-Macaroni* Attempting to smuggle a rope into a jail to help a friend escape, Pulcinella tries to convince the jailer that the rope is only a long strand of macaroni.

◆ *Lazzo of the Hatching Egg* Arlecchino, hatched from an egg, learns to coordinate each part of his independently jointed body.

◆ *Lazzo of Spilling No Wine* Startled, Arlecchino, holding a full glass of wine, executes a complete backward somersault without spilling a drop.

---

* (New York: Performing Arts Journal Publications, 1983).

Cap. Babeo.   Cucuba.

Ribaldry   *Commedia* was a ribald and often riotous comic form, as exemplified by this Callot engraving of Capitano Babbeo and Cucuba.

Gordon also lists scatological and sexual *lazzi,* reporting them "among the most popular" of the repertoire:

◆ *Lazzo of Vomit*   After drinking some of the Dottore's medicine, Arlecchino mimes vomiting.

◆ *Lazzo of the Rising Dagger*   As Pantalone hear about the physical perfection of a certain woman, his dagger begins to rise between his legs.

Performing such *lazzi* is a matter of carefully elaborating the mime, and often improvising dialogue to go with it. In teams of two or more people, develop routines of such *lazzi* that could be inserted into a typical *commedia* plot.

◆ S C E N E   **10–1**

Nicomaco and Sofronia

What follows is an abridged version of a scene in *Clizia* between Nicomaco and his wife, Sofronia. Nicomaco is plotting to have his stupid and ineffectual servant Pirro marry Clizia, so that he can keep Clizia in his house and make her his mistress. Sofronia, naturally, is plotting to stop him.

NICOMACO: Uh-oh, here she comes: Pirro, get out of here fast!

SOFRONIA: I've had to lock Clizia in her room: My son's after her; my husband's after her; the servants are after her—my house is becoming a den of iniquity, for God's sake!

NICOMACO: Where're you going?

SOFRONIA: To church.

NICOMACO: To church? What on earth for? It's not Lent! It's not even Sunday!

SOFRONIA: It's a day in the life of the wicked, all of whom need our prayers. Including you!

NICOMACO: Me? What's wrong with me?

SOFRONIA: Here we've raised this lovely young girl, for which everyone in town admires us, and now you're trying to marry her off to this brainless idiot Pirro! Who can't even support the fleas in his beard! We'll be the laughingstock of Florence.

NICOMACO: Sofronia, darling, you're dead wrong as usual. Pirro's young, he's good-looking, and he loves her. These are the three things a husband should have: youth, looks, and . . . *amore;* who could ask for anything "ahhhh . . . more, eh"?

SOFRONIA: That's not funny! I could like something more! Like more *lire!*

NICOMACO: I know he's not rich, but you know money, it goes from boom to bust, bust to boom, and Pirro's a boomer if I've ever seen one! Indeed, I'm thinking of setting him up.

SOFRONIA: Ha ha ha!

NICOMACO: You're laughing?

SOFRONIA: Who wouldn't? And what are you "setting him up" in?

NICOMACO: What do you mean "in"? In business, of course!

SOFRONIA: In monkey business, I bet! You're going to take the girl away from your son and give her to your steward, right? Something's fishy here, Nicomaco!

NICOMACO: Monkey? Fishy? What are you saying, monkey-fishy?

SOFRONIA: You already know, so I won't tell you.

NICOMACO: What . . . what . . . what do I know?

SOFRONIA: Forget it! Why are you so eager to marry Clizia to Pirro? She's got no dowry, and he's got no prospects! Right?

NICOMACO: Right . . . I guess . . . But I love them both so much, I raised them both; they're both so very . . . so very . . . so very ME! I know they'll be happy together.

SOFRONIA: Happy! Pirro spends all his time drinking and gambling. He would starve to death in the Garden of Eden!

NICOMACO: I told you, I'll set him up!

SOFRONIA: And I told you, you'd just be throwing good money after bad! And you'd convert all our good work into a public scandal! Listen, Nicomaco, we're both involved here: You may have paid the bills for raising Clizia, but I'm the one who brought her up, and I'll have my say about what happens to her! Or else there'll be hell to pay all over town: I'll make sure of that!

NICOMACO: Are you crazy? What are you trying to say? I'm telling you they're getting married tonight, no matter what you do!

SOFRONIA: Maybe yes and maybe no.

NICOMACO: Oho, you're threatening to slander me. Watch out, woman, two can play at that game! You're not all that innocent, you know, helping your dear Cleandro out in his little adventures . . . !

SOFRONIA: What adventures? What are you talking about?

NICOMACO: Oh ho ho! Don't make me say it, dear wife: You know, and I know, and I know that you know, and you know that I know that you know . . . that I . . . that uh . . . that . . . Arghhhh! We're becoming idiots here! Let's make a deal before we make a public spectacle of ourselves.

SOFRONIA: A spectacle, yes, *commedia dell'arte!* And you: old Pantalone! All Florence will be rolling in the aisles!

NICOMACO: Arghhhh! Arghhhh! *[sings]* Sofronia! Sofronia! You're so full of macaronia!*

SOFRONIA: God forgive you, husband. I'm going to church; I'll see you later!

Read the scene aloud with a partner three or four times.

---

* In the original, Machiavelli rhymes *Sofronia* with *soffiona*—a wind machine.

Remember, as with the speeches in the preceding exercise, that the scene takes place in public and that you have a twofold job: first, to convince your spouse to accommodate your interests, and second, to convince any curious passersby that your values are the worthier ones. As with Noah and his wife, Nicomaco should particularly try to get the male passersby on his side, and Sofronia the Florentine wives. So, while seeking to win your argument with your spouse, you should also develop some presentation techniques that will entertain your potential supporters in the town—and therefore in the audience. Humiliate your spouse in public: Make him or her reverse course!

With that in mind, prepare and rehearse the same scene with your partner using the stage directions that follow, which include standard *commedia lazzi* and universal comic business. *Entertain* the audience of passersby, not to prove that you're a comic but to "capture their attention"—to your cause. With the rest of the class on and around the street where this scene is set (some standing, some strolling in the distance, some seated on several sides), play it for all it's worth. Impress your potential supporters both with your truths and with your wit, and try openly, brutally if need be, to win over the Florentine public. Remember, your public and private honor (represented by Nicomaco's lust and Sofronia's marriage) is at stake; lose, and you will be disgraced for the rest of your life!

NICOMACO: *[talking to Pirro]* Uh-oh, here she comes: Pirro, get out of here fast! *[He shoves Pirro, who falls, gets up, falls again, gets up, limps around in a circle until Nicomaco chases him around the stage, as Sofronia enters from the other direction.]*

SOFRONIA: *[speaking to the audience]* I've had to lock Clizia in her room: My son's after her; *[pointing to Nicomaco]* my husband's after her; *[Pirro walks in front of her as he leaves the stage; she points at him]* the servants are after her—my house is becoming a den of iniquity, for God's sake! *[She snarls at her husband and starts off.]*

NICOMACO: Where're you going?

SOFRONIA: To church.

NICOMACO: To church? What on earth for? It's not Lent! It's not even Sunday!

SOFRONIA: It's a day in the life of the wicked, all of whom need our prayers. Including you! *[She falls to her knees and starts to pray vigorously.]*

NICOMACO: Me? *[He too falls to his knees, loudly mocking her praying and making her stop.]* What's wrong with me?

SOFRONIA: *[rising and confronting him directly]* Here we've raised this lovely young girl, for which everyone in town admires us, and now you're trying to marry her off to *[pointing to where Pirro left the stage]* this brainless idiot Pirro! Who can't even support the fleas in his beard! *[Imitates a man trying to pick fleas from his beard. Nicomaco starts to rise; she knocks him down. He starts to rise again; she knocks him down again.]* We'll be the laughingstock of Florence.

NICOMACO: Sofronia, darling, you're dead wrong as usual. *[He starts to rise a third time; she raises her hand, he falls down on his own. She walks away.]* Pirro's young, he's good-looking, and he loves her. *[As she has moved away, Nicomaco slowly rises to his feet during the following.]* These are the three things a husband should have: youth, looks, and *[searching for the Italian word for "love"]* . . . amore; who could ask for anything "ahhhh . . . more, eh"? *[laughs wildly at his pun]*

SOFRONIA: That's not funny! I could like something more! Like more *lire!* *[which she pronounces "leer, eh!" and then echoes his wild laughter]*

NICOMACO: *[in a rage]* I know he's not rich *[she snorts]* but you know money, it goes from boom to bust, bust to boom, and Pirro's a boomer if I've ever seen one! *[she "booms"—farts—around the stage in protest, saying "boom" with each fart.]* Indeed, I'm thinking of setting him up.

SOFRONIA: *[laughs uproariously]* Ha ha ha!

NICOMACO: *[scandalized]* You're laughing?

SOFRONIA: Who wouldn't? *[more laughter]* And what are you "setting him up" IN?

NICOMACO: What do you mean "in"? In business, of course!

SOFRONIA: In monkey business, I bet! *[prancing about like a monkey]* You're going to take the girl away from your son and give her to your steward, right? *[sniffing loudly]* Something's fishy here, Nicomaco!

NICOMACO: *[He sniffs too, taking her literally.]* Monkey? Fishy? What are you saying, monkey-fishy?

SOFRONIA: *[coyly, walking away]* You already know, so I won't tell you.

NICOMACO: *[frightened, following her]* What . . . what . . . what do I know?

SOFRONIA: *[She stops and turns suddenly; he bumps into her and falls.)* Forget it! Why are you so eager to marry Clizia to Pirro? She's got no dowry, and he's got no prospects! Right?

NICOMACO: Right . . . I guess . . . *[He gets up, she again walks away until he restrains her.]* But I love them both so much, I raised them both; they're both so very . . . so very . . . so very ME! I know they'll be happy together.

SOFRONIA: Happy! Pirro spends all his time drinking and gambling. He would starve to death in the Garden of Eden!

NICOMACO: I told you, I'll set him up!

SOFRONIA: And I told you, you'd just be throwing good money after bad! And you'd convert all our good work into a public scandal! *[She points to the audience. Nicomaco, turning to the audience at her gesture, suddenly panics at the thought of creating a scandal. Sofronia turns back to him.]* Listen, Nicomaco, we're both involved here: You may have paid the bills for raising Clizia, but I'm the one who brought her up, and I'll have my say about what happens to her! *[looking out at the audience once again to solicit their approval]* Or else there'll be hell to pay all over town: I'll make sure of that!

NICOMACO: *[Still looking at the audience, he tries to calm them with hand gestures—but then, suddenly panicking more at the thought of losing Clizia, he turns back to Sofronia.]* Are you crazy? What are you trying to say? I'm telling you they're getting married tonight, no matter what you do! *[He turns and starts to leave.]*

SOFRONIA: Maybe yes and maybe no. *[She turns to leave in the opposite direction.]*

NICOMACO: *[His bluff called, he stops and speaks.]* Oho, you're threatening to slander me. *[She stops for a second, then sets out again. He again calls to her—as forcefully as he can.]* Watch out, woman, two can play at that game! *[same business; he shouts at her]* You're not all that innocent, you know, helping your dear Cleandro out in his little adventures . . . !

SOFRONIA: *[stopping for real: She has reason to feel some guilt as well.]*
What adventures? What are you talking about?

NICOMACO: *[feeling, for the first time, that he's on a winning track]* Oh
ho ho! Don't make me say it, dear wife: You know, and I know, and I
know that you know, and you know that I know that you know . . .
[loses his thought] that I . . . that uh . . . that . . . *[breaks down in self-rage]* Arghhhh! We're becoming idiots here! Let's make a deal before we
make a public spectacle of ourselves.

SOFRONIA: A spectacle, yes, *commedia dell'arte!* And you: old Pantalone!
[gesturing to the audience of Florentines] All Florence will be rolling in
the aisles!

NICOMACO: Arghhhh! Arghhhh! *[sings]* Sofronia! Sofronia! You're so full
of macaronia! *[imitates a fart: Pffffffffffffffffffffffffft!]*

SOFRONIA: *[He keeps singing wordlessly, and Sofronia, speaking half to
him and half to the audience, feels she has gotten as much from him as
she can expect at this time.]* God forgive you, husband. I'm going to
church; I'll see you later! *[She storms off, knocking him down in the
process.]*

Stock Characters

Commedia characters are ordinary people—not royalty like Oedipus and
Jocasta, nor biblical figures with divine connections like Noah and his wife.
Nicomaco and Sofronia go to work, cook meals, raise children, gossip with
their neighbors, struggle with their finances, go to church, and die known
only to their immediate circle of family and friends. They're like us, in other
words, and don't present the challenges of the larger-than-life reality you
will find in, say, Teiresias or God.

But they're also *not* like us, for they lack the complexity of thinking and
feeling, and the trail of history, that have gone into the making of our personalities. This is somewhat true for all dramatic figures but particularly for
those we call "stock characters," who are used by dramatists to indicate not
a specific real-life person but a *class* of like-minded and like-behaving individuals. So, while they may be presumed to cook meals, pay bills, and go to
work, we don't see them doing this in the play—unless it is part of the
stereotypical behavior of the part. Neither do we know any of their history.
Nicomaco is a "dirty old man" conniving to win the sexual favors of a
young woman, but Machiavelli gives us no clues as to how he got that way.

A madcap scramble as Pantalone (standing) is both supported and undone by Brighella, Arlecchino, and Il Dottore, as the pert Smeraldina watches the hilarity. (Photo courtesy of Teatro Piccolo.)

Sofronia is a "suffering wife" (*soffrire* is Italian for "to suffer"), but we have no idea how or why she came to that role or what earlier options she may have discarded. These considerations, and the acting questions they provoke, are for another sort of drama. Rather, the character "type" precedes and determines the parameters of the role. The "wily servant" will be a wily servant regardless of his name—which is why *commedia dell'arte* simply dispensed with individual names and called him Arlecchino, and gave him a mask as well, thereby subordinating the actor's individual face to the stock characteristics of the role.

Indeed, stock characters, invented by the Greeks in their New Comedy, were all masked and remained masked in Roman times. And the mask, in all these plays, *is* in a certain sense the character.* Consequently, there is

---

* The Latin word for "mask" is *persona* and is the root of our words *person* and *personality.*

little if any subtle psychology in any *commedia* role. The characters are driven by universal instinct (Nicomaco's lust, Sofronia's jealousy) rather than psychological developments unique to themselves.

This does not mean, however, that stock characters must be played in wholly fixed patterns. Quite to the contrary: The playing of stock characters can be as brilliantly innovative and individual as the actor's imagination allows. One need only remember (if we have seen them) the *commedia* performances of Jim Dale, Bill Irwin, or David Shiner, or imagine those of Jim Carrey, Robin Williams, or Whoopi Goldberg, to realize how brilliantly unique these roles can be in performance. Stock characters demand, above all, outrageously energetic and creative performers, making radical choices in playing—and exaggerating—the aspects of the stereotypical behavior the dramatist was hoping to poke fun at.

And a postscript: "Nicomaco," had you not guessed, is a shorthand version of "Niccolò Machiavelli," who was known to consort with young prostitutes and actresses, including one who performed in the premiere of this play. Stock characters, therefore, while abstractions of individuals, are filled with the breath of real human life.

More *Commedia* Scenes

Scenes in this genre are hard to find because *commedia dell'arte* is largely improvised and unscripted and *commedia erudita* scripts are rare. But you can look at additional scenes in *Clizia* and in Machiavelli's even better known *Mandragola* (*The Mandrake*), and also at the partly scripted plays of two eighteenth-century Venetians with *commedia* roots: Carlo Gozzi (*The King Stag; The Snake Woman*) and Carlo Goldoni (*The Servant of Two Masters,* which Goldoni adapted from an original *commedia dell'arte* version; *The Cunning Widow; The Mistress of the Inn; The Venetian Twins; The Fan*).

And you can *improvise* your own *commedia dell'arte* as well! Using the skeleton of any scene in these plays, or from any Roman comedy, or traditional folk tale from any culture, and mixing in comic *lazzi* and physical and verbal high jinks of your own making, create your own *commedia dell'arte* plot, outlining the main events and character entrances and exits, and, with one or more fellow actors improvising the plot's dialogue with you as you go along, preparing, rehearsing, and staging your mini-masterpiece.

11

Shakespeare and the Elizabethan Theatre

From Italy, the Renaissance spread north, bringing with it a revival of long-lost plays and theatrical insights from ancient Greece and Rome, which soon merged with the popular folk dance, song, storytelling, mime, and acrobatic entertainment of medieval Europe. Nowhere was this combination more thrilling and vigorous than in England, chiefly during the reigns of Queen Elizabeth I (1558–1603) and King James I (1603–1625). Dozens of playwrights became immensely popular during these decades, including John Lyly, Christopher Marlowe, Thomas Kyd, John Webster, Ben Jonson, Thomas Dekker, and of course William Shakespeare, now considered the greatest dramatist not only of his time but of all time.

Like its classical and *commedia* predecessors, Elizabethan drama was largely played in a public theatre, usually outdoors.* The first theatres were trestle stages set up in streets and innyards. By the 1570s, grand open-air public theatres were erected in suburbs north and south of London (playgoing having been outlawed within the city itself). These public theatres seated upwards of three thousand spectators, ranged around the actors on at least three

---

* Technically, "Elizabethan" refers only to the period of Elizabeth's reign; dramas—including some of Shakespeare's—from the time of King James are more properly called "Jacobean." But "Elizabethan" is also used in a general sense to refer to both periods and, for the sake of simplicity, is so here.

Some Elizabethan stage characters   This well-known engraving, made about fifty years after Shakespeare's death, shows costumes and postures of various popular Elizabethan characters, including two of Shakespeare's (Falstaff and Mistress Quickly—here labeled "Hoftes," or Hostess), and probably indicates current costuming of those characters and others.

Basic Elizabethan male attire   The doublet (a vestlike jacket ending in a short skirt) and hose (tights) were basic attire for young men in the Elizabethan era, often with breeches (short pants, often padded) bridging the two. A long-sleeved blouse was usually underneath, and boots, belts, hats, capes, and accessories completed the picture. Stylistic variations, however, were enormous. Pictured is Iris Brooke's reconstruction of a basic male attire for 1595.

sides (some scholars say all four), where they sat in three galleries above the stage, stood on the earthen "pit" at the actors' feet, or, if they could afford it (and the theatre permitted it on that date), sat on the stage itself.

Surrounded by their audience, Elizabethan actors were necessarily virtuoso artists—skilled at holding an audience on all sides with their great skills at singing, dancing, fencing, storytelling, verse and prose speaking, and milking the dramatic styles of both comedy and tragedy to maximum effect. And they were adept at playing characters of both sexes—despite the fact that throughout the entire period, by law all professional actors were male. But make no mistake: Elizabethan actors were emotionally expressive (and impressive) actors as well, engaging their own and the audience's feelings, and, unquestionably, crying real tears onstage when the text demanded it, as it very often did.*

Like their Italian Renaissance counterparts, Elizabethan dramatists often began by revising ancient Roman plays. For example, one of Shakespeare's first plays, *The Comedy of Errors,* was an adaptation of Plautus's *Menaechmi,* eighteen centuries old at the time. Indeed, most Elizabethan plays were adaptations of older plays or of historical chronicles, including

---

* The evidence for this is compelling. See my "Tears (and Acting) in Shakespeare," in Robert Cohen, *More Power to You* (New York: Applause, 2002), pp. 7–18.

Elizabethan ladies, in representative attire as drawn by Iris Brooke.

Greek and Roman history as well as British. But Elizabethan drama diverged from the Italian by dispensing quickly with stock characters, and the plays of Shakespeare, in particular, have given us dramatic roles of extraordinary complexity, individuality, and humanity.

Early in his own time, Shakespeare was identified as a great dramatic poet—equal to the ancients—in both comedy and tragedy. But he also practically invented, and remains the sole true master of, a new genre of drama: the history play, inspired by events in English history from the time of King John. For our first exploration of the genius of his age, we turn to one of Shakespeare's earliest and, in his own time, most successful history plays, *Richard III,* first published in 1597.

◆ S C E N E　　**11–1**

The Past Made Vivid: Richard and Anne

This exchange, from Act 1, Scene 2 of *Richard III,* takes place between Richard, Duke of Gloucester (who when crowned will become King Richard III), and Lady Anne, whose husband Richard has just murdered. To heighten the drama, Shakespeare, counter to the historical record, sets his scene next to the corpse of King Henry VI, Anne's father-in-law, whom Richard has also murdered. The dialogue mixes grief, fury, and sexual adventurism—all in verse—in the brilliant theatricality we have come to associate with the world's most celebrated playwright.

Marco Barricelli plays the crook-backed King Richard in the Oregon Shakespeare Festival's 1993 production of Richard III. (Courtesy Oregon Shakespeare Festival; photo by Christopher Briscoe)

RICHARD: I did not kill your husband.

ANNE: Why, then he is alive.

RICHARD: Nay, he is dead; and slain by Edward's hand.

ANNE: In thy foul throat thou liest: Queen Margaret saw
Thy murd'rous falchion° smoking in his blood;   °*sword*
The which thou once didst bend against her breast,
But that thy brothers beat aside the point.

RICHARD: I was provoked by her sland'rous tongue,
That laid their guilt upon my guiltless shoulders.

ANNE: Thou wast provoked by thy bloody mind,
That never dreamt on aught but butcheries.
Didst thou not kill this king?

RICHARD: I grant ye.

David Troughton plays the title role and Jennifer Ehle plays Lady Anne in this
Royal Shakespeare Company 1995 production of Richard III. (© Clive
Barda/Performing Arts Library)

ANNE: Dost grant me, hedgehog? Then, God grant me too
    Thou mayst be damned for that wicked deed!
    O! he was gentle, mild, and virtuous!

RICHARD: The better for the King of heaven, that hath him.

ANNE: He is in heaven, where thou shalt never come.

RICHARD: Let him thank me, that holp° to send him thither;   °helped
    For he was fitter for that place than earth.

ANNE: And thou unfit for any place but hell.

RICHARD: Yes, one place else, if you will hear me name it.

ANNE: Some dungeon.

RICHARD: Your bed chamber.

ANNE: Ill rest betide° the chamber where thou liest!   °*come to*

RICHARD: So will it, madam, till I lie with you.

The characters' goals are both simple and complex. At the simple level, Richard seeks a sexual encounter with Lady Anne—to "lie with" her. Lady Anne seeks to make Richard suffer ("God grant . . . thou mayst be damned") for murdering her husband and her father-in-law; she wants to get him to confess to those crimes if she can and, at the very least, shame him into a numbing guilt. As these simple goals rely on basic instincts, lust (for Richard) and revenge (for Lady Anne), this scene can develop a ferocious interpersonal intensity.

But there are subtler goals as well. Richard's drive is at least as political as sexual. As a royal prince, he surely would have no trouble acquiring mere sexual gratification, and Lady Anne represents a crucial stepping-stone to his winning the crown: Marrying her could make his claim to the throne appear almost legitimate. Nor is Lady Anne, recently widowed, without political desire. In those times, ousted royals were more likely to be executed than retired to a country estate. Unmarried, Anne would be vulnerable to whoever came to power; married to Richard, she might at least have a protector and access to the royal way of life to which she had surely become accustomed.

So this scene, with a few minor modifications, would be a striking dramatic interchange in any theatrical form: contemporary cinema, TV soap opera, opera, or modern urban drama. But the particular style of Shakespeare's language poses rare—even unprecedented—opportunities for suspenseful, sensual, and emotionally thrilling performances.

Learn, rehearse, and play the scene with a partner before proceeding to the following discussions of the text elements.

Scansion

The exchange between Richard and Anne is a verse text, which means the language has a definable pattern of accented syllables and sometimes a rhyme pattern as well.

The basic elements of dramatic verse are simple to understand: It is language composed in *lines* of a regular length, and each line can be subdivided into a repeating series of *feet,* which are units of a fixed length that have a recognizable and repeated pattern of *accented syllables.*

What is an accented syllable? Generally, it is a syllable spoken with a bit more force and, particularly in dramatic verse, with a slightly raised pitch.

Reading the pattern of the line lengths and accented syllables is called *scansion,* or a scanning of the verse. Thus, for example, scanning Anne's line "And thou unfit for any place but hell" shows a natural speaking rhythm of five paired syllables, each with the second syllable slightly accented: something like "duh DUM, duh DUM, duh DUM, duh DUM, duh DUM." The line could be spoken as something like this (the accented syllables are shown in capitals): "And THOU un-FIT for A-ny PLACE but HELL."

Now, in fact, very few good actors would stress all five of the syllables equally in that line. Some wouldn't stress more than two or three of them—at least as far as the untrained ear could tell. You may instead hear such actors say something like "And THOU unfit for AN-y place but HELL," thus giving *thou* (the person she's angry at) and *hell* (the place she wants him to go) the strongest emphases and the *a* in *any* a light or moderate stress just to punch up the middle of the line.

But if you listen very closely, you might hear that *fit* and *place* are at least micro-stressed, given an emphasis that is barely perceptible but still lends added flavor and sharper distinction to the text.

The "duh DUM" is, in this case, the *verse foot.* This particular type of two-syllable foot, with the second syllable accented, is called *iambic.* Iambic feet are the most common in Elizabethan verse drama, and in most other verse dramas as well—including ancient Greek, neoclassic French, and modern English. Repeated iambic feet are also often employed in ritualized prose, as in the first eight syllables of the Pledge of Allegiance ("i PLEDGE al-LE-giance TO the FLAG") and in the minister's wedding declaration ("i NOW pro-NOUNCE you MAN and WIFE").

A verse scheme that uses lines with five feet is called *pentameter,* from the Greek word for "five." Pentameter is the most common line length in English verse drama.

Iambic pentameter is the most common verse form employed by Shakespeare and other Elizabethan dramatists, and it is the form of Anne's quoted line. When iambic pentameter is not rhymed, it is known as *blank verse.* In fact, the first reference to Shakespeare in print was a rival playwright complaining to his friends in 1592 that the young Shakespeare "supposes he is as well able to bombast out a blank verse as the best of you." And he was.

There are other verse forms used in Elizabethan drama, of course. As to feet: While iambs are the most common, *trochees* (trochaic feet), which also contain two syllables but with the first accented, also appear, often as the first foot of a line. There are also three-syllable feet: *anapests,* which have the last syllable accented (as in the word *underneath*), and *dactyls,* in which the first syllable bears the accent (as in *broccoli*).

As to line length: A four-foot line is called *tetrameter;* a three-foot line *trimeter,* a two-foot line *dimeter,* and a six-foot line (which is the verse form for most French drama) *hexameter.*

As to rhyme: Shakespeare often uses rhyming pentameter couplets, where the last two syllables of two consecutive lines rhyme. And he uses rhymes in more complex ways as well.

Blank verse is the most common form of versification in Shakespeare, but it is not the only one. Later in the same scene between Richard and Anne we have a section of iambic trimeter:

ANNE: I would I knew thy heart.

RICHARD: 'Tis figur'd in my tongue.

ANNE: I fear me both are false.

RICHARD: Then never man was true.

ANNE: Well, well, put up your sword.

RICHARD: Say, then, my peace is made.

ANNE: That shalt thou know hereafter.

RICHARD: But shall I live in hope?

ANNE: All men, I hope, live so.

And the play concludes, as do most Shakespearean dramas, with a rhyming couplet:

Now civil wounds are stopp'd, Peace lives again;
That she may long live here, God say amen!

Verse Variations

Blank verse used in a play is not always regular. Although the earliest dramatic blank verse in English was uniform in its iambic pentameters, as can be seen in the first English play employing this form—Thomas Sackville and Thomas Norton's *Gorboduc* (1561)—most later plays and all of Shakespeare's have a richer poetic texture, one that admits abundant variations or irregularities of both line length and accents. In Scene 11–1, for example, we find:

1. Lines with an extra (eleventh), unaccented syllable. This is called a "feminine ending":* "That laid their guilt upon my guiltless shoulders" and "Let him thank me, that help to send him thither."

---

* So called because it follows the pattern of French lines that end with feminine nouns, such as *chambre* and *monde,* which have an unstressed final syllable.

SWORDS, STAFFS, AND WALKING STICKS

Notice that Anne asks Richard to "put up" his sword. From medieval times until the eighteenth century, men from about age fifteen to fifty commonly wore swords, even in urban settings. One reason was for protection in an era when public safety was not yet secured; another was to establish an image of bravado and manly sophistication. In Shakespeare's works, young men are continually drawing swords upon each other at the slightest provocation (as in the famous

Walking sticks and swords   Notice the swords and walking sticks employed by gentlemen in this Flemish street scene by Jean le Tavernier dating from about 1460. At the upper right, a book is being presented by a kneeling servant to Philip the Good of Burgundy.

opening scene of *Romeo and Juliet*). The sword was worn on the left hip, in a holder or scabbard, and the wearer's left hand commonly rested on the hilt; the right hand was always ready to move to the hilt immediately at the suggestion of an affront or attack.

When the sword itself became unnecessary, either because of improved public safety or the age and infirmity of the man who might carry it, a staff or walking stick was often substituted. The staff, a tall and sometimes decorated pole normally higher than the man himself, implied an official position (as with a "staff of office") and usually conveyed authority; it dates from ancient times, and the blind and holy Teiresias carries one in many productions of *Oedipus*. The walking stick, generally about waist-high, conveyed a dapper urbanity. Staffs and walking sticks alike were useful in negotiating rough cobblestones and unpaved pathways, and for batting away stray dogs and pickpockets. They were nearly ubiquitous as accessories to male attire in Europe for several hundred years, as the Flemish street scene of 1460 shown here indicates.

Actors playing male roles in period dramas, therefore, can spend useful time experimenting with and practicing the carrying and employment of swords, staffs, and walking sticks.

2. Lines with just three feet: "Why, then he is alive" and "Didst thou not kill this king?"

3. Lines in which the pentameter is maintained only by accenting normally unaccented *-ed* endings (as we sometimes do today when pronouncing the word *blessed* as *bless-ed*): "Thou wast provokèd by thy bloody mind." In these cases, the speaking accent is often noted by modern editors with a downward accent over the *e*, as above.

4. A line in which the pentameter rhythm is maintained by accenting the *-ed* ending of one word and shortening a three-syllable word (*slanderous*) into a two-syllable one: "I was provokèd by her sland'rous tongue."

5. Lines simply of prose: "I grant ye" and "Some dungeon."

6. A line of twelve syllables (eleven if *heaven* is pronounced "heav'n") that is best considered prose as well: "The better for the King of heaven that hath him."

7. Lines that would never be spoken as five consecutive iambs, such as "Nay, he is dead; and slain by Edward's hands." The first foot is probably best read as trochaic ("NAY, he"), with the four following feet iambic ("is DEAD and SLAIN by ED-ward's HAND").

Thus Shakespeare's verse, though underlaid by a "standard" pattern, deviates from that pattern almost as often as it follows it.

It isn't, of course, essential to know all the verse forms by their formal names to speak them effectively. There are surely many professional Shakespearean actors who could not define iambic trimeter if you paid them, and perhaps some of Shakespeare's own actors couldn't define it either, learning verse rhythms by experience rather than by instruction. Nonetheless, a deep understanding, as much visceral as cognitive, of the inherent cadences of verse is crucial to conveying the power, sensuality, delicacy, and intellectual complexity of Elizabethan dramatic language.

Playing the Verse

Playing verse is not easily or quickly learned. It is not simply a matter of slavishly following the scansion, which would produce mere singsong. But neither can metrical patterns be willfully overridden without sacrificing much of the text's dramatic power and sensuality. When skillfully handled, blank verse matches meter with meaning and rhythm with emotion, each playing off the other in a compellingly sensual, dynamic tension. A regular iambic rhythm ("duh DUM, duh DUM, duh DUM") also provides a steady "heartbeat" under the dialogue, creating a living presence in the text and the impression of a character brimming with confident assurance. And when the iambs suddenly break down, as happens when a Shakespearean character becomes anxious or confused, it is like a heart monitor going abruptly awry.

Let's see how the verse works in Scene 11–1.

RICHARD: I did not kill your husband.

ANNE: Why, then he is alive.

These first two lines are iambic trimeter fragments, with Richard softening his with a feminine ending, and the masculine ending of Anne's consequently providing a sarcastic jab ("Come off it," the clipped rhythm says)—for they both know that her husband is dead.

RICHARD: Nay, he is dead; and slain by Edward's hand.

Richard's reply, in blank verse but with a trochee instead of an iamb for the first foot, cuts Anne off and brings her back to reality.

ANNE: In thy foul throat thou liest: Queen Margaret saw . . .

This line begins in an iambic pattern (through "liest"), which provides a smooth denunciation of Richard; Anne then shifts essentially to prose for three words ("Queen Margaret saw") to introduce a story, which is her version of what Margaret saw. She goes on:

> Thy murd'rous falchion smoking in his blood;
> The which thou once didst bend against her breast,
> But that thy brothers beat aside the point.

The story, horrific in its imagery, is contained in three lines of iambic pentameter that recount two separate events: the discovery of Richard assassinating Anne's husband, and his earlier attack on Margaret with the same sword. But there's a substituted trochee here, too—in the last foot of the second line, which for sense would have to read "HER breast" to indicate that Richard had attacked not only Anne's husband but, with the same sword, her mother-in-law. A rigid adherence to iambic rhythm at that point ("didst BEND a-GAINST her BREAST") would obscure the meaning of the line.

> RICHARD: I was provokèd by her sland'rous tongue,
>   That laid their guilt upon my guiltless shoulders.

> ANNE: Thou wast provokèd by thy bloody mind,
>   That never dreamt on aught but butcheries.

Here Richard forces the scansion of a line into blank verse and completes the idea with a second line that adds a final unstressed syllable to make a feminine ending, again softening his villainy. Anne, not to be intimidated, parallels his first line, picking up and repudiating his exact words ("I can beat you at this fancy-talk 'provokèd' game!"), then completing her sentence with a searing accusation, with the masculine ending on *butcheries*. The parallel phrasing shows her jockeying not only for political power but also for literary dominance. History, it is said, is written by the winners: Both are fighting for the right to define history (in words), so that they can create a better future for themselves (in actions).

> ANNE: Didst thou not kill this king?

> RICHARD: I grant ye.

Anne starts a line of blank verse, but Richard responds in terse prose, mocking her attempt to versify.

> ANNE: Dost grant me, hedgehog? Then, God grant me too
>   Thou mayst be damnèd for that wicked deed!
>   O! he was gentle, mild, and virtuous!

> RICHARD: The better for the King of heav'n, that hath him.

ANNE: He is in heav'n, where thou shalt never come.

RICHARD: Let him thank me, that holp to send him thither;
  For he was fitter for that place than earth.

ANNE: And thou unfit for any place but hell.

RICHARD: Yes, one place else, if you will hear me name it.

Anne denounces Richard in five reasonably regular verse lines (presuming she expands *damned* to two syllables and contracts *heaven* to one), to which Richard responds in four lines, only one of which can be read as regular blank verse (three have at least eleven syllables), thus continuing to rudely mock her regularity of style. Then his mockery becomes savage:

ANNE: Some dungeon.

RICHARD: Your bed chamber.

Anne, flustered, tries to continue her verbal assault, but her ferocity is undercut by the feminine ending of her response. And Richard, sensing his opportunity, nails the masculine closure:

ANNE: Ill rest betide the chamber where thou liest!

RICHARD: So will it, madam, till I lie with you.

Three lines later, Richard will invite Anne to "leave this keen encounter of our wits, / And fall something into a slower method," and the verse will shift to a more regular pattern. And, yes, he will sleep with her, marry her, and eventually have her executed.

Rhetoric

Playing the verse is only a first step toward meeting the dramatic challenge of Elizabethan dramatists, who were also, by and large, dazzling rhetoricians. Rhetoric, the art of persuasive speech, is fundamental to any theatre that encompasses political or legal debate, as so many plays do. Shakespeare, indeed, was such a master of rhetoric that many scholars believe he must have spent part of his youth working in a lawyer's office. He was certainly well versed in the language of the courts, both judicial ones (he engaged in numerous lawsuits, as did his father) and the royal courts of Queen Elizabeth and King James, where he and his company often performed.

Effective rhetoric—in politics, in courts, or on the stage—is largely dependent on well-turned verbal constructions such as

◆ *Words repeated to build a crescendo:* "government of the people, by the people, for the people"—Abraham Lincoln

- *Words repeated to contrast antithetical ends:* "ask not what your country can do for you; ask what you can do for your country"—John F. Kennedy

- *Poised antonyms:* "give me liberty or give me death"—Patrick Henry

- *Parallel phrasing,* sometimes underlined by alliteration: "not be judged by the color of their skin, but by the content of their character"

—Martin Luther King Jr.

- *Building* of words or phrases, each more potent than the last: "victory at all costs, victory in spite of all terror; victory however long and hard the road may be"—Winston Churchill

In Scene 11–1 we can see repeated words (*heaven, provoked, grant*), building lists of adjectives (*gentle, mild, virtuous*), poised antonyms (*alive/dead, guilt/guiltless, heaven/hell, fitter/unfit*), and parallel phrasings ("I was provoked by her sland'rous tongue" . . . "Thou wast provoked by thy bloody mind"). These rhetorical ingredients can be combined into powerfully persuasive arguments when pointed and accented with great specificity.

Playing and Building the Rhetoric

How do actors do this pointing and accenting, or accentuating? Mainly (but not solely) they use sharply turned inflections, or pitch changes. For example:

RICHARD: I grant ye.

ANNE: Dost ^^grant me, ^^hedgehog? Then, God ^grant ^me ^^too
   Thou mayst be ^^^damnèd for that wicked deed!\

The upward inflections, marked by one or more carets (^) before the syllables to be lifted and pointed, here make a pattern of the two repetitions of the word *grant,* which Anne appropriates from Richard's callous admission of murder, pointedly reusing them to seek a grant in return. Anne's first reuse ("Dost grant me"), sharply pointed, has the edge of sarcasm, tacitly criticizing Richard's casual dismissal of his crime; and her second, attached by alliteration as well as proximity to God ("God grant me"), seeks divine help to overpower that contempt. And Anne's downward inflection at the end of her speech—marked by a downslash (\) after "deed!"—seeks to end the discussion, implying that "there is simply nothing more to be said on the subject."*
   The trading of matched alternatives in the short line exchange

---

* For a much fuller discussion of inflections and their functions in both normal conversation and acting, see *Acting One,* pages 183–189.

ANNE: Some dungeon.

RICHARD: Your ^bed chamber.

is a shocking and effective rhetorical ploy, particularly as it leads the
stunned Lady Anne to walk into a verbal trap:

ANNE: Ill rest betide the chamber where thou liest!

RICHARD: So will it, madam, till I lie with ^you.

Richard's manipulation has forced Anne back into echoing her earlier invective, "In thy foul throat thou liest" (employing a different meaning of *liest*),
and has set him up to turn his evildoing into sexual seduction: When Richard
says "I lie . . ." he is simultaneously confessing deceit and proposing an affair!

ANNE: O, he was ^gentle, ^^mild, and ^^^virtuous!

Describing her dead father-in-law, Henry VI, Anne uses three adjectives.
Gentle basically refers to his rank (he was a gentleman, with the implication
of perfect breeding and manners), *mild* to his demeanor, and *virtuous* to his
moral integrity. In this order, the words increasingly indicate the difference
between Henry and Richard, Henry being roughly equal in gentility (both
men are of royal blood), quite a bit milder (Richard is cruel), but *vastly*
more virtuous—and moral virtue is the critical issue of this scene. Say the
words in any other order and the sentence is weaker: Neither "O, he was
gentle, virtuous, and mild!" nor "O, he was virtuous, mild, and gentle!"
works. The accusations that Richard is merely low-born (non-gentle) and a
hothead (non-mild) are effective only as stepping-stones to the real attack:
that he is utterly immoral (non-virtuous).

Were you simply to say these words flatly, with each adjective having
equal importance (as if saying "the flag is red, white, and blue"), the statement would be a description, not an attack. Create your attack, therefore,
by building your words vocally as Shakespeare did when writing: with continually ascending force and passion.

O, he was ^gentle, ^^mild, and ^^^VIRtuous!

Good rhetoric is concise, controlled, and forceful, the result of precise
word choice, word placement, pointed inflection, and sonic momentum.
Seeming dispassionate, even playful, it can be devastating in propounding an
argument, winning an election, moving troops into life-and-death battle. It is
one of the particular glories of the human mind—and of Elizabethan drama.

The Public Environment

The action of Elizabethan drama takes place in an environment as public as
those theatres that preceded it. The bulk of the scenes unfold in streets,

plazas, taverns, battlefields, courts, parties, trials, weddings, or ceremonies. Lots of people are to be found hanging around the Elizabethan stage. Even in scenes set in a desert (*Timon of Athens*), a deserted island (*The Tempest*), a forest (*A Midsummer Night's Dream*), or the battlements of a castle at midnight (*Hamlet*), there is always the possibility of passersby, including those from both the human and the spirit realms.

When Hamlet says "Now I am alone," he is "alone" with a Globe Theatre audience of up to three thousand persons, all equally lit by the sun lighting him, surrounding him a full 300 degrees from right to left and 90 degrees bottom to top. There was simply no place Richard Burbage, the actor playing Hamlet, could have looked without seeing the packed theatre audience around him. It is no wonder these outdoor theatres, which were the dominant performance spaces of Elizabethan times, were called "public" theatres.*

Scene 11–1 takes place not just between Richard and Anne but also in front of the guards who are carrying the late king's corpse. And while these are nonspeaking characters, they are not nonhearing ones, and everyone in the audience would recognize that the support of such armed forces would prove crucial to any power-seeker in a royal court. Therefore Anne can intensify the forcefulness of her "mild and virtuous" attack because she realizes that her words to Richard are being overheard by the pallbearers still onstage—a secondary audience—and quite possibly by a tertiary audience: any unseen passersby who may be in the vicinity or peeking out their windows to glimpse these quarreling royals. Vigorously attacking Richard in such a public setting, Anne must realize, could actually contribute to his downfall by urging her multiple audiences to remember the late King Henry's virtue and thus enrage the populace against his murder.

So, playing Anne, "use" the presence of these witnesses, both known and potential, as further incentive for your attack. Richard, of course, will be doing the same thing: making clear to everyone in possible hearing range that he is not a man to be crossed lightly.

There's a fourth level of audience as well in this scene. As the apostrophe, O, indicates, the scene also takes place, in Anne's eyes at least, within the view of God, the "King of heaven" (as Richard mockingly calls him) who she hopes will eventually support her quest. And Richard, too, we will later find, has an awareness of a God who might oversee his adventures: "Have mercy, Jesu!" he cries, in a dream at the end of the play. Both Richard and Anne believe they are acting within the context of a divine universe, and their goals are consequently tuned to garner support from a godly as well as a human audience.

Besides God and Jesus, a host of spirit or spiritual characters populate the universe of Elizabethan drama, or at least the minds of Elizabethan dramatic

---

* There were also a few smaller "private" theatres in London late in the period, located indoors and lit by candles. Shakespeare's company owned and performed in one of these, the Blackfriars Theatre, from about 1608 until the end of the era.

characters. Shakespeare's plays are filled with supernatural figures. Ghosts appear onstage (*Hamlet, Macbeth, Richard III*), as do fairies (*A Midsummer Night's Dream, The Tempest*), witches (*Macbeth*), soothsayers (*Julius Caesar, Antony and Cleopatra*), prophets (*Troilus and Cressida*), Greek and Roman goddesses (*As You Like It, The Tempest, Pericles*), fiends (*Henry VI*), apparitions (*Cymbeline*), and the allegorical figure of Time (*The Winter's Tale*). Most of these beings speak, and all become audiences to the human characters in the plays. Their presence must be imagined and played to, even when they are not onstage, by actors playing such characters.

Playing to a spirit audience often means the actor must try to connect to an unseen world. When Lady Macbeth cries "Come, thick night," or King Lear says "Blow, winds!," these are not—onstage at least—mere literary metaphors; the actors playing the roles should actually try, and even expect, to command the spirits of night and the wind.

And when Anne in *Richard III* says "O, he was gentle . . . ," the actor must seek the ear of a divine spirit (God) who, she feels, would be compassionate toward her distress at the injustice she is experiencing.

Does volume help in summoning spirits? Rarely. The most effective way of reaching such audiences (God in Anne's case) is to find the voice that spirit audiences, were they to exist, would listen to and respect. And that's where an actor's imagination, and understanding of human nature, prove essential.

Extending yourself into an Elizabethan text, therefore, means to extend yourself into a spiritual world you yourself probably don't dwell in during your offstage hours, a world that your rational self may regard as superstitious or fantastical. But theatre means bringing that superstition or fantasy into the reality of a character's belief. And this transfer results in making it an audience's belief, as when Peter Pan, in James M. Barrie's play of that name, gets the audience to demonstrate, by their applause, that they, too, "believe in fairies." They don't, of course, outside the theatre—but they will for the dramatic moment if the actors so extend themselves as to live in a world where fairies fly.

Play the Anne–Richard scene several more times. Have classmates play the pallbearers standing silently behind you, occasionally stealing glances at you. Have others play passersby drifting inconspicuously by at a safe distance. Try to win your character's goals by your manipulation of the verse, forceful rhetorical builds, and bold appeals to multiple audiences both seen and unseen.

♦ SCENE   11–2

A Merry War: Beatrice and Benedick

Let's move to something on the lighter side. Beatrice and Benedick are also a warring couple, but in their case the battle is, as described by her uncle in

Jimmy Smits and Kristin Johnston play Benedick and Beatrice in this 2004 production of *Much Ado About Nothing*. (Photo © Michal Daniel)

the opening scene of *Much Ado About Nothing*, "a kind of a merry war," in which the pair engage in "a skirmish of wit" every time they meet. A few lines later in the same scene, Benedick and his companions, returning uninjured from a victorious military engagement, are greeted by Beatrice and her family and friends, including various gentlemen and young ladies. After a round of joyous greetings for the men, Beatrice fires the opening salvo in the "merry war" by commenting on a lame joke Benedick has just uttered:

BEATRICE: I wonder that you will still be talking, Signior Benedick: nobody marks° you.   °*listens to*

BENEDICK: What! my dear Lady Disdain, are you yet living?

BEATRICE: Is it possible Disdain should die while she hath such meet°;
food to feed it as Signior Benedick? Courtesy   °*appropriate*
itself must convert to disdain, if you come in her presence.

BENEDICK: Then is courtesy a turncoat. But it is certain I am loved of all
ladies, only you excepted; and I would I could find in my heart that I
had not a hard heart; for, truly, I love none.

BEATRICE: A dear happiness° to women: they would   °*rare good fortune*
else have been troubled with a pernicious suitor. I thank God and my cold
blood, I am of your humor° for that: I had rather   °*disposition*
hear my dog bark at a crow than a man swear he loves me.

BENEDICK: God keep your ladyship still in that mind; so some gentleman
or other shall 'scape a predestinate° scratched face.   °*preordained*

BEATRICE: Scratching could not make it worse, an 'twere   °*if it were*
such a face as yours were.

BENEDICK: Well, you are a rare parrot-teacher.   °*one who, like a parrot,*
scratches with words
instead of claws

BEATRICE: A bird of my tongue is better than a beast
of yours.   °*I, though a parrot, am better than you, a brute animal.*

BENEDICK: I would my horse had the speed of your tongue, and so good a
continuer. ° But keep your way, i' God's name;   °*so able to keep going*
I have done.

BEATRICE: You always end with a jade's trick.   °*horse's trick, such as I*
know you of old.   *slipping out of the bridle*

Even with the glosses, this dialogue is not, on its surface, easy to understand. Nor are you likely to find the "jokes" funny. But the meaning of this scene is not to be found on its surface, nor are the jokes even remotely funny—out of context. In context, however, the scene is potentially both touching and humorous. Let's explore it.

The first thing actors approaching this scene must realize is (once again) that it takes place in public: amid a crowd of young, glamorous, and unattached men and women, meeting on a particularly celebratory occasion. Romance, one might quickly conclude, is in the air.

Yet a reading of the entire script reveals a deeply personal note: that Beatrice and Benedick love, but do not trust, each other. Beatrice seems to feel that Benedick once betrayed her ("He wears his faith but as the fashion of his hat," she complains just before his entrance), and Benedick distrusts all women as unfaithful to the men who commit to them. What lies beneath this wariness? Shakespeare provides no details, but anyone who has been wounded in love can come up with a thousand possibilities. Those you choose (and Shakespeare does provide some starting points) will determine the specific sort of Beatrice or Benedick you will play.

We're not looking for a definitive "interpretation" of the scene here in this exercise, however. Just learn and rehearse the lines, with a partner, and perform it *in the midst of a crowd of young men and women roughly your age.*

The primary goal for each of you in this opening scene of the play is to impress the *crowd* with your wittiness, attractiveness, friskiness, and boldness. Circulate among them as you speak, getting them on your side in this eternal (but, to you, very particular) battle of the sexes. Impressing the crowd is how you will impress—and silence—the acting partner with whom you are fighting your "merry war." For this is war, no matter how merry, and you must do everything you can to win it!

So impress those of your own sex with how well you represent your side's goals and values. Make them cheer you on and laugh at your bons mots and ripostes. (And, crowd, please *do* cheer on and laugh with your gender representative! As you do so, let the men drift toward the other men, and the women toward the other women, thus becoming two camps, each rooting for its flag-bearer.)

And impress on those of the opposite sex how right your own gender's values are, and how a very special person of the opposite sex will ultimately realize this and come over to your side. In this anti-flirting dialogue, flirt outrageously. Be the sexiest "anti-sex warrior" imaginable.

Try to show not your anger, nor your hurt feelings, but your pride, your wit, your charm, your sexual power, and the rightness of your position.

Of course, your hurt feelings will show before the scene is completed. And, possibly, so will your anger. They will probably come from your partner's being cheered by his backers, and your inevitable sense of failure. So try all the harder *not* to let them show—and not to admit failure. *Try to win the merry war!*

Now you see why the jokes weren't very good when you read them and why it took a dozen glosses to explain the scene—which at the level of content is, as the title says, "about nothing." Shakespeare shows you flailing about, trying to best someone you secretly adore, someone you can't bear to be humiliated by, someone who makes you nervous just to look at. In your nervousness, in your failure to achieve any but the hollowest victory, lies the success of the scene.

In a class situation, let everyone play the scene in turn, mixing partners arbitrarily, and let the "crowd" respond as fully as they wish. Try to win—even if you don't. Try again to win again, even if you continue to fail. "Failure" is built into the scene—Shakespeare knows what he's doing with these lame jokes—but you must never try to fail! Shakespeare doesn't need any help from you on that score; he needs you to try desperately to entertain everyone and let members of the crowd come to their own conclusions as to what's happening.

Introduce props suggesting a party. Set a table with glasses of "champagne" that Beatrice and Benedick can lift as toasts before downing their drinks at appropriate moments.

Move around freely and interact with your partner as well as with the crowd. Let Benedick demonstrate that he is "loved of all ladies" by embracing one or two in the crowd. Let Beatrice show how ugly she thinks Benedick is by boldly pinching his cheeks on "such a face as yours were." Come up with your own, spontaneous business as you run through this scene.

Shakespeare and *Commedia*

We should point out a huge difference between Shakespeare and the *commedia* dramatists that preceded (and in some cases influenced) him. Benedick and Beatrice are not stock characters. They are unique personages, as individually defined as anyone who ever lived; we even feel that we know them as real people, as we never would with Sofronia or Nicomaco. Although Shakespeare's couple are part of an identifiable class of characters (the shy but witty bachelor; the brilliant, awkward, older, and unmarried niece), even these categorizations are more complex than traditional stock, and the categorizations fall pathetically short of a complete description. You can read *Much Ado About Nothing* twenty times, and you will learn more about these characters—their past, their families, their hopes, their fears, their passions—on every reading. With *Clizia,* your twenty readings may afford you new ideas on how to play the roles, but 99 percent of the characters' inner lives will be evident the first time through.

So, though there are places for it later in the play, adapting *lazzi* or inventing slapstick business would be worse than useless in Scene 11–2, where we are getting to know the characters as people, not simply as theatrical figures set out for our entertainment. This is not to rate Shakespearean drama over *commedia*, although you are welcome to do that on your own, but merely to make crystal clear that these are very different sorts of plays.*

---

* Shakespeare's early comedies owe much to *commedia* techniques, particularly *The Comedy of Errors,* which was directly adapted from Plautus's comedy *Menaechmi,* and *The Taming of the Shrew.* But *Much Ado About Nothing* is a later play, with much more complexly conceived characters.

More Elizabethan Scenes

There are four encounters between these two characters: this one from Act 1, Scene 1; more banter (with Beatrice this time pulling the jade's trick) during a dance in Act 2, Scene 1; a mutual declaration of love (but also a discovery of further conflict) in Act 4, Scene 1; and a resolved sharing of goals and desires in Act 5. With one or more partners, rehearse and perform any or all of these scenes.

In *Richard III* the entire scene between Richard and Anne in Act 1, Scene 2 bears consideration, as does the long scene (suitable for cutting) between Richard and Elizabeth in Act 4, Scene 4.

But there are hundreds, if not thousands, of great scenes in Shakespeare, as well as in Jonson, Marlowe, and Webster, easily available at any library, that will provide material for years of acting classes.

For Further Study

Because Shakespeare is both the most-admired and the most-produced dramatist in the United States and many other countries, acting in Shakespearean is a subject in which you eventually may wish to engage at greater depth. For further study, see my *Acting in Shakespeare,* Second Edition (Hanover, NH: Smith and Kraus, 2005).

12

The Theatre of Molière

The French drama of the seventeenth century, often termed "neoclassic" (*neo* means "new") because it sought to follow the rules of the Greek philosopher Aristotle and his *Poetics* of the fourth century B.C., is the first Western drama for which we have rich and authoritative documentation: not only of plays but of costumes, scenery, staging plans, and acting styles. This was also an era when theatrical staging had largely moved indoors, with the stage placed behind a proscenium opening. In short, it was a theatre whose external aspects were, more than any predecessors', most like our own. But the differences were enormous as well.

Jean-Baptiste Poquelin, known as Molière, is to the French national theatre what Shakespeare is to the English. Flourishing both at the court of King Louis XIV and in the public theatre of Paris during the middle decades of the seventeenth century, Molière wrote, directed, produced, and starred in more than thirty plays, most of which remain in the repertories of theatres around the world today. His company, renamed the Comédie Française in 1680, seven years after his death, is the premiere classical theatre in France to this day, and his drama criticism, generally imbedded in plays about the theatre (*The Versailles Rehearsals, The Critique of the School for Wives*), remains among the world's wisest.

And while his works are largely in the genre of comedy (including farces, comedy-ballets, and courtly diversions), he dealt in these plays with some of the most serious, and dangerously controversial, issues of his day, including religious hypocrisy (in *Tartuffe*), freethinking liberalism (*Dom Juan*), incapacitating jealousy (*The Misanthrope*), and embittered avarice (*The Miser*).

Presentational staging   This highly presentational staging, with the four actors arranged in a straight line, the title character seated squarely in the middle and facing the audience, and the orchestra in plain view, is from a 1674 production of Molière's *The Imaginary Invalid* at the palace of Versailles. Notice the long trains of the dresses and the magnificence of the surrounding decor and chandeliers. It was in a performance of this same play a year earlier that Molière, playing the title role, collapsed onstage and died later in the evening.

He also attempted tragedy-ballet (*Psyché*) and, notably, served as the producer of France's two greatest classical tragedians: Pierre Corneille, with whom he collaborated, and Jean Racine, whom he practically discovered. He was truly what the French call *un homme du théâtre,* a man of the stage.

Molière's theatre combines many elements. For Louis XIV, he provided the music and dance entertainments that the king loved to see, and frequently participate in. For the court scholars, he supplied the neoclassic verse that French poets had refined from Aristotle's precepts and also court-comforting satire punctuating bourgeois foibles. For his public audiences, first as a traveling showman in the countryside and subsequently as a royal favorite in Paris, he offered great farcical performances with dull-witted characters and rollicking slapstick humor derived from his associations with *commedia dell'arte,* which crowds love everywhere.* Thus he

---

*   When Molière was given a theatre in Paris, he was at first forced to share it on alternate nights with Louis XIV's favorite *commedia dell'arte* troupe.

Brisart d.   J. Sauvé f.

L'IMPOSTEUR

Hand gestures   In *Tartuffe,* Molière's most serious play, the title character, a religious impostor, is shown hiding under the table. Trying to seduce Elmire, he has been caught by her outraged husband, Orgon, who, still in his hat and cape, has just returned home. Hand gestures underline both actions and reactions. From the frontispiece to the 1682 edition of the play.

provided both high comedy (witty repartee) and low comedy (buffoons and pratfalls), and what is more significant, he provided them in a nearly seamless combination.

Molière wrote plays in both prose and verse. We begin with one of his farcical prose masterpieces, *The Bourgeois Gentleman,* a play so indebted

LE BOURGEOIS GENTILHŌME

Molière as Monsieur Jourdain   The playwright here appears in the title role of *The Bourgeois Gentleman,* surrounded by pretend "Turks." From the frontispiece to the 1682 edition of the play.

to *commedia dell'arte* that one of its characters, the wily servant Coville, is named after his Italian *commedia* predecessor, Coviello. Written on direct command from King Louis XIV for performance at the royal court of Chambord in 1600, the play mocks Monsieur Jourdain, a wealthy member of the bourgeois class (that is, a middle-class craftsman or shop owner) who aspires to be elevated to the social rank of gentleman so as to, among other things, attract a young countess for amorous adventures; he thus hires instructors to teach him the social graces of aristocrats. The play is a comic satire on the theme of social climbing, and Molière, in the title role, proved a great success in both court and public performances of the play.

Physical Comedy: Jourdain and the Philosopher

In one of the classic scenes in *The Bourgeois Gentleman*, from Act 2, a philosopher is trying to teach Jourdain the rudiments of speech. I've provided stage directions (not in the original but implied by the text) to help you visualize the action. The translation is my own.

PHILOSOPHER: What would you like me to teach you?

JOURDAIN: Everything! I adore learning! I am furious at my parents—they never made me study when I was young.

PHILOSOPHER: Yes, I see. *Nam sine doctrina vita est quasi mortis imago.* Of course you know Latin—

JOURDAIN: *[lying through his teeth]* Of course! But pretend I don't— explain it to me.

PHILOSOPHER: Without knowledge, life is the reflection of death.

JOURDAIN: *[beaming beatifically]* Latin is always right.

PHILOSOPHER: Then where shall we begin? With logic?

JOURDAIN: What's that?

PHILOSOPHER: It's what organizes the mind into its three functions.

JOURDAIN: Three functions? What are they?

PHILOSOPHER: The first, the second, and the third.

JOURDAIN: *[confused]* Oh . . .

PHILOSOPHER: The first is to conceptualize, through universal understandings, the second is to evaluate, through categorical reasoning, and the third is to draw conclusions, through identifications and syllogisms.

JOURDAIN: Oh, no. Too hard. I'm afraid logic doesn't suit me very well. Do you have anything jollier?

PHILOSOPHER: Physics, then?

JOURDAIN: What's that?

Celebrated Canadian classical actor William Needles (right) is Monsieur Jourdain, with Rick Tigert as the Philosopher showing how one makes the "little round 'o'." (Photo © Philip Channing)

PHILOSOPHER: Physics is the science of natural order, of the properties of matter: the elements, the metals, the minerals, the stones, the plants and animals; the causes of meteors, the rainbow, the northern lights, the comets, lightning, thunder, thunderclaps, rain, snow, hail, winds, tornadoes . . .

JOURDAIN: *[becoming truly frightened]* A lot of hullabaloo, if you ask me.

PHILOSOPHER: What then?

JOURDAIN: How about spelling?

PHILOSOPHER: Marvelous.

JOURDAIN: And then the almanac, so I can tell when the moon is out and when it's not.

PHILOSOPHER: Very good. But to learn spelling philosophically, we must begin at the beginning, by an understanding of the nature of letters and their various pronunciations. *[making this up as he goes along]* Now first, there are the vowels, so named because they *avow* the voice. And then there are the consonants, so called because they *con-sonate* the vowels, and mark the many measures of vowelization. There are five vowels: ah, eh, ee, aw, yew.* *[He pronounces these in the French manner.]*

JOURDAIN: Yes, I know.

PHILOSOPHER: The sound "ah" is formed by opening the mouth wide— *[he does so, saying]* "ah."

JOURDAIN: *[imitating]* "Ah" . . . "ah" *[nodding vigorously; very pleased with himself]* Yes!

PHILOSOPHER: The sound "eh" is made by closing the jaws. *[opening his mouth wide]* "Ah." *[closing it]* "Eh."

JOURDAIN: *[opening and closing his mouth mechanically as instructed]* "ah"—"eh," "ah"—"eh." My God! You're right! How wonderful learning is!

PHILOSOPHER: And to make an "ee" you close your jaws even further, and spread your cheeks to your ears— *[which he does]* "ah"—"eh"—"ee."

JOURDAIN: *[with exaggerated movements]* "Ah"—"eh"—"ee." "Ee!" *[spreads his cheeks as wide as he can with his fingers]* "Ee!" "Ee!" It's true! Magnificent! Long live philosophy!

PHILOSOPHER: To make an "oh" you must open your jaw and bring to-gether the corners of your lips: "oh."

JOURDAIN: "Oh!" "Oh!" Nothing could be more wonderful than this! *[moving his face in absurdly exaggerated configurations]* "Ah"—"eh"— "ee"—"oh." "Ee"—"oh!" Splendid! *[sounding like a donkey's hee-haw]* "Ee"—"oh!" "Ee—oh!" Wonderful!

PHILOSOPHER: *[nastily, making a circle with his fingers]* The shape of your mouth, you see, is a little round "o."

---

*   The pronunciation of the French *u*—here spelled yew—has no exact equivalent in English spelling. It is basically formed by speaking the *u* in *puke* but with the lips pushed forward and the tongue extended upward so that it nearly touches the hard palate.

JOURDAIN: *[astounded, making the same circle with his finger and tracing his lips in an "o"]* "Oh"—"oh"—"oh"—you're sooooh right. Sooooh! Ah, what a beautiful thing to knooooh something.

PHILOSOPHER: The sound of the French "u" is made by bringing the teeth together, then spreading the lips, then making them come together without quite touching: "yew."

JOURDAIN: "Yew." "Yew." Nothing could be truer: "Yew!"

PHILOSOPHER: *[suddenly makes a grotesque face at Jourdain, who recoils in shock]* It's like making a face at someone: If you want to make fun of somebody, just say "yew" at him and watch him jump! *[He practices this on Jourdain, who finally "gets" it and tries it on the philosopher.]*

JOURDAIN: "Yew!" "Yew!" Oh, it's truuuuuuuuue! Oh, why didn't I take up education earlier. I would have known all this!

Rehearse and perform this scene with a partner. Follow the stage directions if you wish but augment them with others of your own. Wrap yourself in absurdly elegant and colorful clothing: cloak, hat, scarf, high-button or high-heeled shoes. Find an ornate walking stick and practice using it.

Try, as Monsieur (or Madame, if you wish to transgender the role) Jourdain, to impress the Philosopher with your learning, and with your clothing, and with your brilliance, and to also impress *anybody* who might peer into the room—including the audience of your classmates. Try, as the Philosopher, to make Jourdain feel he (or she) is brilliantly succeeding in learning something vitally important, so that you will get a suitable reward. And try at the same time to make him look foolish to anyone peering into the room—including the audience of your classmates—so that no one would mistake you for an admirer of his. Though this scene is largely set in a home interior, it is a large house where servants, guests, and resident family and their friends and lovers continuously come and go, so it is as public a dramatic environment as any.

Molière and *Commedia*

One of the dramaturgical devices Molière adapted from his classical and *commedia* predecessors is the stock character, which results in many of his plays' being named not after their principal characters (like Shakespeare's *Othello, Macbeth,* and *Hamlet,* for example) but after the specific character *types* portrayed (*The Misanthrope, The Miser, The Blunderer, The Affected Ladies, The Bores, The Sicilian, The Imaginary Invalid, The Bourgeois*

Gentleman). And in this scene, the Philosopher has no personal name; he is just a representative of his profession.

Other devices, common to *commedia* and low comedy in general, include the broad physical gags that end up with Monsieur Jourdain tricked into literally making a hee-hawing ass out of himself. The comic success of this scene depends, in large measure, on the actors' skills at rubber-face clowning: the absurd manipulations of lips and cheeks and braying sounds that the Philosopher is able to coax out of the hapless Jourdain. Twentieth-century French philosopher Henri Bergson declared that comedy was essentially an "encrustation of the mechanical upon the living," or portraying a living person as being as rigid as a machine, and the comedies of Molière—as in scenes such as this—were among Bergson's primary examples.

Yet the literary skill and obvious intelligence of Molière's dramaturgy, and the intellectual sophistication of his audiences in the burgeoning scientific era that was soon to develop into a full-fledged Age of Enlightenment, move this material far beyond the single-minded slapstick of *commedia*. While there are elements of a Dottore in Molière's Philosopher, and of a Pantalone beneath Jourdain, a font of wisdom and irony underlies the Philosopher's puffed-up imbecilities, and a whimsical tenderness can be found in the social-climbing Jourdain, whose character, after all, bears a clear resemblance to Molière and his father—both of them coming from the bourgeoisie (Molière's father was an upholsterer) but attaining positions in the court of King Louis XIV.

FRENCH AND RESTORATION GREETINGS

Salutations in the time of Molière, which also became the salutations of the French-influenced English Restoration, elaborated the bows and curtsies of Elizabethan England.

BOWS FOR MEN

The simple: The left foot is swept back as in the Elizabethan bow, though less boldly. The body is inclined and the head cocked slightly to one side, and the right hand is brought upward and palm inward to the heart, as if to say "You have my heart."

The elaborate: The hat is removed with the right hand and tucked under the left arm, as the left foot is swept back (or the right one is advanced) until the feet are perpendicular, the left behind the right, in the dancer's fourth position. At the same time, the body is inclined forward, and the right hand is swept from the left hip in a broad upward circle toward the person being greeted. The hand is then returned, palm inward, to the left hip. On rising, the greeter may continue this circling movement of the right hand and bring the back side of his inwardly curled fingers to his lips, pretending to kiss them, and then continue the arm circle to present the person being greeted with his thusly kissed fingers, palm-side up, before retaking the hat in the left hand.

CURTSIES FOR WOMEN

Essentially French and Restoration curtsies are the same as the Elizabethan but usually preceded with a small step to one side and a head nod in the same direction.

Costume and Deportment

Every age has its wardrobe, but the age of Louis XIV (and of the English Restoration, which followed close upon it—see Lesson 13) was a period of exceptionally glamorous and elaborate costumes and accessories throughout western Europe. Clothing design had become a fully professional craft, and fashion plates (illustrations) of the latest styles were widely circulated. Silks, satins, brocades, lace, ribbons, and pearls were abundant in the clothing of both sexes. Men often wore tricornes (cocked hats), fancy doublets, petticoat breeches, colorful neck cravats, and flounced shirt cuffs under elaborately constructed flared coats or capes, while balancing themselves atop high-heeled, front-buttoned shoes. Women sported elongated bodices (stiffened by wooden or ivory busks to induce an erect posture), bell-shaped skirts, richly embroidered petticoats under open gowns, bosom-revealing décolleté neck-lines, and richly colored makeup. Wildly exaggerated perukes (periwigs) were common for male court dandies, and tall lace headdresses, known as com-modes, encased women's upswept hairstyles. "Showing off" one's costume was an expected social grace in late-seventeenth-century French aristocratic circles, and costume becomes a subject of, not merely an adjunct to, many of the dramas of the day. (In fact, a hilarious scene in which Monsieur Jourdain is fitted into a new court costume, which he is talked into accepting even though the embroidered flowers were mistakenly sewn on upside-down, im-mediately follows this one.) So your standing, walking, sitting, rising, and gesturing are all opportunities to show how fashionable (that is, how witty, how attractive, how rich, how much in royal favor) your character is.

Try it. Climb to the top of the seventeenth-century social ladder by show-ing off your brilliance, your taste, your style, your poise, and your complete consonance with the world of the Sun King himself.

French Verse

To truly understand the art of Molière, and the plays of his time, it is neces-sary to study the intricacy of classical French verse. Not all—or even most—of

Seventeenth-century bows   The out-turned feet, elevated heels, cocked head and smile, and curved fingers were characteristic of the bows of the Restoration era and of the time of Molière, who is pictured in this engraving of his era. (© The Granger Collection New York)

Molière's plays were written in verse, but those that were, which include his most serious and celebrated works, among them *Tartuffe, The Misanthrope,* and *The School for Wives,* followed the model for all neoclassic French dramatists, comic and tragic: the Alexandrine couplet.

The Alexandrine couplet, based on a hexameter, or six-foot, line, is maddeningly complicated,* but fortunately you won't have to learn it in English;

---

*   The Alexandrine line is a six-foot, twelve-syllable iambic line (iambic hexameter), with a momentary pause, known as a *caesura,* after the third foot. In the Alexandrine couplet, the lines rhyme; moreover, from one couplet to the next, the hexameter is both too long and too choppy to be effectively rendered into our language, as Alexander Pope noted in his "Essay on Criticism":

> A needless Alexandrine ends the song,
> That, like a wounded snake, drags its slow length along.

Nearly all modern English verse translations of Molière's verse plays, and of those by Racine and Corneille for that matter, are in rhymed iambic pentameters, not hexameters, as in Scene 12–2 (see also the "Playing Translations" box on pages 413–415).

That you won't have to grapple with the complexity of the Alexandrine, however, does not mean you shouldn't pause to marvel at it, and at the classic French writers' ability to deploy it while writing plays that are masterpieces of logic, credibility, speakability, dramatic momentum, poetic flow, atmospheric texture, and even figurative (if not literal) verisimilitude. Moreover, those playwrights were restrained by many other limitations on their creativity, since royally honored neoclassic critics dictated other "rules"

---

the rhymes alternate between *masculine* rhymes of one syllable ("bait" and "date"), and *feminine* rhymes of two syllables ("parted" and "started"), which add an unstressed syllable to each line's concluding foot. But that's not all: The half-lines on either side of the caesura, called *hemistiches,* must be spoken in precisely equal time durations; moreover, the hemistiches themselves are divided into two *measures,* which must also be spoken in equal time durations. However, the hemistiches need not be divided into equal numbers of syllables; they can be divided three and three, two and four, or one and five, which means that, in the last case, a one-syllable measure must be slowed down in speech to equal the duration of the matching five-syllable measure. Have I lost you yet? It is the accelerating and decelerating of speaking velocity during the measures, in contrast to the rigid time divisions of the measures within the hemistiches (and the hemistiches within the lines), that create the near-infinite variety of rhythm in the Alexandrine couplet (or, more properly, the Alexandrine quatrain, since the pattern extends over four full lines). It is little wonder that traditionally trained French actors take many years to perfect their mastery of this staggeringly complex verse form—which, by the way, is unvarying for every single line in a play. See Maurice Grammont, *Petit traité de versification Française* (Armand Colin, 1965 [1908]).

Of course, the Alexandrine sounds terrific in French, which is a less percussive and more assonant language than English. For anyone who can read it, here's the original French opening of Alceste's long speech ("It's not a stick, Madame . . .") in Scene 12–2. The first couplet ends in feminine rhymes, the second in masculine.

> Non, ce n'est pas, Madame, un bâton qu'il faut prendre,
> Mais un coeur à leurs veux moins facile et moins tendre.
> Je sais que vos appas vous suivent en tous lieux;
> Mais votre accueil retient ceux qu'attirent vos yeux.

supposedly (though not actually) drawn from Aristotle, including demands that a play represent only one day's action, take place in a single locale, be divided into five acts with the stage cleared after each act, and report rather than show acts of physical violence. This is almost like writing a play that is at the same time a crossword puzzle. Nonetheless, it was the achievement not only of Molière but of Corneille, Racine, and, indeed, all the great playwrights and poets of the glorious era of Louis XIV to transcend these dictated parameters of art into a glorious drama of comedy, wit, intelligence, and passion. Perhaps it was the very discipline of writing under such impossible constraints that sharpened their wits to genius level.

Thus the first challenge for the actor in Molière's verse plays is to handle the formality of the outward structure with a feeling for the passion, creativity, and variety within. We examine this challenge in a scene from Molière's masterpiece, *The Misanthrope*.

◆ S C E N E   12–2

Quarreling in Couplets: Alceste and Célimène

Study the following scene. Alceste (pronounced all-SEST) is a youngish man, proud of his integrity and intellectual brilliance; he is in love with Célimène (pronounced SAY-lee-MEN), a pretty, young widow. This is the first scene between them in the play, and as you will quickly see, they are having a fight. The translation is my own.

ALCESTE: Well, Lady Célimène! May I be frank?
   The way you acted yesterday? It stank!
   I must say that I'm totally disgusted.
   Your actions demonstrate you can't be trusted;
   In fact, I've come today to tell you
   Our liaison is off! You—Jezebel, you!
   No matter if I promised otherwise:
   Your conduct leaves no room for compromise!

CÉLIMÈNE: Is that why you came here, to start a fight?
   I thought we talked this all out—just last night!

ALCESTE: Okay!—But you're insatiably driven
   To mass flirtations! They can't be forgiven!
   You bring the whole world into your salon
   Where troops of lovers seek to get it on!

CÉLIMÈNE: You're angry that they find me—affable?
     You think I'm wrong; I think you're laughable!
     What should I do, then, hit them with a stick?
     Drive them from my home? Why are you so thick?

ALCESTE: It's not a stick, Madame,° that you should   °mah-DAHM
     brandish.
     But you must be hard-hearted! Not outlandish!
     They're drawn to you, because you're beautiful,
     But you respond beyond what's dutiful!
     Your racy words, and cooing affectations,
     Lead them to elevated aspirations!
     And you adore them! They're your panting harem;
     This bunch of lisping fops; God, I can't bear 'em!
     Ah, Célimène! I don't know what to do!
     You LIKE to have these phonies chasing you?
     Explain, my dear, what idiotic pleasure
     You take in old Clitandre.° What a treasure!   °clee-TAN-druh
     You like the curling fingernail he's grown?
     Perhaps the horrid wigs he calls his own,
     With cannon curls that fall down to the floor
     Which all the demoiselles° at court adore?   °deh-mwah-ZELZ : young ladies
     Perhaps the codpiece sewn into his hose?
     Those ribboned sleeves on which he wipes his nose?*
     Or maybe it's his phony, flat falsetto?
     Or else his scent: two dabs of Amaretto?

CÉLIMÈNE: You're so infuriatingly UNJUST!
     You know I have him here because I MUST!
     It's for my lawsuit: You know his support—
     His and his friends'—can win my case at court!

ALCESTE: Forget your case! I'd just as soon you lost!
     To have Clitandre's help—you'll pay the cost!

CÉLIMÈNE: Well, you're just jealous, all the world knows that.

ALCESTE: Who's "all the world"? Those you make passes at?

CÉLIMÈNE: I don't see why this makes you so distressed!
     You should be pleased I love them ALL, Aleste!

---

*   These lines give a marvelous picture of the accoutrements of the court dandy in
     the time of Molière. The separate leg hosiery with an open crotch, the privates
     encased in a neomedieval codpiece, was very fashionable courtly male attire in
     the late 1660s.

By not identifying any one as best,
I love, but don't become BY love, possessed!

ALCESTE: Well, that's just fine, my dear, but tell me—say:
Just what from you do I get more than they?

CÉLIMÈNE: The happiness of knowing that you're loved!

ALCESTE: I won't know that—till OUT THE DOOR THEY'RE SHOVED!

CÉLIMÈNE: How selfish of you! No, Alceste, you've heard
All I can say! And that's my final word!

ALCESTE: To me—and to the others too! You love—MANKIND!
For you, dear Célimène, love's REALLY blind!

CÉLIMÈNE: Why, how romantic! Darling, I'm delighted!
You sure can make a girl get all excited!
And just so you won't fret your little head—
I TAKE BACK EVERY SINGLE WORD I SAID!
Oof! What an imbecilic fool you are!
Is this your wish?

ALCESTE: This isn't love: It's war!

Several questions naturally come to mind with this material, the most immediate being: How should the rhymes be played? Should they be emphasized, or simply tossed away, or something in-between? And what do the dramatist's rhymes have to do with the character's situation? Blank verse can almost pass as everyday speech (for example, "I'll have the ham and eggs with toast today"), but rhyming couplets blatantly call attention to themselves and to the artificial contrivance of the form that contains them.

The answer to the question of how to play the rhymes is that rhyming becomes a central *tactic* of the characters in this play and in other plays like it. Rhyming is a Tactic your character uses to win Goals with others. It therefore falls squarely into the GOTE framework described in *Acting One*. Remember, although a play is about real relationships, it always portrays such relationships through a system of theatrical coding. In the system of Molière's rhyming comedies, the rhymes are the characters' efforts to win interpersonal victories by the authority of their brilliant wit and extraordinary linguistic creativity. In short, you must rhyme to win—indeed, you must rhyme *brilliantly* to win. In this case, Alceste and Célimène are using their rhymes to *show off*, with the ultimate goal of gaining the upper hand in a battle of wits.

An explosion of wit—the sparkling wordplay that asserts intellectual superiority, lightness of spirit, and carefree invulnerability—is particularly characteristic of high comedy in the time of Molière, and nothing displays seventeenth-century wit so well as rival characters in a verbal joust. The delightful French film *Ridicule* (1996) portrays French courtiers in the time of King Louis XVI playing wicked rhyming games at dinner parties, ridiculing into social disgrace those failing to instantly improvise a clever rhyming couplet on a specified topic.

So when Alceste says

> Well, Lady Célimène! May I be frank?
> The way you acted yesterday? It stank!

he is, while stating something quite plain and unpleasant (emphasized by the slangy word *stank*), packaging his message in a rhymed couplet that, he hopes, will argue his authority to do so. Of course, Célimène will answer him in kind. And the incessant rhymings become weapons in a continual battle between these two wits, each trying to outdo the other. Thus the rhymes should not be swallowed or buried as though these speeches were written in prose. If Molière had wanted to write the play in prose, he would have done so—he did so on many other occasions. No, Molière wants the rhymes to stand out: He designed the characters to be jockeying for superiority by showing off their verbal dexterity—and hence their brilliance.

Showing off with *every* rhyme, however, would clearly be excessive, since every line in this entire play rhymes with its predecessor or successor. So lines like

> I must say that I'm totally disgusted.
> Your actions demonstrate you can't be trusted

need little underlining of their rhyme. Indeed, as with blank verse, the versifying features (rhythm and rhyme) assert themselves simply as part of a pattern, registering with the audience—and the characters spoken to—as ideas rather than as words. The "showing off" in this case conveys itself through the entire speech, its structure and momentum, rather than the singularity of a single rhyme.

However, when a particularly important line is accompanied by an unusually contrived rhyme, as with

> In fact, I've come today to tell you
> Our liaison is off! You—Jezebel, you!

a pointing of the rhyme could be effective.* Alceste is making a formal pronouncement—ending his affair—followed by an accusation: that Célimène

---

* Of course, all the rhymes in this scene were created by the translator. You are, however, welcome to analyze and present the scene in the original French if you are able, for the identical principles apply.

is, like the biblical queen Jezebel, a woman of low morals. Of course, the accusation is overblown, and Alceste will come panting back. Hence the wit is forced, and the tension between the playful verse and the maddening quarrel it contains becomes the dynamic pulse of the drama as acted and staged.

This is the point of Molière's style in *The Misanthrope,* and of many other formally contrived dramatic scripts as well: The outward style may be precisely measured and controlled, but the inner action must be passionate and chaotic. It is like a boxing match: That the boxers are required to wear padded gloves, avoid hitting below the belt, and stop fighting every time the referee speaks or the bell rings does not mean they aren't, at the same time, trying to pulverize each other. The tension between outer form and inner drive sets up the very vibrations of stylized drama.

And another kind of tension is at work here: between the types of characters represented. Célimène and Alceste do not fight with the same tactics. Célimène responds calmly, as a peacemaker, rebuking Alceste for his unseemly behavior:

> Is that why you came here, to start a fight?
> I thought we talked this all out—just last night!

while Alceste can only bluster:

> Okay!—But you're insatiably driven
> To mass flirtations! They can't be forgiven!

Having declared he'll speak no more, Alceste thinks about it—and then speaks some more! And he persists in what has already been demonstrated to be a useless argument—a repetition of the one they had last night:

> You bring the whole world into your salon
> Where troops of lovers seek to get it on!

Whereupon Célimène simply refuses to join the debate, declaring it—in a fine metatheatrical comment within this comedy—comical.

> You're angry that they find me—affable?
> You think I'm wrong; I think you're laughable!

Then, with wonderfully teasing seductiveness, she reduces Alceste's argument—and Alceste himself—to absurdity:

> What should I do, then, hit them with a stick?
> Drive them from my home? Why are you so thick?

The fact that two people are fighting—even in equally rhyming iambic pentameter—doesn't mean they use the same weapons. Alceste attacks,

Célimène coos; Alceste accuses, Célimène mocks; Alceste denounces Célimène for flirting, Célimène responds by flirting with him.

As noted earlier, characters in Molière have their origins in stock figures but transcend them. Alceste, though he says he's going off to be a hermit by play's end, is not really a misanthrope; what he truly hates is not humankind but the intellectual pretension, gossip, and dishonesty he finds within his social circle. Active and extreme in his predilections, he feels compelled to attack what he despises. Though there is something foolish about Alceste, there is much about him with which we identify: his integrity, his forthrightness, and his hatred of pretense, even if overwrought.

Célimène, while she courts all men's favor, giving each what he desires and offending none—at least to their faces—is no empty-headed flirt. She has a brilliant wit, a profound understanding of practical psychology (particularly with regard to men), a need for allies (a recent widow, she has no apparent family support), and the ability to maintain a serene composure. So as furious as Alceste becomes, he is completely overmatched by Célimène's laughing dismissals of his escalating rage. She doesn't rebut him; she ridicules him with his own desire. Imagine, for example, Célimène imitating Marilyn Monroe in a 1950s film—pouty and wispy and crawling all over him—as she delivers "Why are you so thick?" It's enough to make a misanthrope explode, as Célimène well knows.

These parts were originally played by Molière himself and his famously unfaithful (and much younger) wife, Armande Béjart.* As the battles between the playwright and his bride were known throughout French society, Molière's audiences could easily see the real-life lovers' quarrel underneath the staged drama, Alexandrine couplets and matched hemistiches notwithstanding.

Alceste's speech that begins "It's not a stick" is what French drama scholars call a *tirade* (pronounced tee-RAHD), which, while similar to the English word, in French connotes a long speech that, with exquisite logic and intellectual momentum, persuasively argues a single theme. With a structure that builds each idea upon its predecessor, it makes each detail consequently more hilarious than the one before. Alceste's tirade begins with a brutal instruction:

It's not a stick, Madame, that you should brandish.
But you must be hard-hearted! Not outlandish!

---

* The gossip goes further than that: Armande was widely believed to be the daughter of Molière's longtime mistress Madeleine Béjart, and therefore said by many to be the playwright's own daughter.

then quiets down with a finding of facts that support that instruction:

> They're drawn to you, because you're beautiful,
> But you respond beyond what's dutiful!
> Your racy words, and cooing affectations,
> Lead them to elevated aspirations!

and then completes the first beat with a conclusion:

> And you adore them! They're your panting harem;
> This bunch of lisping fops;

followed by Alceste's emotional, reaction to that conclusion:

> God, I can't bear 'em!

Beginning the second beat, Alceste pretends confusion—"Ah, Célimène! I don't know what to do!"—in order to propose a rhetorical question by which he urges Célimène to rethink her priorities: "You LIKE to have these phonies chasing you?"

The rhetorical question is a ploy: Célimène cannot respond (to say either yes or no would imply that she accepts the definition of her suitors as phonies). That gives the almost-crafty Alceste the opportunity to follow with correlated rhetorical questions about one of her suitors, the pretentious aristocrat Clitandre, hoping to make his point with increasing ferocity as he enumerates Clitandre's absurdly foppish grooming, attire, and behavior:

> Explain, my dear, what idiotic pleasure
> You take in old Clitandre. What a treasure!
> You like the curling fingernail he's grown?
> Perhaps the horrid wigs he calls his own,
> With cannon curls that fall down to the floor
> Which all the demoiselles at court adore?
> Perhaps the codpiece sewn into his hose?
> Those ribboned sleeves on which he wipes his nose?
> Or maybe it's his phony, flat falsetto?
> Or else his scent: two dabs of Amaretto?

A *tirade* must be sustained by the structuring of its parts: the neutral introduction of its topic, the accumulation of evidence, the careful assembling of "proofs," and the clinching windup. Molière was trained as a lawyer,* and his speeches are often crafted as versified legal writs, where the verdict

---

* He received a law degree from the University of Orléans but never practiced.

is expected to come through the jury's response to the attorney's accumulation, organizing, and focusing of details. For an actor to get intellectually lost in such a speech, or to simply slog through it line by line (to "roll it out like a string of sausages" as one actor puts it) is to make both argument and character tedious.

Alceste's windup, however, is hardly a clincher; "two dabs of Amaretto" is just a lame joke (again, in the translator's version), not a convincing explanation: It's by phrases like this we recognize that, for all its seriousness and importance, *The Misanthrope* remains a comedy, and Alceste is essentially a fool—if a noble one. So it's no wonder that Célimène can simply undermine his *tirade* by changing the subject entirely and adding a new piece of information, possibly true and possibly not:

> You're so infuriatingly UNJUST!
> You know I have him here because I MUST!
> It's for my lawsuit: You know his support—
> His and his friends'—can win my case at court!

Alceste is suddenly thrown on the defensive; this lawsuit is clearly something he has not considered. But he doesn't have time to think (owing to the unstoppable momentum of the Alexandrines, and the battle of wits in which pausing means defeat), so he is forced to gamely argue on, despite his obviously unwinnable position.

> Forget your case! I'd just as soon you lost!
> To have Clitandre's help—you'll pay the cost!

And now Célimène is back in charge, and she takes full advantage by making an accusation of her own: "Well, you're just jealous, all the world knows that." The hapless Clitandre has now been taken off the table, and the subject of derision is now none other than Alceste, who can only weakly defend himself by the vaguest of counteraccusations: "Who's 'all the world'? Those you make passes at?"

Célimène the peacemaker now moves in for the kill, promoting as her philosophy a generosity of spirit that seems (to everyone but Alceste) profound, just, and even spiritual, capping her argument with a line that (in this translation) creates closure with literary overtones.

> I don't see why this makes you so distressed!
> You should be pleased I love them ALL, Alceste!
> By not identifying any one as best,
> I love, but don't become BY love possessed!

Alceste is completely flummoxed. It is total defeat; Célimène has seized the apparent high ground, and he knows that no one in Paris—other than himself—is clever enough to see through her argument. Unable to debate successfully against such evident beatitude (and knowing a darker secret—that only he is possessed by love), he retreats, hoping, perhaps, to lull Célimène into overconfidence.

> Well, that's just fine, my dear, but tell me—say:
> Just what from you do I get more than they?

But Célimène has the perfect rejoinder and presses it lovingly on him with the very "cooing affectation" that he has earlier accused her of: "The happiness of knowing that you're loved!"

In the agony of defeat, Alceste tries to terrify her with a shout, certainly accompanied by some would-be-manly strutting: "I won't know that—till OUT THE DOOR THEY'RE SHOVED!"

Alceste has completely and abjectly failed. He began this scene telling Célimène "our liaison is off"; by now he is only demonstrating his undying infatuation. He began by framing his argument rationally and by crafting a skillful *tirade* about his rivals; he is now braying at her like a petulant child. He began with a show of authority; he is now unmasked as impotent and driveling. It's now Célimène's turn to issue an ultimatum, and she does:

> How selfish of you! No, Alceste, you've heard
> All I can say! And that's my final word!

And, unlike Alceste, who said he would speak no more but then continued, Célimène leaves it at that and starts to make her exit. Alceste's position is hopeless. He has come (he said) to end the liaison, and now Célimène is ending it. He calls after her in desperation:

> To me—and to the others too! You love—MANKIND!
> For you, dear Célimène, love's REALLY blind!

And Célimène, far from taking the bait, moves a giant step further. Turning, smiling, and at first pretending to have changed her mind, she coos to him, "Why, how romantic! Darling, I'm delighted!"

But it is almost immediately evident that this cooing is pure sarcasm. With savagely seductive pouts she advances on him, building on his unquenchable desire: "You sure can make a girl get all excited!" Then, having set him up, she brays right back at him with the full force of a woman scorned: "I TAKE BACK EVERY SINGLE WORD I SAID!" Next she stabs him where it hurts most: his intelligence: "Oof! What an imbecilic fool you are!" and concludes by inquiring, "Is this your wish?," seeking closure by blaming the entire argument on him. To which Alceste responds, completing her half-line but addressing it to the audience more than to her: "This isn't love: It's war!"

Using this discussion of the structure and momentum of the *Misanthrope* scene, rehearse it with a partner. Devise movements and business for each of you that will carry the verbal tactics into the physical realm.

Let the rhymes create, as discussed in Lesson 3, a "playing environment" for each of you, in the sense of both "playfulness" ("to play") and "dramatic"

Brisart d.   I Sauué B

LE MISANTROPE

Molière as Alceste   The playwright (right) performs the title role in *The Misanthrope*. Half-seated, perhaps sinking evasively into his chair, he is probably in conversation with the obnoxiously foppish poet, Oronte. Notice the high heels, ruffled cuffs, elaborately brocaded gowns, and the cascading cannon curls of the wigs. No matter how much the misanthrope rails against society, he is a part of it, and dresses (and must move) accordingly. From the frontispiece to the 1682 edition of the play.

("a play"). *Entertain* each other with your rhymes, even as you're fighting, and let each other know that you're an entertaining sort of social person—able to amuse others if not each other. Use your rhymes to make yourself irresistible; make your lover *hate* to lose such a magnificent partner!

How might you dress the parts? An engraving of Molière in the role survives. Despite his vaunted unpretentiousness, his Alceste wears a reasonably typical male costume of the period (see illustration on page 411): loose breeches gathered right below the knee and, peering from an open, richly embroidered coat, billowing and ruffled sleeves; hose into his ribboned, high-heeled shoes; and a simple round-brimmed hat, front cocked up, holding down his peruke, which flows beyond his shoulders. Célimène would have worn something on the order of a long flowing gown with a plunging neckline, and a high headdress; she may well have carried (and used) a folding fan. You may find these garments hard to come by in your contemporary wardrobes, but do come up with ways to capture the shapes and volumes of this period costuming, for it will provide you with dozens of opportunities to match fabric with rhetoric, and sartorial elegance with

Jean-Claude Druout plays Alceste and Maria Blanco Celiménè in this 1985 production of *The Misanthrope* at the Centre Dramatique National in Reims, France. (Photo © Laurencine Lot)

PLAYING TRANSLATIONS

Molière's plays were adapted for the English-speaking stage during his own lifetime, and of course increasingly thereafter, and acting in them—or in any translated plays, for that matter—presents actors and directors with a broad set of options. With an author of Molière's repute, you may have multiple translations to choose from: *The Misanthrope,* for example, is published in several dozen English versions, both in prose and in verse. Which one is the "best"? That depends on the reader, and in this case perhaps on the actor as well; no translation can ever be definitive. The art of translation is subjective, and languages do not pair up precisely with regard to meaning, tone, rhythm, or rhyme: "Translator? Traitor!" says a euphonious Italian proverb. For *The Misanthrope,* the American poet Richard Wilbur's 1954 translation is certainly the best known today, but there are more contemporary as well as more antique ones available, presenting their own challenges and opportunities. You might, as an added exercise, try reading with a partner the following lines from the play's first scene as they appear in a variety of published versions. In the scene, Alceste is arguing with his friend Philinte (pronounced Phil-ANT) about the latter's recent public flattery of and friendliness toward a man they both dislike.

ANONYMOUS, 1716

ALCESTE: I'm your friend no longer—No—I'll have no share in a Corrupt Heart.

PHILINTE: Then you think, Alceste, that I am much to blame?

ALCESTE: To blame? You ought to blush to Death. Such an Action admits no Excuse; and every honest Man must be Scandalized at it.

WALDO FRANK, 1926

ALCESTE: After what I have just seen of you, I tell you candidly that I am no longer your friend. I have no wish to occupy a place in a corrupt heart.

PHILINTE: I am then very much to be blamed from your point of view, Alceste?

ALCESTE: To be blamed? You ought to die from very shame; there is no excuse for such behaviour, and every man of honor must be disgusted at it.

(*Continued*)

(Continued)

RICHARD WILBUR, 1954

ALCESTE: I tell you flatly that our ways must part
   I wish no place in a dishonest heart.

PHILINTE: Why, what have I done, Alceste? Is this quite just?

ALCESTE: My God, you ought to die of self-disgust.
   I call your conduct inexcusable, Sir,
   And every man of honor will concur.

ROBERT COHEN, 1997

ALCESTE: This morning, sir, our friendship was destroyed
   When you pretended to be overjoyed.

PHILINTE: Just when did I do that? Why'm I to blame?

ALCESTE: How can you ask that and not die of shame?
   Your honesty's been permanently bruised,
   And what you did can NEVER be excused!

MARTIN CRIMP, 1996

ALCESTE: And when I see you talking such total shit
   I realise I'm dealing with just one more hypocrite.

"JOHN":   Alceste, don't tell me you're upset.

ALCESTE: Upset? That's the best understatement yet.
   To do that to a man with no coercion
   is a form of social perversion.

semantic sophistication. Pivoting sharply in a flowing gown, or harrumphing off in a frock coat and high heels, conveys a seventeenth-century energy—the furious tension between inward rage and outward formality—that cannot be fully realized in jeans and sneakers.

Stage yourselves. Furniture is written into this play. One or two chairs would be useful; adding a pouf (circular couch or ottoman, permitting reclining) would be even better. Fan gestures—which can be sharply pointed, coyly seductive, fiercely aggressive, and demure by turns (see the "Accessories" box on page 417)—can be usefully employed by Célimène; Alceste's manner of sitting, standing, striding, and collapsing will say as much as Molière's words (as nobody understood better than the actor–dramatist himself).

Go ahead. Have a ball. Rhyme each other into submission.

LESSON

13

Restoration Comedy

English comedy during the Restoration—a four-decade period beginning in 1660, when the English royal family was restored to the throne after a long civil war and a Puritan government—owes far more to the French Molière than to the English Shakespeare, for the English aristocracy, including King Charles II, lived mostly in Paris during the twenty-eight years of Puritan rule. There they acquired not only French manners but a taste for the brilliant theatre of Molière at the court of King Louis XIV. So Restoration comedies, like Molière's, were staged indoors and normally concerned contemporary characters in contemporary settings, most often the same city where they were performed. It was, also like Molière's, a generally aristocratic theatre, even when performed in public houses, and both courtiers and courtesans (elegant prostitutes), often masked, circulated in the audience seeking romantic assignations as much as dramatic entertainment. Caustic wit, amorous adventurism, and the unflagging satire of pretentious fops characterized these English plays, which also featured extravagant costumes, elaborate stage scenery such as had never been seen in England outside of a palace masque, and elegantly turned language. Verse remained the proper language for tragedy, but Restoration comedy was mostly written in very carefully crafted prose.

This was also the era when women made their first appearance as actors on the professional English stage—aided by an official edict of King Charles II, who counted the actress Nell Gwyn among his mistresses—and the backstage liaisons between courtiers and actresses was the stuff of winking London gossip.

The costumes and manners of English Restoration drama are close enough to those of Molière's time and clime to be treated in the same way in a study of acting styles—with, perhaps, the exception that the sniffing of tobacco (snuff) was a habit more to the taste of seventeenth-century English fops than to that of French *galants* of the same era, and the English cavalier preferred a slightly more casual coiffure than the cascading French peruke.

FRENCH AND RESTORATION ACCESSORIES:
THE FAN AND THE HANDKERCHIEF

The decorated fan (for women) and the elegant handkerchief (for men) are essential props for certain courtly characters in the plays of Molière and the English Restoration. Indeed, most English women who considered themselves refined carried fans well into the beginning of the twentieth century. When open, fans could be coquettishly employed to cool the overly amorous body—or to hide the blushingly embarrassed face. When closed, they could rap a naughtily overreaching suitor's knuckles, or indignantly indicate, to an unwelcome visitor, the nearest door. The handkerchief, originally employed to capture the toxic snuff sneezed out the nose by Restoration gentlemen, could be flourished (when held by its center) to show off its expensive lace embroidery, as well as the gracefulness of its bearer's wrists, fingers, and jewelry. The repertoire of fan and handkerchief gestures is almost limitless, and actors specializing in roles from this period often spend years researching and (for the most part) inventing such movements and flourishes.

There is one major difference between Restoration comedy and Molière's, however: Restoration comedy is always about sex. Moreover, it is frankly, openly, and almost solely about sex; it is more graphically sexual, in fact, than any mainstream theatre in world drama between the time of Aristophanes (fifth century B.C.) and the late 1960s.

Aphra Behn, one of the finest dramatists of the Restoration, was the first woman in history to make a living as a playwright. Behn's 1677 comedy, *The Rover,* concerns several young Englishmen visiting the Italian city of Naples, where, as the title character rhapsodizes, "the kind sun has its god-like power still over the wine and woman."

Elegant Restoration attire   Notice the full gowns, bustles, and headdresses of the ladies, and the huge cuffs, extravagant cravats, feathered hats, high-heeled and high-collared shoes, and (usually) powdered periwigs of the gentlemen. The low-hung sword position of the one gentleman, being essentially useless for combat, indicates his urbane gentility.

◆ E x e r c i s e   13–1

Restoration Speeches

Let's look first at a couple of individual speeches from different scenes in *The Rover.*

HELLENA: *[a young woman, preparing to be a nun but still interested in finding a love, to her sister who has already taken a lover]* Now you have provided yourself with a man, you take no care for poor me—prithee tell me, what dost thou see about me that is unfit for love—have I not a world of youth? a humor gay? a beauty passable? a vigor desirable? well shaped? clean limbed? sweet breath'd? and sense enough to know how all these ought to be employed to the best advantage? Yes, I do and will.

· · ·

WILLMORE: *[The Rover himself, a young English cavalier, newly in town and seeking a lover, as Hellena asks him if he likes her face]* Like it! By Heaven, I never saw so much beauty. Oh the charms of those sprightly black eyes, that strangely fair face, full of smiles and dimples! Those soft round melting cherry lips! And small even white teeth! Not to be expressed, but silently adored!—Oh, one look more and strike me dumb, or I shall repeat nothing else till I am mad!

These speeches share the characteristics of the French *tirade* (see Lesson 12); though not as long, they are syntactically complex and rich in detail, and they spin a single, relatively simple idea into rhetorical gold. But the complexity and richness of the language are employed not so much to explore the intellectual ramifications of the speaker's argument as to show off the speaker's splendid wit—and thereby her or his romantic charm.

The tone of superficial understatement overlaying an exuberant boastfulness is characteristic of the entire era. Hellena's speech begins with a mock self-deprecation of her appeal ("poor me"), which is only an excuse to then list seven of her most attractive and sexy qualities, concluding with an eighth: the sense to use them to get a man.

But of course it is not sufficient for Hellena merely to enumerate her charms, she (meaning, of course, the actress playing her) must also *demonstrate* them, and do so convincingly. Hellena is not trying to seduce her sister, of course, but she is trying to convince her that, though she is in training to become a nun, she nonetheless has made a commitment to romance. Only if her sister believes her will she aid in Hellena's quest.

Hellena is also using her sister to *rehearse* her seductive ploys. When a man comes into view, as one surely will, Hellena will have some experience in sexual badinage that surpasses any she might have practiced at the convent.

Women in the class: Learn, rehearse, and perform Hellena's speech.

In your long gown and stiffened bodice, practice movements and expressions that will convince your sister that you have the requisite confidence in your sexual attractiveness to take this holiday from your religious training. Show her that you are—or can quickly become—a temptress. As you become comfortable with the language, flounce around the room, exhibiting your charms along with your petticoats. Use a folding fan to point out your various gifts, as well as to fan the heat of your escalating passion, and to coyly hide behind when the opportunity presents itself.

Rehearse, as the Restoration temptress you wish to become, the seduction of a Restoration man—employing fabric, prop, and text with equal relish.

Imagine a group of attractive young men hiding behind a bush near you, spying on you. Pretending to be unaware of them, try to encourage *their* romantic interest with this speech—which is now only superficially addressed to your sister.

Willmore's speech also begins with a topic phrase ("I never saw so much beauty"), which is also followed by a list: in this case, an enumeration of Hellena's attractions. Is Willmore's list a sincere appraisal? Hardly, nor is it meant to be. His eloquent flattery, in the Restoration era, is itself seductive; the light tone of mockery shows that Willmore is taking great pains

A court dandy   An extravagant court fop, from a 1687 engraving by J. D. de St. Jean. Billowing cuffs, a wig to the waist, and lavish waistcoat decoration—with ample lace and fringe—typify male flamboyance of the era. (© Corbis)

to exaggerate and, therefore, shows his witty refinement along with his appreciation and desire.

When Willmore describes Hellena's teeth as "not to be expressed, but silently adored," and then expresses this thought in anything but silent adoration, his self-contradiction sharply announces the fierceness of his ardor, which is further proclaimed by his wish to be stricken dumb—at the risk of going totally insane for love. No right-minded woman (as Hellena surely is) could possibly be fooled by Willmore's literal declaration, but any Restoration lady, and perhaps many contemporary ladies as well, would be impressed with the energy, imagination, and linguistic dexterity of his over-the-top proposal—particularly if he underlines it with a dashing doff of his hat and an accompanying toss of his long, curling locks.

To whom does Willmore address "Oh, one look more and strike me dumb"? This is clearly an apostrophe (a phrase directed to a person or personified deity or object not physically present) directed either to God or some supernatural spirit, even if tongue-in-cheek. It could, however, be directed right to Hellena, as though she were the goddess of beauty, or at least a stand-in for such a presence.

Men in the class: Learn, rehearse, and perform Willmore's speech. Choose movements and expressions that will convince Hellena you truly adore her features (eyes, face, lips, teeth), and build them, one upon the other, as increasingly aphrodisiac incentives, so that the splendor of her lips throws you into uncontrollable desire, and her teeth, for reasons you do not need to explain, send you into an absolute paroxysm of ecstasy. Then, with a look up to the divine presence, beg for the muteness that can "cure" you of this unbearable infatuation. And top even that with the explanation, looking at Hellena this time, that otherwise you will go utterly insane. Overwhelm *her* with the desire that overwhelms *you*.

As you become comfortable with the language, dress yourself (to the extent possible) in the getup of a Restoration gallant, using any of the following you can find or create: an overlong-sleeved shirt, a fitted vest and tight pants, dress shoes with a visible heel, a floppy hat, a sword in your belt loop, and a long, curly wig. Practice the speech while circling Hellena, doffing your hat to her, holding it close to you (on "never saw such beauty," for example), and then raising it as a challenge to God when invoking him to silence you.

Rehearse, as the gallant you would like the ladies to see, the seduction of a seventeenth-century lady with this speech.

Imagine a group of attractive young women hiding behind a bush near the two of you; imagine that they are spying on you. Pretending to be unaware of them, try to encourage their romantic interest with this speech as well—in case Hellena spurns your approach. Don't worry that they will be jealous of your interest in Hellena. It will only get them more excited, for you are really showing off not your love for any one particular woman but your ability to speak brilliantly about feminine beauty.

◆ S c e n e **13–1**

Sexual Banter: Willmore and Hellena

Rehearse and present this first encounter between Willmore and Hellena from Act 1, Scene 2 of *The Rover*. Willmore has just arrived in Naples, and almost immediately encounters Hellena, who is masked as a gypsy for a carnival masquerade.

WILLMORE: Dear pretty (and I hope) young devil, will you tell an amorous stranger what luck he's like to have?

HELLENA: Have a care how you venture with me, sir, lest I pick your pocket,* which will more vex° your English humour°   °irritate   °disposition
than an Italian fortune will please you.

WILLMORE: How the devil cam'st thou to know my country and humour?

HELLENA: The first I guess by a certain forward impudence, which does not displease me at this time; and the loss of your money will vex you because I hope° you have but very little to lose.   °expect

WILLMORE: Egad,° child, thou'rt i'th'right;   °oh God (a Restoration oath)
it is so little, I dare not offer it thee for a kindness—But cannot you divine what other things of more value I have about me, that I would more willingly part with?

HELLENA: Indeed no, that's the business of a witch and I am but a gypsy yet°—Yet, without looking in your hand, I have a   °still
parlous° guess, 'tis some foolish heart you mean, an   °dangerous
inconstant English heart, as little worth stealing as your purse.

WILLMORE: Nay, then thou dost deal with the devil, that's certain—thou hast guessed as right as if thou hadst been one of that number it° has languished for—I find you'll be better acquainted   °his heart
with it; nor can you take it in a better time, for I am come from sea, child; and Venus not being propitious to me in her own element,†
I have a world of love in store—would° you would be   °I wish
good-natured and take some on't° off my hands?   °of it

HELLENA: Why—I could be inclined that way—but for a foolish vow I am going to make—to die a maid.°   °virgin

WILLMORE: Then thou art damned without redemption; and as I am a good Christian, I ought in charity to divert so wicked a design—therefore prithee, dear creature, let me know quickly when and where I shall begin to set a helping hand to so good a work.

HELLENA: If you should prevail with my tender heart (as I begin to fear you will, for you have horrible loving eyes) there will be difficulty in't that you'll hardly undergo for my sake.

WILLMORE: Faith, child, I have been bred in dangers, and wear a sword that has been employed in a worse cause than for a handsome kind

---

* Gypsies were then believed to be pickpockets.
† Venus, the goddess of love, was born in the sea; Willmore arrived in Naples from the sea.

woman— name the danger—let it be anything but a long siege, and I'll undertake it.

HELLENA: Can you storm?

WILLMORE: Oh, most furiously.

HELLENA: What think you of a nunnery-wall? For he that wins me must gain that first.

WILLMORE: A nun! Oh how I love thee for't! There's no sinner like a young saint. . . . Oh, I'm impatient. Thy lodging, sweetheart, thy lodging, or I'm a dead man.

HELLENA: Why must we be either guilty of fornication or murder, if we converse with you men? And is there no difference between leave° to love me, and leave to lie with me?   °permission

WILLMORE: Faith, child, they were made to go together.

This is a witty wooing scene, not entirely unlike that of Beatrice and Benedick in Scene 11–2; here, however, the emphasis is not on the ambiguity and fragility of human relationships but more simply on the particularities of flirting and sexual conquest. Restoration comedy is known not for exploring the multisided complexities of human emotion, but rather for the delightful ploys of sexual adventurism, mainly expressed through linguistic wit and extravagant behavior. Like other Restoration comedies, *The Rover* is a virtuoso presentation of style and manners.

Moreover, the style and manners are *publicly* deployed. This scene takes place at a masquerade, amid a crowd of revelers. Willmore and Hellena are not merely flirting with each other; they are flirting with the crowd. And, in the larger arena of the Dorset Garden Theatre where the play premiered, they were flirting with the royal and aristocratic audience as well: For an appealing and ambitious actress, a dalliance with the king himself (and a royal income in the bargain) was not outside the realm of possibility.

Willmore begins by setting the topic in a single sentence filled with no less than seven eternal parameters of sexual adventure: beauty, hopefulness, youth, deviltry, desire, novelty, and opportunity: "Dear pretty (and I hope) young devil, will you tell an amorous stranger what luck he's like to have?"

Hellena's riposte, "Have a care how you venture with me, sir, lest I pick your pocket, which will more vex your English humour than an Italian fortune will please you," is not to reject the adventure but to take full charge of what will clearly become a romp: "Pick your pocket" carries the express suggestion that she will penetrate his garments—rather than the other way around! By identifying his country and his interest in (and lack of) money, she gains the immediate upper hand. She will surely be no passive victim to

A Restoration staging   A scene from the original staging in 1707 of Restoration dramatist George Farquhar's *The Beaux' Stratagem*, according to the frontispiece of the 1733 edition.

this would-be Petruchio (the wooing character in Shakespeare's *Taming of the Shrew*, to which Behn's play is openly indebted).

WILLMORE: How the devil cam'st thou to know my country and humour?

HELLENA: The first I guess by a certain forward impudence, which does not displease me at this time; and the loss of your money will vex you because I hope you have but very little to lose.

Hellena extends her advantage by an apparently simple but actually complex response to Willmore's question: identifying his country by his manner (for which she gives him a temporary break) and, then, without giving the "second" explanation to pair with the first, adding a gratuitous dig at his obvious (despite his elegant cavalier costume) poverty.

Willmore comes off the floor with his counter-riposte, employing a Shakespearean allusion as he refuses to be torpedoed by Hellena's wit: "Egad, child, thou'rt i'th'right; it is so little, I dare not offer it thee for a kindness—But cannot you divine what other things of more value I have about me, that I would more willingly part with?" These last four words are an allusion to Hamlet's reply to Polonius's leave-taking in Act 2, Scene 2: "You cannot, sir, take from me anything that I will more willingly part withal," Hamlet says, then slyly adds, "except my life, except my life, except my life." Willmore is slyly offering his "life," in the form of his heart, to Hellena in return for a taste of her sexual favors.

Hellena responds with a riff on Willmore's heart, first framed by locating herself somewhere between witch and gypsy: "Indeed no, that's the business of a witch and I am but a gypsy yet—" and then by repeating the word *yet*, but with the contrary meaning of "but": "Yet, without looking in your hand, I have a parlous guess, 'tis some foolish heart you mean, an inconstant English heart, as little worth stealing as your purse." "Who steals my purse steals trash," Iago says in Shakespeare's *Othello,* so Hellena matches Willmore's literary allusion with one of her own.

To this, Willmore retorts that she is devilishly interested in his heart so he may as well offer it to her. Identifying himself with the sea from which he has just come ashore, and with the Roman goddess of love who was born there, he proclaims: "I have a world of love in store—would you would be good-natured and take some on't off my hands?" The "world of love in store" is a (literally) seminal metaphor; he has earlier said he would not offer his purse for a kindness, but he now offers his love juices were Hellena to be "good-natured" and "take some." One hears few sexual proposals in such politely euphemistic terms in the twenty-first century, but the gist of the offer is no less potent than it would be today.

Hellena has no problem understanding what Willmore intends: "Why—I could be inclined that way—but for a foolish vow I am going to make—to die a maid." She does not decline his offer—and indeed shows some interest in it—but points out a particular obstacle: her "foolish vow" to remain a virgin. This is practically a thrown-down gauntlet: Any Restoration cavalier would eagerly take up the challenge of seducing her from such "foolish" morality. Willmore is clearly up to the task. Turning Christian theology on its head, he argues that chastity is tantamount to damnation and that only religion and charity, not lust, urge him to "divert so wicked a design" by violating it. To that end he invites Hellena to quickly explain "when and where" (on her body, presumably) he may set his "helping hand" so as to undermine her vow.

Hellena's response, "If you should prevail with my tender heart (as I begin to fear you will, for you have horrible loving eyes) there will be difficulty in't

Faye Grant is Hellena and the late Christopher Reeve is Willmore in this
Williamstown Theatre Festival photo of *The Rover*. (Courtesy of Williamstown
Theatre Festival; photo by Nina Krieger)

that you'll hardly undergo for my sake," with its wonderful oxymorons
("horrible loving") showing intertwined fear and desire, encourages
Willmore's pursuit while at the same time warns him how difficult it will be.
To the Restoration gallant and his desired lady—as well as to the Restoration
audience—the greater the challenge, the more powerful was the aphrodisiac
effect.

  In their last two speeches, Willmore and Hellena have named three parts
of the body—hand, heart, eyes—that are predominant in romantic lovemaking. Willmore will now refer to, and perhaps symbolically produce, the
phallic symbol that will take the scene to its next, more explicit level:

Michael Pennington as Mirabell courts Judi Dench as Millamant, while Beryl Reid, as the seated Lady Wishfort, gazes at them nostalgically in a Royal Shakespeare Company production of William Congreve's Restoration comedy *The Way of the World*. (Courtesy of Royal Shakespeare Company; photo by Donald Cooper)

"Faith, child, I have been bred in dangers, and wear a sword that has been employed in a worse cause than for a handsome kind woman—name the danger—let it be anything but a long siege, and I'll undertake it."

What follows is pure symbolic copulation, with "Can you storm?" referring to his lovemaking abilities, the "nunnery-wall" to the female hymen, and "thy lodging" representing Hellena's home, her bed, and her private parts.

Willmore's paradoxical "There's no sinner like a young saint" (that is, there's no lover like a virgin) builds on the earlier opposites of the scene— "pretty devil" and "horrible loving"—and the repetition of "thy lodging" becomes sonic representations of Willmore's phallic thrusts. Having earlier offered Hellena his "life," he now assures her that any denial means his death.

Now spent by the virtually orgasmic ferocity of the wooing, Hellena coolly reflects, with rhetorical questions (half-addressed to the audience, the women who are incorporated in her two uses of the word *we*), on what has just passed: "Why must we be either guilty of fornication or murder, if we converse with you men?"

And then, directly to Willmore, the central issue of the scene, expressed alliteratively: "And is there no difference between leave to love me, and leave to lie with me?" Can there be love without sex? she asks plaintively.

Willmore's reply, beginning with its religious invocation, represents the moral credo of the Restoration: "Faith, child, they were made to go together."

As you rehearse and play this scene with a partner, remember: You are flirting with the audience as well as each other, so flaunt your wit, your education (those Shakespearean allusions!), your good looks, your terrific clothes, and your above-it-all recklessness to the entire crowd.

Dress yourselves in some fashion as described above or illustrated in this or the preceding lesson. Willmore should have a sword (a makeshift broom handle will do) in his belt and a cap in his hand, and Hellena a full, flowing skirt and a folding fan (which can also be stored in her belt).

And do remember, this is not a scene of groping each other. The sex in Restoration comedy is a matter of conversational charm, not physical assault. It is the *control* of sexual passion, and its channeling into the brilliance of banter and reproach, sashay and glance, tantalizing double entendres (words with two meanings) and sly, knowing winks that characterizes the ideal Restoration foreplay. The "real action" occurs, as it does in nearly all drama, safely offstage.

So flirt *outrageously*—with passion, imagination, and delicacy—as you play the scene. And take a cold shower afterward.

14

The Belle Epoque

The Belle Epoque (French for "beautiful era") is the period of European culture from 1890 to 1914: from the final decade of Queen Victoria's rule to the beginning of the First World War. It is the last great age before what we generally think of as modern, and a full century before what we think of as contemporary: an age before radio, television, recorded music, interstate highways, and commercial air travel; the age in which film, still silent, was in its infancy.

In Europe, the Belle Epoque was also an immensely rich era of drama, encompassing major plays by Oscar Wilde, James M. Barrie, and George Bernard Shaw in England; Anton Chekhov, Maxim Gorky, and Leo Tolstoy in Russia; August Strindberg in Sweden; Edmond Rostand and Alfred Jarry in France; and Ferenc Molnár in Hungary. It was also the era when directors rose to prominence in the theatre establishment, creating, blending, and unifying theatrical styles from a wide variety of sources rarely explored previously by playwrights or theatre companies. For the first time, plays were not simply mounted by their authors or leading actors according to accepted tradition, but were reconceived by independent artists eager to make the texts freshly relevant, surprising, revelatory, and sometimes shocking. Perhaps for this reason, this is the first era in which plays were published with extensive stage and acting directions.

Though best known in art circles for the distinctive Art Nouveau style in painting, sculpture, and architecture, the Belle Epoque was not dominated by a single theatrical style: Indeed, it was an era of multiple isms, including expressionism, theatricalism, surrealism, and, yes, naturalism. All had their

---

⚑ Salutations of the Belle Epoque

While handshakes between men and between women (but not between men and women) became common in elegant urban nineteenth-century society, men continued to bow and women to curtsy
throughout the Belle Epoque. The male bow was a simple inclination from the waist, with the feet turned out (heels together) and
the head cocked deferentially to one side. Hands could be clasped
behind the back or below the belly button, and the body could be
angled a full quarter-turn in either direction to give a more dashing
profile. A more formal male bow, associated with Prussia (and carried elsewhere), began with the heels apart so that they could be
smartly clicked together during the descent of the upper torso.

Women might bow as well during this era, or they could curtsy
by first taking a step (to either side) and pointing the foot outward,
then bringing the other foot behind the first, bending the knees,
and inclining the head forward in the direction of the pointed
foot—while at the same time raising both hands toward the heart.

A simple nod of acknowledgment, with the head briefly raised
and then inclined downward and to the side, was even more common than full bows or curtsies for both men and women. And a
maidservant's curtsy would be a mere bob: a quick bend of the
knees and incline of the head, and straight up again to do the mistress's bidding.

The kiss on the hand—"quite continental," as the song says—
became common between European men and women at this time:
the man bowing slightly and lifting, with the back of his own right
hand, the lady's right hand to his slightly pinched (nonmoistened!)
lips. Should the lady's hand inadvertently touch the gentleman's
nose, mortification would result for both parties.

---

heyday, and all have lasted to the present. But it was an era that can be defined by some common characteristics:

◆ It was the last general era of strictly enforced class divisions, which were
   shattered by the First World War and were never again to dominate
   Europe's cultural life to the extent they had done in the age of Queen
   Victoria and Kaiser Wilhelm II.

◆ It was the last era when the capacity for lively, intelligent conversation,
   being the world's main form of entertainment as well as its means for determining wise public policy, was considered a crucial social skill, something to be conscientiously, not randomly, acquired.

◆ It was an age of genteel manners, modeled on court behavior (or at least the public perception of it), which still set the tone of social gatherings in every major European country except France during its Third Republic—which itself possessed an aristocratic and cultural elite (the very word is French), regal all but for an actual crown.

Drama had moved indoors in the age of Molière and the English Restoration. It had largely dropped its verse in the age of Romanticism that followed in the eighteenth and early nineteenth centuries, and it had been toned down from its Romantic exoticisms and grotesqueries by Henrik Ibsen and his followers in the last decades of the nineteenth century. Much of Belle Epoque drama, then, is simply living-room talk. But what talk!

In the following pages, we concern ourselves with three of the greatest dramatists of this era. Though radically different in their stylistic approaches, George Bernard Shaw, Anton Chekhov, and Oscar Wilde, all born within a six-year span and coming into theatrical prominence in the mid-1890s, have proven seminal to the array of theatrical styles prevalent in the twentieth and twenty-first centuries.

George Bernard Shaw

George Bernard Shaw is one of the finest prose writers in the English language, the author of some of the world's best music criticism and drama reviews as well as hundreds of novels, essays, political speeches, published letters, and plays—most of them accompanied by long prefaces, afterwords, dedicatory epistles, or ancillary documents. As a dramatist, he is ranked second in English only to Shakespeare by many critics—and well *above* Shakespeare by his own reckoning.

Shaw forcefully repudiated the notion of "art for art's sake"; he was, instead, an "advanced thinker," an impassioned speaker at political gatherings, and a soapbox orator at London's Hyde Park Corner. His thoughts ranged from politics (he was an avowed socialist and pacifist) to women's rights (the final scene of Shakespeare's *Taming of the Shrew,* he said, was "altogether disgusting to modern sensibility"), eating habits (he was a devout vegetarian and teetotaler), modern drama (he championed the plays of Ibsen), sexual relations (though married, he claimed to be abstinent), and a system of reformed spelling that, among other things, dispensed with most apostrophes. A consummate stylist, Shaw insisted that "effectiveness of assertion," not literary decoration, was the essence of style, and his plays, therefore, are formed around vigorous debates covering a wide range of subjects. In the flash and fire of conflicting assertions lies the Shavian (the adjectival form of his name, pronounced SHAY-vee-un) style, and, as almost all his ideas retain their provocative edge, we are still fascinated—and can still learn from—the arguments Shaw put on the stage a century ago.

◆ E X E R C I S E   14–1

Shaw's Political Speeches

Here are two speeches, each slightly edited, from the final scene of Shaw's *Major Barbara* (1905). The first is by Andrew Undershaft, the owner of a cannon factory; the second is by Barbara, his daughter and the play's title character, a major in the Salvation Army. They are obviously at odds. Undershaft is speaking to Barbara, trying to convince her and her fiancé, Adolphus Cusins (known as "Dolly"), to leave the Salvation Army and join him in the cannon business. In the second speech, Barbara has agreed, and, standing in her father's gun factory, she is seeking to convince Cusins to consider this apparent reversal as an extension of her idealism rather than a mere sellout.

Peter Bowles is captain of industry Andrew Undershaft in the 1998 Picadilly Theatre production of *Major Barbara*. (Photo © Geraint Lewis)

UNDERSHAFT: *[speaking of his cannon factory]* I see no darkness here, no
dreadfulness. In your Salvation shelter I saw poverty, misery, cold and
hunger. You give them bread and treacle and dreams of heaven. I give
from thirty shillings a week to twelve thousand a year. They find their
own dreams; but I look after the drainage. And their souls! I save their
souls just as I saved yours. Oh, yes, I saved your soul; I fed you and
clothed you and housed you. I took care that you should have money
enough to live handsomely—more than enough; so that you could be
wasteful, careless, generous. That saved your soul from the seven deadly
sins. Yes, the deadly seven. *[Counting on his fingers]* Food, clothing, firing,° rent, taxes, respectability and children. Nothing can   °*firewood*
lift those seven millstones from Man's neck but money; and the spirit
cannot soar until the millstones are lifted. I lifted them from your spirit.
I enabled Barbara to become Major Barbara; and I saved her from the
crime of poverty. Yes, I call poverty a crime! The worst of crimes. All
the other crimes are virtues beside it: all the other dishonors are chivalry
itself by comparison. Poverty blights whole cities; spreads horrible pestilences; strikes dead the very souls of all who come within sight, sound,
or smell of it. What you call crime is nothing: a murder here and a theft
there, a blow now and a curse then: what do they matter? they are only
the accidents and illnesses of life: there are not fifty genuine professional
criminals in London. But there are millions of poor people, abject
people, dirty people, ill fed, ill clothed people. They poison us morally
and physically: they kill the happiness of society: they force us to do
away with our own liberties and to organize unnatural cruelties for fear
they should rise against us and drag us down into their abyss. Only
fools fear crime: we all fear poverty!

.   .   .

BARBARA: *[speaking of her father and Bodger, the liquor distiller]*
Undershaft and Bodger: their hands stretch everywhere: when we feed a
starving fellow creature, it is with their bread, because there is no other
bread; when we tend the sick, it is in the hospitals they endow; if we
turn from the churches they build, we must kneel on the stones of the
streets they pave. As long as that lasts, there is no getting away from
them. Turning our backs on Bodger and Undershaft is turning our backs
on life. Oh, Dolly, you thought I was determined to turn my back on
the wicked side of life, but there is no wicked side: life is all one. And I
never wanted to shirk my share in whatever evil must be endured,
whether it be sin or suffering. Oh, I wish I could cure you of middle-
class ideas, Dolly. I have no class: I come straight out of the heart of the
whole people. If I were middle-class I should turn my back on my
father's business; and we should both live in an artistic drawing room,

with you reading the reviews in one corner, and I in the other at the piano, playing Schumann: both very superior persons, and neither of us a bit of use. Sooner than that, I would sweep out the guncotton shed, or be one of Bodger's barmaids. Do you know what would have happened if you had refused Papa's offer? I should have given you up and married the man who accepted it. After all, my dear old mother has more sense than any of you. I felt like her when I saw this place—felt that I must have it—that never, never, never could I let it go. Only she thought it was the houses and the kitchen ranges and the linen and china, when it was really all the human souls to be saved: not weak souls in starved bodies, sobbing with gratitude for a scrap of bread and treacle, but full-fed, quarrelsome, snobbish, uppish creatures, all standing on their little rights and dignities, and thinking that my father ought to be greatly obliged to them for making so much money for him—and so he ought. That is where salvation is really wanted. My father shall never throw it in my teeth again that my converts were bribed with bread. [She is transfigured.] I have got rid of the bribe of bread. I have got rid of the bribe of heaven. Let God's work be done for its own sake: the work he had to create us to do because it cannot be done except by living men and women. When I die, let him be in my debt, not I in his; and let me forgive him as becomes a woman of my rank. Yes, Dolly, the way of life lies through the factory of death. Through the raising of hell to heaven and of man to God, through the unveiling of an eternal light in the Valley of the Shadow. [Seizing Dolly with both hands] Oh, did you think my courage would never come back? did you believe that I was a deserter? that I, who have stood in the streets, and taken my people to my heart, and talked of the holiest and greatest things with them, could ever turn back and chatter foolishly to fashionable people about nothing in a drawing room? Never, never, never, never: Major Barbara will die with the colors.°   ° with military flags flying

As you see immediately, these are both long speeches*—but they can be absolutely captivating with the necessary understanding and work, as they are masterpieces of clear thinking and dramatic momentum. There is a reason for this: Shaw's characters are essentially political orators—as Shaw was himself—and they argue their points with great clarity and rhetorical skill. It is "effectiveness of assertion" that creates the galvanizing theatrical appeal of Shavian rhetoric: It is persuasive, it is captivating, and it commands *increasing* attention as it goes on, leading to a thrilling climax.

---

* In the original, the characters are momentarily interrupted with three or four interjections—single lines or words—by the addressed characters, which I have incorporated into their monologues.

Gemma Redgrave plays the title role in the 1998 Picadilly Theatre's *Major Barbara*. (Photo © Geraint Lewis)

We should also recall that in the days before television, people were used to long speeches. Church sermons in Shaw's day, as in Shakespeare's, could last for two hours. In the famous Lincoln–Douglas debates of 1858, each candidate was allotted *ninety minutes* for his opening remarks (compared with two minutes today) and thirty minutes (versus today's thirty seconds) for his first rebuttal. One of the great challenges of playing Shaw is to recapture the sheer magnitude of argumentative rhetoric, capable of addressing a complex issue in rich detail, and to develop the soaring momentum that reaches a rousing, inspiring conclusion.

Try one of these speeches. Memorize it carefully (allow plenty of time for this) and perfectly: exact word for exact word.

Understand the basic architecture of each speech and how transitions link its structural units. See how each speech begins with a general statement,

The battle of the sexes   A would-be courtier seeks to charm a 1903 feminist at tea. The original caption: "But although you are all known as men-haters, aren't there now and again occasions when you find it *very* hard to live up to your reputation?"

then moves to its particulars, which build in an ascending order of emotionally laden incidents and details, and finally culminates with the speaker's preordained but decidedly passionate conclusion. And there can be no mistake about this last aspect: Shaw's speeches are passionate in their advocacy. That they have structural integrity—assembled as they are from sequentially interrelated ideas, rather than a patchwork of shouting and name-calling—does not in any way diminish the emotional fire of their expression; rather, the sturdy rhetorical structure should enhance your conviction and confidence—and hence, your righteous fervor.

Consider the following guidelines to the organization and rhetorical ploys of each speech, set in **boldface**. Important upglide inflections (pitch-lifted syllables), used to build lists of words or phrases, are indicated by carets (^), with the number of carets indicating the relative extent of the upward shift.

Important downward pitch shifts, indicative of argument closure, are marked with a downslash (\). (See Lesson 11 for a fuller explanation of inflections and builds.)

UNDERSHAFT: *[speaking of his cannon factory]* [seize the stage with a bold attack]   I see no darkness here, no dreadfulness.

[Announce your topic notion]   In your Salvation shelter I saw   [build the following four nouns]   poverty, misery, cold and hunger.

[Lift the following "You" to announce the beginning of a comparison] You give them   [build the following three nouns]   bread and treacle and dreams of heaven.   [Lift even more the following "I" as an antithesis to the preceding "You"]   ^^I give from thirty shillings a week to twelve thousand a year.

[Conclude the topic idea with an arresting metaphor/image, and once again lightly contrast the pronouns]   ^They find their own dreams; but ^^I look after the drainage.

[Expand the topic idea into a theology, so as to match Barbara's soul-saving Salvation Army creed]   And their souls! I save their souls just as I saved yours.

[Then turn theology on its head, redefining Christianity into economic bounty]   Oh, yes,   [build these next three clauses beginning with the word "I"]   I saved your soul; I   [build these three verbs, each followed by the object "you"]   fed you and clothed you and housed you. I took care that you should have money enough to live handsomely—more than enough; so that you could be   [build these three adjectives] wasteful, careless, generous.

[Conclude your new theology with a provocative statement, one that asks "which seven deadly sins"]   That saved your soul from the seven deadly sins.

[Seeing the quizzical looks around you, enumerate the "new" seven deadly sins of your iconoclastic theology]   Yes, the deadly seven. [build the following seven nouns, counting on your fingers—as Shaw requests—to vigorously emphasize the build]   *[Counting on his fingers]* Food, clothing, firing, rent, taxes, respectability and children.

[Putting "children" at the end of that list, implying that having children is the worst sin of all, is a deliberate shock. Take advantage of the shock to make your major point, which answers your topic notion at the opening.]   Nothing can lift those seven millstones from Man's neck but money; and the spirit cannot soar until the millstones are lifted.

[The pointed antithesis of "money" and "spirit"—set up by the repeated notion of lifted millstones—has proven successful; no one now contests your right to go on. Build the following three clauses beginning with the word "I," thus identifying yourself as one who acts—successfully—on the basis of this philosophy.]   ^I lifted them from your spirit. ^^I enabled Barbara to become Major Barbara; and ^^^I saved her from the crime of poverty.

[You've shocked them again: Money is not the root of all evil, but the source of salvation! Having proved that, now prove the opposite: that poverty—the opposite of money—is not sainted but evil.]   Yes, I call poverty a crime! The worst of crimes. All the other crimes are virtues beside it: all the other dishonors are chivalry itself by comparison.

[Build the following three verb clauses, beginning with "blights," "spreads," "strikes"]   Poverty blights whole cities; spreads horrible pestilences; strikes dead the very souls of all who come within   [build the following three nouns]   sight, sound, or smell of it. What you call crime is nothing:

[Build downward the following four nouns, dismissing each as more insignificant than the one preceding]   a ^^^murder here and a ^^theft there, a ^^blow now and a ^curse then: what do they matter? they are only the ^^accidents and ^illnesses of life:

[matter of fact: the baseline from which you are going into your major build of the speech]   there are not fifty genuine professional criminals in London.

[And here it comes]   But there are millions of [start building, first with the following five adjectives]   ^poor people, ^^abject people, ^^^dirty people, ill-^^^^fed, ill-^^^^^clothed people.   [Build further on the six clauses defined by the verbs "poison," "kill," "force," "organize," "rise," "drag," culminating in the emotion-laden noun, "abyss"]   They ^poison us morally and physically: they ^^kill the happiness of society: they ^^^force us to do away with our own liberties and to ^^^^organize unnatural cruelties for fear they should ^^rise against us and ^^^drag us down into their ab ^^^^yss.

[Conclude with the new maxim, worthy of inscribing in the Undershaft Bible]   Only ^^^fools fear crime: we ^^^^^all fear poverty!\

Students of rhetoric will be able to identify the devices used by Undershaft in this speech: *anaphora,* a series of phrases that begin identically ("I lifted . . . I enabled . . . I saved"; "they poison . . . they kill . . . they force"); *epistrophe,* a series of phrases that end identically ("poor people, abject people, dirty people"); and *ploce,* a patterned and emphatic repetition of the same word or words in a single sentence ("nothing can lift those seven millstones from Man's neck but money; and the spirit cannot soar until the millstones are lifted").

But you don't need to know these terms to recognize that a very skillful argumentative hand has shaped Undershaft's speech for maximum effectiveness. Effectiveness of assertion, once again, is the beginning and end of style in the Shaw dramatic canon.

Let us do the same sort of rhetorical analysis for Barbara's speech.

BARBARA: [Seize the stage with your topic sentence: Industrial might is pervasive; we can't solve the world's problems simply by ignoring them.]   Undershaft and Bodger: their hands stretch everywhere:

[Illustrate the topic sentence with details, building the three clauses beginning with "when," "when," and "if"]   ^when we feed a starving fellow ^^creature, it is with their bread, because there is no other bread; ^when we tend the ^^^sick, it is in the hospitals they endow; ^if we turn from the ^^^^churches they build, we must kneel on the stones of the streets they pave.

[Conclude by elaborating, on the basis of this evidence, your topic sentence]   As long as that lasts, there is no getting away from them.\

[Draw Dolly's attention to the major implication—in your lives—of this theme]   Turning our backs on ^Bodger and ^Undershaft is turning our backs on ^^life.

[Contrast past with present]   Oh, Dolly, ^you thought I was determined to turn my back on the wicked side of life, but there   [lift the preferred alternative]   ^^is no wicked side: life is all one. And ^^I [lift negation of "never"—to be picked up again at speech's end]   ^^never wanted to shirk my share in whatever evil must be endured, whether it be ^^sin or ^^^suffering.

[Build on your "life is all one" to a repudiation of the limitations of class consciousness, building these three sentences that employ the word "class"]   Oh, I wish I could ^cure you of middle-class ideas, Dolly. I ^^have no class: I come straight out of the heart of the whole people. If I were ^^^middle-class I should   [build on your refusal to "turn my back" in the last section]   "turn my back" on my father's business; and we should both live in an artistic drawing room,   [build the following four clauses, playing on the antitheses "you," "I," "both," and "neither of us"]   with ^you reading the reviews in one corner, and ^^I in the other at the piano, playing Schumann; ^^^both very superior persons, and ^^^^neither of us a bit of   [strongly punctuate your conclusion of this idea, but without giving up the floor]   ^^^^^use.

[Move to the positive: from what you won't to what you will do, referring to the two industrialists mentioned in your topic sentence]   Sooner than that, I would ^sweep out the guncotton shed, or be one of Bodger's ^^barmaids.\ [Your image—yourself as a common bartender,

given with a commanding downward inflection on the last syllable—so
shocks your fiancé that he is speechless, allowing you to continue. So
pose a rhetorical question]

Do you know what would have happened if you had refused Papa's offer?

[And answer it]   I should have given you up and married the man who
accepted it.

[And explain your answer]   After all, my dear old mother has more
sense than any of you.

[Build the repetition of "felt . . . felt" and then the repetition of "never,
never, never"]   I felt like her when I saw this place—felt that I must
have it—that never, never, never could I let it go. Only she thought it
was the . . .

[build the following four nouns/noun phrases describing your mother's
concerns]   ^houses and the ^^kitchen ranges and the ^^^linen and
^^^^china, when it was really all the   [top the previous build with
your single concern] ^^^^^human souls to be saved:

[Explain by setting up an antithesis]   not ^weak souls in   [build the
words starting with "s"]   ^starved bodies, ^^sobbing with gratitude
for a ^^^scrap of bread and treacle,   [nail the antithesis]   but   [build
the following four adjectives to a great peak on "uppish"—which even
suggests the top of a build]   ^^^full-fed, ^^^quarrelsome, ^^^snob-
bish, ^^^^uppish creatures, all   [enjoy the irony of "standing" vis-à-vis
"little"]   ^^^^^standing on their ^little rights and ^dignities,

[diminish this—and them—by racing through the text here, making
light of their concerns]   and-thinking-that-my-father-ought-to-be-great-
ly-obliged-to-them-for-making-so-much-money-for-him   [a mid-sen-
tence reversal of tone ending with a preliminary downshift: you're now
headed back to your final build]   and so he ought.\

[Return to your life-theme: Lay out the premise]   That is where salvation is really wanted.

[Get personal]   My father shall never throw it in my teeth again that
my converts were bribed with bread. *[She is transfigured.]*

[The ideas begin to speak through you, as in Shaw's description of
transfiguration. Build the escalating phrases beginning with the same
words by lifting the repeated verb, "rid"]   I have got ^rid of the bribe
of bread. I have got ^^rid of the bribe of heaven.

[Move, as your father did, into a new theology]   Let God's work be
done for its own sake: the work he had to create us to do because it
cannot be done except by living men and women.\

[**In this all-but-heretical theology, emphasize your antitheses in the contrasting personal pronouns for yourself and God—"I" and "him;" "me" and "him"**]   When ^I die, let ^^him be in my debt, not I in his; and let ^^^me forgive ^^^^him as becomes a woman of my rank.\

[**Announce your conclusion**]   Yes, Dolly, the way of life lies through the factory of death.\

[**Elaborate your conclusion in theological terms**]   Through the raising of hell to heaven and of man to God, through the unveiling of an eternal light in the Valley of the Shadow.\

[**Having successfully built up your preceding arguments, you were able to end each of your last four statements with commanding downward inflections; Dolly would never dare interrupt you at this point. Congratulations! You've cowed him into following your lead. Now get personal, posing a series of escalating rhetorical questions**]

[Seizing Dolly with both hands] Oh, did you think my courage would never come ^back? did you believe that I was a des^^erter? that I, [**build the three clauses employing the verbs "stood," "taken," and "talked"**]   who have ^stood in the streets, and ^^taken my people to my heart, and ^^^talked of the   [**build the following two adjectives**] ^^holiest and ^^^greatest things with them, could ever ^^^^turn back and chatter   [**build the alliterative and multisyllabic "foolishly" and "fashionable"**]   ^^foolishly to ^^fashionable people about ^^^^^nothing in a ^^^^^drawing room?   [**Explode into the final epizeuxis (immediate word repetition) of "nevers"**]   ^^^^^Never, ^^^^^never, ^^^^^never, ^^^^^never:

[**Conclude with a radical, emotion-laden image**]   Major Barbara will die with the colors.

The rhetorical structure is used not to convince us that you're a good actor but simply to convince us that *you're right!* That you have the solution for world happiness, ethics, and prosperity.

Don't just play these characters, *be* them. Try to convince us of the rightness of your arguments, points of view, and values. And, of course, the best way to convince us of your arguments is to show us that you're *passionate* about them. Shaw's theatre is not a seminar of ideas: It is a struggle to revolutionize the world.

As Shaw was a charismatic and compelling speaker on almost every cultural topic, so are his characters. Mastering a single Shaw speech will raise your persuasive capacity and rhetorical skill in almost every verbal act you undertake for the rest of your life. It will also set you up for excellence in performing in the works of contemporary dramatists whose plays bristle with fiery intellectual debate: writers such as Tony Kushner, Tom Stoppard,

Amy Freed, David Auburn, David Hare, Richard Greenberg, Alan Bennett, and Caryl Churchill.

Work on either of these speeches. Play them to a partner with your classmates gathered around. Use all of Shaw's words and rhetorical devices, and your own passion for your character's ideas, to captivate and convert those around you.

Anton Chekhov

We met Anton Chekhov and *Three Sisters* briefly in Lesson 8. The play was written in 1901, only four years before Shaw's *Major Barbara,* but the styles of these two plays (and their respective playwrights) could hardly be more different.

Whereas Shaw portrayed witty, confident, cogent debaters, eager to express themselves on the vital issues of their time, Chekhov, a doctor by training, studied (and reported on) human malaise: the awkwardness of social behavior, including confusion, indecision, and the bewildering clumsiness of verbal communication, particularly between the sexes. There are few topic sentences or rhetorical flourishes in Chekhov's dialogue but rather an unerring depiction of the deeper meanings that lie buried below language itself, a dramatic communication that we call, after Stanislavsky, *subtext.* Subtext is the text that is thought rather than spoken; it is implicit rather than explicit. It is a combination of hinting, soliciting, wondering, proposing, and shading; it is attractive because it is, if need be, deniable: If your hints are rejected, you cannot be accused of intrusion; if confronted, you can simply say, "I never meant *that!*"

A nineteenth-century Russian, Chekhov was also imbued with the ambient Slavic sentimentality of the era—nostalgia, compassion, and brooding rumination—as well as a wary distrust of smug intellectuality and of clinical, scientific objectivity. Indeed, this is one of the reasons Chekhov spurned the practice of medicine in favor of writing short stories and plays.

It is sometimes convenient, but entirely misleading, to think that Chekhov doesn't have a style but simply "writes the way people speak." It is true that Chekhov's dialogue sounds conversational and lifelike, particularly in its starts and stops, non sequiturs, and misplaced or broken-off expressions— very few of which would ever be found in a Shaw play, much less in a play by Sophocles, Shakespeare, Machiavelli, or Molière. But there is a precise architecture to these seeming conversations, which, though we call them "realistic" or "naturalistic," are crafted with great care. They are, in the first place, refined, the interchanges of a society in which conversing is still regarded as a social grace—particularly the conversations of people in or

Chekhovian realism   The three sisters huddle at a side door of their provincial home as one of the officers prepares to leave town, in the final scene of *Three Sisters*, as sketched by its original stage designer, V. Simov, for the Moscow Art Theatre in 1901.

around the professions: teaching, medicine, and, in *Three Sisters,* the military. Second, they are composed by Chekhov in an elegant impressionistic score that alternates and blends argument with romance, philosophy with jokiness, and laughter with tears—an immensely satisfying symphony of feeling, ideas, and action.

And the action of Chekhov, though generally inner and subtextual rather than blatant and overt, provides powerful storytelling. When performed well, Chekhov's plays are as mesmerizing as any in the dramatic canon. Chekhov's characters seek to win their battles with the same passion and intensity as Shaw's do, and though their battles are more ambiguously defined, and their victories fewer and farther between, they nonetheless struggle to meet life's challenges. That they are defeated on most occasions is Chekhov's genius; that they *try* to win, however, is his—and his actors'—glory. Through all the hemming and hawing of a Chekhov masterpiece, the apparent verbal (and often physical) clumsiness, audiences recognize the lively efforts to impress, the stabs at rhetoric from the less-than-skilled, and the vital passions that cannot be fully expressed.

One might indeed think of Chekhov's characters as trying hard to be Shavian characters but getting distracted, often by their sexual urge (always present in Chekhov, and generally absent in Shaw), or by their overwhelming sensations of loss, dread, and failure.

◆ SCENE   14–1

Chekhov's Symphony of Feeling

Study the following scene from *Three Sisters*. Lieutenant-Colonel Vershinin, recently arrived at a new, provincial garrison from his former posting in Moscow, is visiting with Masha, the eldest of the three Prozorov sisters whom he had met years ago when they lived in Moscow. They are both married now (Masha to Kuligin, a portion of whose earlier scene with her you may have worked on in Lesson 8), but they are also infatuated with each other. In this scene from Act 2, Vershinin and Masha are seen entering a quiet but not entirely walled-off corner of the Prozorov family living room; in mid-conversation as they enter, they sit, while servants can be seen or heard at a distance around them. All stage directions, dashes (—), and ellipses (. . .) are in the original.

MASHA: I don't know. Of course habit does a great deal. After Father's death, for instance, it was a long time before we could get used to having no orderlies in the house. But apart from habit, I think it's a feeling of justice makes me say so. Perhaps it is not so in other places, but in our town the most decent, honorable, and well-bred people are all in the army.

VERSHININ: I am thirsty. I should like some tea.

MASHA: *[glancing at the clock]* They will soon be bringing it. I was married when I was eighteen, and I was afraid of my husband because he was a teacher, and I had only just left school. In those days I thought him an awfully learned, clever, and important person. And now it is not the same, unfortunately. . . .

VERSHININ: Yes. . . . I see. . . .

MASHA: I am not speaking of my husband—I am used to him; but among civilians generally there are so many rude, ill-mannered, badly-brought-up people. Rudeness upsets and distresses me: I am unhappy when I see that a man is not refined, not gentle, not polite enough. When I have to be among the teachers, my husband's colleagues, it makes me quite miserable.

VERSHININ: Yes. . . . But to my mind, it makes no difference whether they are civilians or military men—they are equally uninteresting, in this town, anyway. It's all the same! If one listens to a man of the educated class here, civilian or military, he is worried to death by his wife, worried to death by his house, worried to death by his estate, worried to death by his horses. . . . A Russian is peculiarly given to exalted ideas, but why is it he always falls so short in his life? Why?

MASHA: Why?

VERSHININ: Why is he worried to death by his children and by his wife? And why are his wife and children worried to death by him?

MASHA: You are rather depressed this evening.

VERSHININ: Perhaps. . . . I've had no dinner today, and had nothing to eat since the morning. My daughter is not quite well, and when my little girls are ill I am consumed by anxiety; my conscience reproaches me for having given them such a mother. Oh, if you could have seen her today! She is a wretched creature! We began quarreling at seven o'clock in the morning, and at nine I slammed the door and went away. *[a pause]* I never talk about it. Strange, it's only to you I complain. *[kisses her hand]* Don't be angry with me. . . . Except for you I have no one—no one . . . *[a pause]*

MASHA: What a noise in the stove! Before Father died there was a howling in the chimney. There, just like that.

VERSHININ: Are you superstitious?

MASHA: Yes.

VERSHININ: That's strange. *[kisses her hand]* You are a splendid, wonderful woman. Splendid! Wonderful! It's dark, but I see the light in your eyes.

MASHA: *[moves to another chair]* It's lighter here.

VERSHININ: I love you—love, love . . . I love your eyes, your movements, I see them in my dreams. . . . Splendid, wonderful woman!

MASHA: *[laughing softly]* When you talk to me like that, for some reason I laugh, though I am frightened. . . . Please don't do it again. . . . *[in an undertone]* You may say it, though; I don't mind. . . . *[covers her face with her hands]* I don't mind. . . . Someone is coming. Talk of something else.

The scene begins with a characteristic Chekhovian demurral: "I don't know." We haven't heard the exact question Masha is responding to (it is presumably something about why the sisters like to invite military officers to their home), but the specifics don't really matter: What we soon realize is that Masha doesn't know what to do about Vershinin, her husband, or her life; she's in a quandary and fearful of making the wrong move—in any direction. "I don't know," in fact, is perhaps the commonest expression in Chekhov—just as it is nearly unknown in the plays of Shaw (whose characters *always* know whatever needs to be known).

But quandary or no, Masha wants to look her best and sound her best. And so does Vershinin, whose basic life-confusion is similar, though different in its specifics.

Let's explore a possible subtext—that which the characters are thinking and hoping, though not saying—for this scene. Such a subtext is also often called the character's *inner monologue*. It will be noted here in **bold** type. It represents a nonspoken text, the "inner voice" of the characters, not of the author of the play or this textbook. And since the inner voice of the character must be created by a contemporary actor, the inner monologue will necessarily be in the actor's, not the character's, normal "thinking" language.

MASHA: I don't know.   [I should come up with some sort of eloquent, even philosophical, response here, dammit! And smile, Masha! Let him see your sparkling eyes!]   Of course habit does a great deal.   [What a stupid thing to say! Oh, gosh, he's bored already. Let me play "abandoned orphan" again; let him see how well-off we used to be.]   After Father's death, for instance, it was a long time before we could get used to having no orderlies in the house.   [Uh-oh; he must think I've been spoiled with servants. I'll show him the righteousness of my motives.]   But apart from habit, I think it's a feeling of justice makes me say so.   [He's listening! I should say something nice to him. A compliment?]   Perhaps it is not so in other places, but in our town the most decent,   [Oh, hell, let's go all the way]   honorable, and well-bred people are all in the army. [Oh, please let him say something nice to me in return!]

VERSHININ: [Does she mean me? What can I say? I'll tell her I love her, yes! But how?]   I am thirsty.   [What's the matter with me?! Why can't I just . . . Well, I can't just keep sitting here grinning like an imbecile!] I should like some tea.   [Argh! Coward!]

MASHA: [He hates me!] *[glancing at the clock]* [But how can I get him tea without leaving his side? If I get up, I may never have a chance to talk to him alone again. Then it will be all over.]   They will soon be bringing it. [He's looking at me funny, though. Maybe he's just afraid to talk to me because I'm married. How can he know how unhappy I am? Can't he take a hint? I've been trying to show him what a jerk my husband is for the last two weeks. Well, what have I got to lose?]   I was married when I was eighteen, and I was afraid of my husband because he was a teacher, and I had only just left school. In those days I thought him an awfully learned, clever, and important person.   [I'll laugh, and see if he laughs too. . . . Well, he chuckled a bit! Maybe I'd better lay it out for him.]   And now it is not the same, unfortunately. . . .

VERSHININ: [Whew, she's pushing. I guess we're going there, yes. Wow, her eyes are beautiful. But it's still early for this, this step. . . . I don't know if I can . . . But I've got to say something! She'll think I'm an idiot! I am an idiot! IDIOT!]   Yes. . . . I see. . . .

MASHA: [Oh, I've frightened him! I'll take it back.]   I am not speaking of my husband— [uh-oh, that's too far back. . . . It's not that I find my husband stupid, just boring]   I am used to him; but among civilians generally   [no, I'll show Vershinin how much I hate people exactly like my husband; he'll get it!]   there are so many rude, ill-mannered,   [I'm on a roll: I hate all men but him!] badly-brought-up people. [He's excited! He loves this! I'll really show him how much I love him—by showing how much I hate my moronic husband and all his disgusting friends!] Rudeness upsets and distresses me: I am unhappy when I see that a man is not   [make sure Vershinin realizes I'm really talking about him]   refined, not gentle, not polite enough.   [I love you, Vershinin! I love you, and I'm miserable when I'm with anybody in the world but you!!!] When I have to be among the teachers, my husband's colleagues, it makes me quite miserable.

VERSHININ: [Boy, Masha is hot! When her eyes flash like that, and the blood comes up in her cheeks, I want to hold her, I want to touch her, I want to . . . But do I really want to go down this path? Now? There are so many people here today. And my children . . .]   Yes. . . . [Come on, Vershinin, get off the pot! Agree with her, at least.]   But to my mind, it makes no difference whether they are civilians or military men—they are equally uninteresting, in this town, anyway.   [Yes, this excites her. I'll build on this.]   It's all the same! If one listens to a man of the educated class here, civilian or military, he is worried to death by his wife, worried to death by his house,   [hey, this is great! It's better than sex! I'll keep building] worried to death by his estate,   [uhhhh, where do I go from here?]   worried to death by his horses. . . . [No, it isn't better than sex. It's just stupid rhetoric. I'm just a big phony. I'll never have the courage to make love to this woman. Well, I'll smile.]   A Russian is peculiarly given to exalted ideas, but why is it he always falls so short in his life? [I've completely lost her. Why do I get so intellectual? Dammit! She isn't answering. Come on, Masha, take me off the hook here!] Why?

MASHA: [God, he's fantastic. But what is he talking about? And what does he want me to say? I've got to say SOMETHING!]   Why?

VERSHININ: [She won't answer! She wants me to answer! I've forgotten the question! Something about . . . Yeah, that's it.]   Why is he worried to death by his children and by his wife?   [No! That wasn't it! She doesn't know what I'm talking about, does she?]   And why are his wife and children worried to death by him?   [Oh, God, I've completely lost her now! STUPID!]

MASHA: [He's so deep. And so miserable. But I'm making him miserable, aren't I? Let me see if I can lighten his mood. Smile, Masha!]   You are rather depressed this evening.   [Did I just say that? What an idiot!]

VERSHININ: [Thank God, she's let me off the hook!] Perhaps. . . . [Well, a second chance. I'll just blame everything on my wife; that's what we have in common: Blame the spouse! But I can't seem depressed—that will make her blame herself. I'll laugh! Ha! Ha!] I've had no dinner today, and had nothing to eat since the morning. [Ha! Ha! Good, she's laughing with me! I'll try to laugh this off as well; we're just two old married folk, complaining about our spouses! Ha! Ha! Haha!] My daughter is not quite well, and when my little girls are ill I am consumed by anxiety; my conscience reproaches me for having given them such a mother. [Hahahah! Oh, well said, Vershinin! This is a lot better than blaming yourself. Pour it on, boy!] Oh, if you could have seen her today! [This is really funny!] She is a wretched creature! [And this is even funnier.] We began quarreling at seven o'clock in the morning, [and now I'll show her what a hero I was in meeting this challenge!] and at nine I slammed the door and went away. *[a pause]* [Masha's not laughing anymore, but this is exhilarating . . . she's moved. I think she loves me. I've never seen a woman look at me like this before.] I never talk about it. [Oh, hell, let her know.] Strange, it's only to you I complain. [Go for it, guy! On the hand. Formal. She can't complain about this. It only means what she makes of it.] *[kisses her hand]* Don't be angry with me. . . . [She's not angry at all. She's crying! Tell her! Tell her! You'll never have another chance! It's now or never!] Except for you I have no one— [TELL HER AGAIN!] no one . . . *[a pause]*

MASHA: [I've waited all my life for this, but what . . . What do I do now? I SHOULD SMILE! I'm not going to have an affair, am I? Or am I? What am I supposed to do? KEEP SMILING! Does he pick me up and carry me away now? Am I supposed to kiss his hand? Why doesn't he DO something? He's just staring into my eyes, waiting, waiting, for, for what? I can't just sit silently here smiling like an idiot! I'm starting to cry, dammit! . . . Ah, thank God, something to talk about.] What a noise in the stove! [He must think I'm crazy, changing the subject like that! I'd better explain why it's important. But it's not important! Well, I'll lie, what the hell.] Before Father died there was a howling in the chimney. [He bought it. Why not? There's the sound again . . .] There, just like that.

VERSHININ: [All right, the cat's out of the bag, there's no stopping now. But what should I say? Damn the noise in the chimney; she probably made it up.] Are you superstitious? [Why did I ask her that?]

MASHA: [I think he's hoping that I say "yes"] Yes.

VERSHININ: [Pure instinct to ask her that! Yes: howling, chimney, father dying . . . It's fate, isn't it? We're fated. She's a creature of fate, not bound by conventional morality. I'll test her.] That's strange! [She's smiling again! She agrees; she's strange! I'm strange too! So let's throw caution to that strange wind engulfing us! Her father's dead, we're both

strange, and the winds of fate are blowing us away! I'll kiss her hand
again. Her beautiful hand!] *[kisses her hand]*   You are a splendid, wonderful woman. [Elaborate, Vershinin!] Splendid! [Come on,
dammit, elaborate!] Wonderful! [Well, I'm not Cyrano, but she
seems to be buying it anyway. I'll think of something real cool to tell
her.]   It's dark, but I see the light in your eyes.

MASHA: [I'm completely paralyzed. I can't move. But does this mean we
have to have sex now? He's beautiful. This is funny. This is like in a
play. Let me see if I can get up.] *[moves to another chair]* [I better explain why I just did that.]   It's lighter here.

VERSHININ: [God, I haven't done this in ten years.]   I love you—
[Elaborate, idiot!] love, love . . . I love your eyes, your movements,
[now I'm on track] I see them in my dreams. . . . [Does this mean we
have to sleep together?]   Splendid, wonderful woman! [Didn't I just
say that?]

MASHA: [God, he's better at this than I thought! If he thinks I'm helpless, I
could be ruined. Show control, Masha, show you're a woman of the
world. Laugh a little . . .] *[laughing softly]* [That was too much! Let him
know you LOVE this.]   When you talk to me like that, for some reason
I laugh, though   ["be gentle, baby, I've never done this"]   I am frightened. . . . [What does he think: I'm a loose woman?]   Please don't do it
again . . . [Oh God, he's taking me seriously! He's moving away. NO!
COME BACK!] *[in an undertone]* You may say it, though; I don't mind.
. . . [I'll submit; it's all his doing; I had nothing to do with this. I'm sim-
ply blown by fate; it was the howling in the chimney; IT'S NOT MY
FAULT!] *[covers her face with her hands]*   I don't mind. . . . [A NOISE!
And it IS my fault! Shut up! I'm a fallen woman!]   Someone is coming.
Talk of something else.

It should be clear, even if an entirely different subtext were to elicit these
lines, that the action of *Three Sisters* takes place largely *in the minds of the
characters*—though such inner action is of course exemplified by the behavior (body language, expression, movement, gesture, inflection, tone of
voice) of the actors in performance. The ideal of naturalistic acting is simply
to vigorously use a character's tactics in pursuit of his or her goals, but you
must also enter into the specific world of the characters to see how those
goals, and more specifically the tactics, have evolved. Masha's and
Vershinin's tactics are probably different from yours and those of your fellow classmates. They may include

◆ Expressed gentility of spirit and refinement of manners appropriate
  among the professional and landowning classes in late tsarist Russia

- Regular entertaining of many visitors, for extended afternoons and evenings, and without set programs or activities, in the country homes of these classes
- Formal clothing and formal modes of behavior and conversation, expected when entertaining visitors in such homes
- Appreciation of the art of philosophizing: generalizing principles out of daily life occurrences
- Fascination with "the Russian character," an enduring topic of profound conversation
- Unquestioned acceptance (by the majority of the professional and landowning class) of the inborn superiority of the upper classes
- Admiration of military officers, selected from aristocratic and gentleman ranks: generally well-traveled and educated
- A polite disdain for working and servant classes; exceptions are rare but noteworthy when they occur

The direct contrast of this formal and refined code of conduct with the internal confusion—bordering on chaos—of the human souls Chekhov depicts creates the paralyzing ambivalence of the typical Chekhov character, whose aspirations run directly counter to his or her fears and feelings of inadequacy. The fears and feelings contribute, to Chekhov's (and thereby the actor's) work, a profound sadness, but the social refinement, and the will to transcend despair, create the bright Chekhovian gaiety. "Laughter through tears" is the cliché by which actors know Chekhov's demand, but the cliché is also a fundamental truth: Chekhov's characters are trying, often desperately, to seize their share of happiness. They may fail, by play's end, but the struggle goes on right up to the final curtain—and beyond. It is, finally, the laughter that should be played by Chekhov's actors, for the tears will take care of themselves.

Oscar Wilde

Of all the playwrights of the modern (that is, post-1850) theatre, probably none more exemplifies the word *style* to the ordinary playgoer than Oscar Wilde. If Shaw repudiated art for art's sake, Wilde embraced it. Indeed, his personal life was a work of art—and controversy. Satirized in a 1891 Gilbert and Sullivan operetta as a man who would "walk down Picadilly [a main shopping street in London] / with a poppy or a lily / in his medieval hand," Wilde was famously flamboyant, reportedly explaining to a New York customs officer that "I have nothing to declare except my genius." It was indeed his inability to restrain himself from such witty and flippant remarks that, during notorious trials related to his homosexuality, alienated the author from the British court and public and led to his career-dooming incarceration—as is brilliantly documented in Moises Kaufman's 1997 play, *Gross Indecency: The Three Trials of Oscar Wilde.*

A true belletrist (person of letters) of the Belle Epoque, Wilde earned wide public notoriety in a wide variety of literary fields: as horror novelist (*The Picture of Dorian Gray*), prison poet ("The Ballad of Reading Gaol"), and dramatist whose works range from Victorian melodramas to political satires to the macabre tragedy of *Salome* (revived in Los Angeles in 2006 by actor Al Pacino). But none of Wilde's plays endure with the vitality of his brilliant comedy of manners, *The Importance of Being Earnest,* often considered the wittiest play ever written, and probably today's single-most-produced English-language drama between Shakespeare's age and the twentieth century.

"Comedy of manners" generally describes a style of relentlessly witty dramas modeled after Restoration comedy (see Lesson 13) and the eighteenth-century plays of Richard Brinsley Sheridan (*School for Scandal, The Rivals)* and Oliver Goldsmith (*She Stoops to Conquer).* Essentially, a comedy of manners depicts, with great charm and verve, and often a barely hidden satirical edge, the elegant diction, wry put-downs, and ironic epigrams of cultured urban aristocrats. Elements of such comedy certainly appear frequently in George Bernard Shaw (*Misalliance* and *Getting Married* have brilliant scenes in this style), but no English play fulfills the model as does *The Importance of Being Earnest.** Even the title of Wilde's play is a witty play on words, for the play's most fundamental subject, as Peter Thompson points out in the *Cambridge Guide to Theatre,* is the importance of *not* being Earnest—"Earnest" being, in this play, the name of a fictitious character rather than a synonym for "serious" or "sincere."

Few writers have created scenes of such continuously amusing repartee between characters of the same sex. Such scenes are typical of the style because their characters can be superficially chummy while socially competitive: the veneer of agreeability covering a spirited rivalry. The following two scenes from *Earnest* are between young aristocrats.

◆ S C E N E   14–2

Wilde's Comedy of (Male) Manners

ALGERNON: How are you, my dear Ernest? What brings you up to town?

JACK: Oh, pleasure, pleasure! What else should bring one anywhere? Eating as usual, I see, Algy!

---

* I cannot help noting that all of these "English" playwrights—Wilde, Sheridan, Goldsmith, and Shaw—were actually Irishmen.

ALGERNON: *[Stiffly.]* I believe it is customary in good society to take some slight refreshment at five o'clock. Where have you been since last Thursday?

JACK: *[Sitting down on the sofa.]* In the country.

ALGERNON: What on earth do you do there?

JACK: *[Pulling off his gloves.]* When one is in town one amuses oneself. When one is in the country one amuses other people. It is excessively boring.

ALGERNON: And who are the people you amuse?

JACK: *[Airily.]*   Oh, neighbors, neighbors.

ALGERNON: Got nice neighbors in your part of Shropshire?

JACK: Perfectly horrid! Never speak to one of them.

ALGERNON: How immensely you must amuse them! *[Goes over and takes sandwich.]* By the way, Shropshire is your county, is it not?

JACK: Eh? Shropshire? Yes, of course. Hallo! Why all these cups? Why cucumber sandwiches? Why such reckless extravagance in one so young? Who is coming to tea?

ALGERNON: Oh! merely Aunt Augusta and Gwendolen.

JACK: How perfectly delightful!

ALGERNON: Yes, that is all very well; but I am afraid Aunt Augusta won't quite approve of your being here.

JACK: May I ask why?

ALGERNON: My dear fellow, the way you flirt with Gwendolen is perfectly disgraceful. It is almost as bad as the way Gwendolen flirts with you.

JACK: I am in love with Gwendolen. I have come up to town expressly to propose to her.

ALGERNON: I thought you had come up for pleasure?. . . I call that business.

JACK: How utterly unromantic you are!

ALGERNON: I really don't see anything romantic in proposing. It is very romantic to be in love. But there is nothing romantic about a definite proposal. Why, one may be accepted. One usually is, I believe. Then the excitement is all over. The very essence of romance is uncertainty. If ever I get married, I'll certainly try to forget the fact.

JACK: I have no doubt about that, dear Algy. The Divorce Court was specially invented for people whose memories are so curiously constituted.

ALGERNON: Oh! there is no use speculating on that subject. Divorces are made in Heaven

◆ SCENE   14–3

Wilde's Comedy of (Female) Manners

CECILY: *[Rather shy and confidingly.]* Dearest Gwendolen, there is no reason why I should make a secret of it to you. Our little county newspaper is sure to chronicle the fact next week. Mr. Ernest Worthing and I are engaged to be married.

GWENDOLEN: *[Quite politely, rising.]* My darling Cecily, I think there must be some slight error. Mr. Ernest Worthing is engaged to me. The announcement will appear in the *Morning Post* on Saturday at the latest.

CECILY: *[Very politely, rising.]* I am afraid you must be under some misconception. Ernest proposed to me exactly ten minutes ago. *[Shows diary.]*

GWENDOLEN: *[Examines diary through her lorgnette carefully.]* It is certainly very curious, for he asked me to be his wife yesterday afternoon at 5.30. If you would care to verify the incident, pray do so. *[Produces diary of her own.]* I never travel without my diary. One should always have something sensational to read in the train. I am so sorry, dear Cecily, if it is any disappointment to you, but I am afraid I have the prior claim.

CECILY: It would distress me more than I can tell you, dear Gwendolen, if it caused you any mental or physical anguish, but I feel bound to point out that since Ernest proposed to you he clearly has changed his mind.

GWENDOLEN: *[Meditatively.]* If the poor fellow has been entrapped into any foolish promise I shall consider it my duty to rescue him at once, and with a firm hand.

CECILY: *[Thoughtfully and sadly.]* Whatever unfortunate entanglement my dear boy may have got into, I will never reproach him with it after we are married.

GWENDOLEN: Do you allude to me, Miss Cardew, as an entanglement? You are presumptuous. On an occasion of this kind it becomes more than a moral duty to speak one's mind. It becomes a pleasure.

CECILY: Do you suggest, Miss Fairfax, that I entrapped Ernest into an engagement? How dare you? This is no time for wearing the shallow mask of manners. When I see a spade I call it a spade.

GWENDOLEN: *[Satirically.]* I am glad to say that I have never seen a spade. It is obvious that our social spheres have been widely different.

With a partner of the same sex, choose roles and read the scene aloud. Then reverse roles and do it again. And again. And again! Then learn the lines *exactly as written* and rehearse the scene for performance, imagining an elegant morning room in a London apartment (for the first scene) or an elegant garden in a country manor (for the second) as your setting.

Perhaps the greatest difficulty in learning to play a comedy of manners is *to make it seem as though you have been speaking this way for your entire adult life.* Simple repetition will enable you to get a start on speaking the speech of these upper-class English men and women who are (quite probably) more or less your own age.

"Manners," in a comedy devoted to them, are not seen by the characters as affectations. The characters in *Earnest* do not consider themselves superficial, even if we do. Indeed, they think of *other* characters in the play as superficial—as those who, as Cecily says, wear "the shallow mask of manners," and who, as Jack says, exhibit "reckless extravagance." Rather, the Wildean characters in this play believe themselves committed, as Gwendolyn declares, to "a moral duty to speak one's mind." In other words, they consider themselves to be just as sincere and unaffected as we think *we* are. Thus actors playing these roles must also play their characters' *belief in their own sincerity.*

Making your initial headway toward performing this play does not require rigorous historical research.* Other than a few strictly British references, its language is easily understood by the average American reader. What is crucial for the beginning actor approaching this material is rather finding a comfort level with a level of social pride—particularly pride in one's "proper" linguistic and pronunciation skills—that is rarely seen in contemporary American society, where pride in "improper" speech is far more common (as, for instance, in performance modes such as hip-hop and stand-up comedy).

In a professional production, directors normally require this play to be done with an upper-class English accent (sometimes known as "Received

---

* Shropshire is a hilly and picturesque region west of London; a lorgnette is a pair of glasses that fashionable people of era held up to their eyes with a stick; and "tea" here refers to a traditional afternoon snack, usually tea and delicate sandwiches served on formal china, that was enjoyed during the era by upper-class persons in what Algy calls "good society."

Pronunciation"). If you and your partner are not already adept at this, you should probably forgo it. Your comfort level with the language is more crucial, at this entry point to style, than are professional dialect skills.

Concentrate instead on these elements:

◆ Imagine your acting partner as your social inferior—in dress, deportment, intelligence, and language style. Allow this attitude to make you feel, by contrast, superior. Don't affect an attitude of superiority, however; just imagine the inferiority of the other.

◆ Imagine those who may pop into the room—servants, for example—as *very* inferior, and imagine that they are in awe of your social standing, speech patterns, wealth, breeding, and overall elegance.

◆ Practice all Wilde's stage directions—pulling off your gloves, reading through your lorgnette, taking a sandwich from a silver tray, sitting on a sofa—until you can execute them with maximum grace, skill, and elegance. Imagine you are doing this before an audience of inferiors—and giving, by your example, important demonstrations of proper manners and social etiquette.

◆ Practice moving and speaking with Wilde's adverbial instructions: stiffly, airily, meditatively, carefully, thoughtfully, quite politely, *very* politely (and notice the difference between the two). And do more than merely follow these adverbs. *Teach* your acting partner—and everyone watching you—how these adverbs *should* be executed in the best societies.

◆ With the beaming confidence of one who believes that his or her own words are golden, smilingly ridicule the "shallower" opinions and expressions (on romance, on the country, on country newspapers) of those characters surrounding you. There is no need to sneer, argue, plead, or whine: All others are inferior, and you (in your own mind!) only need to lead by example. Maintain your smile throughout; allow no one to see that you have been bested, or ever could be bested. Never seek pity!

Following those tips, and learning Wilde's language *exactly,* seek to make your acting partner follow your lead in all things, while also amusing any servants or unexpected visitors who may happen to be passing through. Play this scene before an audience and realize that they, too, are your inferiors.

15

The Hypertheatre

The final two decades of the nineteenth century were the high-water mark of realistic theatre, particularly in Europe, where André Antoine formed his Free Theatre (Théâtre Libre), which was so realistic it was known as "Antoine's back"—for Antoine was so inclined to realism that, as an actor, he turned his back to the audience when speaking to characters upstage of him. A counter-revolution practically exploded at the turn of the twentieth century, however, when authors and directors, professing the goals of symbolism, surrealism, expressionism, and other isms, sought to restore extravagant theatrical imagination to their dramatic creations. The counterrevolution was so successful that many of the early realist giants, including playwrights Henrik Ibsen, August Strindberg, and even George Bernard Shaw, began writing surrealist, fantastical, and even (in the case of Shaw) self-satirizing works.

What all these works had in common was an open exploitation of the theatrical medium, which often turned the theatre from being a mere vehicle for drama into the subject of drama itself. Characters, instead of pretending to interact with each other within a room in which—as was said at the time—"the fourth wall had been removed," now began to face the audience and address them directly, often breaking into song, verse, vaudeville routines, or didactic speeches. Audiences were confronted with plays that included references to other plays and actors who would comment on the roles they were playing. Often the actors were traditional performers—clowns, orators, and mimes—playing on antique stages contained within the newer plays that framed them.

In the mid-twentieth century, Romanian–French playwright Eugene Ionesco coined the term *antitheatre* for dramatic works, such as his own, that repudiated the notion that an actor should consistently and authentically represent a human character. His plays were consequently called "absurd," and the term stuck, defining a new genre of his particularly antirealistic style. At the same time but for different reasons, German playwright–director Bertolt Brecht also repudiated realism, using the term *verfremdung,* "distancing" (initially translated as "alienation"*) to describe an acting style in which actors would make clear that they were *not* the characters they played and were only "playing" them from a distance. As Ionesco's drama became known as the "theatre of the absurd," Brecht's is called the "theatre of distancing."

But while Ionesco and Brecht—and like dramatists of their time—sought to transcend realism, they were not opposed to theatre.† Far from it: Rather than standing against theatre, Ionesco's and Brecht's plays *incorporated* "the theatrical" into their dramas and gloried in manipulating the theatre's theatricality for philosophical or social purposes.

What should we call this genre? Scholars generally use the terms *metatheatre* (*meta* means "beyond") to describe plays that turn on themselves and comment on their own dramatic form. Shakespeare provides classic examples, as when the actor playing Hamlet talks to actors playing the Players about the art of playing, and or when the actor playing Fabian in *Twelfth Night* exclaims, "If this were played upon a stage now, I could condemn it as an improbable fiction." But the twentieth century took this to more extreme levels that affect not just the way the play is written but the way it is played, and for this reason I prefer the term *hypertheatre,* because it incorporates and seeks to heighten (*hyper* means "above," "over") every aspect of theatrical performance: acting, directing, and design. Hypertheatre is an unashamedly *theatricalized* theatre, and it demands a hypertheatricalized form of acting.

Hypertheatre is not new. There is nothing in Ionesco or Brecht that cannot be found in the 2,500-year-old plays of Aristophanes, a Greek master of Old Comedy who, from the fifth century B.C., employed dramatic formats and characters in the same fashion. But since the end of World War II, the hypertheatre has become a dominant theatrical format, popular onstage, and generating several of the techniques of what many critics refer to as postmodern drama.

We next look at—and work with—the two significant trends that formed the foundation blocks of hypertheatre.

---

* The translation *alienation* is still used, but *distancing* or *estrangement* is less misleading, as Brecht's notion is nearly the opposite of "social disaffection," which is the most common understanding of *alienation* in contemporary casual speech.
† "In the end I realized that I did not write 'antitheatre' but theatre," said Ionesco, claiming that he was really creating a "new-classicism." Cited in Rosette C. Lamonte, *Ionesco's Imperatives: The Politics of Culture* (Ann Arbor: University of Michigan Press, 1993), p. 201.

Mr. and Mrs. Martin in the original (and ongoing) Nicolas Bataille production of *The Bald Soprano* at the Théâtre de la Huchette, shown here in a 1985 performance. (Photo © Laurencine Lot)

Eugene Ionesco: Theatre of the Absurd

Theatre of the absurd was defined by Martin Esslin in his 1962 book of that title, which covered plays of several stylistically linked dramatists, principally Eugene Ionesco and Samuel Beckett. The Romanian-born Ionesco and the Irish-born Beckett lived and wrote most of their work in Paris, mainly in the last half of the twentieth century. Neither writer used the term *absurd* to describe their works (nor did most of the others Esslin charted), but the term stuck to identify plays of the era that treated the universe as essentially incomprehensible.*

---

*   The term *absurd* originated in Albert Camus's 1942 essay, *The Myth of Sisyphus,* in which the French philosopher–playwright proposed that humans are unable to stop seeking answers about the universe even after they discover it is useless do so. This "absurd condition," Camus proposed, is like the destiny of the mythical Sisyphus—always pushing his rock up the mountain despite knowing that when it gets to the top it will roll down the other side.

Although Beckett, both by common consensus and by the distinction of a Nobel Prize for Literature, is by far the greatest of the absurdist authors, Ionesco is absurdism's most characteristic theatrical practitioner and was the first to make a powerful appearance on the world stage. His *Bald Soprano,* which initially premiered in Paris in 1950, returned to the Paris stage in 1957 where it continues to run to this present day. It has been translated into dozens of languages and is one of the great classics of the contemporary world stage.

Below is a selection from that play, in its English translation by Donald M. Allen. See if you can determine why this play has been running continuously for more than fifty years.

◆ S C E N E   **15–1**

Theatre of the Absurd: Mr. and Mrs. Martin

[MR. AND MRS. MARTIN *sit facing each other, without speaking. They smile timidly at each other.*]

MR. MARTIN: Excuse me, madam, but it seems to me, unless I'm mistaken, that I've met you somewhere before.

MRS. MARTIN: I too, sir. It seems to me that I've met you somewhere before.

MR. MARTIN: Was it, by any chance, at Manchester that I caught a glimpse of you, madam?

MRS. MARTIN: That is very possible. I am originally from the city of Manchester. But I do not have a good memory, sir. I cannot say whether it was there that I caught a glimpse of you or not!

MR. MARTIN: Good God, that's curious! I, too, am originally from the city of Manchester, madam!

MRS. MARTIN: That is curious!

MR. MARTIN: Isn't that curious! Only, I, madam, I left the city of Manchester about five weeks ago.

MRS. MARTIN: That is curious! What a bizarre coincidence! I, too, sir, I left the city of Manchester about five weeks ago.

MR. MARTIN: Madam, I took the 8:30 morning train which arrives in London at 4:45.

MRS. MARTIN: That is curious! How very bizarre! And what a coincidence! I took the same train, sir, I too.

MR. MARTIN: Good Lord, how curious! Perhaps then, madam, it was on the train that I saw you?

MRS. MARTIN: It is indeed possible; that is, not unlikely. It is plausible and, after all, why not!—But I don't recall it, sir!

MR. MARTIN: I traveled second class, madam. There is no second class in England, but I always travel second class.

MRS. MARTIN: That is curious! How very bizarre! And what a coincidence! I, too, sir, I traveled second class.

MR. MARTIN: How curious that is! Perhaps we did meet in second class, my dear lady!

MRS. MARTIN: That is certainly possible, and it is not at all unlikely. But I do not remember very well, my dear sir!

MR. MARTIN: My seat was in coach No. 8, compartment 6, my dear lady.

MRS. MARTIN: How curious that is! My seat was also in coach No. 8, compartment 6, my dear sir!

MR. MARTIN: How curious that is and what a bizarre coincidence! Perhaps we met in compartment 6, my dear lady?

MRS. MARTIN: It is indeed possible, after all! But I do not recall it, my dear sir!

MR. MARTIN: To tell the truth, my dear lady, I do not remember it either, but it is possible that we caught a glimpse of each other there, and as I think of it, it seems to me even very likely.

MRS. MARTIN: Oh! truly, of course, truly, sir!

MR. MARTIN: How curious it is! I had seat No. 3, next to the window, my dear lady.

MRS. MARTIN: Oh good Lord, how curious and bizarre! I had seat No 6, next to the window, across from you, my dear sir.

MR. MARTIN: Good God, how curious that is and what a coincidence! We were then seated facing each other, my dear lady! It is there that we must have seen each other!

MRS. MARTIN: How curious it is! It is possible, but I do not recall it, sir!

MR. MARTIN: To tell the truth, my dear lady, I do not remember it either. However, it is very possible that we saw each other on that occasion.

MRS. MARTIN: It is true, but I am not at all sure of it, sir.

MR. MARTIN: Dear madam, were you not the lady who asked me to place her suitcase in the luggage rack and who thanked me and gave me permission to smoke?

MRS. MARTIN: But of course, that must have been I, sir. How curious it is, how curious it is, and what a coincidence!

MR. MARTIN: How curious it is, how bizarre, what a coincidence! And well, well, it was perhaps at that moment that we came to know each other, madam?

MRS. MARTIN: How curious it is and what a coincidence! It is indeed possible, my dear sir! However, I do not believe that I recall it.

MR. MARTIN: Nor do I, madam. [*A moment of silence. The clock strikes twice, then once.*] Since coming to London, I have resided in Bromfield Street, my dear lady.

MRS. MARTIN: How curious that is, how bizarre! I, too, since coming to London, I have resided in Bromfield Street, my dear sir.

MR. MARTIN: How curious that is, well then, well then, perhaps we have seen each other in Bromfield Street, my dear lady.

MRS. MARTIN: How curious that is, how bizarre! It is indeed possible, after all! But I do not recall it my dear sir.

MR. MARTIN: I reside at No. 19, my dear lady.

MRS. MARTIN: How curious that is. I also reside at No. 19, my dear sir.

MR. MARTIN: Well then, well then, well then, well then, perhaps we have seen each other in that house, dear lady?

MRS. MARTIN: It is indeed possible but I do not recall it, dear sir.

MR. MARTIN: My flat is on the fifth floor, No. 8, my dear lady.

MRS. MARTIN: How curious it is, good Lord, how bizarre! And what a coincidence! I too reside on the fifth floor, in flat No. 8, dear sir!

MR. MARTIN: [*musing*] How curious it is, how curious it is, how curious it is, and what a coincidence! You know, in my bedroom there is a bed, and it is covered with a green eiderdown.° This room, with the bed   °*quilt* and the green eiderdown, is at the end of the corridor between the w.c.° and the bookcase, dear lady.   °*toilet*

MRS. MARTIN: What a coincidence, good Lord, what a coincidence! My
bedroom, too, has a bed with a green eiderdown and is at the end of the
corridor, between the w.c., dear sir, and the bookcase.

MR. MARTIN: How bizarre, curious, strange! Then, madam, we live in
the same room and we sleep in the same bed, dear lady. It is perhaps
there that we have met!

MRS. MARTIN: How curious it is and what a coincidence! It is indeed
possible that we have met there, and perhaps even last night. But I do
not recall it, dear sir!

MR. MARTIN: I have a little girl, my little daughter, she lives with me,
dear lady. She is two years old, she's blond, she has a white eye and a
red eye, she is very pretty, her name is Alice, dear lady.

MRS. MARTIN: What a bizarre coincidence! I, too, have a little girl. She is
two years old, has a white eye and a red eye, she is very pretty, and her
name is Alice too, dear sir!

MR. MARTIN: How curious it is and what a coincidence! And bizarre!
Perhaps they are the same, dear lady!

MRS. MARTIN: How curious it is! It is indeed possible, dear sir. [*A rather
long moment of silence. The clock strikes 29 times.*]

MR. MARTIN: [*after having reflected at length, gets up slowly and unhur-
riedly, moves toward Mrs. Martin, who, surprised by his solemn air, has
also gotten up very quietly.*] Then, dear lady, I believe that there can be
no doubt about it, we have seen each other before and you are my own
wife. Elizabeth, I have found you again.

[*MRS. MARTIN approaches MR. MARTIN without haste. They embrace
without expression. The clock strikes once, very loud. The MARTINS do
not hear it.*]

MRS. MARTIN: Donald, it's you, darling!

[They sit together in the same armchair, their arms around each
other, and fall asleep.]

It is easy to see why, in comparison to earlier playwrights discussed in this
book, Ionesco's work may at first glance be passed off as a joke: "absurd" in
the ordinary sense of the word. But that is not the case: No mere joke can attract a paying audience eight times a week for fifty-plus years. Made vividly
theatrical by inspired acting and directing (primarily by Nicolas Bataille,

who both directed and played Mr. Martin), *Bald Soprano* created an electrifying impact on Parisian audiences, and proved fundamental to the birth of hypertheatre.

What is hypertheatrical about it? First, *Bald Soprano* is obviously not a normal human conversation but a totally theatrical one. It was written not from life, nor to be perceived as life, but as a text to be perceived as text—a theatrical contrivance based on the art of performance itself.

The specific form of Mr. and Mrs. Martin's exchange—filled as it is with repetitions of clichés and nonsensical phrases—is, on its surface, a cross between French vaudeville and English music-hall banter, influenced, the author explained, by the popular Guignol puppet shows for children (still played regularly in the Luxembourg Gardens in Paris) that Ionesco had adored as a four-year-old. The playwright also acknowledged his debt to early Marx Brothers films, also wildly popular in France during his early years.

There are other classic performative patterns in this dialogue, however. It is an abstraction of a blind-date conversation or a courting ritual, in which each participant begins with the tiniest verbal overtures that head toward a meeting of minds en route to a meeting of bodies. It is a mystery drama: a whodunit in which Mr. and Mrs. Martin collectively seek to close in on a secret "truth" that eludes them until the last minute. It is a parody of "proper English reserve" as seen by a radical continental iconoclast. And, perhaps most important, it is the failed effort to approach the messy and inchoate reality of human life (sex, marriage, creation of new life) within the intellectual medium of language.

In this last sense, it is not only absurd in the sense of Camus's essay, but "nauseating," in the language of existentialist philosopher Jean-Paul Sartre, who was also flourishing in Paris at this time. Sartre centered his notion on humanity's attempt to encapsulate *existence* (essentially reality, as perceived by our senses) and *essence* (essentially language, as perceived by our mind). The effort, Sartre maintained, was doomed, and pursuing it makes us want to throw up. For his part, Ionesco was inspired to write the play because of his failed attempt to learn English from an English–French Conversation Manual for Beginners. "The language had become disjointed," he reported; "words, now absurd, had been emptied of their content.* He converted Camus's and Sartre's philosophical notions into hypertheatre.

But Ionesco's works are not nauseating; the absurdity of life, to him, provides dramatic fodder that is both theatrically funny and philosophically challenging.

---

* Eugene Ionesco, *Notes and Counternotes,* trans. Donald Watson (New York: Grove Press, 1964), pp. 178–179.

Ionesco's theatre is not a declaration of the absurdity of human life, but rather its exploitation in theatrical zaniness, where words are emptied of their content, characters divorced from their psychology, and the basic processes of life are replaced by music-hall patter and Marx Brothers shenanigans.

In *The Bald Soprano* we see life, therefore, not through subtext or rhetoric but through the dramaturgical *pattern* itself: in this scene, a relentless, if glacially slow, dramatic build.

It begins with silence, then timid smiles, and then an apologetic overture:

MR. MARTIN: Excuse me, madam. . .

followed immediately by a redundant qualifier:

. . . it seems to me, unless I'm mistaken . . .

This most hesitant of beginnings—a parody, unquestionably, of what the French consider the ridiculous reserve of English gentlemen—concludes with the most common of pickup lines:

. . . that I've met you somewhere before?

The entire scene that follows—all fifty-one speeches—is an unremittingly steady escalation of invocations (questions and statements implying questions) leading toward the answer to that initial timorous question, "I've met you somewhere before?*

The tools of this build are repetition, circumlocution, and cliché. Each character selects, and builds upon, phrases of the other.

"I am originally from the city of Manchester. . . ."

"Good God, that's curious! I, too, am originally from the city of Manchester. . ."

"That is curious!"

"Isn't that curious! Only, I, madam, I left the city of Manchester about five weeks ago."

Notice that not merely are single words merely repeated. Whole phrases are repeated ("city of Manchester," for instance—when simply "Manchester" or even "there" would suffice in a real-life conversation).

---

* It turns out to be the *wrong* answer, actually. It will later be revealed that the daughter they speak of is not "theirs" at all, for Donald's daughter has a white right eye and a red left one, and Elizabeth's daughter has the reverse! The absurd triumphs again.

In some repetitions words are rearranged,

"That is curious!"
"Isn't that curious?"

and some phrases are overelaborated in an almost biblical manner:

"Only, I, madam, I left. . . ."

(Compare from the Book of Job: "I only am alone escaped to tell thee.")

In his stage directions for the play, Ionesco asks that the actors speak "in voices that are drawling, monotonous, a little singsong, without nuances."* This heightens the scene's tension by not escalating it too readily. Thus, as the repetitions begin to compound themselves, "curious," "bizarre," and "coincidence" become like drumbeats, first appearing singly, then in various combinations ("That is curious! How very bizarre! And what a coincidence!" "How curious it is, how bizarre, what a coincidence!"), then in self-repetition ("How curious it is, how curious it is, and what a coincidence!" "How curious it is, how curious it is, how curious it is, and what a coincidence!"), and finally as a flurry of repetitions, "Well then, well then, well then, well then, perhaps we have seen each other," which culminate in the original inquiry, "I've met you . . . before?"

Escalating numbers intensify the pattern as Mr. and Mrs. Martin narrow toward their goals. "Coach No. 8, compartment 6," "coach No. 8, compartment 6," they cry, and "seat No. 3" "seat No. 6." "No. 19," "No. 19," as their excitement builds. "The end of the corridor, between the w.c. and the bookcase, dear lady!" says Mr. Martin. "The end of the corridor, between the w.c., dear sir, and the bookcase!" responds Mrs. Martin, in what is now leaving the banter of the music hall for the pure stichomythia (series of one-line exchanges) of ancient Greek tragedy. The rising action is clearly heading toward a climax.

What kind of climax? Ionesco insists that his actors be outwardly restrained up to the end of the dialogue. This restraint is part of the brilliance of his style, for it keeps the parody of English reserve alive. But it holds back the erupting volcano of the couple's emotions, which is fundamental to the couplings of everyday life. There is no question but that the characters reach a "proper English orgasm" at the end of this scene, for as Mr. and Mrs. Martin rise and embrace each other, though their manners are properly restrained, the clock strikes with a sound that, in the author's words, "must be so loud that it makes the audience jump."

The volcanic tension between the fire of inner passion and the shell of outer formality is the great dialectic (conflict of forces) of all dramaturgy,

---

* *Four Plays,* trans. Donald M. Allen (New York: Grove Press, 1988), p. 15.

and nowhere is it so blatantly portrayed as in Ionesco. Here, with both psychology and rational argument removed, the dramaturgic pattern—a slow, steady build, fueled by suppressed sexual desire that is simultaneously suppressed by English propriety—dominates the scene.*

With a partner, rehearse and play it.

Since hypertheatrical dramatic pattern, not realistic characters or rhetorical argument, is primarily involved here, this is your opportunity to work on purely theatrical performance techniques: character voices and character walks mentioned in Lesson 5, for example, and, perhaps with some assistance and coaching, dialects and other vocal or physical extensions of your own normal persona. Find theatrical costuming and props that are not realistic English but hyper-English; create business and behavior that is in keeping with this hypertreatment.

Learn your lines *precisely*. This will be no easy task, as the usual technique—learning lines by focusing on their meaning—is all but useless because most of the lines mean the same thing. Yet precise line-learning remains essential, since it is the linguistic and stylistic *variations* of the lines that enable you to make the escalating build of not three or four but *twenty-five* graduated steps—in sync with your partner's twenty-five. Each step should show your anticipated progress to your orgasmic/explosive goal, your mounting excitement in the face of potential victory, and your increasingly difficult struggle to contain the chaos within you while at the same time seeking its release.

With your partner, see how you can make these tiny increments—the graduated "building steps" to victory—while still constraining yourself within the outward manners of a proper English gentleman or gentlewoman. At some moments, your emotional build may come out as heightened vocal releases on repeated phrases. At others, you will intensify your linguistic propriety by employing verbal constructions that elevate your speech to a higher social level.

Consider, for example, these portions of two consecutive speeches by Mrs. Martin (as separated by a portion of Mr. Martin's intervening speech):

"But of course, that must have been ^^I, sir. How curious it is, how curious it is, and what a coincidence!"

(MR. MARTIN: How curious it is, how bizarre, what a coincidence!. . .)

---

* By play's end, however, the volcano has exploded, with the Martins "completely infuriated, screaming in each other's ears." Ionesco's hypertheatre is, in some ways, a violent parody of the comedy of manners—Oscar Wilde gone mad.

"How ^^curious it is and what a co^^^incidence! It is indeed possible, my ^^dear sir!. . ."

In your first line, you lift the word "I" so as to point out that you are using the correct construction (the nominative case *I,* rather than the objective case *me,* is the proper direct object of "been"). Your correct grammatical usage thus separates you from more common speakers, while your "sir" indicates your presumption of an elevated social class. In your second speech, though, you emphasize your growing attraction to Mr. Martin by lifting your words ^^*curious* and co^^*incidence,* since you have picked up and repeated them from his previous speech; your rising enthusiasm shows that you both are approaching a passionate accord. As does your expression ^^*dear sir,* which adds a "dear" to the plainer *sir* with which you previously addressed him.

In like manner, build all your lines, one by one, both on the inside (by moving closer and closer to your emotional climax) and on the outside (by becoming increasingly more properly English). Do this in concert with your partner, who will simultaneously be building in response. Then climax your scene by the formal embrace the author directs. (Don't worry about the inner orgasm: the clock strike that makes the audience jump will represent it perfectly.) Then, when you collapse with your partner into the armchair, you will have created the scene's "absurd" conclusion, a postcoital denouement.

Bertolt Brecht: Theatre of Distancing

Think for a moment of a fifteen-second TV commercial dramatization. A groaning husband turns to his wife and says, "Oh, I have a terrible headache." His wife smiles knowingly, picks up a bottle of medicine, and turns to him saying, "Here, honey, try some of this!" But even in these five seconds, you know from the acting that the actor playing the husband does *not actually have a headache,* and you know that the woman playing the wife is smiling not because she can cure a headache but simply because *she has been paid to smile.* And you know all this *because of the style of their acting.* The commercial actors are, as it were, "winking" at us while they're performing. Their words are a bit overpronounced, their grimaces and expressions are a bit cartoonish, and they somehow seem to be looking out at the viewers from behind their characters to ask: "You get this, don't you?"

Are they bad actors? Not at all. They're doing what TV commercials require. Were we to get involved in the man's headache, or the couple's relationship, we'd lose the sole point of the commercial, which is to sell medicine. The "winking" style basically tells us, "This skit isn't about us, it's about the product," at which point the commercial segues into cartoon figures, marketing jingles, and pictures and texts that let you know what the product looks like, where you can buy it, and how to recognize it on the drugstore shelf.

The "winking" actor in the commercial demonstrates pure Brechtian acting. It is "distanced" acting because the performer deliberately separates the actor's self from his or her dramatized character, so that the viewer can focus solely on the message.

No twentieth-century playwright has influenced the modern theatre as much as Bertolt Brecht. This is not because his plays are so universally admired—although they continue to be performed around the world—but because of his radical assault on notions of acting unquestioningly accepted since the time of Plato and elevated to almost religious status by Stanislavsky and his followers in Europe and America after World War I. It was Stanislavsky's goal that the actor should ignore the audience and simply live the life of his or her character onstage—a notion that became the cornerstone of "Method" acting as further developed in America under Group Theatre members and Actors Studio teachers Lee Strasberg and Sanford Meisner. It was Brecht's quite opposite notion that the actor should maintain a discrete "distance" from his or her character, *representing* the character's action while at the same time retaining a direct relationship between his or her own (acting) self and the theatre audience. The Brechtian actor does not allow himself to become completely transformed on the stage into the character he is portraying, Brecht said. Instead, the actor stands alongside the role and, in the dramatist's famous analogy, presents the role to us "like a bystander describing an accident."* Why? Because to Brecht—as to the producers of television commercials—the *message* of the drama—which for him was political, not commercial—was far more important than the psychology or reality of the play's individual characters. Brecht refused to sweep up his audience in a rhapsody of feeling; rather, he wanted them to concentrate on what they should do to correct the social problems he was addressing.

Brecht took advantage of his position as playwright–director to fashion plays that took advantage of his acting theory. Anticipating the TV commercial (not yet invented, of course), he incorporated into his dramatic

---

* Quotations from John Willett, *The Theatre of Bertolt Brecht* (London: Methuan, 1959), p. 180.

work songs, poems, and lectures addressed directly to the audience; slide projections announcing scene titles and stage descriptions; stage lights and scenery moved and operated by onstage technicians in plain sight; and nondramatic staging formats that included boxing arenas, lecture halls, vaudeville houses, and cabarets. Like Ionesco and other hypertheatrical playwrights, Brecht wholly avoided realistic scenery and conventional plots. His plays were instead artistic and literary collages that displayed ideas, images, and bold stage actions in a vigorous theatrical combination that remains dominant in Europe today and important in America as well.

Seen in the long run, Brecht's innovations were not as original as they at first glance appeared. Songs, poems, asides, signs, and visibly operated stage machinery were common in Shakespeare's plays as well. But Brecht was certainly radical in his deliberate departure from the theatre of his day, dominated as it was by Stanislavskian realism. Brecht sought a theatre for a "scientific age" and achieved precisely that. His theatre was a laboratory for social study, public debate, and political change.

Brecht's ideas on acting were and remain controversial. He did not apply them consistently and backed away from some of them toward the end of his life. He acknowledged that despite his best efforts, many of his actors—including his actress–wife, Helene Weigel—evoked waves of sympathy from the audience in their "Brechtian" performances. But his insistence on delivering a message rather than having his actors sentimentalize their roles with personal feelings, or try to sweep the audience away in a bathos of emotion, marked a major shift in acting style that has major repercussions in acting to this very day.

Here is a (slightly edited) scene from Brecht's "parable" of *The Good Person of Szechuan,* as translated by Eric Bentley, who first brought Brecht's work to American readers and audiences.* In the play, Shen Te, the title character, is a poor Chinese prostitute who, in the opening scene, is given a large sum of money by three gods who have become sympathetic to her attempt to be a good person in a society riddled with destitution. As Shen Te tries to improve her lot by opening a tobacco shop, she encounters others in her city who take advantage of her—including, in this scene, the failed pilot, Yang Sun. Yang, dressed in rags and about to hang himself, is first seen shooing away two other prostitutes. When they leave, Shen Te enters and sees him throwing the rope over a willow branch.

---

* (New York: Grove Press, 1965), where the play was titled (less correctly) *The Good Woman of Sezuan.*

◆ S C E N E   15–2

Distancing in Szechuan

YANG SUN (*to the prostitutes*):   Move on there! This is a park, not a whorehouse! (*They leave. He speaks to the audience.*) Even in the farthest corner of the park, even when it's raining, you can't get rid of them. (*He spits.*)

SHEN TE (*she has come in and overhears this*):   And what right have you to scold them? (*But at this point she sees the rope.*) Oh!

YANG SUN: What are you staring at?

SHEN TE: That rope. What is it for?

YANG SUN: Think! Think! I haven't a penny. Even if I had, I wouldn't spend it on you. I'd buy a drink of water.

The rain starts.

SHEN TE (*still looking at the rope*):   What is the rope for? You mustn't!

YANG SUN: What's it to you? Clear out!

SHEN TE: It's raining.

YANG SUN: Well, don't try to come under this tree.

SHEN TE: Oh, no. (*She stays in the rain.*)

YANG SUN: Now go away. (*Pause.*) For one thing I don't like your looks, you're bowlegged.

SHEN TE: That's not true!

YANG SUN: Well, don't show 'em to me. Look, it's raining. You better come under this tree.

Slowly, she takes shelter under the tree.

SHEN TE: Why did you want to do it.

YANG SUN: You really want to know? (*Pause.*) To get rid of you! (*Pause.*) You know what a flyer is?

SHEN TE: Oh yes. I've met a lot of pilots. At the tearoom.

YANG SUN: You call *them* flyers? Think they know what a machine is? Just 'cause they have leather helmets? They give the airfield director a bribe, that's the way *those* fellows got up in the air! Try one of them out sometime. "Go up to two thousand feet," tell them, "then let it fall, then pick it up again with a flick of the wrist at the last moment." Know what he'll say to that? "It's not in my contract." Then again, there's the landing problem. It's like landing on your own backside. It's no different, planes are human. Those fools don't understand. (*Pause.*) And I'm the biggest fool for reading the book on flying in the Peking school and skipping the page where it says: "We've got enough flyers and we don't need you." I'm a mail pilot with no mail. You understand that?

SHEN TE (*shyly*):   Yes, I do.

YANG SUN: No you don't. You'd never understand that.

SHEN TE: When we were little we had a crane with a broken wing. He made friends with us and was very good-natured about our jokes. He would strut along behind us and call out to stop us going too fast for him. But every spring and autumn when the cranes flew over the village in great swarms, he got quite restless. (*Pause.*) I understand that. (*She bursts out crying.*)

YANG SUN: Don't!

SHEN TE (*quieting down*):   No.

YANG SUN: It's bad for the complexion.

SHEN TE (*sniffling*):   I've stopped.

She dries her tears on her big sleeve. Leaning against the tree, but not looking at her, Yang Sun reaches for her face.

YANG SUN: You can't even wipe your own face. (*He is wiping it for her with his handkerchief. Pause.*)

SHEN TE (*still sobbing*):   I don't know *anything!*

YANG SUN: You interrupted me! What for?

SHEN TE: It's such a rainy day. You only wanted to do . . . *that* because it's such a rainy day. (*To the audience:*)

In our country
The evenings should never be somber
High bridges over rivers
The gray hour between night and morning
And the long, long winter:
Such things are dangerous

For, with all the misery,
A very little is enough
And men throw away an unbearable life.

Pause

YANG SUN: Talk about yourself for a change.

SHEN TE: What about me? I have a shop.

YANG SUN: You have a shop, have you? Never thought of walking the streets?°   °*becoming a prostitute*

SHEN TE: I did walk the streets. Now I have a shop.

YANG SUN (*ironically*):   A gift of the gods, I suppose!

SHEN TE: How did you know?

YANG SUN (*even more ironically*):   One fine evening the gods turned up saying: here's some money!

SHEN TE (*quickly*):   One fine morning.

YANG SUN (*fed up*):   This isn't much of an entertainment . . . What do you know about love?

SHEN TE: Everything.

YANG SUN: Nothing. (*Pause.*) Or d'you just mean you enjoyed it?

SHEN TE: No.

YANG SUN (*without turning to look at her, he strokes her cheek with his hand*):   You like that?

SHEN TE: Yes.

YANG SUN (*breaking off*):   You're easily satisfied, I must say. (*Pause.*) What a town!

You can quickly see that Brecht has used direct narrative address (characters speaking directly to the audience), which in this case includes both ironic prose and free-verse poetry, that violates both the format and tone of realism. Shen Te also recites a Chinese parable about a crane, and Yang Sun tells a long-winded story about his failure to get hired as a pilot, both of which are more literary than conversational.

But there's more distance yet: The characters and setting are purportedly Asian, but the roles were not written to be played by Asian actors, and "Szechuan" (today, Sichuan) is not a Chinese city at all but a rural province.

Yang Sun and Shen Te on a bench in the Bern production.

Brecht had never been to China, did little or no research on China for his play, and there is little about *Szechuan* that is specifically Chinese. The play's "tree"—as Brecht specified elsewhere—is simply an abstracted stage construction, not to be treelike in appearance, and the rain is also intended to be indicated primarily by the actors' mimed reactions rather than simulated by realistic sound effects or actual falling water. The reference to "gods" as real beings—and speaking contemporary slang—creates a further dissonance between what we see on the stage and what we imagine would happen in a traditional Chinese (or a staged Chekhovian) portrayal of the same situation.

Finally, this scene's inner actions (the two characters' falling in love, Yang Sun's intended suicide) are indicated not by the performance of psychological ambiguities or complications but by precise physical gestures. Brecht used the term *gestus* for such highly specific and controlled gestures (plus certain vocal actions) that would each convey a single, explicit meaning. Thus Yang Sun's tossing the rope over the "branch," spitting on the ground, wiping Shen Te's face with his handkerchief, then with his hand, are not merely random samples of the miscellaneous physical movements an actor or character may make, but visual and vocal signifiers with which Brecht composes the dramatic arc of his play.

Learn and play with a partner this scene from *The Good Person of Szechuan*. In rehearsing and performing it, do the following:

◆ Segue effortlessly from speaking to your partner and speaking to the audience, but make quite clear *to whom you are speaking* as you do. Treat the audience *as persons watching the play,* and lead them through the narrative of your character's thoughts—and your own as well. In other words, when as Shen Te you say "In our country," you mean both the Szechuan of Shen Te and *your own* country (e.g., America) as well—and you understand the audience will heed both meanings as do you.

◆ Overpronounce your words a bit. Make them, and your meaning of them, *super-clear*—not only to your acting partner but to any other characters who may be overhearing you. Imagine that the prostitutes who left the scene earlier are now in the theatre audience, hoping to hear what you have to say. Let them hear—and *make sure they understand* what you mean.

◆ Use gestures that are explicit and exact, not muddied or ambiguous. When, as Yang Sun, you throw the rope over the "branch" (which you may mime), make the throw in a single, unfussy motion. Tie a noose on the rope's other end with a single, swift, self-choreographed movement. When, as Shen Te, you burst out crying, fully enact this bursting of tears— as if you were *showing Yang Sun how a fictional Shen Te may have cried.* Don't worry whether or not you "feel" like crying when you do this. Perform the act of crying whether you feel it or not; remember that, to Brecht, the important thing is that *the story is told, the message is heard,* not that the actor fills the role with his or her own sincere emotion.*

◆ As Shen Te, find within yourself a poetic voice for your poem and an Aesopian voice for your parable. As Yang Sun, find the coarse, boisterous voices for the airmen whose dialogue you enact in your speech about the flying school. *Perform* these vocal presentations, both for each other and for the audience, and segue from these performative voices to more conversational voices when you segue to more colloquial and personal exchanges.

◆ Capture, if you can, the edge of irony and even whimsy both characters have in their speeches. For even as characters they engage in actions that in real life would be tumultuous, as actors they are always conscious that they are telling a story and relaying a parable of persons of another age and race. Their resulting dialogue, therefore, should always have a twinkle

---

* We gather from essays and correspondence of the time that Brecht's actors did on occasion feel real feelings and cry real tears, but that this emotion was mainly the result of their long training and experience more than their working to "emote" or dredge up previous life experiences.

in the eye. "I don't like your looks, you're bowlegged," for example, is not a line you would expect from a real person about to hang himself.

♦ "Wink" at the audience with your mind's eye. As Yang Sun, mock your coarseness in a way that tells the audience "I'm showing you a coarse guy" (just as the husband in the commercial tells the viewers "I'm *showing* you a guy with a headache; I'm not the guy myself"). As Shen Te, say the line "A very little is enough" with a look that says "I, the actress playing this role, know more about how to live with very little than this fictional character I'm playing does."

Verfremdung in Everyday Life

One of the reasons Brecht's style of acting continues to hold sway in the twenty-first century is that a "distanced" manner of behaving is now widely realized as being as common in real life as it is on the stage. In his important 1961 essay "Role Distance," psychologist Erving Goffman points out that a human in real life often creates actions that "effectively convey some disdainful detachment of the [person] from a role he is performing."* Goffman traces this detachment to childhood. A typical three-year-old boy, Goffman finds, when riding a merry-go-round, will embrace his role to the maximum, "living the life" of the cowboy in a manner that Stanislavsky would find appealing. By age five, however; "irreverence begins." The same boy, Goffman points out, now "leans back, stands on the saddle, holds on to the horse's wooden ear, and says by his actions: 'Whatever I am, I'm not just someone who can barely manage to stay on a wooden horse.'" For the five-year-old, Goffman discovered, the interest in fully "inhabiting" such roles has ended and is replaced by "a dutiful regard for [displaying] one's own character."

Understanding Goffman's notion, and his other discoveries of our very human "performances" in everyday life, has helped forge the understanding that what Brecht proposed was not contrary to the natural life of human beings but rather fundamental to it. The Brechtian actor is not unlike the adult in normal adult life who, while engaged in performing a professional or social "role" (such as waitress or party host), shows evidence of his or

---

* Erving Goffman, *Encounters: Two Studies in the Sociology of Interaction* (Indianapolis: Bobbs-Merrill, 1961). For further discussion, see my "Role Distance: On Stage and on the Merry-Go-Round," *Journal of Dramatic Theory and Criticism,"* Fall 2004, pp. 115–124.

her own identity by "winking" beneath the role's mask ("I'm not really a waitress; I'm really a not-yet-discovered movie star"). The Stanislavskian actor, in Brecht's contrasting terms, is still a child.

Brecht's influence in contemporary theatre has in any event become incalculable. In the half century since his death (1956), speeches directly addressed to the audience, ideographic gesture and mime, characters commenting on their roles in the play, dramatic action broken into short and discontinuous scenes, theatrical technology brought out into the open, and the inclusion of poems, songs, and signs into a completely serious text have become so common that they rarely even provoke remarks from audiences, much less critics. And the wry, distanced, self-referential acting we call "Brechtian" has become common not only in the theatre but in film and television acting as well.

16

Contemporary Styles

It is hard to see the styles of one's own era, perhaps because they seem so normal. No one in the 1950s, for example, was particularly conscious of dressing in a 1950s style. Only decades later, when invited to a "'50s party," might people have seriously reflected on what 1950s style actually was.

Likewise, neither Aeschylus nor Euripides would have been consciously trying to write a "classical Greek tragedy." They were simply writing plays as they knew them; the term "classical Greek tragedy" was defined much later. And the same is true for medieval mystery plays, Italian *commedia erudita,* French neoclassic tragedy, and even twentieth-century theatre of the absurd. In each case, the works came first and the categorization of style later—sometimes much later.

A case may be made, however, that contemporary theatrical "style" is more varied and less reducible to categorization than dramas of the past. Today's playwrights gleefully process and amalgamate styles developed all over the world and from every era, so that various combinations of many styles—Greek myth, Victorian melodrama, Shakespearean comedy, kabuki dance, African chant, Chinese opera, circus trapeze, official court transcripts, scientific debate—now find their way into contemporary dramas. And theories of alienation, absurdity, deconstruction, nonlinearity, interculturalism, interextualism, and metadrama directly inform dramaturgical approaches. Moreover, our age values novelty and originality in the arts; thus the artist gains fame by violating conventions rather than perfecting them. It is always a surprise for students to learn that, in the nineteenth century, the term "unexceptional" was used as a mark of *praise* in a theatrical review. Today it would be the gravest condemnation.

It is fair to say, then, that contemporary theatre artists are free—and encouraged—to create their own styles and are not absolutely tied to any single historical or geographical base. And actors are certainly asked to dig into this smorgasbord of styles from all eras and mind-sets.

In this chapter, therefore, we look at four contemporary dramatic styles, exemplified by widely differing—but Pulitzer Prize–winning—American plays from the 1990s. Playing these styles does not require the same intensity of historical research, for these plays are set in the present or in the recent past, and the purely historical aspects of character deportment, behavior, and dress are abundantly around us still. But this familiarity only increases the complexity and subtlety of the actors' challenges as they extend themselves into the specific styles and characters portrayed in these interactions between a gay man and a Mormon wife, a rural black man, an urban black woman, a dying female professor and an ambitious young male doctor, and a transvestite playing himself as a teenage boy confronting as SS officer. Each of these characters comes from his or her own world, and with his or her own personal appeal and limitations, and moves out into a world that proves quite different, problematical, and filled with challenges. You will have something in common with all of these characters, I hope; with none of them, however, will you have everything in common.

Clashing Cultures

Tony Kushner's two-part *Angels in America* is the most honored American play since 1950, having won not only the 1993 Pulitzer Prize for Drama but no less than *two* Tony Awards for Best Play (its two parts premiering on Broadway in consecutive seasons).

Kushner, born in 1956, creates a new category for his play, spelled out in its subtitle: "A Gay Fantasia on National Themes." And indeed, everyone in the play operates within the unique "fantasia" of Kushner's imagination: Actors play many roles (living and dead, natural and supernatural, often of differing genders and ages), scenes overlap each other and take place simultaneously on different areas of the stage, and characters talk to the audience, appear in each other's dreams, climb up to heaven, and return from the dead. And, while the issues addressed by the play are extremely powerful (sexual betrayal, the spread of AIDS, homophobia and religious persecution, death and transfiguration), the duration exhausting (about eight hours), and the tone often savage, the play is, at many times, enormously funny. Kushner's language is often as wickedly clever as Shaw's and often, too, as brilliantly elliptical, and awkwardly stammered, as Chekhov's. There is good reason, in other words, to consider this the one true dramatic masterpiece of the 1990s.

Cynthia Mace is Harper and Stephen Spinella is Prior in the world premiere of
Angels in America at the Los Angeles Mark Taper Forum, 1992. (Photo by Jay
Thompson)

Two different American subcultures come together in this work: gay
males in New York City, and Mormons (members of the Church of Jesus
Christ of Latter-Day Saints) from Utah. Although none of the play's characters should be considered precisely typical, nearly all of them show the influence of prevailing—and conflicting—cultural attitudes. Indeed, that is
the axis on which most of the play's scenes turn.

This scene, from *Part One: Millennium Approaches,* is a fantasy conversation between Prior Walter and Harper Pitt. Prior, Kushner tells us, "occasionally works as a club designer or caterer, otherwise lives very modestly
but with great style off a small trust fund." He has also recently discovered
himself to be HIV positive. In his dream he is dressed in women's clothing,
presumably preparing for a drag performance. Harper is a young woman
from Utah, a member of the Mormon church, who has followed her husband, Joe, to New York; she is described by Kushner as "an agoraphobic
with a mild Valium addiction."

*[Prior is at a fantastic makeup table, having a dream, applying the face.
Harper is having a pill-induced hallucination. For some reason, Prior
has appeared in this one. Or Harper has appeared in Prior's dream. It is
bewildering.]*

PRIOR *[alone, putting on makeup, then examining the results in the mirror;
to the audience]:*   "I'm ready for my closeup, Mr. DeMille."

One wants to move through life with elegance and grace, blossoming in-frequently but with exquisite taste, and perfect timing, like a rare bloom, a zebra orchid. . . . One wants . . . But one so seldom gets what one wants, does one? No. One does not. One gets fucked. Over. One . . . dies at thirty, robbed of . . . decades of majesty. Fuck this shit. Fuck this shit.

[He almost crumbles; he pulls himself together; he studies his handiwork in the mirror]

I look like a corpse. A corpsette. Oh my queen; you know you've hit rock-bottom when even drag is a drag.

[Harper appears.]

HARPER: Are you . . . Who are you?

PRIOR: Who are you?

HARPER: What are you doing in my hallucination?

PRIOR: I'm not in your hallucination. You're in my dream.

HARPER: You're wearing makeup.

PRIOR: So are you.

HARPER: But you're a man.

PRIOR *[Feigning dismay, shock, he mimes slashing his throat with his lipstick and dies, fabulously tragic. Then]*:   The hands and feet give it away.

HARPER: There must be some mistake here. I don't recognize you. You're not . . . Are you my . . . some sort of imaginary friend?

PRIOR: No. Aren't you too old to have imaginary friends?

HARPER: I have emotional problems. I took too many pills. Why are you wearing makeup?

PRIOR: I was in the process of applying the face, trying to make myself feel better—I swiped the new fall colors at the Clinique counter at Macy's. *[showing her]*

HARPER: You stole these?

PRIOR: I was out of cash; it was an emotional emergency!

HARPER: Joe will be so angry. I promised him. No more pills.

PRIOR: These pills you keep alluding to?

HARPER: Valium. I take Valium. Lots of Valium.

PRIOR: And you're dancing as fast as you can.*

---

*   An allusion to a 1979 book by Barbara Gordon about Valium addiction.

HARPER: I'm not *addicted*. I don't believe in addiction, and I never . . . well, I *never* drink. And I *never* take drugs.

PRIOR: Well, smell *you*, Nancy Drew. *

HARPER: Except Valium.

PRIOR: Except Valium; in wee fistfuls.

HARPER: It's terrible. Mormons are not supposed to be addicted to anything. I'm a Mormon.

PRIOR: I'm a homosexual.

HARPER: Oh! In my church we don't believe in homosexuals.

PRIOR: In my church we don't believe in Mormons.

HARPER: What church do . . . oh! *[She laughs]* I get it.
   I don't understand this. If I didn't ever see you before and I don't think I did then I don't think you should be here, in this hallucination, because in my experience the mind, which is where hallucinations come from, shouldn't be able to make up anything that wasn't there to start with, that didn't enter it from experience, from the real world. Imagination can't create anything new, can it? It only recycles bits and pieces from the world and reassembles them into visions. . . . Am I making sense right now?

PRIOR: Given the circumstances, yes.

HARPER: So when we think we've escaped the unbearable ordinariness and, well, untruthfulness of our lives, it's really only the same old ordinariness and falseness rearranged into the appearance of novelty and truth. Nothing unknown is knowable. Don't you think it's depressing?

PRIOR: The limitations of the imagination?

HARPER: Yes.

PRIOR: It's something you learn after your second theme party: It's All Been Done Before.

HARPER: The world. Finite. Terribly, terribly . . . Well . . . This is the most depressing hallucination I've ever had.

PRIOR: Apologies. I do try to be amusing.

HARPER: Oh, well, don't apologize, you . . . I can't expect someone who's really sick to entertain me.

PRIOR: How on earth did you know . . .

---

* The wholesome young heroine of a series of children's mystery novels.

HARPER: Oh that happens. This is the very threshold of revelation sometimes. You can see things . . . how sick you are. Do you see anything
about me?

PRIOR: Yes.

HARPER: What?

PRIOR: You are amazingly unhappy.

HARPER: Oh big deal. You meet a Valium addict and you figure out she's
unhappy. That doesn't count. Of course I . . . Something else. Something
surprising.

PRIOR: Something surprising.

HARPER: Yes.

PRIOR: Your husband's a homo.

[pause]

HARPER: Oh, ridiculous. *[pause, then very quietly]* Really?

PRIOR: *[shrugs]*   Threshold of revelation.

In Kushner's "gay fantasia," hallucinations and dreams are as real and
vibrant as earthly dialogue, and direct address makes the audience a participant in the struggles as well as the "performances" of the characters. The
playwright even calls this "bewildering" in his stage direction, but it needn't
bewilder us: It is what we accept as the reality—the world—of his play. And
the play, while considered "contemporary," is in fact set in 1985–1986,
during the Reagan era, which makes it increasingly subject to historical
evaluation as the years go by.

Within this overall style, Kushner creates separate subcultural styles:
here the drag queen and the Mormon wife. Few gay American males are
drag queens, of course, and not all drag queens adore diva actresses, catty
profanity, florid imagery, or quoting from old movies like *Sunset Boulevard*.
But there is a distinct drag queen subculture nonetheless (it was first portrayed theatrically in Lanford Wilson's brilliant *Madness of Lady Bright* in
1964), and any actor playing Prior Walter should understand the common
practices and attitudes of that subculture. Reading Wilson's play, seeing
drag performances live or on film, and experiencing or reading in the literature of the subculture are all useful in understanding the goals, motivations,
and favored tactics of a character such as Prior.

Cultural—and subcultural—behaviors are learned, of course. In life,
they are learned by observation and emulation; this is how a group of
relatively generic fifth-grade boys can, six years later, become diversely
identified as jocks, nerds, stoners, preppies, and skinheads. Whatever

genetic predisposition may have led to these identifications, the practical cause was each boy's increased association with a particular group, leading to emulation of group dress, behavior, and attitudes and an increasing desire to fit in with—and be defined by—the chosen group. This would be how a "real" Prior Walter would become what we see in the play; the actor must undergo a similar process, though usually in imagination and rehearsal.

Of course Prior's chosen style doesn't fully, or even principally, define him. He is also a member of other subcultures: descendants of *Mayflower* Americans and AIDS patients among them. And he rebels against his drag queen subculture, finds it a drag, and transcends it in supernatural ways. Prior is an individual, whose brilliant wit and deep (though often disguised) compassion make him unlike not only any other drag queen but any other human being in the world.

Similarly, not all Mormon wives—nor even most of them—are unhappy, or in denial about their husband's sexuality, or addicted to drugs, all of which Harper appears to be. But the Mormon church is an association of men and women who regularly express, and who seek to teach their children, spiritual values that promote heterosexual life and that forbid homosexuality, alcohol, drugs, and profanity. Clearly the character of Harper, seen as a real person (even in a "fantasia"), would have been affected by her Mormon upbringing and her continuing Mormon beliefs and attitudes. An actor playing Harper would therefore wish to study Mormon society, either through direct experience or through literature, films, conversations with members of that faith, and other sources, in order to understand and truthfully perform the mind-set of her complex character.

But of course Harper, too, is not defined just by her Mormon beliefs and heritage. She has made the move to New York with her husband, she has accepted this conversation (and the jokey byplay) with the admitted homosexual whom her church would shun, and she has confessed to him her violations of her church's rules against drugs. Like Prior, she is a combination of her individual mind-set, goals, and desires (her "character"), and her culturally derived channels of dress, deportment, language, and attitudes (her "style").

Let's look at key moments in the scene itself, seeing how the characters employ many of the devices we have explored in the historical sections of *Acting Two*—language styles, rhetorical ploys, rhyme, assonance, voices of the supernatural, a *tirade,* and, above all, *performative behaviors* (behaviors taking the form of a public performance, or a quotation or satire of a public performance)—in order to achieve their goals. In this, we will be doing as much a literary as an acting analysis, but these analyses will provide guidelines for creating your own performance in the scene.

[Prior is at a fantastic makeup table, having a dream, applying the face. . . .] "I'm ready for my closeup, Mr. DeMille."

Prior begins the scene not just dressed as a woman, but speaking the words of the character Norma Desmond, a delusional old silent-film actress played by Gloria Swanson in the celebrated 1950 film *Sunset Boulevard*. The actor's research, here, clearly requires viewing this film. Prior is, according to Kushner, speaking to the "audience," but which audience? Through the imaginary mirror, the actor playing Prior is clearly speaking to the theatre audience that is watching him in real time. But in his imagination, Prior might also be addressing a drag show nightclub audience—in the role of Desmond. Perhaps Prior is rehearsing a line from an actual drag act. It is at moments like these that performative behavior becomes a crucial part of the play's style: not just Prior performing in drag but performing a specific character in another dramatic work. Such expropriation of another's performance can permit—indeed, often demands—"overacting," but this is no artistic sin, because it is your *character* doing the overacting, not you. You are only acting the overacting of Prior Walter—who is satirizing Norma Desmond's acting!

Some of this performative behavior spills over, though not in quotation marks (as with the Desmond line), as Prior continues—now directly to the theatre audience—his speech—during which he oscillates between being Prior and being Desmond:

One wants to move through life with elegance and grace, blossoming infrequently but with exquisite taste, and perfect timing, like a rare bloom, a zebra orchid . . . One wants . . . But one so seldom gets what one wants, does one? No. One does not. One gets fucked. Over. One . . . dies at thirty, robbed of . . . decades of majesty. Fuck this shit. Fuck this shit.

[He almost crumbles; he pulls himself together; he studies his handiwork in the mirror]

I look like a corpse. A corpsette. Oh my queen; you know you've hit rock-bottom when even drag is a drag.

This speech, filled with Chekhovian repetitions and trail-offs ("One wants . . ."), rhetorical questions ("does one?"), abstract philosophical musings (identified by the impersonal "one") quickly brought to earth by savage profanity ("One gets fucked"), whimsical wordplay ("corpsette"; "even drag is a drag"), is a deliberate and dazzling literary display: Prior bravely showing off his brilliant mind in order to hide (from us? from himself?) his deteriorating body. The performative speech—delivered before a mirror—may make us think, perhaps, of the mirror-inspired monologue in Act 4, Scene 1 of Shakespeare's *Richard II*: "Give me that glass, and therein will I read. / No deeper wrinkles yet? Hath sorrow struck / So many blows upon this face of mine, / And made no deeper wounds?", or Mimi's glorious aria in the death-throes of tuberculosis in Puccini's *La Bohème*.

With Harper's entrance, Kushner moves to an exchange of single lines, each rhetorically linked with its predecessor by one or more words:

HARPER: Are you . . . Who are you?

PRIOR: Who are you?

HARPER: What are you doing in my hallucination?

PRIOR: I'm not in your hallucination. You're in my dream.

HARPER: You're wearing makeup.

PRIOR: So are you.

HARPER: But you're a man.

PRIOR *[Feigning dismay, shock, he mimes slashing his throat with his lip-stick and dies, fabulously tragic. Then]:*   The hands and feet give it away.

Each plays on the other's speech, partly copying, partly mocking, and partly restating it, thereby trying to seize control not only of the topic but of the tone. Prior caps the exchange, however, by a *physical* response to Harper's last provocation: a gesture. And it is also a *performative* gesture, bringing into play his cross-gendered attire and a Grand Guignol (or slasher film, if you prefer) theatricalized bloodletting, which he then immediately deflates with a cliché. He is not really dead, he is not really female, and the most obvious things about him ("hands and feet," the well-known give-aways of transvestites) have betrayed him.

Prior and Harper subsequently play off their problems and genders. To Harper's girlish fantasy ("imaginary friend"), Prior poses his familiarity with girls' fiction ("Nancy Drew"); to her "emotional problems," he responds with his "emotional emergency." She matches his brand-name makeup (Clinique) with a brand-name medication (Valium); he counters her church with his sexual orientation. And as they trade what superficially seem like catty insults, they grow inevitably closer: Their dialogue, their repetition of each other's words and phrases, their mutual performative act, become a strong dramatic bond, blending their larger subcultures into a new, shared one—that consists, at the moment, of just the two of them.

Emboldened by their increasingly parallel discourse, Harper confesses with a rhetorical flourish (a bit of epistrophe—phrases ending with the same word), her drug problem to this strange new person who somehow, unlikely as it may first have appeared, increasingly seems to be her friend:

HARPER: Valium. I take Valium. Lots of Valium. *[. . .]* I'm not *addicted.* I don't believe in addiction, and I never . . . well, I *never* drink. And I *never* take drugs.

PRIOR: Well, smell *you,* Nancy Drew.

The euphemistic attack line, abjuring the f-word and sweetened with a rhyme *(you/Drew)* leaves Harper more amused than insulted. We are given to presume she *did* read Nancy Drew books as a child and has never met a *man* who ever did. She's emboldened further toward confession: "Except Valium."

Prior repeats her phrase, then ironically both amplifies and takes the edge off it with an adjective that has baby-talk overtones (as in Lesson 1), creating an even deeper trust and leading to their paired revelations:

PRIOR: Except Valium; in wee fistfuls.

HARPER: It's terrible. Mormons are not supposed to be addicted to anything. I'm a Mormon.

PRIOR: I'm a homosexual.

The paired revelations are followed by their subcultures' paired objections:

HARPER: Oh! In my church we don't believe in homosexuals.

PRIOR: In my church we don't believe in Mormons.

HARPER: What church do . . . oh! *[She laughs]* I get it.

The laughter is of recognition and admission: the recognition that the two of them aren't as different as she had thought and the admission that reliance on their individual subcultures won't be enough to sustain them through their present crises. None of this, of course, is said directly through the *meaning* of the lines; rather, it is expressed, and unambiguously ex-pressed (as meaning alone can rarely if ever be), in the *style* of the language and actions the actors employ.

Harper continues with a *tirade* (see Lesson 12) in which she tries to come to terms with the fantasia Kushner has placed her in:

I don't understand this. If I didn't ever see you before and I don't think I did then I don't think you should be here, in this hallucination, because in my experience the mind, which is where hallucinations come from, shouldn't be able to make up anything that wasn't there to start with, that didn't enter it from experience, from the real world. Imagination can't cre-ate anything new, can it? It only recycles bits and pieces from the world and reassembles them into visions . . . Am I making sense right now?

And Prior, fascinated, hoping to find some answer himself, keeps her going: "Given the circumstances, yes."
Which she does:

So when we think we've escaped the unbearable ordinariness and, well, untruthfulness of our lives, it's really only the same old ordinariness and falseness rearranged into the appearance of novelty and truth. Nothing unknown is knowable.

The *tirade* is complete, but it is unfulfilling. Imagination—which includes transvestite performance and drug-induced hallucination—can only recycle the world; it can't remake it, and it certainly can't cure AIDS. Harper is left only to see whether Prior shares her conclusion, which he does. And, true to his performative nature (he's a pro at being funny), he tries to lighten her mood; it's probably the sort of line that suggested to homosexual men, around the 1940s, the appellation "gay": "It's something you learn after your second theme party: It's All Been Done Before."

But Harper, still brooding about her addiction and how it violently conflicts with her religious beliefs, will not be cheered up: "The world. Finite. Terribly, terribly . . . Well . . . This is the most depressing hallucination I've ever had."

Prior responds, "Apologies. I do try to be amusing"—a distant allusion, perhaps, to a self-deprecating line from a song by gay playwright Noel Coward: "The most I've had is just / A talent to amuse."

Prior and Harper share the insights that their emotional and, now, psychological proximity have gained them. For both are, at bottom, spiritual creatures: This is, after all, a play about angels.

HARPER: Oh, well, don't apologize, you . . . I can't expect someone who's really sick to entertain me.

PRIOR: How on earth did you know . . .

HARPER: Oh that happens. This is the very threshold of revelation sometimes. You can see things . . . how sick you are. Do you see anything about me?

PRIOR: Yes.

HARPER: What?

PRIOR: You are amazingly unhappy.

Now it's Harper's turn to make the jest, lighten the mood, show a little just-learned New York sarcasm: "Oh big deal. You meet a Valium addict and you figure out she's unhappy. That doesn't count."

The bonding is nearly complete. Harper has bought in to Prior's subculture; she shares his language and attitude. And she can trust him with the worst: She asks him to tell her something about herself that's surprising.

PRIOR: Something surprising.

HARPER: Yes.

PRIOR: Your husband's a homo.

[pause]

HARPER: Oh, ridiculous. *[pause, then very quietly]* Really?

And, with a studied-casual acknowledgment *("shrugs")* to the profound tie that now binds them, he repeats her phrase: "Threshold of revelation."

Angels in America is a play of extraordinary sensitivity, conveyed through far more than just cleverness and open-heartedness. It is a masterpiece of intricately blended styles and characters who communicate through every act of performance: speaking, sighing, crying, laughing, quoting, miming, pretending, revealing, hiding, loving, and suffering.

The discussion in the preceding pages, which in several ways is an analysis of Kushner's art, provides cues for the actors' performance on nearly every line, by showing how you can use not merely the meanings of the words but their shapes and forms as well to seek to achieve your character's goal. How do you shape your words, and your body, to express your opinions and contradict your opponent's, but still get the help you need (and the love you want) from other human beings? These are the issues for both Prior and Harper, coming from very different backgrounds but seeking the shared experience—and revelation—they both desire.

◆ S C E N E   16–1

Prior and Harper

Prepare and perform the scene between Prior and Harper. Get yourselves a dressing table with a mirror frame. Dress the roles—not to "explain" your characters to the classroom audience but to get the feel of your characters: Prior in a satin bathrobe and barefoot, and Harper in what you consider to be a prim, country-wifely outfit—with shoes to match. Perform your characters' actions as though your own subculture were watching you from afar (Harper's mother and minister; Prior's lover and former lovers). Imagine the theatre audience (with or without looking at them) as members of your subculture—until your acting partner becomes more dominant in your life at this particular moment.

Luxuriate in the wonderful, if different, world of your character, and relish any area in which your character's world may be preferable to your own.

Use the rhetoric and poetry of your part to better your character's lot and to create a new friend in your acting partner.

Clashing Subcultures

August Wilson died in 2005, having just completed his massive, ten-play cycle of plays, covering, individually, each decade of African American life in the twentieth century. This towering masterwork, which won Wilson two Pulitzer Prizes and seven Tony Award nominations during the twenty years of its composition, is unprecedented in achieving sustained success—with theatre audiences as well as drama critics.

Surely no one—black or white—can perform Wilson's plays without a profound understanding of American black culture and its complex roots. As Wilson said,

> Black Americans have their own culture. While we all do the same things, we all do them differently. We decorate our houses differently, bury our dead differently. Sometimes the differences aren't all that great, but if you ever went to a Black funeral and then to a white funeral, you'll definitely know that there are two distinct, separate cultures at work. Neither is better than the other one. They're just two different ways of approaching life.

Describing this difference as it appears in the dialogue of his plays, Wilson added an illuminating anecdote:

> I once had some problems with some producers of *Fences* because of repetition. For instance, Troy says to Rose, "What're you cookin' there?" [She replies] "I got some chicken. I'm cookin' up some chicken with collard greens." "You already said that," the producers said. "Why are you repeating that?" But that's the way Black folks say it. The language is the language of the people, and you can't deny them that. To deny them that is . . . denying them their humanity, trying to make them into somebody else. . . . We can say exactly the same things as others, but we say them differently because we're a different people."*

We will see repetition masterfully used in the scene that follows.

But the difference is hardly limited to speech. Wilson's plays—and indeed most plays in the African American repertory—are more often driven by character than plot, and by emotional exchange rather than dispassionate debate. And while Wilson's reproduction of black American speech is superb, his is not a mere stenographic transcription of black conversation: Wilson began his career as a poet, and even though his theatre is often naturalistic like Chekhov's, it is not rigidly so. There is often a level of spirituality in his work (there's a ghost in *The Piano Lesson,* for example) and always a profound musicality.

In *The Piano Lesson,* set in the 1930s, Boy Willie, from rural Mississippi, comes up to his sister Berniece's house in Pittsburgh (the city where most of

---

* Both quotes are from "Men, Women, and Culture: A Conversation with August Wilson," an interview conducted by Nathan L. Grant, 1993. Published at http://blues.fdl.uc.edu/www/amdrama/wilsonint.html.

Wilson's plays are set) to sell watermelons; he's also trying to talk Berniece into selling the family's heirloom piano so he can buy the Mississippi property where their family worked. Boy Willie is described by Wilson as "thirty years old. He has an infectious grin and a boyishness that is apt for his name. He is brash and impulsive, talkative and somewhat crude in speech and manner." In this scene, from Act 2, Scene 3, having gone out with a buddy, Lymon, to "find some women" at a local bar, Boy Willie has met Grace and is bringing her back to Berniece's house.

Both characters are African American. Both have been drinking prior to this scene, but neither should be considered intoxicated.

Read through the scene.

[Boy Willie enters the darkened house with Grace]

BOY WILLIE: Come on in. This my sister's house. My sister live here. Come on, I ain't gonna bite you.

GRACE: Put some light on. I can't see.

BOY WILLIE: You don't need to see nothing, baby. This here is all you need to see. All you need to do is see me. If you can't see me you can feel me in the dark. How's that, sugar? *[He attempts to kiss her.]*

GRACE: Go on now . . . wait!

BOY WILLIE: Just give me one little old kiss.

GRACE: *[pushing him away]* Come on, now. Where I'm gonna sleep at?

BOY WILLIE: We got to sleep out here on the couch. Come on, my sister don't mind. Lymon come back he just got to sleep on the floor. He run off with Dolly somewhere he better stay there. Come on, sugar.

GRACE: Wait now . . . you ain't told me nothing about no couch. I thought you had a bed. Both of us can't sleep on that little old couch.

BOY WILLIE: It don't make no difference. We can sleep on the floor. Let Lymon sleep on the couch.

GRACE: You ain't told me nothing about no couch.

BOY WILLIE: What difference it make? You just wanna be with me.

GRACE: I don't want to be with you on no couch. Ain't you got no bed?

BOY WILLIE: You don't need no bed, woman. My granddaddy used to take women on the backs of horses. What you need a bed for? You just want to be with me.

GRACE: You sure is country. I didn't know you was this country.

BOY WILLIE: There's a lot of things you don't know about me. Come on, let me show you what this country boy can do.

Victor Mack is Boy Willie and Terrilyn Towns is Grace in a South Coast Repertory production of August Wilson's *The Piano Lesson*. (Photo © Henry di Rocco)

GRACE: Let's go back to my place. I got a room with a bed if Leroy don't come back there.

BOY WILLIE: Who's Leroy? You ain't said nothing about no Leroy.

GRACE: He used to be my man. He ain't coming back. He gone off with some other gal.

BOY WILLIE: You let him have your key?

GRACE: He ain't coming back.

BOY WILLIE: Did you let him have your key?

GRACE: He got a key but he ain't coming back. He took off with some other gal.

BOY WLLIE: I don't wanna go nowhere he might come. Let's stay here. Come on, sugar. *[He pulls her over to the couch]* Let me heist your hood and check your oil. See if your battery needs charged. *[He pulls her to him. They kiss and tug at each other's clothing.]*

This scene is about young people quarreling about sex: whether to have it, where to have it, how to have it, and when to have it. In this it is not unlike any of hundreds of American plays, such as Tennessee Williams's *Streetcar Named Desire,* Sam Shepard's *Fool for Love,* Eric Bogosian's *subUrbia,* Wendy Wasserstein's *Heidi Chronicles,* and Lanford Wilson's *Burn This.* But August Wilson, naturally, layers this situation with a particularly African American style, in both language and tone. Wilson's commitment to explore black culture is both political and aesthetic; he is a playwright who refuses to synthesize races, gloss over cultural differences, or minimize cultural glories. "I find in black life a very elegant kind of logical language, based on the logical order of things," he says.

But logical language does not mean factually logical. As it turns out, Boy Willie's sister *does* mind, and, when they end up at Grace's home, her boyfriend Leroy *does* show up. "There's the idea of metaphor," Wilson continues. "When you ask a question, instead of getting an answer to the question, you get . . . ideas . . . opinions about everything, a little explanation. You get all these kinds of things just from one question."

And under the umbrella of African American culture, Wilson portrays, in this scene, two of its idealized subcultures: Willie's southern, rural (or, as Grace calls it, "country") style and Grace's northern, big-city attitude. And of course he portrays two idealized genders as well, with men (in this case) primarily interested in sex, and women primarily in material comfort. Neither Grace nor Boy Willie should be reduced to mere stereotypes, however, as both are complex characters trying to escape such typing. In the very act of having their conversation, each character is trying to shed the idealized role of his or her upbringing or environment: Though they dare not show it openly, Willie is fascinated by Grace's urban sophistication, and Grace is enchanted by Willie's countrified brashness and naïveté. Thus this scene is not merely an argument about sex, it is a negotiation, within the framework of an overarching culture, of differing substyles and language codes.

Their opening exchange is not simply an argument about lights or furniture; it's about "How are you going to treat me?" And the questions are posed not in the content but in the style of the language: Boy Willie calling Grace by pet names ("baby," "sugar") and Grace complaining that she's not being *treated* as the "baby" or "sugar" he's calling her.

Boy Willie makes a macho move, showing how he controls his older sister and can easily order his buddy Lymon around: "We got to sleep out here on the couch. Come on, my sister don't mind. Lymon come back he just got to sleep on the floor. He run off with Dolly somewhere he better stay there."

He concludes by repeating his order ("Come on") and softening it by repeating an endearment: "Come on, sugar."

Grace is all big-city legalisms and facts: "Wait now . . . you ain't told me nothing about no couch. I thought you had a bed. Both of us can't sleep on that little old couch."

Willie tries his best to get around her argument, but he fails miserably: "It don't make no difference. We can sleep on the floor. Let Lymon sleep on the couch." He's humiliated. He's blown it.

But this is not about a couch! Grace doesn't really care about the furniture arrangements; she just doesn't want to spend the night with a man who can't provide a proper setting. It's bad enough he's called "Boy" Willie: If she's going to sleep with him, she at least needs him to show some resourcefulness and authority. She wants him to be a man! Grace persists, amplifying her demand with a triple negative for emphasis: "You ain't told me nothing about no couch."

Willie realizes there's no arguing with her. Where is the delightful young woman who responded to him earlier in the saloon? ("She real nice. Laugh a lot. Lot of fun to be with" is how Lymon thought of her on that occasion.) Willie tries valiantly—but rather foolishly—to call on the promise of that earlier encounter: "What difference it make? You just wanna be with me."

It's loggerheads: How can Boy Willie tell Grace what *she* wants? And Willie knows it. But Grace has run out of tactics now. She can't simply acquiesce to a childish plea, and she still wants to be treated right by a man she can admire. All she can do is repeat her demand: "I don't want to be with you on no couch. Ain't you got no bed?"

And so Boy Willie summons his nerve to become the man he realizes she's looking for: "You don't need no bed, woman. My granddaddy used to take women on the backs of horses. What you need a bed for? You just want to be with me." A man like his grandfather. A man from Mississippi. A man on horseback! These Pittsburgh girls have never made love to a real man like this.

Grace is stunned: confused, excited, revolted, overwhelmed. How does a city girl deal with such rural hyperbole? Boy Willie is just kidding, isn't he? Or do they really do it on horseback in Mississippi? Graphic images fly through her mind—she can't stop them. But she's no fool. Or is she? Grace temporizes, testing the waters further before making a commitment: "You sure is country. I didn't know you was this country."

Now sure of success, Willie gallops ahead. He finds the biggest, sexiest, movie-star voice he can come up with, exaggerating his down-home southern accent and plunging to his lowest, most resonant vocal register: "There's a lot of things you don't know about me. Come on, let me show you what this country boy can do."

Grace is hooked. But she needs to save face too. She's no doormat. In two brief lines she makes clear: OK, but in my place and in my bed and, in case things get out of hand, I've got a boyfriend who'll beat you to a pulp: "Let's go back to my place. I got a room with a bed if Leroy don't come back there."

Uh-oh! The horse has disappeared. Boy Willie has another obstacle to overcome. "Who's Leroy? You ain't said nothing about no Leroy."

Leroy, Grace makes clear, is no Boy Leroy: "He used to be my man. He ain't coming back. He gone off with some other gal."

Boy Willie fences with her about the logistics of this potential problem, with each rephrasing and repeating the other's words in a mini-fugue of keys and comings, *k* and *g* consonants:

BOY WILLIE: You let him have your key?

GRACE: He ain't coming back.

BOY WILLIE: Did you let him have your key?

GRACE: He got a key but he ain't coming back. He took off with some other gal.

Relieved that she's been dumped by Leroy, Boy Willie now feels strong enough to reassert his authority, even in retreat. He explains, then orders, then seduces, employing the pet name with which he began the scene: "I don't wanna go nowhere he might come. Let's stay here. Come on, sugar." He concludes with a peroration: a line of wonderful bravado and creative sexual imagery ("the idea of metaphor," Wilson has said) that locks in his victory: "Let me heist your hood and check your oil. See if your battery needs charged."

Only this grand speech *doesn't* lock in a victory! In the very next moment, Willie's sister comes down and kicks them out of the house, whereupon they go to Grace's home and Leroy interrupts them, forcing Willie to flee the premises.

August Wilson is America's Chekhov, revealing both the awkwardness and loveliness of human imperfection. His characters are sensually detailed, made so by the rich texture and style of the language, by which they imply (and we infer) an almost infinite subtext.

◆ SCENE   16–2

Boy Willie and Grace

With a partner, prepare and present the scene between Boy Willie and Grace.

Play your character's background, era, and goals, not your own. Look at old magazines to find what African Americans might have worn for a night out in the city during the depression years—with particular attention to Boy Willie's rural roots. Find a couch in your prop room, if possible, for use in rehearsing and presenting the scene—and use it in your staging.

Clashing Professions

Margaret Edson, born in 1961, won the Pulitzer Prize for *Wit,* her first and still only play, in 1999. It is a powerful drama concerning a brilliant and somewhat authoritarian professor of English literature, Vivian Bearing, who is dying of ovarian cancer in a research hospital. The play jumps back and forth in time and alternates between starkly realistic portrayals of her suffering to her reflections—often whimsical—largely given directly to the audience; these concern not only her current medical plight but her life, her academic career, and, more surprisingly, the strange play she finds herself in.

In the following scene, Vivian is being attended by Jason Posner, a young research physician who was once an undergraduate student in her literature class, which was on the poetry of John Donne, her specialty.

Note: While Vivian is described as being fifty years old at the point this scene takes place, over the course of the play she plays herself at various ages from five onward, so it is does not inordinately strain credulity for her to be played by a college-age actor.

With a partner, read the scene aloud, for familiarity, before moving on.

VIVIAN [*sits weakly in a wheelchair; to the audience*]:
This is my playes last scene, here heavens appoint
My pilgrimages last mile; and my race
Idly, yet quickly runne, hath this last pace,
My spans last inch, my minutes last point,
And gluttonous death will instantly unjoynt
My body, and soule
John Donne. 1609.
I have always particularly liked that poem. In the abstract. Now I find the image of "my minutes last point" a little too, shall we say, *pointed.*

I don't mean to complain, but I am becoming very sick. Very, very sick. Ultimately sick, as it were.

In everything I have done, I have been steadfast, resolute—some would say in the extreme. Now, as you can see, I am distinguishing myself in illness.

I have survived eight treatments of Hexamethophosphacil and Vinplatin at the *full* dose, ladies and gentlemen. I have broken the record. I have become something of a celebrity. Kelekian* and Jason are simply delighted. I

---

* Her doctor.

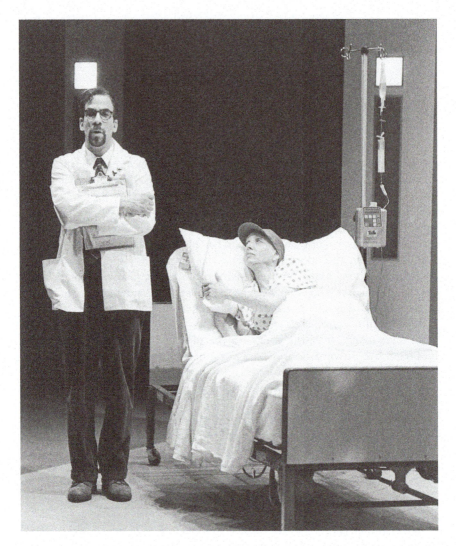

Linda Alper is Vivian and Jonathan Toppo is Jason in this 2000 production of Margaret Edson's *Wit* by the Oregon Shakespeare Festival. (Courtesy of Oregon Shakespeare Festival; photo by David Cooper).

think they foresee celebrity status for themselves upon the appearance of the journal article they will no doubt write about me.

But I flatter myself. The article will not be about *me,* it will be about my ovaries. It will be about my peritoneal cavity, which, despite their best intentions, is now crawling with cancer.

What we have come to think of as *me* is, in fact, just the specimen jar, just the dust jacket, just the white piece of paper that bears the little black marks.

My next line is supposed to be something like this:
"It is such a *relief* to get back to my room after those infernal tests."
This is hardly true.

It would be a relief to be a cheerleader on her way to Daytona Beach for Spring Break.

To get back to my room after those infernal tests is just the next thing that happens.
[She returns to her bed.]

Oh, God. It is such a relief to get back to my goddamn room after those goddamn tests.

[Jason enters.]

JASON: Professor Bearing. Just want to check the I&O.°   °*intake and outgo of fluids*

Four-fifty, six, five. Okay. How are you feeling today?   *[He makes notations on his clipboard throughout the scene.]*

VIVIAN: Fine.

JASON: That's great. Just great.

VIVIAN: How are my fluids?

JASON: Pretty good. No kidney involvement yet. That's pretty amazing, with Hex and Vin.

VIVIAN: How will you know when the kidneys are involved?

JASON: Lots of in, not much out.

VIVIAN: That simple.

JASON: Oh, no way. Compromised kidney function is a highly complex reaction. I'm simplifying for you.

VIVIAN: Thank you.

JASON: We're supposed to.

VIVIAN: Bedside manner.

JASON: Yeah, there's a whole course on it in med school. It's required. Colossal waste of time for researchers. *[He turns to go.]*

VIVIAN: I can imagine. *[Trying to ask something important]* Jason?

JASON: Huh?

VIVIAN: *[Not sure of herself]* Ah, what . . . *[Quickly]* What were you just saying?

JASON: When?

VIVIAN: Never mind.

JASON: Professor Bearing?

VIVIAN: Yes.

JASON: Are you experiencing confusion? Short-term memory loss?

VIVIAN: No.

JASON: Sure?

VIVIAN: Yes. *[Pause]* I was just wondering: why cancer?

JASON: Why cancer?

VIVIAN: Why not open-heart surgery?

JASON: Oh, yeah, why not *plumbing.* Why not run a *lube rack,* for all the surgeons know about *Homo sapiens sapiens.* No way. Cancer's the only thing I ever wanted.

VIVIAN: *[Intrigued]* Huh.

JASON: No, really. Cancer is . . . *[searching]*

VIVIAN: *[Helping]* Awesome.

JASON: *[Pause]* Yeah. Yeah, that's right. It is. It is awesome. How does it do it? The intercellular regulatory mechanisms—especially for proliferation and differentiation—the malignant neoplasia just don't get it. You grow normal cells in tissue culture in the lab, and they replicate just enough to make a nice, confluent monolayer. They divide twenty times, or fifty times, but eventually they conk out. You grow cancer cells, and they never stop. No contact inhibition whatsoever. They just pile up, just keep replicating forever. *[Pause]* That's got a funny name. Know what it is?

VIVIAN: No. What?

JASON: Immortality in culture.

VIVIAN: Sounds like a symposium.

JASON: It's an error in judgment, in a molecular way. But *why?* Even on the protistic level the normal cell–cell interactions are so subtle they'll take your breath away. Golden-brown algae, for instance, the lowest multicellular life form on earth—they're *idiots*—and it's incredible. It's perfect. So what's up with the cancer cells? Smartest guys in the world, with the best labs, funding—they don't know what to make of it.

VIVIAN: What about you?

JASON: Me? Oh, I've got a couple of ideas, things I'm kicking around. Wait till I get a lab of my own. If I can survive this . . . *fellowship.*

VIVIAN: The part with the human beings.

JASON: Everybody's got to go through it. All the great researchers. They want us to be able to converse intelligently with the clinicians. As though *researchers* were the impediments. The clinicians are such troglodytes. So smarmy. Like we have to hold hands to discuss creatinine clearance. Just cut the crap, I say.

VIVIAN: Are you going to be sorry when I— Do you ever miss people?

JASON: Everybody asks that. Especially girls.

VIVIAN: What do you tell them?

JASON: I tell them yes.

VIVIAN: Are they persuaded?

JASON: Some.

VIVIAN: Some. I see. *[With great difficulty]* And what do you say when a patient is . . . apprehensive . . . frightened?

JASON: Of who?

VIVIAN: I just . . . Never mind.

JASON: Professor Bearing, who is the President of the United States?

VIVIAN: I'm fine, really. It's all right.

JASON: You sure? I could order a test—

VIVIAN: No! No, I'm fine. Just a little tired.

JASON: Okay. Look. Gotta go. Keep pushing the fluids. Try for 2,000 a day, okay?

VIVIAN: Okay. To use your word. Okay.

Now study the scene in more detail.

In addition to the metatheatrical stylization of the dramaturgy (Vivian speaking to the audience, specifically about the play she is in), this scene also carries the weight of professional jargon, as both characters see the world in terms of their professional training and experience (in literary criticism and medical research). Actors in these roles, therefore, must master not only the vocabulary of each part (which is at minimum the meaning, pronunciation, and importance of each term) but the *professional mind-set* of their characters. The actor playing Vivian must be able to read the John Donne poem as a professor of English poetry would. The actor playing Jason must be able to rattle casually on, with seemingly absolute assurance, about intercellular regulatory mechanisms. No one could play either of these roles without doing research on the professions involved and practicing the jargon in the lines until they could speak it with both fluidity and apparent conviction.

Indeed, playing roles of this nature practically requires that the actor take an accelerated "training course" in the profession portrayed, a course that, however short (and rehearsal time often allows little beyond a few days or even hours), nonetheless explores not just what persons in the profession actually do but what they seek, what they worry about, and what they pride themselves on. The actors playing Vivian and Jason must, above all, allow us to accept them as authentic and fully dimensional *professionals in their fields:* Without this, the life-and-death and moral issues of the play will not be very convincing.

Read through the scene aloud a second time, stopping at each of the discussion points to read and discuss each fragment. Then read it aloud again. And again—until you feel reasonably comfortable with the professional language and the points raised in this text, and in your own discussion.

> This is my playes last scene, here heavens appoint
> My pilgrimages last mile; and my race
> Idly, yet quickly runne, hath this last pace,
> My spans last inch, my minutes last point,
> And gluttonous death will instantly unjoynt
> My body, and soule
> John Donne. 1609.

Spoken by a dying woman, the Donne poem excerpt is doubly sad; but that it is a speech in a play about the last scene of another "play" (one we already know will end with the speaker's death) gives it a certain wittiness (befitting Edson's title) that beautifully balances the pathos, making Vivian an ironic commentator on her own despair. Edson immeasurably helps the actor in this role by beginning the speech without introduction; unless we (the audience) are ourselves Donne fanciers, we have no idea Vivian is reciting a Donne poem, or indeed any poem at all, until the first rhyme is completed at the end of the third line. So we are momentarily confused, not knowing exactly what to think or how to feel until the poem concludes and is identified, with its sadness and ironic commentary intermixed.

The actor exploits this confusion, as does the character. Both are performing for us, and our ease at sympathizing with Vivian's plight comes, in part, from knowing that the actor playing the part is presumably not, herself, dying of ovarian cancer. So when Vivian identifies the author and date of the poem at the end, we all relax, knowing both that the character will die today but the actor (and we) will not and that these lines were written a long time ago and will not apply to us until a long time from now.

Vivian continues with her ironic commentary on her self-mourning, showing, in her very verbosity (punning *point* and *pointed;* emending *very, very* to *ultimately;* insisting on her dispassionate objectivity with the distancing "as it were"; unnecessarily pairing a synonym, *resolute,* to *steadfast*), an attempt to conquer the fear of death through rhetoric: an effort to talk her way out of the grave:

> I have always particularly liked that poem. In the abstract. Now I find the image of "my minutes last point" a little too, shall we say, *pointed*.
> I don't mean to complain, but I am becoming very sick. Very, very sick. Ultimately sick, as it were.
> In everything I have done, I have been steadfast, resolute—some would say in the extreme. Now, as you can see, I am distinguishing myself in illness.

She will conquer her fear of cancer by acquiring medical expertise, particularly the ability to pronounce the complicated names of chemical compounds so effortlessly as to follow them with "ladies and gentlemen," as though they were part of a Mistress of Ceremonies cabaret routine: "I have survived eight treatments of Hexamethophosphacil and Vinplatin at the *full* dose, ladies and gentlemen. I have broken the record." Boldly, she rises to the top of her ironic form: "I have become something of a celebrity. Kelekian and Jason are simply delighted. I think they foresee celebrity status for themselves upon the appearance of the journal article they will no doubt write about me."
And then, just as boldly, she falls; her medical expertise can only describe, not reverse, her physical affliction:

> But I flatter myself. The article will not be about *me*, it will be about my ovaries. It will be about my peritoneal cavity, which, despite their best intentions, is now crawling with cancer. What we have come to think of as *me* is, in fact, just the specimen jar, just the dust jacket, just the white piece of paper that bears the little black marks.

Vivian can no longer maintain her performative, professorial lecture mode, and, quite brilliantly, Edson now has her step outside the play she's in, and into the world of hypertheatre:

> My next line is supposed to be something like this:
> "It is such a *relief* to get back to my room after those infernal tests."
> This is hardly true.
> It would be a *relief* to be a cheerleader on her way to Daytona Beach for Spring Break.
> To get back to my room after those infernal tests is just the next thing that happens.

But quickly, we return to the hospital bed, where Vivian is once again a victim, away from her professorial pulpit. And her language suffers. Her despair even mangles the line she was "supposed" to deliver, which now has a pair of "ad libbed" *goddamn*s. *Infernal* is too professorial a word to issue from her lips once the physical torment returns; only a vulgarity (though a relatively sedate one) can suffice: "Oh, God. It is such a relief to get back to my goddamn room after those goddamn tests."

Jason at first makes light of his learning, using abbreviations ("I&O"; "Hex and Vin") and repeated euphemisms ("Okay"; "Great. Just great") in an effort to simplify and to improve his bedside manner. Vivian calls him on it; she doesn't want to be treated like a child:

JASON: Professor Bearing. Just want to check the I&O. Four-fifty, six, five. Okay. How are you feeling today? *[He makes notations on his clip-board throughout the scene.]*

VIVIAN: Fine.

JASON: That's great. Just great.

VIVIAN: How are my fluids?

JASON: Pretty good. No kidney involvement yet. That's pretty amazing, with Hex and Vin.

VIVIAN: How will you know when the kidneys are involved?

JASON: Lots of in, not much out.

VIVIAN: That simple.

JASON: Oh, no way. Compromised kidney function is a highly complex reaction. I'm simplifying for you.

VIVIAN: Thank you.

Jason can't let it go at that. Though it's his job to minister to the patient, he needs some ministering himself. He proceeds to gratuitously tell the dying Vivian *his* problems, seeking her sympathy as a fellow intellectual with an implicit shrug: "We're supposed to."

Her response is deliberately brief: just the term, not her feeling about it, letting Jason do all the interpreting.

VIVIAN: Bedside manner.

JASON: Yeah, there's a whole course on it in med school. It's required. Colossal waste of time for researchers. *[He turns to go.]*

Jason's "Yeah" (in lieu of "Yes") begins a subtle relaxation of his official style, as he begins to treat Vivian not as a patient but more as an honorary colleague, conspiratorially indicating his contempt for the caregiving role he's required to play and begging for sympathy: Vivian, he is saying, should be sorry for *him* for having to waste his time being sympathetic toward *her*. A transition occurs between them as they now jostle for control of the dia-logue. Chekhovian hesitations, questions unanswered, or answered by other questions ("Huh?" "When?"), proliferate:

VIVIAN: I can imagine. *[Trying to ask something important]* Jason?

JASON: Huh?

VIVIAN: *[Not sure of herself]* Ah, what . . . *[Quickly]* What were you just saying?

JASON: When?

VIVIAN: Never mind.

Alarmed at what he might have opened himself up to, Jason tries to seize the high ground by becoming doctorlike, probing her, asking medical questions to reestablish his authority.

JASON: Professor Bearing?

VIVIAN: Yes.

JASON: Are you experiencing confusion? Short-term memory loss?

VIVIAN: No.

JASON: Sure?

VIVIAN: Yes. *[Pause]*

And Vivian comes to the point: Let's talk about *you* instead of me: "I was just wondering: why cancer? [. . .] Why not open-heart surgery?" And Jason, thrilled to be the subject of her inquiry (something that would have been impossible when he was her undistinguished student), reveals his intellectual brilliance—and emotional tone-deafness—through adolescent sarcasm: "Oh, yeah, why not *plumbing.* Why not run a *lube rack,* for all the surgeons know about *Homo sapiens sapiens.* No way. Cancer's the only thing I ever wanted." The paradox—lost on Jason—is overwhelming: What he *wants* is precisely what's killing her.

VIVIAN: *[Intrigued]* Huh.

JASON: No, really. Cancer is . . . *[searching]*

Vivian finds the perfect teenage adjective for the era: "Awesome." And he finds the perfect affirmative: "Yeah." Now Jason, still not catching her sarcasm (indeed, he proudly repeats the supplied adjective), is in high gear, showing off, along with his unlettered slang ("Yeah"; "conk out"), all the scientific language he has picked up since he left her English class. There will be no more simplifying, nor no gentle easing of the horror to a woman who is dying of the very process he's giddily boasting about:

Yeah, that's right. It is. It is awesome. How does it do it? The intercellular regulatory mechanisms—especially for proliferation and differentiation—the malignant neoplasia just don't get it. You grow normal cells in tissue culture in the lab, and they replicate just enough to make a nice, confluent monolayer. They divide twenty times, or fifty times, but eventually they conk out. You grow cancer cells, and they never stop. No contact inhibition whatsoever. They just pile up, just keep replicating forever.

And now he feels bold enough to enter her world: a world of words, images, poetry. The English student is becoming the English teacher:

JASON: That's got a funny name. Know what it is?

VIVIAN: No. What?

JASON: Immortality in culture.

VIVIAN: Sounds like a symposium.

Nailing his point with medical terminology that he knows she cannot contest (who besides medical researchers knows what *protistic* means?), Jason flies: He is now an expert on errors in judgment, on subtlety, on perfection; and he can now show his contempt for "idiots" with ferocity (Edson has italicized the word to indicate this). Can we not see, in this italicized *idiots,* that this is how Jason himself once felt—as one of Vivian's literature students? Like the lowest life form on earth:

> It's an error in judgment, in a molecular way. But *why?* Even on the protistic level the normal cell–cell interactions are so subtle they'll take your breath away. Golden-brown algae, for instance, the lowest multi-cellular life form on earth—they're *idiots*—and it's incredible. It's perfect. So what's up with the cancer cells? Smartest guys in the world, with the best labs, funding—they don't know what to make of it.

No sentimentalist herself (remember the irony of her comments on the Donne poem), Vivian sees something of herself in this cocky young intellectual. Still a teacher, she wants to teach him something she never got to in her class.

VIVIAN: What about you?

JASON: Me? Oh, I've got a couple of ideas, things I'm kicking around. Wait till I get a lab of my own. If I can survive this . . . *fellowship.*

He is again unaware of his insensitivity: He's complaining about the difficulty of (figuratively) "surviving" his fellowship—to a person who cannot (literally!) survive cancer. She finally makes him aware of it: "The part with the human beings."

She has succeeded, and Jason's tone changes. But he's not going to retreat. Perhaps he knows she enjoys this discourse. Perhaps he knows she
admires his tactless honesty. Once the "bedside manner" game has been
discarded, there's no sense pretending it's anything other than fiction.

JASON: Everybody's got to go through it. All the great researchers. They
    want us to be able to converse intelligently with the clinicians. As
    though *researchers* were the impediments. The clinicians are such
    troglodytes. So smarmy. Like we have to hold hands to discuss creati-
    nine clearance. Just cut the crap, I say.

The "cut the crap" was to her. In other words, empathy is worthless;
clinicians are phonies; we both know it; you didn't hold my hand in the
Donne class, and I'm not going to hold yours now; let's at least respect each
other's intelligence—and honesty.
The scene finally plays out as a simple and frank discussion, with a subtext—of impending death and the limits of professional expertise (literary
or medical) to ameliorate death—shared fully between them.

VIVIAN: Are you going to be sorry when I—Do you ever miss people?

JASON: Everybody asks that. Especially girls.

VIVIAN: What do you tell them?

JASON: I tell them yes.

VIVIAN: Are they persuaded?

No false bravado here, but no self-effacement either.

JASON: Some.

VIVIAN: Some. I see. *[With great difficulty]* And what do you say when a
    patient is . . . apprehensive . . . frightened?

JASON: Of who?

VIVIAN: I just . . . Never mind.

It's too much for him. He becomes doctorly again—this time, however,
mainly to end the dialogue before it gets too deep (for him, not for her):

JASON: Professor Bearing, who is the President of the United States?

VIVIAN: I'm fine, really. It's all right.

JASON: You sure? I could order a test—

VIVIAN: No! No, I'm fine. Just a little tired.

This is just the answer he was hoping for.

JASON: Okay. Look. Gotta go. Keep pushing the fluids. Try for 2,000 a day, okay?

VIVIAN: Okay. To use your word. Okay.

◆ S C E N E   16–3

Vivian and Jason

Now memorize, prepare, and rehearse the scene between Vivian and Jason for presentation in line with your work to this point.

Take time on your own to research the medical and scholarly language so that you can feel these words are truly coming out of your *brain,* not just your mouth. Say the difficult words in different contexts: Make up five sentences using the words *protistic* and *peritoneal cavity,* for example, and practice using them in a mock conversation (or drop them into a *real* conversation) until you can feel that it is *you* choosing to speak this way. Study and discuss with others (including your partner, if you wish) the poetry of John Donne, so you feel you can speak about Donne's work from the background of your own perspective, not just Edson's or her character's.

Dress and stage the scene: A bed would help the actor playing Vivian to feel the awkward vulnerability of a flat-on-her-back patient towered over by a standing doctor (who was once her student). And wearing a hospital gown would also help induce, in that actor, the reality of the social discomfort into which Vivian has now been thrown. A buttoned-to-the-neck white coat, or some equivalent, would help the actor playing Jason assume the clinical air that for him is a struggle to maintain.

And if the actor playing Vivian were wearing no underwear beneath the hospital gown, which would of course be the case in a real situation, her feeling of vulnerability (to exposure, or to a doctor's sudden and casual probing) would be powerfully intensified.

All of these dressings—the bed, the gown, the lack of underwear—can be simply imagined, of course. Acting always involves imagination, and as a practical matter, the no-underwear suggestion is probably better imagined (at least in a classroom setting) than actually employed.* But the support of key furniture and costume elements, particularly when they determine the physical relationships (standing, sitting, lying) and power relationships (relatively dressed

---

*   In the play as performed, Vivian is wearing no underwear, as is revealed in a momentary vignette when she lets her gown fall to the floor as the play ends. "[S]he is naked and beautiful, reaching for the light," Edson writes in the stage direction.

and undressed) of the characters, is not mere storytelling for the audience, nor is it an acting gimmick: It conjures key elements of the situation's reality and the obstacles against which the actors must forcefully struggle, all of which will greatly intensify the acting.

Imagining the ovarian tumor destroying you, or the tasks that stand between you and a career as a brilliant medical researcher, will be a sufficient challenge in any case.

Play the scene with your partner and seek to achieve your character's goals in the context of the professional language, hospital staging, and character subtext that you and your partner have derived from these and your own discussions.

Solo Performer, Multiple Roles

The final scene in this lesson is from Doug Wright's 2004 Pulitzer Prize winner, *I Am My Own Wife*. This play is nothing less than a tour de force for any actor, because each of the play's thirty-five roles—male and female, old and young, German, American, French, English, and Japanese—is played by the same actor with only a single costume change. "Distinctions between characters," Wright explains in an opening stage direction, "are made by changes in the tonal qualities and pitch of the actor's voice; through his stance, his posture, and his repository of gestures. Often, his transformations are accomplished with lightning speed and minimal suggestion; a raised eyebrow or an unexpected smile."

Solo performances (plays performed by a single actor) have become a significant trend of the contemporary stage. In recent decades Robert Morse captivated Broadway audiences as Truman Capote in Jay Presson Allen's *Tru*, Pauline Collins did the same as a fictional housewife in Willy Russell's *Shirley Valentine*, as did Alec McCowen in his own dramatic narration of *The Gospel of St. Paul*. But the degree of difficulty is much higher when the solo performer performs multiple roles, as when Sherry Glaser played five members of her family in *Family Secrets*, when Lili Tomlin created thirteen women, four men, and a dog in Jane Wagner's *The Search for Signs of Intelligent Life in the Universe*, and when Jefferson Mays soloed in *Wife*. Playing multiple characters challenges the actor to master nearly every lesson in *Acting Two*, as it requires her or him to make and reverse multiple self-extensions, with dazzling speed.

My Own Wife presents the true story of German transvestite Charlotte von Mahlsdorf, an antique fancier who, during and after World War II, survived both Nazi and Communist regimes. Wright traveled to Berlin to interview her in the 1990s, and his resulting play includes himself as "Doug," the young, gay American playwright who elicits her story as we watch it.

Jefferson Mays plays all the roles in *I Am My Own Wife*, shown here in the play's off-Broadway premiere. (Photo © Joan Marcus)

Study, rehearse, and see what you can create with this fragment (slightly abridged) from the play's opening scenes. It includes five characters: Charlotte as a woman at age sixty-five; Charlotte as a boy (Young Lothar) at sixteen; Doug; a Nazi SS Officer; and a Nazi SS Commander. Although Wright designates the sole actor as male, for strictly classroom purposes any actor may study, rehearse, and perform this fragment. Character descriptions in parentheses are Wright's, drawn from elsewhere in the 2005 published edition.

Supertitle: Are You a Boy or a Girl?
(*Standing before us is Charlotte von Mahlsdorf. Charlotte is, in fact, a man, roughly sixty-five years old. She wears a simple black house dress with*

peasant stitching, a kerchief on her head, and an elegant strand of pearls. When she speaks, it's in broken English, but the cadences of her voice are delicate; there's a musical lilt to her inflection. She has a German accent.)

CHARLOTTE: *[speaking to the audience]* The last days of the World War were the most dangerous time for me because I refused to carry a weapon or to wear a uniform. Instead, I had my hair long and blonde and my mother's coat and the shoes of a girl. And so I was—in Germany, we say *"Freiwild."* Like the Jews, we were wild game.

Berlin was destroyed. I was walking about—the houses were all broken and the street was full of rubble. Yes. And there was coming Russian airplanes with the Splatter bombs—so close, you could see the pilot with the helmet and goggles. And there was standing an air raid shelter. And so I went inside. I was sitting there maybe half an hour. And I could hear the bombs, and the old building was shaking. And in came four SS Officers. Infantry police. *Die Kettenhunde. . . .*

(She becomes the SS Officer, and plays out the scene in real time.)

SS OFFICER: *(Doctrinaire)* All deserters shall be shot.

CHARLOTTE: And they wanted to shoot me. I looked down; I didn't want to see them shoot. I thought, "I'll wait until I feel it." But when I looked to the ground, I saw the boots of a Commander. *(Her gaze rises as she sizes up the Commander with both awe and dread.)* And he looked at me.

SS COMMANDER: Are you a boy or a girl?

CHARLOTTE: And I thought, "If they shoot me, what's the difference between a boy and a girl, because dead is dead!"

(She becomes a child and answers:)

YOUNG LOTHAR: I am a boy.

SS COMMANDER: How old are you then?

YOUNG LOTHAR: Sixteen.

CHARLOTTE: And he turned around to face the Execution Squad Commander.

SS COMMANDER: *(With some measure of self-contempt.)* We are not so far gone that we have to shoot school children.

CHARLOTTE: And this was my salvation.

Supertitle: Listening
(Charlotte becomes Doug, a playwright, in his mid thirties, with an eager-to-please manner and a somewhat mellifluous voice.)

DOUG: *[he is writing a letter to Charlotte]* My dear Charlotte. Enclosed please find two antique cylinders. Your favorite: John Philip Sousa. *El Capitan* and *Semper Fidelis*. They're Blue Amberols,[*] so you should be able to play them on your Edison Standard. I—meanwhile—am listening to our interview tapes every chance I get. (*Then, with feeling*) You are teaching me a history I never knew I had. Thank you. (*A pause.*) Tape Seven. January 26, 1993.

CHARLOTTE: *Heute habe ich einen Spitznamen fur dich.*

DOUG: A nickname? For me?

CHARLOTTE: "Thomas Alva Edison."

I Am My Own Wife is clearly influenced by Brecht's drama, with its abrupt transitions, projected supertitles captioning individual scenes, and characters alternating speeches to each other with direct remarks to the audience. The play also includes stylistic elements we have seen earlier in this union: transvestitism as in *Angels in America,* interaction of subcultures and language patterns as in *The Piano Lesson,* and professional jargon (the Blue Amberols) and self-referentiality (being a play about its own playwright gathering material for this play) of *Wit.* But it also reflects almost every theme of *Acting Two:* requiring its sole actor to extend into genders, languages, ages, and countries other than his or her own. And it also cautions, particularly on one line, "with feeling."

So I'm not going to provide any suggestions for playing this fragment. Let it rather become your "final examination" for all the lessons of *Acting Two*—and your retention of the lessons of *Acting One.*

Follow the playwright's instructions, and segue from one character to another by your "changes in . . . tonal qualities and pitch, . . . stance, . . . posture, . . . gestures . . . and minimal suggestion." Do it in front of a mirror, or a good friend, and practice until you can make the distinctions clean, precise, and immediately identifiable. Then practice to make sure that every character is also "you," and that when you answer as Young Lothar, it is *your* life that you are saving when the SS Commander asks you what your sex is.

Buy a copy of this astonishing play. On your own (for this is a work you can develop on your own), rehearse and privately perform larger and larger fragments—until, perhaps, you are able to write to the Dramatists Play Service for performance rights, and perform the entire play in a theatre of your choosing.

---

[*] Wax cylinders used with early Edison phonographs.

L'Envoi

As both acting teacher and author, I have a single overriding goal: to have the actor not only say the playwright's lines but appear to think them up as well. To me, great acting is getting the audience to believe that you are not only speaking Hamlet's lines but making all of his decisions: where to go, what to wear, and how to dress your hair, tie your shoelaces, and greet your friends—even though in reality these decisions were made ahead of time by the playwright, the director, the costume designer, and a whole host of people, including you in your earlier research and rehearsals.

The goal of acting is to look as though you're doing all of this right now, right before us, and in fact most great actors feel that they *are* doing it right now, right before us, even in plays written hundreds or even thousands of years ago. But this is not as easy as it sounds, as you surely have found out by now.

This immediacy of action is probably even more important in a classic play, or in a musical comedy or farce, than in the gritty realistic contemporary dramas that are written out of our own immediate experience. For while you might actually *be* the sort of contemporary college student portrayed in the current new play, you're obviously not an ancient Athenian *tyrannus,* nor a royal widow, nor, I hope, a cancer-ridden English professor specializing in John Donne. So you've got to think the part as well as do the part, and that's the long-range purpose behind the exercises, discussions, and scenes in *Acting Two.*

I don't presume, of course, that addressing this single goal answers all the questions and problems of acting, or even most of them, but it does focus the dialogue that goes on in the classroom and rehearsal hall. It is by thinking the characters' thoughts that you integrate your real emotional impulses with the structured dramaturgy of the play, no matter how seemingly artificial or stylized it may appear at first glance. This will help you find the level of emotional improvisation, and even the confusion, that remains at the heart of the dramatic text, no matter how sharply configured its externals may be. Ultimately, I hope you will learn how to work at the precise point where unconscious emotion flows into structured language and dramaturgy, for that's where the greatest acting lies.

Playing style and character is learned only by a great deal of practice. After all, characters are presumed to have grown up in their roles: Play a fifty-year-old Renaissance Italian, and you are playing someone who has had at least forty-five years of daily learning to be that person. Such tasks as convincing your *tyrannus* that you speak with the authority of the gods, or negotiating your way to the crown of England, or bedding the most interesting Englishman in Naples without losing your self-respect, or speaking medical jargon with authority—these take people years to master, if they ever do. And performing these roles with passion, acuity, brio, and complete unselfconsciousness takes the confidence that only experience can bring.

The work in *Acting Two* is therefore inexhaustible: Let me assure you that you can get better at every speech and scene herein for at least the next twenty years. Some roles are easily worth a lifetime of preparation; they are mountains that—to paraphrase Charles Laughton on the role of Lear—can be scaled only by stepping over the corpses of those who have so far failed to reach the summits. But do not be dissuaded, for the greatness is in the effort.

I have led you on different paths in approaching the different scenes, suggesting ways, for example, to find different-from-ordinary voices for Teiresias and Oedipus, comic physical business for Nicomaco and Sofronia, versified dueling for Richard and Anne, a performative minidance for Willmore and Hellena, rhetorical tropes for Barbara and Undershaft, subtext for Masha and Vershinin, distanced "winking" for Shen Te and Yang Sun, professional jargon for Jason and Vivian. We've dealt with medieval, Elizabethan, and French neoclassic verse, well-turned and halting prose, Kushner's and the Bible's angels, age and youth, city and country, tragic and farcical—all coming together, and coming into conflict, in the diversity of theatre.

And all different. There is no one way to play style because style comes from many sources: the historical period, the specific environment, the author's literary proclivities, the world of the characters, and the subcultures within that world.

And there is no single approach to character. You can quickly see that some playwrights create characters of psychological complexity and depth: Chekhov, Shakespeare, and August Wilson are clearly examples. Other dramatists who can be equally championed—Machiavelli, Molière, Shaw, and Brecht, for example—draw more on their character's theatrical, behavioral, or social positions. An understanding of the variety of theatrical construction—the way roles are created by their authors—can be immensely useful in helping you find where to look first and how to build a role that blends your appropriate features with those of the part as the dramatist conceived it.

There is no single key to performing on the stage. It is all of these things, and it is all of you.

A Glossary
of Acting Terms

Note: Some of the following terms are not used in this text. They are, however, words you may hear while pursuing studies in acting. All words are described only as they pertain to acting and to the theatre.

action   everything an actor does onstage. Distinguish between outward actions (Romeo kneeling before Juliet) and inner actions (Romeo falling in love with Juliet).

action cue   a word in the speech preceding yours that initially prompts you to speak in response. See also **line cue**.

arc (of a role)   the overall **action** of a character during a play, and the way in which the character changes and develops during the course of that play.

aside   a character's brief remark, often witty, delivered directly to the audience. Other characters onstage are presumed not to hear it. A **presentational** technique, most common in comedies from the sixteenth to the nineteenth century. See also **soliloquy**.

beat   the smallest unit of action. Said to derive from the classroom teaching of Richard Boleslavsky, a disciple of Stanislavsky's, who, when referring to each little "bit" of an actor's action, pronounced it in his Polish accent. Also, as occasionally seen in stage directions, a short but pregnant pause in the dialogue; shorthand for "wait a beat before speaking."

blocking   arranging the major movements of actors onstage, such as entrances, exits, stage crosses, sitting, standing, going up and down stairs. In full play productions, this is often initiated by a director.

business or **stage business**   hand or other small movements that actors make, often with props, that although normally incidental to the plot convey lifelike behavior. Examples include putting on reading glasses, lighting and smoking a cigarette, and dusting bookshelves. Initiated by both actors and directors to add texture and detail to performance.

cheating out (or **cheating**)   angling the body partly toward the audience, while still presuming to face the character you are in conversation with. "Cheat out a bit," a director might say so that the audience can see your face better. Though a common staging technique, it may seriously inhibit the intensity of personal interaction between actors.

communion   to Stanislavsky, the desirable state of full emotional rapport among actors in a play.

cue   in general, the line preceding your own that "cues" you to speak. See also **action cue** and **line cue.**

downstage   the front of the stage in a proscenium theatre; that part nearest the audience. "Cross downstage" is the director's instruction to move forward.

emotional memory   reliving situations in your own life while performing, often with the aid of **substitution,** in the hope of arousing your own emotions while acting a role. An age-old technique, made prominent by Stanislavsky in his early writing, but later discarded by him. Also known as *affective memory* and *emotional recall.*

empathy   the sense of personal identification the audience may develop with one or more characters in a play. The capacity of the audience to share feelings with, care for, and root for a dramatic character—in the person of an actor.

end-inflection   the inflection at the end of a line or word. Rising end-inflections tend to propel action and ideas forward, falling end-inflections tend to conclude them.

expectation   as used in this book, the actor's assumption of his or her character's belief that victory is possible (even when the actor knows, from reading the script, that failure will be the result). A technique that energizes the actor during the performance and tends to create **empathy** in the audience.

eye contact   two actors looking into each other's eyes.

goal   as used in this book, the character's quest at any given moment; what the character wants to achieve. In the conventional translation of Stanislavsky, the **objective.** Also sometimes called the *intention* or the intended *victory.*

improvisation   acting without a fixed text; playing a character's actions but with your own spontaneously invented words. Often used as a rehearsal technique; sometimes used as a theatre form in itself.

indicating displaying, rather than experiencing, emotion onstage. Considered an acting flaw, as the audience can see that the emotion derives not from the action of the play but simply from the actor's desire to emote, to simply "indicate," in a mechanical fashion, the feelings of her or his character.

inductive tactic an interactive tactic intended to induce a change in another character's (actor's) behavior. Smiling, befriending, seducing, and charming are all inductive (as opposed to **threatening**) **tactics**.

indulging when in the grip of an emotion, in performance, sustaining it purely for its presumed dramatic impact on the audience. Considered an acting flaw as it does not advance or contribute to the action of the play. "Don't indulge it," a director might say.

inflection the change in pitch within a spoken line. See **end-inflection.**

inner actions actions of a play that cannot be described simply by recounting the actor's words or outward movements, but are internal shifts: mental decisions, mood swings, emotional upheavals, and so on.

intention see **goal**

lift in speech delivery, to raise the pitch of a specific syllable.

line cue specifically, the last syllable of the last line preceding your own.

"Magic If" Stanislavsky's invention: The actor plays "as if" he or she were in the character's situation. Playing Juliet, you play "as if" you were in love with the actor playing Romeo. Playing Hamlet, you play "as if" the actress across from you was your mother and she wanted you to drop out of school and stay home.

moment-to-moment the action of a scene or play in each individual moment, plus the minute changes in situation that occur from "moment to moment." Generally used in contrast to more general, unchanging emotional states, or relatively static character attitudes.

naturalistic a dramatic (and acting) style that seeks, as much as possible, to represent ordinary life onstage.

objective the best-known translation of Stanislavsky's term *zadacha* (problem). See **goal.**

other in the terminology of this book, a person (or person-like image—a god or ghost, say) from whose changed outlook or behavior your character seeks to achieve a goal.

pointing physically pointing, with a finger, open hand, head toss, or other gesture, at a person (place, object) to indicate, often with emphasis, the person (place, object) intended.

practical props props that actually have to work during performance; for example, a television set or cell phone that is seen to operate during the play.

presentational acting that is openly "presented" to the audience without the illusion that the dialogue is simply a conversation between the characters. Normally considered an acting flaw in naturalism but not necessarily in other forms of drama. **Soliloquies, asides, takes,** and many musical numbers are openly presentational to the audience.

prima donna   an actor, female or male, whose arrogance and selfishness breed resentment among fellow workers. Literally, "first lady," and originally derived from certain overly demanding opera stars.

props or **properties**   small and usually hand-carried objects—for example, combs, pistols, pocket watches, telephones—used by actors during performance.

proscenium theatre   technically, a theatre that has a proscenium arch dividing the audience from the stage; used more generally, and in this glossary, to describe a staging orientation that has the audience on one side of the action only.

"real"   acting that convinces the audience it is genuine human behavior, performed on the stage but fully experienced by the actors. Placed in quotation marks here because acting is always, in fact, at least partly an illusion, and the "reality" of acting, no matter how spontaneous it seems, is always in part contrived. That the actors show up at the theatre at the same time the audience does is, in fact, the beginning of the contrivance of drama. Still, "Be more real" is a frequent directorial command, meaning, among other things: "Experience this more personally" or "Put more of yourself into it." (Or, as some cynics might say, "Seem to be more real.")

realistic   generally, but not uniformly, **naturalistic.** Acting (and drama) that is like ordinary life in most respects, though occasionally presentational.

representational   used as the opposite of **presentational,** and referring to acting that fundamentally seeks to humanly represent, rather than theatrically present, a dramatic character. The difference, however, is generally a matter of degree rather than pure opposition.

resonance   the voice's quality of "re-sounding" through the throat and nasal passages. Resonance amplifies the vocal sound and gives it strength, tone, timbre, and personal quality.

result   often used to indicate the outcome of a drama and what the actor should avoid playing before it occurs. "Don't play the result" means to play as though you're going to win (see **expectation**) even if the play dictates that you will eventually fail. "Play the action, not the result," is a common director's instruction.

soliloquy   a speech given directly to the audience, ordinarily with no one else onstage. Common in ancient and Elizabethan drama and in modern drama as well. Usually played as a direct address to the audience, sometimes played as a character thinking aloud in the audience's presence.

spine   see **superobjective**

stage left   in a **proscenium theatre,**   the actor's left, while facing the audience. "Cross left," when said by the director to the actor on such a stage, means cross to *your* (the actor's) left.

stage right   the actor's right. See above.

stakes   the emotional level of an acting performance. As in poker, where the term originated, "raising the stakes" in acting means that you have more to lose and more to win; thus you will be led to a greater emotional commitment to achieving your goals.

Stanislavsky   Konstantin Stanislavsky (also spelled Stanislavski), 1863–1938. Russian cofounder/director of the Moscow Art Theatre in 1897, creator of the world's first and best known systematized study of the acting art.

Strasberg   Lee Strasberg (1901–1982). Austrian-born acting teacher, artistic director of the Actors Studio, and developer of what came to be known as "Method acting," an approach based on the early teachings of **Stanislavsky.**

substitution   consciously imagining a person or event from your real life in the place of your actual acting partner, or the situation of the play, in order to stimulate real emotion. Often used in the **emotional memory** technique.

subtext   the hidden meanings of a dramatic text, comprising its **inner actions** and the unstated **goals** of the characters.

superobjective   Stanislavsky's term (actually *sverkhzadacha,* or "superproblem") that represents the character's long-range **goal** for the entire play. Also sometimes called the *spine* of the role.

tactics   in this book, the means by which a character seeks to achieve his or her **goal.** Tactics can be **inductive** or **threatening.**

take   as a noun, a quick, quizzical, or comical look at the audience or another actor. A **presentational** technique, often used in farce and *commedia dell'arte.*

targets of attention   persons, places, or objects the character focuses on.

threatening tactics   tactics a character may use to achieve a **goal** by implying force, violence, intimidation. Almost all characters can be seen to use threatening tactics at some point, although **inductive tactics** are more commonly used by most characters.

three-quarters   a stage position in a **proscenium theatre,** where the actor is facing halfway toward the actor to her or his side and halfway toward the audience. Thus the audience is essentially seeing a three-quarter view of the actor. See **cheating out.**

upstage   the opposite of **downstage;** the back part of the stage in a **proscenium theatre;** the part farthest from the audience. Derives from the eighteenth century, when the stage was slanted ("raked") toward the audience, with the rear of the stage higher than the front.

upstaging   to deliberately go upstage of an actor with whom you are sharing a scene, in order to make that actor face upstage to maintain the illusion of **eye contact,** or even a genuine conversation. Considered—if done for this purpose—selfish behavior worthy only of a **prima donna.**

virtuosity   great technical skill, in acting or any performing art.

vocal fold/vocal cord   interchangeable terms referring to the organs in the throat that, under the proper stimulus, generate sound.

INDEX